Days of the Lord

THE LITURGICAL YEAR

Days of the Lord

THE LITURGICAL YEAR

Volume 6.

Ordinary Time, Year C

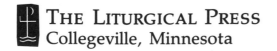

THE LITURGICAL PRESS
Collegeville, Minnesota

The English translation of Volume 6 of this series is by Gregory LaNave and Donald Molloy. The original French text of *Days of the Lord (Jours du Seigneur*, Brepols: Publications de Saint-André, 1988) was written by the authors of the *Missel dominical de l'assemblée* and *Missel de l'assemblée pour la semaine* under the direction of Robert Gantoy and Romain Swaeles, Benedictines of Saint-André de Clerlande.

ACKNOWLEDGMENTS
Excerpts from the English translation of *Lectionary for Mass* © 1969, International Committee on English in the Liturgy, Inc. (ICEL); excerpts from the English translation of *The Roman Missal* © 1973, ICEL; excerpts from the English translation of *The Liturgy of the Hours* © 1974, ICEL. All rights reserved.

Scripture selections are taken from the New American Bible *Lectionary for Mass*, © 1970 by the Confraternity of Christian Doctrine, Washington, D.C., and are used by license of said copyright owner. All rights reserved. No part of the New American Bible *Lectionary for Mass* may be reproduced in any form without written permission from the copyright owner.

Scripture quotations are from the *New American Bible with Revised New Testament*, © 1986 Confraternity of Christian Doctrine. The text of the Old Testament in *The New American Bible with Revised New Testament* was published in *The New American Bible*, © 1970 Confraternity of Christian Doctrine. Other quotations, as indicated, are from *The Jerusalem Bible*, © 1966 by Darton, Longman & Todd, Ltd. and Doubleday & Company, Inc.

Cover design by Monica Bokinskie.

Library of Congress Cataloging-in-Publication Data

(Revised for v. 6)

Jours du Seigneur. English.
    Days of the Lord.

    Translation of: Jours du Seigneur.
    Includes bibliographical references.
    Contents: v. 1. Advent, Christmas,
Epiphany —   — v. 6. Ordinary Time, C.
    1. Church year. 2. Catholic Church—Liturgy.
I. Title.
BX1970.J67313 1990   264'.02034   90-22253
ISBN 0-8146-1904-5 (v. 6)
ISBN 0-8146-1899-5 (v. 1)

Contents

Ordinary Time C

The third year of the liturgical cycle—Year C—is characterized by its use of the Gospel According to Luke, which the Lectionary begins on the First Sunday of Advent. However, the Third Gospel is read consecutively during Ordinary Time, from the first verse of chapter 1 to the nineteenth verse of chapter 21. Two sections are not read during Ordinary Time. The first is concerned with the infancy narrative (1:5–3:22), which is quite naturally read during Christmas; the mission of John the Baptist (reserved for Advent); and the baptism of the Lord, which is read on the feast that closes the season of Christmas-Epiphany. The other, from the final chapters (22:1–24:33), concerns the passion, resurrection, Jesus' appearances, and the sending forth of the apostles. These passages are read in their entirety elsewhere during the year (Passion Sunday and Eastertime).[1]

All in all, more than sixty percent of Luke's Gospel is read on the Sundays of Year C, and half of this on the Sundays in Ordinary Time.[2]

The first readings for these Sundays are taken from the Old Testament and are chosen according to the theme of the Gospel. Eighteen of the Old Testament's forty-six books (Gen, Exod, Deut, 1 Sam, 2 Sam, 1 Kgs, 2 Kgs, Neh, 2 Macc, Eccl, Wis, Sir, Isa, Jer, Amos, Hab, Zech, Mal) have had selections taken from them.[3]

The second readings come from seven of the thirteen Pauline Epistles (1 Cor, Gal, Col, 2 Thess, 1 Tim, 2 Tim, Phlm) and the Letter to the Hebrews.

As with the other liturgical years, the Gospel for the First Sunday of Ordinary Time comes from John.[4] At the beginning of Year C, the text is that of ''the beginning of his signs at Cana in Galilee,'' by which Jesus revealed his glory and awoke the faith of his disciples. The next Sunday begins the reading from Luke, which is the unifying element of Year C.

The evangelist himself said that he wrote a ''narrative'' (Luke 1:3). Note also that the Lectionary has carefully chosen the passages from the Gospels that are to be read each Sunday. In what follows, one can distinguish several separate sequences of readings that have their own internal coherence.[5] The point is that the series of Sundays in Ordinary Time is not a jumble of unconnected liturgies, but an itinerary that leads us, step by step, toward the celebration of Christ, the king of the universe.

Practical Scheme of the Gospel According to Luke

Ancient authors did not write their books according to the same scheme by which we read them. Unlike us, they did not divide their books clearly into chapters and paragraphs.[1] Nevertheless, they composed with great care, in an orderly fashion, editing according to personal guidelines based on the intentions for which they wrote. Their editorial work took a great deal of talent, as we can clearly see in Luke. If we try to divide the work into chapters and paragraphs, as in our modern books, we will meet with insurmountable difficulties, and no "scheme" should be imposed to the exclusion of all others. In fact, exegetes are not in agreement on the scheme of Luke's Gospel, though they all do distinguish certain sections, e.g., the infancy narrative, chapter 15 with its parables of mercy, and the gospel of the passion and resurrection.

The "scheme" we suggest here does not pretend to be the solution of such difficult problems. It has a simple, practical goal: to allow the reader to have a general view of the first of Luke's books.[2]

Prologue (Luke 1:1-4)

1. Prelude: The Gospel of Jesus' Infancy (Luke 1:5–2:52)
Announcement to Zechariah (1:5-25)
Announcement to Mary (1:26-38)
Elizabeth's praise of Mary (1:39-45)
Mary's praise of God (1:46-56)
Birth of John the Baptist (1:57-79)
Birth of Jesus (2:1-21)
First journey to the Temple (2:22-40)
Second journey to the Temple (2:41-52)

2. Jesus in Galilee (Luke 3:1–9:50)
Prelude to the mission (3:1–4:13)
Ministry and imprisonment of John (3:1-20)

2

Baptism of Jesus (3:21-22)
Genealogy of Jesus (3:23-38)
Temptation of Jesus (4:1-13)

A. First manifestations (4:14–5:16)

Nazareth: at the synagogue (4:14-30)
Capernaum: at the synagogue (4:31-41)
Galilee (4:42–5:16)

B. Five controversies (5:17–6:11)

Healing of a paralytic (5:17-26)
Dining with sinners (5:27-32)
Discussion about the harvest (5:33-39)
Picking grain on the sabbath (6:1-5)
Healing on the sabbath (6:6-11)

C. Discourse-program (6:12-49)

Choice of the Twelve (6:12-16)
Fame as a miracle-worker (6:17-19)
Sermon on the plain (6:20-49)

D. The deeds of the Messiah (7:1-50)

Healing of a servant (7:1-10)
Resurrection of a widow's son (7:11-17)
Questions from John's disciples (7:18-35)
Pardon of a sinful woman (7:36-50)

E. The sower assembles a community (8:1-21)

The audience (8:1-3)
The sower (8:4-15)
The lamp (8:16-18)
The true family of Jesus (8:19-21)

F. New works of Jesus (8:22-56)

Authority over:
    nature (8:22-25)
    demons (8:26-39)
    sickness (18:40-48)
    death (8:49-56)

G. Climax and end of Galilean ministry (9:1-50)

Mission of the Twelve (9:1-6)
Herod and Jesus (9:7-9)
Multiplication of the loaves (9:10-17)
Peter's confession (9:18-21)
First announcement of the passion (9:22-27)
Transfiguration (9:28-36)
Healing of possessed boy (9:37-43a)
Second announcement of the passion (9:43b-45)
Instruction of the disciples (9:46-50)

3. *Jesus' Journey to Jerusalem (Luke 9:51–19:27)*

A. Departure and mission of disciples (9:51–10:24)

Rejected at a Samaritan village (9:51-56)
To follow Jesus unconditionally (9:57-62)
Mission of the seventy-two disciples (10:1-24)

B. Conditions of entering into life (10:25–11:13)

Love of God and neighbor (10:25-28)
The good Samaritan and the neighbor (10:29-37)
Martha and Mary before the Word (10:38-42)
Prayer (11:1-13)

C. Jesus defends himself (11:14-54)

He expels demons (11:14-23)
He guards against their return (11:24-26)
He is greater than Jonah (11:29-32)
He transforms by his light (11:33-36)
He attacks the Pharisees (11:37-54)

D. Warnings to the disciples (12:1-53)

Against hypocrisy (12:1-3)
Encouragement and vigilance (12:4-12)
Beware of riches! (12:13-21)
Against uneasiness (12:22-34)
Vigilance and fidelity (12:35-48)
The time to decide (12:49-53)

E. New teachings for the crowds (12:54–13:35)

The signs of the times (12:54-59)
The barren fig-tree (13:1-9)
Healing of a possessed woman (13:10-17)
The mustard-seed (13:18-19)
The yeast (13:20-21)
Rejection by the Jews and call to pagans (13:22-30)
Apostrophe to Herod (13:31-33)
Lament over Jerusalem (13:34-35)

F. Supper in the house of a notable Pharisee (14:1-24)

Healing of a man with dropsy on the Sabbath (14:1-6)
Seats at table (14:7-11)
Invitations (14:12-14)
The behavior of the invited (14:15-24)

G. Exigencies and supreme mercy (14:25–17:10)

Renunciation of possessions (14:25-27)
Do not lose flavor (14:28-33)
Parables of mercy (5:1-32)
The dishonest steward (16:1-12)
Exigencies of the kingdom (16:13-18)
The rich man and Lazarus (16:19-31)
Scandal (17:1-3a)
Brotherly correction (17:3b-4)
The strength of faith (17:5-6)
The gratuity of service (17:7-10)

H. Last halt before the entry (17:11–19:27)

Healing of ten lepers (17:11-19)
The coming of the kingdom and the Son of Man (17:20-37)
The judge and the widow's petition (18:1-8)
The Pharisee and the publican (18:9-14)
Jesus and the little children (18:15-17)
The call of the rich official (18:18-30)
Third announcement of the passion (18:31-34)
Healing of the blind man at Jericho (18:35-43)
Zacchaeus (19:1-10)
Parable of the gold coins (19:11-27)

4. Jesus at Jerusalem (Luke 19:28–24:53)

A. At Jerusalem with the whole people (19:28–21:38)

Solemn entry (19:28-40)
Lament for Jerusalem (19:41-44)
Discourse in the Temple (19:45–21:4)
Discourse on the last things and the fall of Jerusalem (21:5-38)

B. From the Supper to the Mount of Olives (22:1-46)

Conspiracy and treason (22:1-6)
Preparation and celebration of the Last Supper (22:7-20)
Announcement of Judas' treason (22:21-23)
Dispute over rank (22:24-30)
Prediction of Peter's denial (22:31-34)
The tragedy of the hour (22:35-38)
On the mount of Olives (22:39-46)

C. From the trial to the tomb (22:47–23:56)

The Jewish trial (22:47-71)
The Roman trial (23:1-25)
The execution (23:26-56)

D. Resurrection and exaltation (24:1-53)

The empty tomb and the announcement to the women (24:1-8)
Incredulity of the disciples (24:9-12)
On the road to Emmaus (24:13-35)
Official appearance at Jerusalem (24:36-49)
Ascension (24:50-53)

The Lectionary Texts

	First Reading	Psalm	Epistle	Gospel
2nd Sunday	Isa 62:1-5	96	1 Cor 12:4-11	John 2:1-12
3rd Sunday	Neh 8:2-4a, 5-6, 8-10	19	1 Cor 12:12-30	Luke 1:1-4; 4:14-21
4th Sunday	Jer 1:4-5, 17-19	71	1 Cor 12:31–13:13	Luke 4:21-30
5th Sunday	Isa 6:1-2a, 3-8	138	1 Cor 15:1-11	Luke 5:1-11
6th Sunday	Jer 17:5-8	1	1 Cor 15:12, 16-20	Luke 6:17, 20-26
7th Sunday	1 Sam 26:2, 7-9, 12-13, 22-23	103	1 Cor 15:45-49	Luke 6:27-38
8th Sunday	Sir 27:4-7	92	1 Cor 15:54-58	Luke 6:39-45
9th Sunday	1 Kgs 8:41-43	117	Gal 1:1-2, 6-10	Luke 7:1-10
10th Sunday	1 Kgs 17:17-24	30	Gal 1:11-19	Luke 7:11-17
11th Sunday	2 Sam 12:7-10, 13	32	Gal 2:16, 19-21	Luke 7:36–8:3
12th Sunday	Zech 12:10-11	63	Gal 3:26-29	Luke 9:18-24
13th Sunday	1 Kgs 19:16b, 19-21	16	Gal 5:1, 13-18	Luke 9:51-62
14th Sunday	Isa 66:10-14c	66	Gal 6:14-18	Luke 10:1-12, 17-20
15th Sunday	Deut 30:10-14	69	Col 1:15-20	Luke 10:25-37
16th Sunday	Gen 18:1-10a	15	Col 1:24-28	Luke 10:38-42
17th Sunday	Gen 18:20-32	138	Col 2:12-14	Luke 11:1-13
18th Sunday	Eccl 1:2; 2:21-23	95	Col 3:1-5, 9-11	Luke 12:13-21
19th Sunday	Wis 18:6-9	33	Heb 11:1-2, 8-19	Luke 12:32-48
20th Sunday	Jer 38:4-6, 8-10	40	Heb 12:1-4	Luke 12:49-53
21st Sunday	Isa 66:18-21	117	Heb 12:5-7, 11-13	Luke 13:22-30
22nd Sunday	Sir 3:17-18, 20, 28-29	68	Heb 12:18-19, 22-24a	Luke 14:1a, 7-14
23rd Sunday	Wis 9:13-18	90	Phlm 9b-10, 12-17	Luke 14:25-33
24th Sunday	Exod 32:7-11, 13-14	51	1 Tim 1:12-17	Luke 15:1-32
25th Sunday	Amos 8:4-7	113	1 Tim 2:1-8	Luke 16:1-13
26th Sunday	Amos 6:1a, 4-7	146	1 Tim 6:11-16	Luke 16:19-31
27th Sunday	Hab 1:2-3; 2:2-4	95	2 Tim 1:6-8, 13-14	Luke 17:5-10
28th Sunday	2 Kgs 5:14-17	98	2 Tim 2:8-13	Luke 17:11-19
29th Sunday	Exod 17:8-13	121	2 Tim 3:14–4:2	Luke 18:1-8
30th Sunday	Sir 35:12-14, 16-18	34	2 Tim 4:6-8, 16-18	Luke 18:9-14
31st Sunday	Wis 11:22–12:1	145	2 Thess 1:11–2:2	Luke 19:1-10
32nd Sunday	2 Macc 7:1-2, 9-14	17	2 Thess 2:16–3:5	Luke 20:27-38
33rd Sunday	Mal 3:19-20a	98	2 Thess 3:7-12	Luke 21:5-19

The Sequences of the Sundays in Ordinary Time C

This division is based on the Gospel readings that form the skeletal outline of each Sunday's Liturgy of the Word. It is not meant to exclude all other possible divisions, but is based on the "scheme" of Luke's Gospel and the selection of texts made by the Lectionary.

2nd Sunday

Isa 62:1-5	1 Cor 12:4-11	John 2:1-12

3rd, 4th, and 5th Sundays

Neh 8:2-4a, 5-6, 8-10	1 Cor 12:12-30	Luke 1:1-4; 4:14-21
Jer 1:4-5, 17-19	1 Cor 12:31–13:13	Luke 4:21-30
Isa 6:1-2a, 3-8	1 Cor 15:1-11	Luke 5:1-11

6th, 7th, and 8th Sundays

Jer 17:5-81	1 Cor 15:12, 16-20	Luke 6:17, 20-26
1 Sam 26:2, 7-9, 12-13, 22-23	1 Cor 15:45-49	Luke 6:27-38
Sir 27:4-7	1 Cor 15:54-58	Luke 6:39-45

9th, 10th, and 11th Sundays

1 Kgs 8:41-43	Gal 1:1-2, 6-10	Luke 7:1-10
1 Kgs 17:17-24	Gal 1:11-19	Luke 7:11-17
2 Sam 12:7-10, 13	Gal 2:16, 19-21	Luke 7:36–8:3

12th, 13th, and 14th Sundays

Zech 12:10-11	Gal 3:26-29	Luke 9:18-24
1 Kgs 19:16b, 19-21	Gal 5:1, 13-18	Luke 9:51-62
Isa 66:10-14c	Gal 6:14-18	Luke 10:1-12, 17-20

15th, 16th, and 17th Sundays

Deut 30:10-14	Col 1:15-20	Luke 10:25-37
Gen 18:1-10a	Col 1:24-28	Luke 10:38-42
Gen 18:20-32	Col 2:12-14	Luke 11:1-13

18th, 19th, 20th, and 21st Sundays

Eccl 1:2; 2:21-23	Col 3:1-5, 9-11	Luke 12:13-21
Wis 18:6-9	Heb 11:1-2, 8-19	Luke 12:32-48
Jer 38:4-6, 8-10	Heb 12:1-4	Luke 12:49-53
Isa 66:18-21	Heb 12:5-7, 11-13	Luke 13:22-30

22nd, 23rd, and 24th Sundays

Sir 3:17-18, 20, 28-29	Heb 12:18-19, 22-24a	Luke 14:1a, 7-14
Wis 9:13-18b	Phlm 9b-10, 12-17	Luke 14:25-33
Exod 32:7-11, 13-14	1 Tim 1:12-17	Luke 15:1-32

25th and 26th Sundays

Amos 8:4-7	1 Tim 2:1-8	Luke 16:1-13
Amos 6:1a, 4-7	1 Tim 6:11-16	Luke 16:19-31

27th and 28th Sundays

Hab 1:2-3; 2:2-4	2 Tim 1:6-8, 13-14	Luke 17:5-10
2 Kgs 5:14-17	2 Tim 2:8-13	Luke 17:11-19

29th, 30th, and 31st Sundays

Exod 17:8-13	2 Tim 3:14–4:2	Luke 18:1-8
Sir 35:12-14, 16-18	2 Tim 4:6-8, 16-18	Luke 18:9-14
Wis 11:22–12:1	2 Thess 1:11–2:2	Luke 19:1-10

32nd and 33rd Sundays

2 Macc 7:1-2, 9-14	2 Thess 2:16–3:5	Luke 20:27-38
Mal 3:19-20a	2 Thess 3:7-12	Luke 21:5-19

34th Sunday: Solemnity of Christ the King

2 Sam 5:1-3	Col 1:12-20	Luke 23:35-43

Whenever the term Sunday is used in this volume, it refers to a Sunday in Ordinary Time, Year C. References to other Sundays from the various liturgical seasons are to be considered from Year C.

Second Sunday in Ordinary Time

The Sign of Cana

Each year, the Second Sunday of Ordinary Time has its own particular integrity.[1] It is like an ornate gateway, which might be called an "icon of greeting" taken from the Gospel According to John, in front of which the liturgy has us pause before beginning the long road of "green Sundays." This icon depicts Jesus being pointed out by John the Baptist: "Behold, the Lamb of God, who takes away the sin of the world" (John 1:29-34—Year A); Jesus being followed by John's disciples, John and Andrew (John 1:35-42—Year B); and, this year, Jesus working his "first sign" at Cana in Galilee at a wedding to which he, his mother Mary, and his disciples had been invited (John 2:1-12).

The "sign of Cana" is important not just because it is the first of the signs that Jesus accomplished. If it is thought of from that point of view, it does not reveal its true scope, the depth of its meaning, especially within the context of the liturgy, after the celebration of the Baptism of the Lord and at the threshold of Ordinary Time C. This "Sunday of Cana" is the pivot point or hinge between two periods of the liturgical year. To dwell a little while before this icon, to retain a mental impression of it, allows for a better subsequent reading of Luke's Gospel, which is the warp and woof of the Sunday celebrations throughout Ordinary Time.

In its symbolic dimension, the miracle of Cana allows one to see all at once what is implied in Jesus' coming into this world. While celebrating his baptism, we have contemplated the founder and ruler of the new people coming out of the Jordan and receiving the spirit. One week later, the Sunday celebration focuses on the divine glory that is at work in the world since Jesus' first miracle, ready to be extended, thanks to his ministry, to all who believe in him. The hour of God's wedding with humanity has sounded, the wine of the universal feast needs only to be drawn, the Bride is already present at the side of the one who is manifesting his glory.

Circumstances that may appear to be of only anecdotal interest reveal the true meaning and importance of the "first sign" accomplished by Jesus in the context of a wedding feast.

The Nuptials of God and His People

The theme of wedding or marriage occupies an extremely important place in the Bible; no image has been found that better expresses and symbolizes the union, the joining of life and destiny, ordained by God between himself and his chosen people. It is a covenant that involved fidelity, reciprocal trust, mutual giving, the love of God for his people and of the people for their God. The initiative of God, to which his people freely responded, created a bond between them that could not be broken, for God never takes back his love. The prophets constantly resorted to the image of a marriage, without the least embarrassment.

This marriage relationship certainly follows a rocky course, with its ups and downs, times of serious tension, even ruptures. But never divorce, because of the eternal faithfulness of God, who always leads his errant Spouse back to him, pardoning even the worst affronts. The prophets thus speak of adultery, prostitution, repudiation, renewals of grace, and new betrothals. Consider, for instance, the Book of Hosea—one of the oldest prophetic writings[2]—the vocabulary and nuptial imagery of which exerted tremendous influence on prophecy,[3] even in the New Testament.[4] And what about the extraordinary Song of Songs, one of the most beautiful love poems ever written, whose profound symbolism clearly illuminates the nuptials between God and his people. Mystics like John of the Cross have always been able to penetrate to the true depth of this mystery![5]

One must be aware of all this biblical background while listening to the passage from the Book of Isaiah which, from so many possibilities, the Lectionary has designated for this Sunday (Isa 62:1-5).

The divine initiative is clearly marked. It is God who "gives a new name." The free imposition of a name is not just any act, even if we don't often reflect on it. It expresses what I want or might want some person (or even some thing) to be, whom I call by such a name; it actually bestows a certain kind of existence. When a little child gives a name to an inappropriate object, for example, a stuffed animal, it is not necessarily a matter of confusion or ignorance, especially when, despite all our attempts to correct him or her, the child insists on the name, wanting the animal to be what the child has decided to call it: the child creates it as such. When, for the first time, a child says "Papa" or "Mama," he or she recognizes their existence as father and mother; in the child's eyes, they become what they are, but what they would not fully be if the child did not name them as such.

For God, to name and to create are, in a very real sense, the same thing: "God said, 'Let there be light,' and there was light. . . . God called the light 'day,' and the darkness he called 'night.' Thus evening came, and morning followed—the first day" (Gen 1:3, 5).

He it is who decides on the names of certain children who will fulfill his plan of salvation: John, Jesus (Luke 1:13, 31). A "new name" establishes a new mission, creates a new personality: Jesus gives Simon the name Peter (Luke 6:14). When they enter into glory, the elect will receive "a white amulet upon which is inscribed a new name, which no one knows except the one who receives it" (Rev 2:17).

The "new name" given by the Lord himself to Jerusalem makes her a new city, for God has pardoned her. Thus she becomes "City of Justice," "Faithful City," "City of the Lord," "Frequented," "My Delight."[6]

"Called" to become what she is, "Forsaken," repudiated on account of her infidelity, prostitution, and adultery, she is raised again to the rank of "My Delight," chosen before all others. "Desolate," sterile far from her Spouse, she rediscovers her name, "Espoused," the bride of God himself, "Joy of her God!" What a remarkable change! The mercy of God has done this: "Where sin increased, grace overflowed all the more" (Rom 5:20).

There are great ramifications to this fidelity or infidelity, the estrangement of the people from their God or their return to him who never ceases to love them. When "the blessed of the Lord" are far from him and are scattered among the nations because of their adultery, the pagans jeer: "Where is their God?" (Ps 79:10); "They put their faith in him, and he has abandoned them." The credibility of the Lord is in jeopardy. Then, his holiness leads him to gather his own, to encourage them to repent of their infidelity, to forgive them, to bind them to himself again. So, as the prophet says: "Nations shall behold your vindication, and all kings your glory."

This vindication and glory are made manifest in a way that the prophet could never have imagined: the covenant of God has been opened to all the nations, without restriction! The whole earth sings to the Lord a new song and blesses his name, for the wonders of God are extended to the whole world.

> *Proclaim his marvelous deeds to all the nations.*
>
> Sing to the LORD a new song;
>   sing to the LORD, all you lands.
> Sing to the LORD; bless his name.

Announce his salvation, day after day.
  Tell his glory among the nations;
Among all peoples, his wondrous deeds.

Give to the LORD, you families of nations,
  give to the LORD glory and praise;
  give to the LORD the glory due his name!

Worship the LORD in holy attire.
  Tremble before him, all the earth;
Say among the nations: The LORD is king.
  He governs the peoples with equity.
  (Ps 96:1-2a, 2b-3, 7-8a, 9a, 10ac).

A Wedding Feast at Cana in Galilee

It comes as no surprise that John would have accorded particular importance to the "first sign" accomplished at Cana in Galilee: it was among
the festivities at a wedding that Jesus changed water into wine: this was
only a few days after John had followed him and spent a week with him.[7]
But John edited his Gospel toward the end of his life, after having reflected
for a long time on the events he witnessed, and having spoken many
times about them in his preaching and teaching. Clearly, it was in the
light of both later events and his well-developed faith that he spoke of
"the beginning of the signs that Jesus accomplished." It is important,
therefore, to listen to this story very closely.

"The Mother of Jesus Was There"

This is the first thing John says, even before noting that "Jesus and his
disciples were also invited to the wedding." In fact, Mary plays both a
discreet and effective role, since it is she who notices the lack of wine
and tells her son of it. She implicitly asks him to do something about it.
This is really extraordinary faith and confidence, since Jesus had not yet
performed any sign! She did not take as a refusal her son's strange response: "My hour has not yet come." She simply said to the servants:
"Do whatever he tells you." What a wonderful intuition of faith. Mary
knew that Jesus could not be insensible to the distress of those who had
invited him and his disciples; that he wouldn't allow the feast to be ruined
by a lack of wine. But, more importantly, she must have seen that her
son's presence at the wedding feast had some meaning with respect to
his mission.

In any case, John was aware of it, since he had seen the water changed
into wine. Also, he was, from this moment on, conscious of Mary's place
in the economy of salvation. The Fourth Gospel contains no details of

Jesus' birth; up till this point, nothing has been said about Mary. And behold, she appears just at the moment of the "first sign" worked by Jesus! We are accustomed to address Mary as "Mother of the Savior," "Mother of God." These titles do express her supreme and unique status. John points up her role at the beginning of Jesus' ministry: she introduced, so to speak, her son—the Son of God—to the sight of all by giving him the first chance to manifest his glory, to accomplish the "first sign" of salvation.[8]

It is important not to misunderstand Jesus' seemingly irritable, even wearied, response: "Woman, how does your concern affect me? My hour has not yet come." What hasn't been said about this incident! Especially that Mary, far from letting herself be rebuked, pursued her purpose by speaking to the disciples as if Jesus had agreed to her request, effectively forcing his hand. Consequently, Marian piety can find tremendous warrant: the power of Mary's intercession has been limitless since Cana.

However legitimate this piety may be, John is not speaking of Mary in the role of intercessor. The Fourth Gospel mentions Mary on only two occasions: here at Cana and at the foot of the cross (John 19:25-26). In both cases, Jesus addresses her as "woman," a rather unusual thing for a son to call his mother, but which does not, in itself, contain any nuance of disrespect. At Calvary, it has a solemn character.[9] At this final moment, Jesus proclaimed the singular role of Mary. Whether John saw it as such or not, the Christian today will readily, and quite rightly, regard the appellation "woman" as recalling the first woman. The man called her "Eve, because she became the mother of all the living." Mary is such in a very different sense: the woman whose child would crush the head of the one who caused the fall of the first Eve (Gen 3:20, 15—solemnity of the Immaculate Conception of the Virgin Mary).

Beginning of the Signs and the Hour of Jesus
In the Fourth Gospel, the "hour" of Jesus always has to do with the plan of God, which is accomplished by the Son fulfilling the will of the Father.[10] In its primary sense, this "hour" is that of Jesus' Passover, when "all is finished," when, because of Jesus' glorification, the Spirit is given to those who believe in him, when the glory of God and his Christ shines forth (John 19:30; 7:39; 16:5-7).

At Cana, this "hour has not yet come." And yet, it is "the beginning of the signs that Jesus accomplished." His glory already is "revealed," and "his disciples began to believe in him." By means of these subtle indications, John invites us to contemplate the work and revelation of Jesus in its integrity, from first manifestation to final fulfillment.

Mary's presence at the beginning and end of this uninterrupted course of events has, therefore, great symbolic meaning. Her intervention at Cana expresses the urgency of the people of the new era, who are impatient to see Christ's glory. Standing at the foot of the cross, she is the symbol of the Church, which recognizes, in the crucified Christ, the Son glorified by the Father, and adores him in silence. This woman thus appears as the perfect model of the believer: "Blessed are you who believed!" (Luke 1:45). "Blessed are those who have not seen and have believed" (John 20:29). In order to attain the fullness of faith, one must become, in some fashion, like John at Calvary (John 19:26-27), the "son" of this mother of believers. To paraphrase a formula from Cyprian, one could say that, in order to have God for Father through Christ our brother, one must have Mary for mother.[11]

She is the Daughter of Zion, the image of the Church straining to see the realization of the promises, joining in the realization of God's plan of salvation. Not so much because of what she does, but because of what she is: attentive to the needs of other people in the course of salvation history; open to the meaning of signs that reveal the glory of God and his Christ; looking ahead, with her son, to the hour when the hope of humanity longing for its liberation will be fully satisfied.

The Wine of the Wedding Feast

In response to Mary's intervention, Jesus caused to be filled with water "six stone water jars there for Jewish ceremonial washings, each holding twenty to thirty gallons.". . . "Draw some out now and bring it to the headwaiter." It was wine of excellent quality, better even than what had been served up to that point.

Everything about this scene is remarkable. First of all, there was a simplicity with which the miracle took place. Jesus merely gave the servants an order that must have been incomprehensible but easy enough to fulfill. One might wonder why they were not surprised to draw forth wine where they had poured water. No one seemed to be surprised. Where did this wine come from? The headwaiter never asked. The only remark he made that indicates any surprise is to the bridegroom, whom he reproached with having kept back the good wine till that time! The superabundance of the divine gift surpasses all bounds. And then, the wine's quality is such that the headwaiter found it excessive!

But everything has significance here.

In the Bible, wine, because of all that it symbolizes, is one of God's most precious gifts. It "gladdens men's hearts" (Ps 104:15) and that of God himself.[12] It is a blessing from heaven.[13] It eases the curse that lies over the earth and the labor that goes with tilling the soil.[14]

On the religious level, wine has special significance. Its lack evokes the great punishments that God reserves for those who offend him.[15] On the other hand, its abundance suggests the joy and happiness of the messianic age.[16]

It is with this biblical perspective that the "sign" of water changed into wine takes on its meaning. The feast at Cana, in which Mary, Jesus, and the disciples were involved, evokes the banquet and the overflowing joy of messianic times. The Apocalypse of Baruch, an apocryphal writing composed around A.D. 96, and therefore roughly contemporaneous with the Fourth Gospel, says that "each vine will bear a thousand branches, each branch will bear a thousand clusters, each cluster will have a thousand grapes, and each grape will yield a kor of wine."[17]

Finally, the good wine "kept till now"—is it not that which Jesus, when his hour will come, will make the blood of the new covenant, served at the sacramental supper of the eternal wedding banquet? We know that John does not recount the institution of the Eucharist, but his Gospel is nonetheless the most Eucharistic of the four. Certainly, we should not try to find Eucharistic allusions strewn everywhere, to be detected only by the initiate. And yet, read within the framework of the liturgy, where the "sign"—the sacrament—par excellence is celebrated, the Gospel of the wedding at Cana awakens Eucharistic resonances within us.

This is put most admirably by Ephraim, deacon of Edessa and doctor of the Church (c. 306-373):

> The wine he offers, Christ makes excellent, to suggest the treasures hidden in his life-giving blood. The first sign he accomplishes is the wine that gladdens the celebrants; the significance is that his blood rejoices the nations. All earthly joys come together in wine; all of salvation is joined in the mystery of his blood. He offers the sweet wine that transforms hearts, as they believe in the inebriating doctrine that transforms them.[18]

Epiphany of the Glory of Jesus and Faith of the Disciples

At Cana, "Jesus revealed his glory, and his disciples began to believe in him."

This is not merely a conclusion to a Gospel passage. It must rather be understood as a question. As if, when we finish contemplating this icon, someone were to say to us: "Behold: such was the first of Jesus' signs. It took place at Cana in Galilee. Can you see the glory of the one in whom you believe?''

But suppose someone were then to ask: "What glory? How does it appear in such a simple, though certainly extraordinary miracle? The word 'glory' seems ill-chosen.'' In modern usage, "glory" means "great renown publicly spread, associated with merits, actions, or works judged to be extraordinary.'' Several synonyms are: celebrity, honor, prestige, etc. All this excites admiration—but faith?

Contrary to our usage, "glory" in the Bible has to do not with a person's prestige and renown, but with interior worth, one's "power.'' It is this that inspires respect and confidence.

"Glory" in an absolute sense is attributed to God alone. He alone truly carries "power.'' Because of his omnipresence we say, "Holy, holy, holy Lord, God of power and might. Heaven and earth are filled with your glory.'' Recalling Isaiah's vision of God's glory in the Temple, John regards it as a prophetic vision of the glory of Christ (Isa 6:1-4; John 12:41).

Because he was near to God from the beginning, the only Son is the means by which we know God—his "glory''—whom no one has seen: this glory, "which he holds from his Father,'' shone in him, and we have seen it (John 1:1, 14, 18). To understand the "signs" properly, one must start "at the beginning,'' at Cana in Galilee, at a wedding feast. "Don't you understand?,'' the evangelist says to us. "Surely you see the meaning and importance of this first sign? Reread the Gospel with an eye to the significance of the wedding feast, the wine, etc., and also what we do in the Eucharist.''

> When Christ changed the water into wine by his power, the crowd rejoiced, delighting in the taste of this wine. Today, it is at the banquet of the Church that we are all seated, for the wine is changed into the blood of Christ, and we drink it with blessed joy, glorifying the great bridegroom. For the true bridegroom is the son of Mary, the Word from all eternity, who has taken the form of a slave and who created all in his wisdom.[19]

Thus we have here a "mystery of faith,'' i.e., a "sign" that reveals Jesus in his true status—his "glory''—and at the same time demands our involvement along with the disciples who believe in him.

There will be other "signs." John speaks of seven[20] that he has selected among countless others, too numerous to report (John 20:30). Each of them is full of the revelation of the glory of Christ. But, because of its multiple symbolism, that of Cana is the "first,'' in every sense of the term.

When the hour is come, the Father will glorify his Son on the cross and the Son will glorify him (John 17:1). But the glory of the Father and the Son shines on those who believe in him (John 17:22), and it will overwhelm the community of the disciples in the Church, which will receive it, grace following upon grace, and sharing it with all through the Church's life witness and proclamation of the gospel.[21]

The liturgical year causes us symbolically to travel this path of glory, from the "beginning of the signs" to the sign of Easter and the descent of the Spirit at Pentecost, which begins the Ordinary Time of the Church.

No other icon could better adorn the gateway that leads to Year C. Luke is, in fact, the evangelist who most insists on the manifestation of God's glory, from the announcement to Mary of the birth of the Savior to his nativity in the poor surroundings of Bethlehem, from Christ's baptism to his transfiguration, throughout his ministry up through the resurrection. And the Book of Acts will emphasize its diffusion in the Church and in the world.

Unity of Spirit, Diversity of Gifts

We also begin this Sunday a series of "semicontinuous" readings from the First Letter of Paul to the Corinthians (lasting through the Eighth Sunday). The Lectionary contains almost all of chapters 12, 13, and 15.

Corinth was a relatively new, large city. Destroyed in 146 B.C., it was rebuilt one hundred years later. It was a wealthy city owing to its position on the isthmus between the Aegean and Adriatic seas. It was also a cosmopolitan city, visited by people from all over the world, a city full of contrasts: ostentatious wealth for some, misery and squalor for most. One could say that the lower stratum of the population was composed of slaves! A city where the best and the worst live shoulder to shoulder: astonishing intellectual activity and fertile ground for many doctrines; mystery religions and worship of Aphrodite with sacred prostitution; and the development of all kinds of sects.

During an eighteen-month journey (A.D. 50-52), Paul proclaimed the gospel in this city (see Acts 18:1-8). The community that his preaching assembled was composed of a small number of rich and poor, the downtrodden, and slaves (1 Cor 1:26, 28; 7:21; 11:21-22).

It was a vibrant and fervent community, but—is this so surprising?—exposed to many dangers because of its surroundings: internal division and quarrels (1:11-12; 6:1-11); the allure of pagan doctrines (1:19–2:10); sexual deviations (6:12-20); ignorance about the gifts of the Spirit (chs.

12, 13, 14); assemblies thrown into disarray because of the introduction of certain elements of "mystery" religions (14:26-38); and even perversion of the fundamental gifts of the Christian faith (ch. 15). In short, a community that, because of the surrounding paganism, somewhat resembles Christian communities today, which are assailed by similar dangers.

This letter, which probably dates from the spring of A.D. 56, is structured in the following manner:

Greeting and thanksgiving (1:1-9)

1. The divisions in the Corinthian community (1:10–4:21)
2. The case of incest (5:1-13)
3. Appeals to pagan courts (6:1-11)
4. Fornication (6:12-20)
5. Marriage and virginity (ch. 7)
6. Food consecrated to idols (8:1–11:1)
7. The way to hold religious assemblies (11:2–14:40)
8. The resurrection of the dead (ch. 15)

Recommendations, greetings, conclusion (ch. 16)

Chapter 12, read in its entirety between this Sunday and next, belongs to the section on proper order in the assembly (11:2–14:40).

We know very well the preceding passage, on the Lord's Supper (11:23-37), which is read every year on Holy Thursday and during Year C on the solemnity of the Body and Blood of Christ.

Here the question concerns "spiritual gifts," "forms of service," "workings," and their manifestations in the assembly.

Their apparent variety—the apostle is content to list them quickly—is a blessing that the Church would not know how to do without. "But one and the same Spirit produces all of these, distributing them individually to each person as he wishes" (v.11). Each time he mentions one of these "gifts," "forms of service," or "workings," Paul repeats that it is always "the same Spirit," "the same Lord," and "the same God." It would be impossible to insist more emphatically on their common origin.

Consequently, it would be absurd, in the Church and the assembly, to talk of rights and authority, when it is a question of various gifts disposed of only by the will of God.

On the other hand, there is no room for untimely exhibitions that arise from an uncontrolled self-centeredness: neither seemingly delirious shouts of praise, like in some modern-day circles, nor the spontaneity preached and practiced by others.

Who would not agree that these strong words from the apostle should be of interest today?

> *Alleluia! Alleluia!*
> God has called us with the gospel;
> the people won for him by Jesus Christ our Lord.
> *Alleluia!*

The Gospel acclamation sets the tone of this Sunday very well and succinctly expresses the mystery.

The "sign" of Cana is not merely an episode from Jesus' life, recounting one day when he happened to be invited to a wedding. It is a revelation of the glory of Christ, which is the source and object of our faith, as well as an invitation to contemplate the glory of the Lord throughout Ordinary Time, which begins today.

At the same time, it is a revelation of the poverty—"they have no wine"—to which the Lord brings an end, definitively, by filling us with an abundance of new wine.

He himself, henceforth, will be the master of the feast, the Bridegroom who shares his table with those who believe in him.

In his Church, as among those gathered in his name, thanks to the diversity of "spiritual gifts," "forms of service," and "workings," believers cease to be a group of individuals. They are, and must ceaselessly become, a community gathered in living unity, upon which comes the one Spirit.

When this happens, the glory of God is revealed: believers—for whom Mary is the model—express it, so that all others may see it.

From the Third to the Fifth Sunday in Ordinary Time

The Gospels—more generally, the whole of the biblical writings—were composed according to the criteria of their literary genre, as well as the intention and personal genius of the author, which is indissolubly linked to the time of composition.[1] This is particularly the case with Luke.

He wrote one work in two volumes that are quite connected: the Gospel and the Acts of the Apostles. The "prologue," which is found at the beginning of the first book (Luke 1:1-4—Third Sunday) acts as an introduction for both of them.

The author speaks of this as a historical work: "a narrative of the events that have been fulfilled among us, just as those who were eyewitnesses from the beginning . . . I too have decided, after investigating everything accurately anew, to write it down in an orderly sequence for you" (Luke 1:1-3 = *ibid.*).

But at the same time, he notes that the "eyewitnesses" have become "ministers of the word," and that his decision to write has a very precise goal: that the reader may "realize the certainty of the teachings" received (4 = *ibid.*).

Such are Luke's distinctive perspective and method. Without ignoring the historical veracity of his work, the resulting character of the account composed by Luke is quite in line with his intention; at once to show the soundness of the received teachings, and to make the reader understand the meaning and import "of the events that have been fulfilled among us."

His work is certainly neither a chronicle nor a "history"—in the modern sense of the word—of Jesus (Gospel) and the primitive Church (Acts). Nor should we imagine that Luke's sequence of events is historically or geographically correct. If that were the case, the author would have left the reader the full responsibility—and the risk—of trying to discover on his or her own the meaning of events, of recognizing in them the hand of God, and of rooting out what is significant regarding faith. This was clearly not his intention.[2] And yet one can legitimately speak of the account as being "accurately investigated," "ordered."

In the Gospel According to Luke, we can see a definite progression: the stories of Jesus' infancy (1:5–2:52) and the prelude to the mission (3:1–4:13); the first part of the mission (properly so-called) 4:14–9:50; the "journey to Jerusalem" (9:51–19:28); the third part of Jesus' mission

(19:29–24:53). But this is more a framework than a plan, at least in the sense of which we speak of it today.[3]

On the other hand, it is possible to see, in the "semicontinuous" reading contained in the Sunday Lectionary, a series of small groups (if not in fact of distinct units) that have an internal coherence.[4] Such is the case with the readings from the Third, Fourth, and Fifth Sundays of Ordinary Time (Luke 1:1-4; 4:14-21/4:21-30/5:1-11). To point out their unity—or rather their coherence—without forgetting that each of these passages is proclaimed in the context of a liturgical celebration along with other scriptural texts, one could present them as: The mystery of the Word: revealed and proclaimed with sovereign authority and in a decisive manner by the Messiah of God (Third Sunday); in the face of which one has to choose (Fourth Sunday); to the service of which Jesus himself has called those whom he instituted as "fishers" of men (Fifth Sunday).

In its own way, the Old Testament (first reading) enlightens this mystery directly, indirectly, or by contrast.

Finally, the three excerpts from the First Letter of Paul to the Corinthians show how the Christian community experiences—must experience—unity with its diversity of functions (Third Sunday); according to a proper hierarchy of charisms (Fourth Sunday); faithful to the teaching transmitted and received (Fifth Sunday).

Third Sunday

Jesus Christ, the Amen of God

It may be pointless to insist on the place and the role, in "revealed" religion, of the Word of God proclaimed by the prophets, studied and meditated on by the sages, inscribed in the book par excellence, which we call the "Bible." But perhaps it is worth the trouble to recall that, in the history of the people of God, the creative Word (Gen 1) is to be heard directly, through the proclamation of Scripture every time Israel is solemnly gathered together for a reawakening of the covenant: at the restoration of the Temple under Solomon (1 Kgs 8) and the worship under Hezekiah (2 Chr 29–30), at the "discovery" of the book of the law under Josiah (2 Kgs 23) and the inauguration of Judaism after the Exile (Neh 8–9).

A Liturgy of the Word

The first reading of this Third Sunday recalls the solemn Liturgy of the Word that took place on this last occasion (Neh 8:1-10). It contains several important keys for unlocking the meaning and significance of what happened, much later, when Jesus entered the synagogue of Nazareth one sabbath and read the book that was handed him, as well as for understanding what happens every Sunday in the Christian assembly.

The assembling of all the people: men, women, and children who are old enough to understand; the solemn enthronement of the Book of the Law; the reading given by the scribe Esdras "on a wooden platform"; the standing assembly; the benediction of God and of the people who, "hands raised high," cry out "Amen! Amen!," then kneel and prostrate themselves before God; the reading by Esdras; the translation and teaching by the Levites sprinkled throughout the assembly; finally, the dismissal of the assembly in joy and thanksgiving. Out of these elements, we can draw interesting and fruitful reflections for the Liturgy of the Word today.

The liturgical celebration is not meant to be leisure-time. On the contrary, it insists that we enter more deeply into the Liturgy of the Word, from the beginning of Ordinary Time. After this reading has stirred us up, the liturgy has us sing four verses from the second half of Psalm 19:

Your words, O LORD, are spirit and life.

The law of the LORD is perfect,
  refreshing the soul;
The decree of the LORD is trustworthy,
  giving wisdom to the simple.
The precepts of the LORD are right,
  rejoicing the heart;
The command of the LORD is clear,
  enlightening the eye.
The fear of the LORD is pure,
  enduring forever;
The ordinances of the LORD are true,
  all of them just.
Let the words of my mouth and the thought of my heart
  find favor before you,
O LORD, my rock and my redeemer.

Roles and Charisms in the Body of Christ

Next, we read a passage from the First Letter of Paul to the Corinthians (12:12-30), which follows immediately after the passage that was read last Sunday (12:4-11). It turns our attention to the mystery of the Church, of all ecclesial communities, of the assembly gathered here and now.

Here it deals with the unity in diversity of the "spiritual gifts," "forms of service," "workings" (12:4-6), but seen from a different angle, for it is always from the source—from on high—that the apostle envisages the most concrete reality: "It was in one Spirit that all . . . were baptized." Hence the central affirmation: "You, then, are the body of Christ. Every one of you is a member of it."

The realism—mystical, concrete, practical—of this affirmation proceeds from the comparison developed in verses 16-26. On the one hand, the body is not the sum of its individual members, but a whole, unified reality, of which each member is an integral part. At the same time, the "body" must be understood here, as elsewhere (Rom 6:6 and 12:1, for example), in the sense of a "person" whose "body" is the necessary locus of his or her existence, action, relation to God, others, and the world. In addition, Christ is, through the Spirit, the principal unifier of this "body-person." The apostle goes quite far with this understanding. Really, the reader is waiting for him to say: "This is the case with the Church and the assembly." Instead, he writes: "Now you are Christ's body"! What is at issue here is not first and foremost the functional good of a harmonious assembly ordered in the form of a living being, but the very mystery of Christ and his person. The Church is in his image, a reflection of what he is in himself.

One can and must make certain distinctions: "first . . . second . . . third . . ." (v. 28). But they do not evoke different categories of "members," of "spiritual gifts," of "forms of service" or "workings," more or less "indispensable" or "honorable" (vv. 22-23), in the way that one might speak of a well-structured social body. We have here a diversity in forms of service in a living organism that embraces them in its unity. Their anarchic development, the atrophying of such and such a member can damage the vitality of the whole body.

Today, This Word

And now, see how the Gospel (Luke 4:14-21), today as yesterday, focuses on Jesus, the Christ, the herald of the good news that he solemnly proclaims and fulfills: "All . . . looked intently at him."

This scene takes place in the ultra-common setting of the liturgy in the synagogue on the sabbath. But the surface simplicity of the event throws into relief its novelty and grandeur.

A man like others, well known to the people in this, his hometown. Like so many others before and after him, he went up to read the book that was presented him. He "found"⁵ a passage that many people, if not everyone, knew by heart, having heard it read many times before.

But suddenly, in the silence, after the book was returned to the servant and the reader was seated, came this extraordinary statement: "Today this scripture passage is fulfilled in your hearing."

After so many centuries, during which we have become accustomed to it, it still retains its power of novelty and revelation. The proclamation of the gospel is always based on the reading of the Law enlightened by prophecy. But this continuity comes across something new: Jesus, the "anointed," on whom the Spirit rested, "sent to bring glad tidings to the poor," whose appearance inaugurates the new age of salvation. Jesus, the eternally living Word of God, the "Amen" of the Father, fulfillment of the Scriptures, on whom our eyes are fixed.

> Blessed assembly whom Scripture attests all had their eyes fixed on Jesus! How I wish that this assembly might receive similar testimony, that all, catechumens and faithful, women, men, and children have their eyes, not of the body but of the soul, filled with the sight of Jesus! When you look at him, his light and his contemplation will lighten your faces, and you will be able to say: "The light of your face has left its imprint on us, O Lord!"⁶

The book is still read in the assembly. In the Church, there are, first of all, the "apostles" who announce the good news; secondly, there are the "prophets" who, in its light, interpret the signs of the times; and third, the "teachers," then all those whose various gifts are put at the service of the entire body. But each of us, whatever our vocation and place in the Church and the assembly, must—above all—learn from Jesus to "read" the Book.

May the liturgy of this Sunday remind us of and turn us toward Jesus when we open the Book that the Church gives us! May we keep our attention fixed on him when the reading is made in the assembly!

> You want me to read; and you want me to read in a certain way. "He stood up to read"; my first task seems to be to open the holy books and to look for you in them. "He was handed a scroll of the prophet Isaiah"; the Church constantly presents the holy Scriptures to my attention, to my meditation, and it is from her that I receive the Book with respect and faith. Yet it is not on "my" reading, but on "your" reading of the Book that I must try to fix my thought. It is in seeing you read, in hearing you read, that I may learn "how" to read. The roles are reversed. It is now to you that your servant poses the question: "How do you read?"
>
> You come to Nazareth. It is the day of the Sabbath. According to your custom, you enter the synagogue. I enter it with you. There, you offer to read the Book yourself. You then want to explain the Word of God. I translate this into Christian terms: you have confided to your holy Church the deposit of inspired Scriptures. I have no wish to read the Word without your Church or against your Church: she is the supreme and infallible interpreter of what was written under the Spirit's power. Yet you welcome me, both in the "synagogue" and in the privacy of my room, with the intensely personal welcome of the Word. How should I understand this? Lord, each time I take the Bible in my hands, may I see that I lift you, and may you teach me to "read."[7]

Then, kneeling, prostrate before the Lord, we may, with the whole Church, sing in faith and thanksgiving:

> Today, we celebrate Jesus Christ who
> died for our sins
> AMEN!
> rose from the dead
> AMEN!
> and we await him till he returns
> AMEN!

Christ, the Sign of Contradiction

Last Sunday, the liturgical assembly ended in the joy and happiness of an extraordinary good news proclaimed by Jesus with sovereign authority. After having read in the Book of Isaiah the prophecy announcing "a year of favor from the Lord," Jesus declared: "Today, this scripture passage is fulfilled in your hearing."

One might expect that what happened "today" would arouse the crowds in the synagogue of Nazareth, causing the swelling of a tidal wave in converts to follow Jesus. One might expect to see Jesus' preaching give the lie to the proverb: "No prophet is accepted in his own native place" (Luke 4:24).

Much more often than not, Scripture testifies to the rejections the prophets faced, their troubles, the numerous persecutions they endured, and the deaths to which faithfulness to their mission so often led them.

I Am With You

However, it is not upon such things that the first reading dwells, but rather on the help that, from their first call, God grants to his messengers (Jer 1:4-5, 17-19).

When one understands the mission of Jeremiah, one of the greatest prophets, it is not surprising that God should have initially assured him that he would be with him in his trials, making him "a fortified city, a pillar of iron, a wall of brass." For he was told to challenge the deepest convictions of his fellow citizens, to stand firm in the face of lies and slander, to upbraid the people for their laxity, in short, to go "against the whole land: against Judah's kings and princes, against its priests and people" who treated him very harshly. He knew the agonizing loneliness of a man of the Word, and of a Gethsemane, having been thrown into a deep hole where he could hardly think about the renewal that it was his mission to proclaim.

Hesitant, troubled in the depths of his being, bowed down under an overwhelming responsibility, hounded on all sides, he never stopped speaking with the tenacity of a timid person; he remained an upright man. He learned the cost of being a prophet and, by his suffering, he learned obedience to God.

This would not have been possible had he not been firmly assured, throughout, of God's promise. Some days, to be sure, he could barely utter this message: "Be not crushed on their account, as though I would leave you crushed before them." Like Jesus on the cross repeating Psalm 22: "My God, my God, why have you forsaken me . . . I will proclaim your name to my brethren; in the midst of the assembly I will praise you . . . For dominion is the LORD's and he rules the nations."

An absolutely extraordinary mission, certainly, but no less necessary today in the life of individual Christians, ecclesial communities, and the Church, whose prophetic mission can only be undertaken in the faith and hope of which Psalm 71 sings.

I will sing of your salvation.

In you, O LORD, I take refuge;
  let me never be put to shame.
In your justice rescue me, and deliver me;
  incline your ear to me, and save me.

Be my rock of refuge,
  a stronghold to give me safety,
  for you are my rock and my fortress.
O my God, rescue me from the hand of the wicked.

For you are my hope, O LORD;
  my trust, O God, from my youth.
On you I depend from birth;
  from my mother's womb you are my strength.

My mouth shall declare your justice,
  day by day your salvation.
O God, you have taught me from my youth,
  and till the present I proclaim your wondrous deeds.

The Royal Way of Charity

Jeremiah evokes the figure of Christ. From the prophet, herald of the good news, the epistle draws us back briefly to the ecclesial community assembled by Jesus, the body animated by the Spirit on which God freely bestows his gifts (1 Cor 12:31–13:13).

The various gifts of which the apostle spoke in the readings for the previous two Sundays (1 Cor 12:4-11; 12:12-30) are certainly of great value; the "body" could not do without them. Nevertheless, there is a "way which surpasses all the others." And so we have the marvelous hymn to love that all Christians should know by heart, that they may keep themselves on its path.

This hymn is clearly divided into three parts: the superiority of love (vv. 1-3); its works (vv. 4-7); its lasting quality (vv. 8-13).

Love here first means fraternal love, but love for God is present everywhere, especially in verse 13, which speaks of faith and hope.[8] Of course, it would not be love in the Christian sense of the word, if love of neighbor were not intimately bound up with love for God: the two commandments really become one. We can be inclined to forget this, and therefore regard the way of love as an independent road, an easy shortcut, by which one can avoid the other roads, with their wearisome toil.

In fact, the apostle has no intention of offering a "better way" in the sense of an easier, less burdensome itinerary. This impassioned text is inserted between chapters 12 and 14, which treat very well of the indispensable gifts of the Spirit and the proper way of using, in the Church and the community, the various "forms of service" and "workings" (1 Cor 12:4-6—Second Sunday). Without love, these things have no value.

The apostle affirms this with extraordinary vigor. Without love, the gifts (speaking in tongues, the gift of prophecy, full knowledge and comprehension of all mysteries), the most complete generosity ("giving everything I have to feed the poor"), even the sacrifice of one's own life ("handing over my body to be burned") are nothing.

With no less spirit, the apostle, in four verses, speaks of several concrete manifestations of authentic love. Many New Testament texts can be called to mind here.

Finally comes the strophe (vv. 8-13) on the unfailing durability of love situated with respect to the realities that it surpasses (prophecy, tongues, knowledge) and the faith-hope-love trilogy, "three things that last," but of which "the greatest is love."

A royal way that leads to union with God from where we are, love is the path of sanctity accessible to everyone with the grace of the Lord. It is not enough to know it: one must be fully and confidently set on its sure path.

This is what Thérèse of Lisieux found in chapter 13 of the First Letter to the Corinthians.

Finally I have found peace. Regarding the mystical body of the Church, I had not seen myself as one of the members described by St. Paul, or rather I did not wish to see myself in the whole. Charity gave me the key to my vocation. I understood that if the Church had a body, composed of different members, all necessary and noble, the Church must have a heart, and that this heart was burning with love. I understood that love alone moves the members of the Church, that if love were to die out, the apostles would not proclaim the gospel, the martyrs would refuse to shed their blood. I understood that love encompassed all vocations, that love was all, that it embraced all times and places; in a word, that it was eternal.

Then, in the excess of my delirious joy, I cried out: O Jesus, my love; I have finally found my vocation, and it is love.

Yes, I have found my place in the Church, and this place, O my God, you have given me. In the heart of the Church, my Mother, I will be love; thus I will be all, thus my dream will come true.[9]

Truly, the Love of which the apostle speaks with so much fire, yet in a quite concrete manner, is not a mere human sentiment, even a generous and noble one, but grace, in the strongest sense of the word, that is to say, "a free gift of God" for salvation. It has its beginning and end in God, Father, Son, and Spirit, who is Love. The Spirit communicates it. It allows one to enter, through the Son, into communion with the Father. In short, the mystery of love is indissolubly linked with the mystery of the Trinity that we confess in faith.[10]

A Prophet Scorned in His Own Country

The Gospel (Luke 4:21-30) leads us back to the synagogue of Nazareth that we had left last Sunday after Jesus declared: "Today this scripture passage is fulfilled in your hearing."

Matthew (13:54-58) and Mark (6:1-6) also report the hostile reactions of the people of Nazareth to Jesus' preaching in their synagogue, albeit in much milder form.[11] But these reactions have a particular significance in Luke.

First of all, the reactions did not flow from Jesus' general teaching, but specifically from the implications of a decisive revelatory proclamation: the oracle of Isaiah 61:1-2 is fulfilled today. It is impossible to mistake Jesus' meaning: it is he who proclaimed the prophecy; it is in him and through him that the decisive age of salvation begins.

In addition, for the evangelist, this "today" is clearly that of the Church: Luke wrote his book for believers who belonged neither to the generation nor the milieu of the townspeople to whom Jesus spoke at Nazareth.[12]

That such a revelation should provoke astonishment is not surprising. There clearly was a disproportion between this "appealing discourse" and the human condition of the one who proclaimed it: "Is this not Joseph's son?"

Such astonishment can be a form of skepticism, whether recognized as such or not, that constantly demands proofs, but will never be satisfied, because it is never open to being convinced. To say to someone "Physician, heal thyself" is to reject him out of hand and definitively. The demand for evidence can hide an adamant refusal to be convinced.

Moreover, in citing the proverb "No prophet is accepted in his own native place," Jesus was not voicing a truism. There would be nothing more to say if it were a matter of the confirmation of a common experience. Rather, it is a pronouncement like the apostrophe against the cities on the lake: "Woe to you, Chorazin! Woe to you, Bethsaida! For if the mighty deeds done in your midst had been done in Tyre and Sidon, they would long ago have repented, sitting in sackcloth and ashes. But it will be more tolerable for Tyre and Sidon at the judgment than for you. And as for you, Capernaum, 'Will you be exalted to heaven? You will go down to the netherworld' " (Luke 10:13-15).

From the beginning of the Church—as witnessed by Acts—until the present day, many who should have been the first to welcome the good news and its preachers have reacted like the inhabitants of Nazareth! And not only because they know the spokesperson—the "prophet"—too well, but because they cannot bear the thought that people outside their own family or milieu can share with, or even see before them, the same grace, the same privilege. "What you did at Capernaum," this city rife with paganism . . .

> When the Son of Man went into the place where he belonged, his own people did not receive him. The "patriotism" of this elected people should have consisted in faith in God and in his word, and therefore also in his new word, but the incarnate Word did not encounter this faith. This people believed that its relations with God had long been defined and that there was nothing to change about them; they figured that the fact that there was a covenant concluded with God meant that they did not need to approach him more clearly and that they could henceforth dispense with what God wished to say to them. The Son found no faith among the people who believed in his Father, for Israel already thought of itself as "believing." He found this faith in a centurion who belonged to the pagan army that had occupied the land. He was lost in admiration, he who knew everything from eternity. This admiration accompanied the Son of Man throughout his life; his heart was moved to think that so many who seemed to be

outside were inside, that those who were born citizens of the kingdom would be thrown out into darkness, that unconditional faith often sprang more readily from the heart of the "unbeliever" than from the heart of those who were always orthodox and that heaven finds sincere penitence in sinners rather than in those who believe they have no need of it.

All these considerations retain their value today. The limits of the kingdom of God do not coincide with those of people who separate the confessions or who draw a line of demarcation between "practicing" and "non-practicing" Catholics. This does not necessarily mean that the will of God is not that one be Catholic and "practicing," but that among Catholics, not all are true children of the kingdom. The book of life does not accord purely and simply with religious statistics, parish registers, and lists of members of Catholic associations. . . .[13]

Chauvinism and provincialism are incompatible with the universal proclamation of prophecy, with the mission of Jesus and the Church, with the gospel, with God's way of acting. Luke, as we know, insists on this point: Acts witnesses that the mission must consistently extend its frontiers. The Church earnestly desires Christian assemblies to hear and respond to God's way, conformed to by Jesus and of which he is the model: "There were many widows in Israel in the days of Elijah, yet . . . Recall, too, the many lepers in Israel in the time of Elisha the prophet; yet. . ."

The universality of salvation! God's concern for all goes quite far; even so far as to leave the ninety-nine sheep to go and search for the lost one (Luke 15:3-7—Twenty-fourth Sunday).

Jesus was not satisfied merely with proclaiming this in various ways; he readily "compromised" himself in such a way as to excite astonishment, anger, and malignant slander: "Look, he is a glutton and a drunkard, a friend of tax collectors and sinners" (Luke 7:34). They "rose up and drove him out of the town, and led him to the brow of the hill on which their town had been built, to hurl him down headlong. But he passed through the midst of them and went away" (Luke 4:29-30).

His road leads to Jerusalem, to which, from the beginning, he journeys "resolutely." Nothing can hold him back: neither the murderous intentions of his fellow citizens nor the refusal of the Samaritans who would not receive him in their village "because the destination of his journey was Jerusalem" (Luke 9:53—Thirteenth Sunday).

Jesus would not let himself be deterred by anyone or anything, "continuing . . . today, tomorrow, and the following day" (Luke 13:33) up to Jerusalem where "everything written by the prophets about the Son of Man will be fulfilled" (Luke 18:31).

It is through death that he will "pass over" to return to his Father after his resurrection. On that day, a criminal who deserved his condemnation, hanging by his side, would hear him say: "Amen, I say to you, today you will be with me in Paradise." "The centurion who witnessed what had happened glorified God and said, 'This man was innocent beyond doubt,'" while "all his acquaintances stood at a distance, including the women who had followed him from Galilee and saw these events" (Luke 23:39-43, 47, 49—Passion [Palm] Sunday, Year C).

All this can be read between the lines of the story of Jesus' preaching in the synagogue at Nazareth, as is clearly Luke's intention in writing a "narrative" that points up the reliability, the coherence of the received teachings, and the call to salvation addressed to all.

Truly, the beginning of the Gospel According to Luke is not oriented toward a "history" of Jesus in the sense of an impartial relation of a train of events. Luke can certainly be called a historian: he has his information from reliable witnesses. But his "history" must be read in light of the cross of Christ. Its full meaning is revealed in the context of the celebration of the Passover of the Lord. It calls for faith in Jesus, and leads to more authentic faith in him, without hesitation.

Jesus came as a "sign of contradiction" that forces us to choose (Luke 2:34—feast of the Holy Family B). This is what the liturgy for this Sunday reminds us about.

At the same time, it urges each of us, as well as every assembled community and the whole Church, to enter more deeply, day to day, into the mystery of the love of God and of neighbor, of the love that "surpasses all the others."

Jesus Alone Is Master and Lord of the Fishers of Men

In his relation to God and his mission, Jesus is and will always be alone. It is in and through him alone that the mystery of salvation is fulfilled "today." It is with regard to him alone that we must make our decisions. And yet he shares his mission with certain individuals whom he makes fishers of men. Yesterday, it was the invisible God who called the prophets and made them his spokespersons. Henceforth Jesus will choose those who will be sent to announce the good news of salvation.

The Calling of a Prophet
The Old Testament delights in evoking the initiative of God, who chooses and sends his prophets: Abraham (Gen 12), Moses (Exod 3), Amos (Amos 7), Jeremiah (Jer 1), Ezekiel (Ezek 3), and others. Along with the common features that can be found in each of these stories are the particular characteristics of each, having to do with the personality of the messenger, his particular mission and the concrete circumstances in which he would exercise it.[14]

The calling of Isaiah is connected with a vision in the Temple. Isaiah "sees" God, the lord and king of the universe.[15] The "high and lofty throne," the "train" of the cloak that "filled the Temple," evoke the incomparable majesty and dignity of the one who dwells in the midst of his people and leads them through their history.

The God of majesty is the thrice-holy God. The seraphim, those mysterious, fiery beings, are his throne. Acclaiming them was doubtlessly a practice before Isaiah's time in worship and has been part of the Christian liturgy throughout the centuries. It is a practice filled with the prophet's theology of the sanctity of God. But in the liturgical framework of this Sunday, we will remember above all the universality of the reign of the "God of the universe," whose glory fills the earth, whose sovereign might is revealed, in the vision, by the clamorous shout that shook the hinges of the doors while smoke filled the Temple.

35

How could anyone help feel his or her utter frailty and the unworthiness of the people?

But God purifies Isaiah, who has the audacity to calmly say: "Here I am . . . send me."

With Psalm 138 and the refrain "In the sight of the angels I will sing your praises, LORD" the assembly echoes the acclamation of the seraphim. It gives thanks and joins the whole universe with its praise. And by bowing toward the throne of the glory of God, it acknowledges that everything comes from him, that each believer has a share in his universal victory:

> *In the sight of the angels I will sing your praises, LORD.*
>
> I will give thanks to you, O LORD, with all my heart,
>   [for you have heard the words of my mouth;]
>   in the presence of the angels I will sing your praise;
> I will worship at your holy temple
>   and give thanks to your name.
>
> Because of your kindness and your truth;
>   for you have made great above all things
>   your name and your promise.
> When I called, you answered me;
>   you built up strength within me.
>
> All the kings of the earth shall give thanks to you, O LORD,
>   when they hear the words of your mouth;
> And they shall sing of the ways of the LORD:
>   "Great is the glory of the LORD."
>
> Your right hand saves me.
>   The LORD will complete what he has done for me;
> Your kindness, O LORD, endures forever;
>   forsake not the work of your hands.
> (Ps 138:1-8)

A profession of faith, recall of the past (anamnesis), invocation (epiclesis)—this psalm is a veritable cosmic liturgy.

The Ministry of an Apostle

In the second reading (1 Cor 15:1-11), Paul reminds the Corinthians who have received the gospel that to be saved, they must guard the object of the good news from all impurity. This reminder is valuable to us as a condensed form of the "symbol of the Apostles": "Christ died for our sins in accordance with the scriptures . . . he was buried . . . he was raised on the third day in accordance with the scriptures"; he appeared to the witnesses he had chosen.

Paul is one of them. He is certainly conscious of not being worthy of the title of apostle, because of his persecution of the Church of God; however, in question here is not personal dignity. His election is pure grace from God, as is the zeal which he is to use to accomplish his mission. An unconditional gift, disposed of most freely. To the Lord, Isaiah simply responds: "Send me." Saul is content to say to Jesus: "What shall I do?" (Acts 22:10).

The Lord and Peter's Boat

Now see the Master who, from where he is seated in Peter's boat, teaches the crowds with his sovereign authority (Luke 5:1-11).

The scene drawn by the evangelist has a striking, solemn, hieratic quality. We should pause over it, for in ways that are distinctively his own, Luke says many important things.

Jesus is seated in a boat that Simon, at his request, has anchored some little distance from the shore. His voice carries to the bank where the crowds are gathered to hear the word of God. This is not a meaningless scene, but one that belongs to the Gospel; it is a parable in action. Actually, it allows us to contemplate in Jesus the Lord who teaches the word to the Church and to the countless multitudes to whom the good news must still be proclaimed.

Peter lends his boat, as he will later lend his voice, though never substituting it for Jesus'.

The evangelist passes without transition from the title of Master to that of Lord. Luke wants the reader to realize, from the beginning, the true identity of the Master and Lord whose teaching the Gospel faithfully transmits, as it has been received from tradition (Luke 1:1-4—Third Sunday). Drawing Simon and his companions from his teaching as he had previously drawn them from their work, Jesus directs them to go out on the lake and cast the nets they had been drying.

The demand was so unexpected (to say the least!) that Simon couldn't refrain from pointing out: "Master, we have worked hard all night long and have caught nothing." But, having said this, he did not hesitate: "but at your command, I will lower the nets." He caught so many fish that he had to call his companions to help, "and [they] filled both boats so that they were in danger of sinking."

Simon, whom the evangelist will henceforth refer to as Peter, the name that Jesus will give him, was immediately seized with "fright" at this manifestation of the divine, ". . . as well as James and John, Zebedee's sons, who were partners with Simon." He saw with his own eyes the one whom he recognized as the Lord! He is sitting in Simon's boat! Simon can only fall at his feet and beg him to leave, for he is a "sinful man."

All manifestations of the divine excite a profound feeling of holy terror, for the creature is in the presence of his God. The Bible never misses such an occasion: for example, the stories of the calling of the prophets, which we have seen in the first reading. But we can also think of Mary being "greatly troubled" at the announcement of the angel (Luke 1:29).

In every case, in one way or another, a word is said that is not meant only to calm the fearful heart, but to authenticate the revelation in some way: "Do not be afraid" says Jesus to Simon as the angel said to Mary (Luke 1:30).

Finally, we see the revelation of the vocation and the mission: "From now on you will be catching men."

Coming after the miraculous catch, this declaration points out that his success will surpass imagination and that it will come from the Lord and the faithfulness of Peter, who cast his nets when told to do so.

The story ends with the response of Peter and his companions. Returning their boats to the shore, they left everything and followed Jesus.

To follow Jesus is to become his disciple.[16] Luke notes the radical nature of this decision in stating that the disciples had to leave "everything" to follow him; some of those to whom Jesus called "Come and follow me" balked at this sacrifice.

The story of the miraculous catch, such as it is found in Luke, clearly has an Easter flavor. In fact, in the Fourth Gospel, this scene comes after the resurrection (John 21:1-14). But, as we have already noted, this Gospel is not strictly chronological. Luke stated clearly at the beginning that he wanted to compose a narrative to show the reader the reliability of the instruction he had received (Luke 1:3-4).

This reader Luke is addressing is a Christian who not only possesses Easter faith, but who lives in a Church community where, through the apostles and their successors, the work of the resurrected Christ is continued.

> "Master, we have been hard at it all night long and have caught nothing; but if you say so, I will lower the nets." I too, Lord, know that for me it is night when you do not govern. No matter what, it is still night for me. I have cast the net of the word at Epiphany, and I have caught nothing yet. I have cast it during the day. I await your order, on your command I will cast the nets.
>
> O vain presumption! O wondrous humility! They had caught nothing till then; at the voice of the Lord, they made a marvelous catch of fish. This

is not the work of human eloquence, but the blessing of the heavenly call. Peace to human arguments: it is by faith that the people believe. The nets are full and the fish cannot escape. The companions who were in another boat are called to the rescue.[17]

By placing the miraculous catch, the calling of Peter and his companions, and their response at the beginning, Luke indicates in what spirit the Gospel is to be read.

As the story ends, one can clearly see that the central figure is Jesus. Master and Lord who alone teaches with truth and authority, he is and remains at the origin of the preaching and mission of the Church. It is he who calls the "fishers of men." To follow him is to leave everything behind.

Paul, who never knew the historical Jesus, says that every apostle proclaims the good news transmitted to him; the resurrection is the foundational event of the apostolate and its mission, the heart of faith and its central object; no one can claim the title of apostle who has not been called by the grace of God.

The coherence of the Third, Fourth, and Fifth Sundays of Ordinary Time, Year C, is based on the fact that Luke, from the beginning, placed the Christian assembly in the presence of the person of Jesus and his mystery that is unfolded today in the Church and in the world.

This Jesus is the Messiah, herald of the good news and the divine grace, whose revelation inaugurates the era of salvation; Jesus, the prophet, the sign of contradiction to whom no one can remain neutral; Jesus, Master and Lord at the origin of the mission, who calls his disciples to follow him while abandoning everything to become "fishers of men" in this world; Jesus, his person and mystery, on whom shines the light of earlier Scripture, who preaches conversion to all.

Today we still cast the net. And Christ fills it. And Christ calls to conversion men who are found "in the depths of the sea," as the psalm has it (Ps 69:15), that is to say, among the waves and tempests of the world.[18]

Throughout the three extracts from his First Letter to the Corinthians, Paul sounds the urgent call. He addresses all the members of the Christian communities assembled through faith in the gospel.

The Church is the living body of Christ; the diversity of graces, gifts, and services that it cannot do without, come from the one Spirit. Let each of us examine the way we place them at the service of all!

And may we never forget that, without love, there is nothing, absolutely nothing of any value!

From the Sixth to the Eighth Sunday in Ordinary Time

During the Sixth, Seventh, and Eighth weeks, the Lectionary contains a large portion of chapter 6 of Luke's Gospel (twenty-seven of forty-nine verses). In fact, nearly the entire "Sermon on the Plain" (Luke 6:17-49), rather like the "Sermon on the Mount" in Matthew, is included. Thus we have a third "unit" in this semicontinuous reading of Luke.

The unit begins with the Beatitudes (vv. 20-26—Sixth Sunday), continuing with the words of Jesus on love for enemies, mercy, and benevolence (vv. 27-38—Seventh Sunday), and ending with an instruction on proper zeal (vv. 39-45—Eighth Sunday).

Also, during these three Sundays, we finish the semicontinuous reading of chapters 12 to 15 of the First Letter to the Corinthians. Next will come the Letter to the Galatians.

Sixth Sunday

The Paradoxical Happiness of Jesus' Disciples

Choose Life and Happiness

"Cursed . . . Blessed." These words, which occur respectively at the beginning of the two paragraphs that constitute this very short—four verses—first reading, immediately awaken our attention and set up the text in a striking antithesis (Jer 17:5-8).

The parallelism of these two paragraphs is truly remarkable. They have the same number of lines. Their construction is practically identical. Very nearly, each proposition in the first has its antithetical formulation in the second. It is immediately recognizable as a "wise saying." The first sentence says what should be obvious: "the Word of the Lord"; which, as proclaimed in the liturgy, and thus outside the context of the Book of Jeremiah, must be understood as being of general value and significance: "Always and everywhere is this so."

Blessedness or cursedness is tied to whether a person puts his or her confidence in the Lord or, turning from him, relies on "strength in flesh," in other words, on a being that is weak, fragile, and mortal.

The "confidence" here is expectant hope, which involves one's whole life, to which one holds fast through every trial.

This "confidence in God" accompanies faith in the one who calls himself "I Am," in whom, consequently, we may truly take refuge, on whom we can and must rely, and base our whole life.

Therefore, to place this "trust in human beings," "seeking strength in flesh," as solid as it may seem, whatever the powers at its disposal may be—strength, wealth, influence, relations, personal qualities, etc.—is objectively impiety, blasphemy, folly. The prophetic books and the psalms constantly speak of the enemy to the person who fears and relies on the Lord as one who puts his or her confidence in other things.[1] The same error must be safeguarded against both in religious institutions and the Law, in which we can be inclined to put the reliance that belongs to God alone:

41

Put not your trust in the deceitful words: "This is the temple of the LORD! The temple of the LORD! The temple of the LORD!" . . . I will do to this house named after me, in which you trust . . . just as I did to Shiloh. (Jer 7:4, 14)

How can you say, "We are wise,
  we have the law of the LORD"? . . .
The wise are confounded,
  dismayed and ensnared;
Since they have rejected the word of the LORD,
  of what avail is their wisdom? (Jer 8:8-9)

To express the contrast between the unhappiness of the one who relies "in human beings" and the happiness of the one who puts his trust "in the LORD," Jeremiah uses very evocative imagery. His intent is undoubtedly to point out how enviable is the condition of the person who is truly "blessed," and to lure his listeners to the path that leads to this blessedness.

Many passages from the Old Testament say the same thing, often with similar imagery. Thus, for example:[2]

In God I trust without fear;
  what can flesh do against me? (Ps 56:5)

God indeed is my savior;
  I am confident and unafraid.
My strength and my courage is the LORD,
  and he has been my savior.
With joy you will draw water
  at the fountain of salvation. (Isa 12:2-3)

The just man shall flourish like the palm tree,
  like a cedar of Lebanon shall he grow.
They shall bear fruit even in old age;
  vigorous and sturdy shall they be.
(Ps 92:13, 15)

The New Testament has the same view. Of the man who delights in the law of the Lord, Psalm 1 says: "Whatever he does, prospers." And Paul writes: "All things work for good for those who love God" (Rom 8:28).

In order to continue our meditation on this "Word of the Lord" received in faith, one psalm immediately suggests itself: the one that opens the Psalter and seems to be inspired by the oracle of Jeremiah 17, with a refrain that is forever on the lips of the one who puts his trust in the Lord.

Happy are they who hope in the LORD.

Happy the man who follows not
  the counsel of the wicked

Nor walks in the way of sinners,
   nor sits in the company of the insolent,
But delights in the law of the LORD
   and meditates on his law day and night.

He is like a tree
   planted near running water,
That yields its fruit in due season,
   and whose leaves never fade.
   [Whatever he does, prospers.]

Not so the wicked, not so;
   they are like chaff which the wind drives away.
For the LORD watches over the way of the just,
   but the way of the wicked vanishes.
(Ps 1)

The Assurance of the Christian

The epistle—continuing our reading of chapter 15 of the First Letter of Paul to the Corinthians (1 Cor 15:12, 16-20)—speaks about the basis for the Christian's assurance.

The apostle has reported the good news, the message that "by God's favor" he was commissioned to announce: "that Christ died for our sins in accordance with the scriptures; that he was buried; that he was raised on the third day in accordance with the scriptures . . . " And, he said, if you keep the gospel I have proclaimed to you, "You are being saved, unless you believed in vain" (1 Cor 15:1-8—Fifth Sunday).

He reiterates this last point in vociferously affirming that the destiny and conduct of Christians is intimately bound up with the resurrection of Christ, the fundamental and central object of the apostolic preaching and faith.

To believe in the resurrection of Christ entails belief in the resurrection of the dead. To deny one is to deny the other.

He concludes: "if Christ has not been raised, your faith is in vain; you are still in your sins. Then those who have fallen asleep in Christ have perished. If for this life only we have hoped in Christ, we are the most pitiable people of all" (vv. 17-19).

As in the first reading, we have an opposition between "the unhappy and the happy." But here, what differentiates their relative condition is faith in the resurrection of the dead and of Christ.

The hope of Christians, their certitude of not being confounded, the assurance of life in full, which death cannot cut short, rests on this certitude.

If we are not raised, "then Christ died for nothing" (1 Cor 15:13). If he is not raised for us, he is not raised at all, for there is no reason for him to be raised for himself. In him, the cosmos is resurrected, in him heaven is resurrected, in him earth is resurrected; for there will be "a new heaven and a new earth" (Rev 21:1). But what need does he have of resurrection, since the bonds of death cannot hold him? For though he died as man, he was nevertheless free in hell. Do you wish to know how he was free? "I am numbered among those who go down into the Pit, a man bereft of strength" (Ps 88:4). He was free enough to raise himself, according to what is written: "Destroy this temple, and in three days I will raise it again" (John 2:19). And free enough that he descended in order to free others.[3]

Jesus' Sermon on the Plain

It is toward Jesus that the Gospel turns our eyes. Jesus who himself proclaims the good news with the solemnity and authority that we have already seen in the Gospels of the previous Sundays.

The passage from Luke for the Sixth Sunday (Luke 6:17, 20-26) starts with the beginning of the "Sermon on the Plain." It is worthwhile, however, to remember how this selection is situated in Luke's Gospel, especially with regard to the sequence just concluded (Luke 6:12-16).

"In those days," says Luke, "he departed to the mountain to pray and he spent the night in prayer to God." Now, each time Luke shows Jesus at prayer, it is at an important, even a decisive, point in his mission.[4]

This time, it is a matter of a choice of twelve of the disciples to whom he went "when day came" and whom he "named apostles":[5] an important decision, both for Jesus' immediate mission and its later development.[6] But the fact that Luke mentions Jesus' prayer points up that the "Sermon on the Plain," which comes immediately afterward, is of extreme importance.

The beginning of the following sequence (the first verse of the Gospel for this Sixth Sunday) forms, in its simplicity, an imprint that is both majestic and hieratic. Luke indicates this with a marvelous handling of the staging: extremely spare but, at the same time and perhaps for that very reason, remarkably solemn. We feel that something is going to happen, and wait for it breathlessly.

First we see Jesus. He descends the mountain with those who have been selected as the apostles. He stops in the plain.

Only at this moment do we find that there are "many of his disciples" and "a large crowd of people" there. A substantial increase in audience size since the synagogue at Nazareth! (Luke 4:14-21—Third Sunday).

Being thrifty with his details, the evangelist mentions that this "crowd" was made up of "people" from all over. From "all Judea and Jerusalem" and even "the coast of Tyre and Sidon," Gentile countries! It is a "crowd"—one whole people—which already suggests all the nations to which the Anointed One of the Lord has come to announce "today," "a year of favor" (Luke 4:19, 21—Third Sunday). Indeed, Jesus is not a prophet sent only to the people of his own country (Luke 4:21-30—Fourth Sunday).

A sea of humanity—the whole world in some way—into which the "fishers of men," who came down from the mountain with him, "by his order" must enter "without fear" and throw their nets (Luke 5:1-11—Fifth Sunday).

In several lines that have the feel of a "summary"—verses 18 and 19, which are omitted by the Lectionary—Luke shows how, as Jesus proclaimed at Nazareth, "today" is fulfilled the word of Scripture taken from Isaiah. Of these "people," whose extraordinary diversity of origin he has noted, the evangelist says: they "came to hear him and to be healed of their diseases; and even those who were tormented by unclean spirits were cured. Everyone in the crowd sought to touch him because power came forth from him and healed them all" (Luke 6:18-19).

Again, what a contrast to what happened at Nazareth! Jesus had returned to the place "where he had grown up." He entered the synagogue of his town. He spoke to his people. Scandalized by what he said, they led him to an escarpment of a hill outside the village and conspired to throw him to his death (Luke 4:14-20, 21-30—Third and Fourth Sundays).

Here, we see the multitudes who have come to him, eager to listen, confident in the "power which came forth from him and healed them all." Far from wanting to steer clear of him, "everyone in the crowd sought to touch him."

At the Crossroads

One can hardly grow weary of contemplating this picture, painted in all its grandeur and simplicity, full of meaning and revelation. But Jesus focuses on his disciples, urging them to listen attentively to what he will say, hinting at the seriousness of his discourse. They are aware of this from the first part of the "Sermon of the Plain," which is in the form of eight sentences: four begin with "Blessed are you . . . " and four with "Woe to you . . . ."[7]

One is struck by the similarity with the passage from Jeremiah (first reading): "Blessed . . . cursed the man . . . ." But also by the differences. There, it was a wise saying that, as useful for all people, did not single out any particular category of persons. It dealt with confidence placed in God or "in human beings," "in strength of flesh."

The Way of Happiness

Here, Jesus speaks directly to a concrete audience, to the Twelve, to the disciples, to "the crowd" who surround him. He says to them: "Blessed are *you* . . ."

Even more, he is speaking to people "now" who are in unenviable, even miserable situations: the poor, the hungry, the afflicted, the outcast, the downtrodden.

The "today" of which Jesus spoke at Nazareth was opposed to the "yesterday" which preceded his coming. That was the day of his advent, the realization of the salvation promised, through Isaiah, to the poor, to prisoners, to the blind and oppressed (Third Sunday).

The "now" of the "Sermon on the Plain" is one of trial, of witnessing in the face of misfortune, which is the lot of Christians and the Church. Jesus warns them of it, of their fate in this "today" that will last from his departure till his return: "They will seize and persecute you, they will hand you over to the synagogues and to prisons, and they will have you led before kings and governors because of my name. It will lead to your giving testimony. . . . You will even be handed over by parents, brothers, relatives, and friends, and they will put some of you to death. You will be hated by all because of my name" (Luke 21:12-13, 16-17—Wednesday of the Thirty-fourth Week).

The announcement of this "now" of the trial is connected with a promise that is no less firm: "Remember, you are not to prepare your defense beforehand, for I myself shall give you a wisdom in speaking that all your adversaries will be powerless to resist or refute. . . . but not a hair on your head will be destroyed. By your perseverance you will secure your lives" (Luke 21:14-15, 18-19—*ibid*.).

Jesus also assures his disciples that there will be a complete reversal of the situation: since the kingdom of God belongs to them—their greatest treasure in "present" poverty—their tears will be changed to laughter, their miserable condition today will lead to great joy and recompense "in heaven." "On the day they do so, rejoice and exult."

But what is "that day"? According to Luke's conception, it is the time when each person will perceive the end of his trials in life: on that day, entering into the kingdom, he will know perfect joy, which is his recompense. At any rate, this is clearly the intention of the parable of the rich man and the beggar Lazarus (Luke 16:19-31—Twenty-sixth Sunday). In fact, it is in death that their positions are reversed: the beggar, "carried by angels to the bosom of Abraham," finds consolation, while the rich man is in "the abode of the dead where he was in torment" after having been "well off in his lifetime." This amounts to what Jesus said to the thief crucified with him, who was about to leave his sorrowful life: "Amen, I say to you, today you will be with me in Paradise" (Luke 23:35-43—Thirty-fourth Sunday and Passion [Palm] Sunday).

It is in this solemn promise that martyrs of all times and places put their hope and find their strength.

What will separate us from the love of Christ? Will anguish, or distress, or persecution, or famine, or nakedness, or peril, or the sword? . . . No, in all these things we conquer overwhelmingly through him who loved us. (Rom 8:35, 37).

If tribulation comes, we will say to God: "When I am in trouble, you come to my relief" (Ps 4:1). If there is worldly agony, which comes from the needs of the body, we will search the expanse of the wisdom and knowledge of God, in which the world will not find itself crowded in. I will go to the immense fields of the divine Scriptures; I will search the spiritual intelligence of the word of God, and no agony will trouble me anymore. Through the vast spaces of the mystical and spiritual intelligence, I will spur myself to the gallop. If I suffer persecution and if I confess my Christ before men, I am assured that he will confess me before his heavenly Father (cf. Matt 10:32).

I will not fear danger: "The LORD is my light and my salvation; whom should I fear? The LORD is my life's refuge; of whom should I be afraid?" (Ps 27:1).

The earthly sword cannot frighten me, for I have with me a stronger sword, that of the Spirit who is the Word of God. With me is God's word, "living and effective, sharper than any two-edged sword" (Heb 4:12). If therefore the sword of the world is poised over my head, it makes me worthy of greater love with respect to God. For I will say to him: as it is written, "For your sake we are being slain all the day; we are looked upon as sheep to be slaughtered" (Rom 8:36).

It is not enough for me to die or be tortured only one hour for Christ, but the whole day, that is to say, throughout my whole life. For if I pass my life in persecutions and dangers, I will say that "I consider the sufferings of this present time are as nothing compared with the glory to be revealed for us'' (Rom 8:18).

Brief is the time of this life; short are the moments we spend in persecutions; but perpetual and eternal is what we await in glory. And ''in all these things,'' says the apostle, ''we conquer overwhelmingly through him who loved us.''[8]

The Dilemma to Avoid

Also in this section are the four antitheses that are commonly known as ''maledictions.'' The term is not especially well chosen. ''Malediction'' is defined literally as a phrase by which one expresses a desire for someone's harm, especially in calling down the wrath of God upon him; hence, a condemnation pronounced by God on the evildoer. Such is not the case here.

In calling the rich ''woeful,'' those who are replete with goods ''now,'' those of whom ''all speak well,'' Jesus does not condemn them, nor swear that they are evildoers. He affirms that they are on a bad path, whose outcome is fatal: they have no consolation to await after this life; they will be hungry; they will experience mourning and misery.

Likewise, by declaring others ''blessed,'' Jesus affirmed, with sure divine foreknowledge, that their condition will lead them to joy and recompense in heaven. But the word ''beatitude,'' which refers to a state, merely adds to the confusion.

Again, it is to the parable of the rich man and Lazarus that one must turn. The former was not cursed, but the ''happiness'' known during this life makes his unhappiness ''in the abode of the dead'' like the ''misery'' of which Lazarus partook on this earth, he who was granted a place ''in Abraham's bosom.''

In spite of the ''you'' (the rich who are satisfied, etc.), the ''woeful'' of whom Jesus speaks are certainly not in his audience, which is composed of apostles, disciples, and the crowd of people who ''came to hear him and to be healed of their diseases'' (v. 18). This way of speaking falls within a genre always used in the Bible when pronouncing an apostrophe on those who are called ''woeful.''

''Woe'' to the rich, those who are ''full,'' those who need nothing ''now,'' because they have what they are looking for: it simply is not possible for them to wait for anything else. ''Woe'' to them, because they put their confidence in perishable goods that death destroys, while they fail to store up ''treasure in heaven'' in sharing with the poor, in choosing between false gold and true good, for they cannot serve both God and Mammon. Luke is particularly insistent on this point (Luke 12:13-40; 16:1-13, 19-34).

The parallelism with the beatitudes is perfect. There is no lack of clear distinction between the beatitude of those who are hated, rejected, insulted, treated with contempt "because of the Son of Man," and those whom Jesus declares "Woe to you when all speak well of you." One would have expected Jesus to speak about them as persecutors, those who inflict suffering on others. But no: they are "woeful" because "all speak well" of them, which was formerly the way the false prophets were treated.

This is what is surprising. Is it shameful to have a good opinion of oneself? And should one therefore be suspicious of whatever the world calls good?

Without including the fourth commandment of the Decalogue—"Honor your father and your mother, that you may have a long life in the land which the LORD, your God, is giving you" (Exod 20:12)—there are many passages in the Bible that speak of "honor," of the blessedness of the just. Thus, with regard to David, "He died at a ripe old age, rich in years and wealth and glory" (1 Chr 29:28). Likewise, for example, for Jehoshaphat (2 Chr 17:5; 18:1), Hezekiah (2 Chr 32:33), Judas and his brothers (1 Macc 5:65). Paul writes: "There will be glory, honor, and peace for everyone who does good" (Rom 2:10). To the question "LORD, who shall sojourn in your tent? Who shall dwell on your holy mountain?" Psalm 15 responds "he who walks blamelessly and does justice . . . while he honors those who fear the LORD" (Ps 15:1, 2, 4). Finally, the First Letter of Peter, reprising Proverbs 24:21, prescribes: "Give honor to all, love the community, fear God, honor the king" (1 Pet 2:17).

From the viewpoint of Greek culture, Luke knows the value attached to a good opinion of oneself, and the esteem granted—quite naturally—to eulogies offered to those who have good reputations.

But he also knows that Christians are disciples of the Lord who died on the cross like a slave after having suffered humiliation after humiliation during his passion. He remembers this saying of Jesus: "No disciple is superior to the teacher" (Luke 6:40—Eighth Sunday). He has seen his Christian brothers slandered, treated with contempt, and he has recalled that the apostles, leaving the great council where they had been beaten like dogs rejoiced "that they had been found worthy to suffer dishonor for the sake of the name" (Acts 5:40-41—Third Sunday of Easter). Therefore, "Woe to you when all speak well of you" is the antithesis of the fourth beatitude: "Blessed are you when people hate you, when they exclude and insult you and denounce your name as evil on account of the Son of Man," he who was "mocked and insulted and spat upon," "beaten," "treated contemptuously" (Luke 18:32; 22:63; 23:11).

"Blessed" are those who receive the preaching of Christ crucified "a stumbling block to Jews and foolishness to Gentiles" (1 Cor 1:23), who want nothing "except Jesus Christ, and him crucified" (1 Cor 2:2), who are glad to be "crucified with Christ" (Gal 2:19). For Jesus said to all: "If anyone wishes to come after me, he must deny himself and take up his cross daily and follow me. For whoever wishes to save his life will lose it, but whoever loses his life for my sake will save it. What profit is there for one to gain the whole world yet lose or forfeit himself?" (Luke 9:23-25).

The Liturgy of the Word of the Sixth Sunday in Ordinary Time situates the assembly at the center of the Christian life and mystery, which gain their meaning from the life and mystery of Christ.

"It is necessary for us to undergo many hardships to enter the kingdom of God" (Acts 14:22—Fifth Sunday of Easter): an uncontestable "law."

Christian life does not imply masochism, or complacency in the face of suffering, persecution, insults. "The hungry he has filled with good things" *(Magnificat)*. Jesus healed the sick, fed the crowds, comforted all those who were weak. Peter was miraculously freed from prison (Acts 12:1-19), and while Paul and Silas prayed, their chains were broken (Acts 16:25-40). From its origins till the present day, the Church, the Christian communities, the believers have not ceased to help the poor, to defend the oppressed, the outcasts, those judged to be worthless.

By proclaiming them "blessed," Jesus assures them that God is with them and that justice will be reestablished on "that day" when they will enter into the kingdom that has been prepared for them. Their assurance is based on their trust in God.

And yet, the perspective here is not "moral" but Christological. Their fate is linked with that of Christ dead and risen, humbled in his mortal life and exalted into glory. Today like yesterday.

> One must be ready for martyrdom. There was a time when we would read the acts of the martyrs with veneration, as a history that moved and strengthened us. Today, whoever decides to live the fullness of the gospel must prepare to be a martyr. The worst that can happen is that one be abused

and killed "for the name of Jesus Christ." This is the fulfillment of the word of the Lord: "I have told you this so that you may not fall away. . . . The hour is coming when everyone who kills you will think he is offering worship to God. . . . I have told you this so that when their hour comes you may remember that I told you." (John 16:1, 2, 4). It is the Spirit that brings about this joyous detachment in the face of martyrdom. Jesus promised the Spirit to his apostle so that they could preach "with power"—as the fruit of experience and palpable contemplation—and so that they could go to martyrdom in joy . . . Hard times demand strong men, who live by persevering in hope. Therefore they must be poor and contemplative men, totally dispossessed of their personal security, relying only on God, with the capacity to discover daily the working of the Lord in history and to enter joyfully into the service of men for the creation of a more brotherly, more Christian world . . . These men have experienced God in the desert and have tasted of the cross. That is why they are able, in this night, to read the signs of the times, to decide to give their lives for their friends, and, above all, to be happy to suffer for the name of Jesus and to participate deeply in his Easter mystery. For, in fidelity to the Word, they have understood that difficult times are the most providential and the most evangelical, and that it is necessary to live in the contemplation and serenity of the cross.[9]

It is Christ resurrected from the dead that the Church proclaims, he who is the sure token of our own resurrection.

He toward whom the Christian assembly turns this Sunday, with confidence:

Lord, be my rock of safety, the stronghold that saves me. For the honor of your name, lead me and guide me.
(Ps 31:3-4—Entrance Antiphon)

He who is celebrated in every Christian Eucharist this Sunday and forever:

Glory to you who were dead,
Glory to you who are living,
Our Savior and our God!

To Love Without Measure— Without Judging— Even One's Enemies

Assured by the grace of God of a paradoxical happiness, the disciples of Christ are called to adopt, with regard to others, no less paradoxical a position. Last Sunday's Gospel foreshadowed it. The sight of the rich, the satisfied, those who live in joy and of whom the whole world speaks well, far from exciting the envy of the poor, comforts, in the knowledge of their happiness, those who are now hungry, who mourn, who are hated, rejected, and despised as worthless. These are the happy ones; the others are unhappy. And this is because of Christ rejected, despised, mocked, insulted, put to death, but resurrected. Because he placed his trust in God, he was the first, "greatly exalted," proclaimed "Lord to the glory of God the Father," exalted to his right hand (Phil 2:6-11: Passion [Palm] Sunday).

In contemplating Christ, the disciples will learn how to perceive the true value in all things and all situations. And their behavior will be modeled on that of God revealed through Jesus.

God Will Render to Each According to His or Her Due

The passage from the Book of Samuel selected for the first reading this Sunday recalls how David spared Saul in his mercy (1 Sam 26:2, 7-9, 12-13, 22-23).[10]

To avenge oneself on an evildoer, at least to exact an equal punishment, is a fairly spontaneous reaction. To renounce punishment is not so.[11] The Bible thus testifies to the long and patient efforts that were necessary to gradually educate the individual and collective conscience.

Genesis (4:23-24) reports that Lamech boasted that he would be avenged seventy-seven times, killing "a man for wounding me, a boy for bruising me."

Very quickly, ancient laws enforced proportionate limits to "vengeance" and punishment. Thus, the law speaks of retaliation equal to the wrong

52

inflicted (Exod 21:23-25). In order to prevent precipitous application of the law, the right of asylum was instituted. It set up places where an involuntary murderer could flee to take refuge (Exod 21:12-13; Num 35:9-29; Deut 19:1-12). Sheltered from the vindictiveness of an individual or the lynching instincts of a mob, the guilty man gave himself up to the justice of the society. All of this was still very harsh, of course. But to be greatly scandalized over it reflects poor understanding. So many centuries later, do we not still often face—in fact and in thought—the "law of retaliation"? We find it even among Christians who regard vengeance as a legitimate, or even necessary, part of the law.

On the other hand, the Bible urges everyone to renounce personal retribution against those who have wronged them: "Say not, 'I will repay evil!' Trust in the LORD and he will help you" (Prov 20:22).

Of course, the just often invoke the "vengeance" of God (Jer 12:3; 15:15; 17:18; Ps 5:11; etc.). But one must understand that this reaction is inspired by passionate devotion to God and his will. It is intolerable that the impious should impudently offer affront to the Lord!

Other texts in these and older books go even further: "If your enemy be hungry, give him food to eat, if he be thirsty, give him to drink; for live coals you will heap on his head, and the LORD will vindicate you" (Prov 25:21-22); "You shall not bear hatred for your brother in your heart. . . . Take no revenge and cherish no grudge against your fellow countrymen. You shall love your neighbor as yourself. I am the LORD" (Lev 19:17-18). And even: "Forgive your neighbor's injustice; then when you pray, your own sins will be forgiven" (Sir 28:2).

David almost forgot this when he surprised Saul while he was sleeping. But, calling God to mind, he did not wish to lay hands on the king who had received the Lord's anointing. David placed his trust in the Lord. Thus could he say to Saul: "As I valued your life highly today, so may the LORD value my life highly and deliver me from all difficulties" (1 Sam 26:24).

The psalmist explained David's attitude well in the "Te Deum" that he put on his lips: "when the LORD had rescued him from the grasp of all his enemies and from the hand of Saul":[12]

> The LORD *rewarded me according to my justice;*
>   *according to the cleanness of my hands he requited me;*
>
> For I kept the ways of the LORD
>   and was not disloyal to my God;

For his ordinances were all present to me,
  and his statutes I put not from me . . .

Toward the faithful you are faithful,
  toward the wholehearted you are wholehearted,
Toward the sincere you are sincere,
  but toward the crooked you are astute;
For lowly people you save
  but haughty eyes you bring low . . .

God's way is unerring,
  the promise of the LORD is fire-tried;
he is a shield to all who take refuge in him.
(Ps 18:21-23, 26-28, 31)

David, a type of Christ, is thus also a model for the believer who, by his fidelity to the Word, allows God to change his heart of stone into a heart of flesh. The recollection of such an action as David's inspires the Christians assembled for the Sunday Eucharist to make their own the psalmist's profession of faith and thanksgiving. A profession of faith and thanksgiving which implies that they be truly proclaimed, that is to say, proclaimed by one's commitment to the path of kindness and pity:

The LORD is kind and merciful.

Bless the LORD, O my soul;
  and all my being, bless his holy name.
Bless the LORD, O my soul,
  and forget not all his benefits.

He pardons all your iniquities,
  he heals all your ills.
He redeems your life from destruction,
  he crowns you with kindness and compassion.

Merciful and gracious is the LORD,
  slow to anger and abounding in kindness.
Not according to our sins does he deal with us,
  nor does he requite us according to our crimes.

As far as the east is from the west,
  so far has he put our transgressions from us.
As a father has compassion on his children,
  so the LORD has compassion on those who fear him.
(Ps 103:1-2, 3-4, 8, 10, 12-13)

Children of Earth and Heaven
Molded out of clay, we show the marks of our origin. But we also knows that we are called to ''bear the likeness of the man from heaven.'' Thus

all people live in tension between what they are and what they will be.

The third passage[13] selected by the Lectionary from the First Letter to the Corinthians (15:45-49), treats again of the resurrection of the dead, and more specifically, the resurrection of the body. This has always been a problem. Whatever conception one has of humankind, and especially the body—prison of the soul or concrete and sensible expression of the person—one runs afoul of the experience that the body, more or less decrepit with age and sickness, finally breaks down and disappears after death. All attempts at visualizing its resurrection lead to an impasse. St. Paul is well aware of this. Yes, he says, every person born of flesh, from the line of the first Adam, comes from the earth: everyone is perishable.

But Christ, come from heaven, became "a life-giving spirit." "Heavenly men are like the man of heaven," and will therefore be in his image. Faith assures us of this. It does not repudiate the evidence of experience. But it has to do with a path whose outcome is unimaginable. It is of this that the apostle speaks. You believe that Christ has risen. You know that his resurrection was not a return to the condition of the first Adam into which he became incarnate. Therefore resurrection is not the recommencement of life in an earthly condition or in a world similar to ours, though it is as free from hardship as one could imagine. It is to be completely transformed and filled with the Spirit, in the image of the resurrected Christ. An unthinkable transformation, certainly, but guaranteed by faith in the resurrected Christ whom we know to be living and who gives life to the living and the dead.

This text steadfastly insists on the double solidarity of all people in their earthly condition and in Jesus Christ raised from the dead.

What gives us this solidarity with the resurrected Christ has not yet been said. But we have the visible basis of it in baptism, the sacrament of second birth that, symbolically and really, joins us to the death of Christ that we may rise with him and be made creatures "from heaven," coheirs with Christ.

We come to this visible life by bodily birth, and that is why we are wholly corruptible. As to future life, we will be transformed by the power of the Spirit, and that is why we will be raised incorruptible. And since this will only be realized then, Christ our Lord desired to transport us to that state in a symbolic manner here and now, by giving us baptism and new birth in him. This spiritual birth is the present figure of the resurrection and of the regeneration that must be fully realized in us, when we will pass into that life. This is why baptism is also called regeneration.[14]

To Return Good for Evil

Last Sunday's Gospel spoke of the paradoxical happiness of a disciple of Jesus. Luke—our text this Sunday—immediately recounts what Jesus declares to the multitude that came to hear him. He teaches how those who are paradoxically called "blessed" must behave, while they "now" live in poverty, destitution, affliction, scorned by all, objects of hate and persecution (Luke 6:27-38).

Drawing out the implications of the fourth "beatitude," Jesus says that one should bear hate, insults and scorn patiently, without seeking to be avenged or even to enact justice oneself. He teaches that one must "love your enemies, do good to those who hate you, bless those who curse you, pray for those who mistreat you. To the person who strikes you on one cheek, offer the other one as well, and from the person who takes your cloak, do not withhold even your tunic. Give to everyone who asks of you, and from the one who takes what is yours do not demand it back." In short, one must always and everywhere return good for evil.

Ignoring for the moment the extraordinary, even heroic, effort this can entail, let us look at some immediate, obvious objections to such a radical teaching. It will ultimately happen, of course, that good will vanquish evil. But Jesus goes beyond authorizing that we not seek to exact equal retribution, praying for our enemies, giving to those who ask of us, indeed going so far as to ordain that we suffer aggression without retaliating, that we give to those who steal from us and give the other cheek to those who strike us! Isn't this passive complicity and indeed positive encouragement to violence? And what implication would this have for a third person? Must they refrain from acting and abandon victims to the power of their aggressors?

It would not be fair to make a mockery of Jesus' very serious words, to dismiss them after presenting them as a defense of a kind of pacifism that would endanger the peace, justice, and freedom of individuals and groups, indeed even of whole nations. They do not absolutely authorize inaction, passivity, still less an attitude of personal or collective resignation in the face of injustice, violence, and extortion; the whole Gospel testifies to the way in which the tradition has understood this. We cannot forget that in the synagogue at Nazareth Jesus proclaimed that he was sent to bring freedom to prisoners and the oppressed, those whom he is now calling "happy" (Luke 4:14-21—Third Sunday). Clearly, he healed the sick and consoled the afflicted; he "went about doing good" (Acts 10:38—Baptism of the Lord).

In the attempt to correctly understand the Beatitudes and what they entail for believers, for Christian communities, and the Church, endless discussion has proved more harmful than useful; history, not only that of the distant past, indicates this all too clearly! We have seen too much complacency when there was a need for action. Occasionally, whether it is intended or not—and it is sometimes intended—the Beatitudes become alibis for noninvolvement and lack of commitment to the "Son of Man." Nowadays, the poor and oppressed are not only left to their oppressors. They are told that their oppression is part of the nature of things, that their power to better their situation is vitiated, even in their own minds.

The Gospel says quite clearly: "Do to others as you would have them do to you." This is a general rule—"the golden rule"—which is to be applied always and everywhere, without exception. It demands that we act toward others without being solicited, that we offer friendship and pardon constantly, without asking or hoping for anything in return, even simple recognition. Such behavior, especially as a habit, seems entirely unreasonable. Christians certainly do not have exclusive rights to this; to imagine otherwise would be unjust and untrue. But mustn't this always be their way of acting? They have heard Jesus proclaim: "Then your reward will be great and you will be children of the Most High, for he himself is kind to the ungrateful and the wicked."[15] They are called to be, in this world, the witnesses of God.

> Mercy is the image of God, and the merciful are, in fact, a God dwelling on the earth. As God is merciful to all, without distinction, so the merciful must share benefits equally. My son, be merciful and share your goods with all, so that you may be elevated to divinity: for, as I have told you, the merciful person is another God on the earth.[16]

Do they not regularly say the "Our Father"?

"Forgive, and you will be forgiven," says Christ in the Gospel of Luke (6:37). And you, what do you say in prayer? What we are trying to explain: "Forgive us our offenses as we forgive!" What you say, that you must do. If you do not do so, you will perish.

What then? When an enemy begs mercy of you, forgive him immediately, and when your enemy besets you most strongly, lift your eyes to the Lord your God and his word: "Father, forgive them, they know not what they do!" (Luke 23:34).

But perhaps you will say: "He was able to do this because he is the Christ, the only Son of God, the Word made flesh! How can I, a weak and sinful person, imitate him?'' Our Lord's example is too lofty for you? Consider that of your companion. They stoned Stephen, and on his knees in the midst of the stones, he prayed for his enemies and said: ''Lord, do not hold this sin against them!'' (Acts 7:60). They pelted him with stones, and he prayed for them. This is what I wish for you: elevate your hearts and love your enemies![17]

The Gospel for this Sunday ends with the order to give without measure, ''for the measure you measure with will be measured back to you.'' What astonishing disproportion! How incommensurate the gift of a person, even when one has given his or her own life, compared with the infinite gift of God! This paradox is certainly the greatest and most provocative in the passage read this Sunday.

The Bible is not a collection of doctrines or moral teachings. It is God's self-revelation: his person, his action in and for the world, his plan of salvation and its fulfillment.

In Jesus, this revelation has not simply taken a decisive turn; it has been manifested by this ''second Adam,'' ''from heaven,'' by his person, teaching and behavior.

Human conduct has always been based and modeled on God, as he is in himself—the Holy One—and as he is revealed.

The Bible speaks of God: in this sense it is ''theology.'' The ''morality'' it tries to inculcate is likewise ''theological.''

Christ, ''life-giving spirit,'' guarantees not only that we will, at the resurrection ''bear the likeness of the man from heaven.'' He shows us, in his person, how, both today and in the promised future, we are to act like God, ''good to the ungrateful and the wicked,'' ''compassionate.'' He is not content to teach this merely with the voice of authority. He displays it in every moment of his life:

> . . . though he was in the form of God,
> [he] did not regard equality with God
>   something to be grasped.
> Rather, he emptied himself,
> taking the form of a slave,
> coming in human likeness;
> and found human in appearance,
> he humbled himself,
> becoming obedient to death,
>   even death on a cross!
> Because of this, God greatly exalted him
> and bestowed on him the name

that is above every name . . .
(Phil 2:6-9—Passion [Palm] Sunday).

We need not look elsewhere, beyond him, for justification of what he asks all his disciples: to love without measure, without reckoning, even their enemies.

The Zeal of the Disciples

The teaching of Jesus—as sublime as it truly is—and its exigencies—folly to human wisdom—are taken directly from life. What remarkable knowledge he has of the human heart!

After proclaiming the paradoxical happiness of the disciples and teaching them to love even their enemies without measure or calculation, the Gospel turns to the responsible members of the community to speak to them "in parables" of the daily conditions of a proper zeal, both communal and active.

The Reliable Test of Speech

The first reading for the Eighth Sunday is a short extract—four verses—of the book attributed to the author "Ben Sirach the Wise."[18] This collection of sayings was, until recently, known as "Ecclesiasticus," a name given to it by Christians since the time of Cyprian (bishop of Carthage, martyred in 258) because it was used to instruct catechumens.[19]

The four sentences read this Sunday concern speech (Sir 27:4-7), a common theme among the knowledgeable of all times and peoples: words, or simply "language," can be the best or the worst of things.

Ben Sirach knows this. He is acquainted with and denounces all the sins of speech: lies and gossip (19:4-12), thoughtless swearing (23:7-15), quarrels (28:8-12), and, above all, hypocrisy (28:13-16). Nevertheless, he holds speech in high esteem. It has a power that cannot be resisted for very long, which will inevitably lead it back to its proper use. Sooner or later, people who attempt to use it to disguise and hide their thoughts will be caught in its snare. They will be unmasked by the very words that they had tried to hide behind. Thus one has a sure means of coming to an accurate opinion of someone: "Praise no man before he speaks, for it is then that men are tested" (v. 7). Then can one truly discern.

Still, how does one sift through someone's words? Are they truth or lies? wisdom or folly?

"The test of what the potter molds is in the furnace." To be sure, some pottery cracks, shatters, even melts. It is in the oven that enamel reveals its true colors. Some pieces come out of the baking more beautiful than one could have imagined. In short, the potter only knows the quality of his work after it has passed through fire. The same is true of a person's words. It is prudent not to pass judgment on a subject—especially not to eulogize someone—before his test.

Anyone familiar with the Bible will not be surprised at the importance accorded to one's words for their ability to reveal one's true nature. We know, in fact, that in the Bible, speech and being go together. First of all in God who speaks, as opposed to dumb idols (Isa 41:21; 45:20-25; 46:7); who reveals himself through his Word, the first gift that he makes (Gen 1) of himself that is always effective. One knows his thought, will, and plans by listening to his Word. His silence, which is always disquieting (Ezek 3:26; Hab 1:13; Job 30:20; Ps 83:1; 109:1), is punishment (Isa 64:11), insofar as it indicates estrangement (Ps 35:22). The definitive silence of God characterizes hell (Ps 94:17).

Created in the image of God, humans are beings gifted with speech that despite the evil use they may make of it, always retains the imprint of its divine origin. It cannot be mastered to the point that it will not ultimately reveal the truth, for better or worse.

The Letter of James vigorously denounces indiscreet use of speech. ''If anyone does not fall short in speech, he is a perfect man . . . The tongue is also a fire. It exists among our members as a world of malice, defiling the whole body and setting the entire course of our lives on fire, itself set on fire by Gehenna. . . . no human being can tame the tongue. It is a restless evil, full of deadly poison'' (James 3:2-8—Saturday II, Sixth Week). The whole ascetic tradition is inspired by this doctrine.[20]

But one also reads, in this very same letter, that language serves to ''bless the Lord and Father'' (James 3:9).

LORD, it is good to give thanks to you.

It is good to give thanks to the LORD,
  to sing praise to your name, Most High,
To proclaim your kindness at dawn
  and your faithfulness throughout the night. . . .

The just man shall flourish like the palm tree,
  like a cedar of Lebanon shall he grow.
They that are planted in the house of the LORD
  shall flourish in the courts of our God.

They shall bear fruit even in old age;
  vigorous and sturdy shall they be,

Declaring how just is the LORD,
  my Rock, in whom there is no wrong.
(Ps 92:2-3, 13-16)

The Victory of Life

The second reading is the end of chapter 15 of the First Letter of Paul to the Corinthians (15:54-58). These five verses are in the form of a hymn and final exhortation at the end of a lengthy exposition on the resurrection of the dead.

The victory of life over death proceeds from the word of Scripture. Thus "that which is corruptible must clothe itself with incorruptibility, and that which is mortal must clothe itself with immortality." The assurance of his faith is such that, already, the apostle celebrates this triumph of life. He urges us to give thanks "to God who has given us the victory through our Lord Jesus Christ."

"O death, where is your sting? The sting of death is sin"—an enigmatic phrase. The apostle is doubtlessly speaking of death not in itself, but as it has become because of sin: formidable, capable in some way of poisoning all of life.

This is why he immediately says "your toil is not in vain." Provoked by this "sting" of death, one must be "steadfast," "persevering," "fully engaged in the work of the Lord," knowing that at the end of the road is life, immortality, "the victory through our Lord Jesus Christ."

An Active Disciple

Last Sunday's Gospel ended with the exhortation to show mercy, not to judge and condemn but to pardon, to give generously (Luke 6:36-38).

The next section (Luke 6:39-41) begins with a completely different issue. It is a question now of those who "guide" the others. Luke alone calls those who are responsible for the community "guides"; even today, in the East, the superior of a monastery is called "hegoumene" or "hygomene" (from the Greek "hegoumenos"). Those with such responsibility must be clear-sighted: "Can a blind man act as guide to a blind man? Will they not both fall into a ditch?"

The disciple must not try to be greater than his master, but attempt to imitate "the one who is well formed." This applies to all, and thus to the "guides," for their Master is Jesus, who welcomed sinners, granting them pardon because he was truly merciful, like the Father (Luke 5:20-24; 7:47-49).

The following speech (Luke 6:41-42) deals with relations among members of the community. Its meaning is clear: it is a continuation of the exhortation not to judge (v. 37).

To see the splinter in another's eye while ignoring the wooden beam in one's own is to behave as "a hypocrite."[21] The term is a harsh one, seeing that Luke uses it for the crowds who cannot recognize the time of salvation, and to refer to those who try to stop Jesus from healing the sick on the sabbath (Luke 12:56; 13:15). It thus indicates a radical misunderstanding of the truth. Here, Jesus is speaking to the disciples. But to focus on the splinter in another's eye without seeing the beam in one's own—is this not tantamount to revoking the Master's teaching, to act in flagrant contradiction to the Gospel that says: "Be merciful, just as your Father is merciful. Stop judging and you will not be judged. Stop condemning and you will not be condemned. Forgive and you will be forgiven" (Luke 6:36-37—Seventh Sunday)? Is it not to reveal that despite appearances, one is a "rotten tree"?

The Gospel adds, "A good tree does not bear rotten fruit, nor does a rotten tree bear good fruit" (v. 43).

It is in deeds that one recognizes the true disciple, that one can judge him. "For people do not pick figs from thornbushes, nor do they gather grapes from brambles" (v. 44). "Every tree that does not produce good fruit will be cut down and thrown into the fire" (Luke 3:9).

This stern warning should make a community inquire after the value of its practice. A bishop like John Chrysostom doesn't mince words about it:

> The Church is in an extremely critical state, and you think that all is going well. The fact is that we are plunged into countless sins, and we do not even know it!
>
> You wonder why. We have churches, money, and everything else. There are places for assembly, people come there every day; surely this is not nothing?
>
> But it is not thus that we judge the state of the Church. Then how?, you ask.
>
> Whether we lead a truly Christian life. Whether every day we make ourselves spiritually more rich, bearing fruit, whether great or small; if we are not content simply with fulfilling the law and expediting our religious duties.
>
> Who is a better person, after having frequented the church all month?
>
> This is what we must look for! After all, even what appears to be a good action is only a bad action, when one does not follow it up.
>
> Do you believe that the truly Christian life consists in not missing an office? This is nothing, if we do not derive profit from it. If we bring nothing to fruition through it, it would be better to stay at home.[22]

But the root, the source of all—acts as well as words—is the good or bad heart from which people draw good and evil.

Therefore, it is with the heart that one must listen to the Word in order to produce good and plentiful fruit, it is in the heart that one must meditate on and treasure it.[23] "He said to them in reply, 'My mother and my brothers are those who hear the word of God and act on it'" (Luke 8:21—Tuesday of the Twenty-fifth week).

The three readings of this Eighth Sunday of Ordinary Time shed their light on what it is to be and to act as a disciple of Jesus in the very depths of one's soul and the community of believers.

People without duplicity, whose speech, which they have received from the God-Word, reveal the purity of their hearts, their intentions, their sentiments (First Reading).

One must be animated with the proper zeal. Clear-sighted, as opposed to the "hypocrites," one does not reprove others without first correcting him—or herself.

Active, it is manifested in deeds that arise from the heart (Gospel).

They know that on the last day, when death will be swallowed up, the fruits of their labor will appear. Everything that is corruptible will be thrown off. They will retain only the pure gold of truth and charity. Then will they be able to join their voices to the hymn of the victory of life over death.

This sequence of three Sundays makes the Christian assembly travel a route whose atmosphere is very well expressed by the opening antiphons:

> Lord, be my rock of safety, the stronghold that saves me. For the honor of your name, lead me and guide me.
> (Ps 31:3-4—Sixth Sunday)

> Lord, your mercy is my hope, my heart rejoices in your saving power. I will sing to the Lord for his goodness to me.
> (Ps 13:6—Seventh Sunday)

> The Lord has been my strength; he has led me into freedom. He saved me because he loves me.
> (Ps 18:19-20—Eighth Sunday)

It is toward the Lord that all the texts turn our eyes, our prayer and adoration, even when they shed light on the road traveled by the disciples.

He alone can proclaim with assurance and authority the paradoxical happiness of his disciples who hear him.

He alone can demand that they be disciples animated with a zeal that has no hint of false enthusiasm, and is both communal and active.

But, in all this, it is he himself who is revealed: the beloved Son, joy of the blessed, seated at the right hand of the Father; the just man persecuted, killed for sinners, forgiving his executioners on the cross; the Son of Man who gave all for humankind, even his own life.

This is why the Church and every Christian community gives thanks to the Father most holy, God eternal and all-powerful, joining their voices to those of the angels and saints.

From the Ninth to the Eleventh Sunday in Ordinary Time

Between the ''Sermon on the Plain'' (Luke 6:20-49), from which we have read large sections during the three preceding Sundays, and the first teaching in parables (Luke 8:4-18), we find, in the Third Gospel, a series of stories in part peculiar to Luke (7:1–8:3).[1] From this section, the Lectionary has selected the healing of the centurion's servant (Luke 7:1-10), the raising of the son of the widow of Naim (Luke 7:11-17), and the incident of the pardoned sinful woman (Luke 7:36-50), thus comprising thirty-one of fifty verses in chapter 7.

After this comes a short review of Jesus' activity (Luke 8:1-3). Luke enjoys inserting such small tableaux into the framework of his story. These ''summaries'' act as conclusions to what precedes and as introductions to what follows, thus linking the two sections. They play the same role as a brief, slow sequence in a film; to recollect where one is and to have a slight pause before continuing. The rhythm of the passage focuses us: the great sweeping swathes and panoramas of the transition section evoke what has preceded and prepares us for what will follow.

Jesus has revealed himself in the synagogue at Nazareth ''in the power of the Spirit,'' he has proclaimed that ''today'' is fulfilled the prophetic oracle announcing ''a year of favor from the Lord.'' On the lakeshore, he has chosen the disciples to make them fishers of men (Third, Fourth, Fifth Sundays).

In the plain, he has solemnly promulgated the charter of the kingdom, declaring the radical exigencies of the ''law of love,'' of the communal and active zeal that the disciples must exhibit in their lives (Sixth, Seventh, Eighth Sundays).

''When he had finished all his words to the people''—the ''Sermon on the Plain''—Luke tells us that Jesus first entered Capernaum, where he healed a slave belonging to a Roman centurion. He then went to a village called Naim, where he recalled a widow's only son to life. Finally, he entered the house of a Pharisee who had invited him to dinner, where he forgave the sins of ''a sinful woman in the city'' who, weeping, poured over Jesus' feet ''an alabaster flask of ointment'' (Ninth, Tenth, Eleventh Sundays).

These three significant episodes show that ''the power of the Spirit'' gives to Jesus' words not only a sovereign authority for teaching but also the power to effect what he says.

Therefore it is constantly the question of Jesus' identity that is the center of attention.[2] Both by his teaching and acts, he reveals who he is.[3] It remains our duty to be open to this revelation and to receive it.[4]

By healing the centurion's slave, by giving life to the son of the widow of Naim, by forgiving a woman "her many sins," Jesus reveals that "the year of favor" that he institutes is for all, that God alone determines how his gifts shall be given, that salvation, far from being merited, is received gratuitously.

The Ninth Sunday begins our reading of Paul's Letter to the Galatians, where the apostle finds himself obliged to recall that the gospel is perverted when the universality and gratuity of salvation that it proclaims are compromised. This epistle contains one hundred forty-nine verses divided into six chapters. The Lectionary has selected, for the Ninth, Tenth, and Eleventh Sundays, short excerpts from the first two chapters: seventeen verses from chapter 1 (out of twenty-four) and four verses from chapter 2 (out of twenty-one).[5]

As always in Ordinary Time, the first reading is selected from the Old Testament to complement the Gospel of the day. Thus we have, for these three Sundays, two excerpts from the First Book of Kings, and one from the Second Book of Samuel.

Such is the general structure of the Liturgy of the Word for the Ninth, Tenth, and Eleventh Sundays of Ordinary Time, Year C, which forms a new sequence that has its own internal coherence.

Ninth Sunday

A Boundless Salvation

From his first appearance at the synagogue in Nazareth, after his sojourn in the desert, Jesus proclaimed, citing the examples of Elijah and Elisha, that the benefits of God know no boundaries. He even went so far as to claim that strangers welcome a prophet more than do the people of his homeland. Because of this, everyone in the synagogue became furious, and rising up, they "led him to the brow of the hill on which their town had been built, to hurl him down headlong" (Luke 4:14-30—Third and Fourth Sundays).

God Welcomes the Prayers of All

The first reading (1 Kgs 8:41-43) is a brief excerpt from the long and beautiful prayer of Solomon on the day of the dedication of the Temple, as he faced the altar in the presence of the whole people, his hands lifted toward heaven (1 Kgs 8:22-61).

The king prays first for himself (vv. 22-29), then for the people, that God may always listen to their prayer (vv. 30-40), and finally for foreigners (vv. 41-43).[6]

The "universal" import of Solomon's prayer depends on our understanding of the word "foreigner."

The Bible recognizes two categories of "foreigners," denoted by two different Hebrew words. The first designates one who, not belonging to the race of Abraham, comes to dwell in their land or seeks refuge there (fleeing a vendetta, for example), whether temporarily or permanently. Even today, in our country, we recognize this type of "immigrant," who is called in Hebrew *ger*, that is, "come from elsewhere."

The second term used *(nokri)* designates a "foreigner," properly speaking, one whom various circumstances have brought into the land: commercial or diplomatic relations, wars, military postings (mercenaries during their time of service), etc.[7] Now, it is for the former, foreigners properly so-called, that Solomon prays. For these "foreigners," having understood at least confusedly about the "strong hand" and the "long arm" of the Lord, would come to the Temple to invoke his intervention on their behalf. In fact, after the Babylonian Exile, many "sons of foreigners," without fully adhering to the Law and without being circumcised, recognized the name of the Lord and served him. As the prophet had announced: "Them I will . . . make joyful in my house of prayer. . . . For my house shall be called a house of prayer for all peoples" (Isa 56:7).

In the Greco-Roman era—at the time of Jesus and the apostolic Church—there was a vast movement of people who were called "proselytes." Jesus himself recognized the zeal of those who traveled sea and land in order to spread Judaism (Matt 23:15). Some of them wrote books with this intention or in order to refute objections and calumnies, among them the Jewish philosopher Philo of Alexandria (c. 13 B.C.–A.D. 54) and the historian Flavius Josephus of Jerusalem (A.D. 37–95), author of *Antiquities of the Jews*.

King Solomon could not foresee such a spreading of the name of the Lord. Yet he hoped that all peoples on earth would recognize the name and adore the Lord. His universalism, though, is still "centripetal," centered on Jerusalem and the Temple. This universality is of a spiritual order. There is no trace here of domination, of tribute or other levies. The only concern is for conversion. It is proper to say, then, that for Solomon, all people—"foreigners"—can have access to salvation. As the author of the beautiful Psalm 87, he sees Zion as the fatherland, the mother of all peoples:

His foundation upon the holy mountains the LORD loves,

The gates of Zion,
 more than any dwelling of Jacob.
Glorious things are said of you,
 O city of God!
I tell of Egypt and Babylon
 among those that know the LORD;

Of Philistia, Tyre, Ethiopia:
 "This man was born there."
And of Zion they shall say:
 "One and all were born in her;

And he who has established her
 is the Most High LORD."

They shall note, when the peoples are enrolled:
 "This man was born there."
And all shall sing, in their festive dance:
 "My home is within you."

This psalmic hymn would go well after this reading. The Lectionary has chosen instead the shortest psalm, Psalm 117, which directly prolongs Solomon's prayer:

> *Go out to all the world and tell the good news.*

> Praise the LORD, all you nations;
>   glorify him, all you peoples!
> For steadfast is his kindness toward us,
>   and the fidelity of the LORD endures forever.

Fidelity to the Gospel Alone

The Letter of Paul to the Galatians, which we begin to read this Sunday, is not, as is usual, addressed to any specific local Church, but to the "churches in Galatia." This is a kind of "circulating letter," destined for small, dispersed communities that were doubtlessly related to each other.[8]

The tone and style of the address is striking. Paul underlines his apostolic status. Moreover, he declares that he has not been "sent from human beings nor through a human being," but directly by Jesus Christ resurrected from the dead by God the Father. Such evocation, at the beginning of the letter, of his singular calling—to which he will return more explicitly (Gal 1:11-19—Tenth Sunday) and which the Churches know well enough (Acts 9:1-19—January 25, feast of the Conversion of Paul)—sets the writer up in all his authority. We might guess that if Paul is going to speak in such a manner, the situation must be very serious.[9]

Also notable is the abrupt way in which the apostle comes to the heart of the matter. Paul's other letters typically begin with a mention of his rejoicing in seeing an increase in the faith among his correspondents. Here, there is nothing of the sort. Without any transition, without the least warning, he vehemently expresses his astonishment over what has happened in the Churches of Galatia. This is a true crisis, a shipwreck of the faith, a desertion, the abandonment of the message of grace preached to the Galatians, and an exodus to another gospel! As if it were possible to have another! "O stupid Galatians! Who has bewitched you?" he will write a little later (Gal 3:1). This was wholly unexpected and thus extremely distressing!

To take up another gospel! This is a thing of such enormity that the Galatians in all probability were not aware they were doing it. Hence the claim that they are truly "so stupid" (Gal 3:3). But what is the concern here? Fools enough to believe the first preacher that comes to them, they stupidly let themselves be deceived by "some who wish to alter the gospel of Christ."

Such is a sacrilegious enterprise that renders whoever is devoted to it anathema, i.e., excluded from the privilege—the grace—of salvation. No less does Paul call this curse upon himself if he were to be guilty of proclaiming a different gospel. *Reductio ad absurdum?* Yes, in a certain sense. But above all an unyielding affirmation that a choice must be made: either "the gospel preached by me" or the doctrines of "troublemakers among you." There is no other alternative or any amalgam possible between the gospel and the other doctrines. Either Paul or these are "anathema." Neither more nor less!

His choice is made: not at all trying to win approval and to seek to ingratiate himself with all, but to seek the approval of God and to be "serving Christ."[10]

The reading of the Ninth Sunday holds to this. But it would be a mistake to take the beginning of the Letter to the Galatians merely as testimony to a serious crisis that shook the Churches of Asia Minor around A.D. 56–57.

Are not Christians today often at the mercy of the first teaching that comes their way, imperiled by doctrines that purport to have come from an angel, by theories and practices that bind them to a slavery from which the good news had freed them? Especially when preachers make a point of rigorous observances—fasting, prayer, etc.—isn't it common to suppose, like the Galatians, that they are preaching progress and not the abandonment of the gospel? And yet . . .

A Pagan, Model for Believers

The gospel is not a collection of doctrines and precepts. Jesus' teaching is inseparable from his person and action. Words and deeds must be understood as closely linked. This is what Luke suggests at the beginning of the Gospel for the Ninth Sunday (Luke 7:1-1.), by situating the acts of Jesus "when he had finished all his words to the people," which was the "Sermon on the Plain."

In itself, the story presents no difficulties, and we can be tempted to listen to it only distractedly, like a story we have heard hundreds of times. However, it is worthwhile to reread it while paying attention to the details that indicate the intention of the evangelist when he included it.

Capernaum was, as we know, the departure point of Jesus' mission when the hostility and rejection he received in Nazareth forced him to leave the village "where he had grown up" (Luke 4:16, 28-29, 31-44). Capernaum, on the shores of Lake Genesareth, was a border city with a customs bureau and a military outpost.

A "captain of a hundred"—a "centurion" says the Lectionary—probably a mercenary, certainly a pagan, "who had a slave who was ill and about to die, and . . . was valuable to him."[11]

Like so many others, this officer has heard of the miracles accomplished by Jesus in Capernaum and the surrounding area, of which Luke speaks (Luke 4:37-41; 5:12-16; 6:6-11, 17-19). He therefore thinks that Jesus could, by coming near him, save the sick man, who is near death. But he sends "some Jewish elders" to petition him, which they do readily: "He deserves to have you do this for him, for he loves our nation and he built our synagogue for us."

In Acts, Luke speaks of another officer, Cornelius—a Roman, "centurion of the Cohort called the Italica"—who "used to give alms generously to the Jewish people" but was himself a "proselyte" (Acts 10:1-2). Still, this insistence on the intervention of "Jewish elders" fits with Luke's intention. He knows very well, and points out, that the gospel came to the pagans through the mediation of Israel. The first preachers were all Jews, and in every pagan town they entered, they first contacted the Jewish community and preached in the synagogue—especially Paul, whose missions are recorded in Acts.

Jesus does not hesitate to go with the envoys. This is another typical feature of Luke and of the missionary perspective of his book: one cannot hesitate to respond to a pagan's appeal. Again, we remember Paul.

When Jesus is near the house, the officer sends messengers again, though this time they are friends of his, to bring a personal message. And what a message! Such a profession of faith!

More than a protestation of humility, "Lord . . . I am not worthy" is recognition of the absolute gratuity of God's gift, to which we can claim no right. Jesus has uncontested power over the sick man.

We may rightly sense that the evangelist has retained these words because they are exemplary for Christian faith. Those who know the power of the Word can and must proclaim always: "Lord, in the strongest sense of the term, I am not worthy, but only say the word."[12] Moreover, in the story itself, the central figure, on whom our gaze rests, is Jesus, not the other, anonymous characters. If the figure of the centurion is distinguished from the others (though he, too, is anonymous), it is as a type of person. This is what the evangelist wants us to remember about him. Who was he? Where did he come from? What was his name? What happened to him? These questions and others like them arise from legitimate curiosity. In the gospel, the announcement of the good news, what counts and must be remembered are the characteristics that make a person a model for Christians of all times, and the faith-journey which can be exemplary for them. Are we not "pagans," saved by grace?

But as always, it is Jesus who is at the center, it is toward him—his words, behavior, initiative—that the evangelist turns our eyes. For the gospel is not simply a recitation of historical events—edifying though they might be—but the revelation of the one who came to manifest the Father and accomplish his plan of salvation.

The Bible gradually reveals the universality of this plan of salvation. It does so most concretely by showing how God excludes no one from his benefits, his intervention. The Old Testament is full of striking examples testifying to this. Elijah, during the drought and famine, "was sent . . . to a widow of Zarephath in the land of Sidon"; "during the time of Elisha the prophet . . . not one [of the lepers] was cleansed, but only Naaman the Syrian" (Luke 4:25-27—Fourth Sunday).

The prayer made on the day of the dedication of the Temple by Solomon, the wisest of the wise, opens up the broad perspective of salvation for all. Certain that this corresponds to God's desire, the king asks him to hearken to "all that the foreigner asks of you" who will come to pray in this newly constructed Temple. Furthermore, he foresees "all the peoples of the earth" receiving the grace of recognizing the name of the Lord and adoring him.

Solomon can only imagine this universality of salvation with Jerusalem and the Temple its center. But it is unconditional, requiring no tribute or allegiance whatsoever to the first beneficiaries of revelation. The only things that matter are conversion to the only true God and recognition of his name (First Reading).

There is no hint of any syncretism, a kind of "ecumenism" that hides a mixture of many religions.

Paul, the apostle to the Gentiles, forced himself remorselessly to travel the world to announce the gospel, "the power of God for the salvation of everyone who believes . . . " (Rom 1:16). "For there is no distinction between Jew and Greek; the same Lord is Lord of all, enriching all who call upon him. For 'everyone who calls on the name of the Lord will be saved' " (Rom 10:12-13). God is the God not only of the Jews but of the pagans as well (Rom 3:29). This preaching brought the apostle persecution after persecution. He remained faithful, however, because were he to have sought the approbation of men rather than God, he would not have been serving God (Gal 1:10).

But the one he preaches is Jesus and Jesus crucified. To await another salvation or to accept other pretended means of salvation is an extraordinary aberration! This would be to forsake "the one who called you by [the] grace [of Christ] for a different gospel" going over to another gospel, "altering the gospel of Christ." "Anathema" is the one who dares to do so. The true universality is that of salvation based on faith in Christ as Savior (Epistle).

Jesus' healing of the centurion's slave is more than an illustration of this; it is a demonstration in action.

All people, whether foreigner or pagan, must become open to the possibility of finding in Jesus healing for themselves or for those near them who are otherwise doomed to certain death.

The encounter with the Savior occurs through mediation. Therefore, those who already know or have encountered him must not hide themselves.

Faith does away with all distance between Jesus and those who turn toward him. Salvation is no reward for merit—"I am not worthy"—but a free gift of divine mercy.

> Isn't all this very important for us? It is certainly possible that we underestimate the grace of Christ working in the Church, but at the same time we can be tempted to feel that we alone are the elect, that the members of the Church are the only sons of the kingdom. Then, by his example, Jesus tells us: May you also be men who impartially acknowledge truth, goodness, honesty, greatness, faithfulness, courage, wherever you find them. Have nothing to do with partiality. You must see the light wherever it is. It can exist anywhere, and this without prejudice to the truth of the Church. Faith teaches us that the grace of God is not limited to the visible Church of Christ, that the grace of God blows through every last alleyway in the world and that it will find in every place hearts where this faith and this grace work for supernatural salvation. We Catholics have, therefore, no right to think that because we are children of the true Church that there is no grace or divine charity elsewhere than in our hearts. Yes, we must always accept what has been said to us—particularly in this Gospel—that the sons of the kingdom can share in the status of those who are rejected, while others, coming from everywhere, who apparently have not been called, will be among the elect.[13]

Admiration of Jesus is an important trait to hold onto. It is toward those who follow—the readers of the gospel, disciples today—that he turns. It is to them that he says: "Not even in Israel have I found such faith!" Not that others' faith eclipses their own, but the former must prick them to increase. May our faith grow, stimulated by vigorous emulation of the faith we find in others.

Apostolic times saw the enthusiastic reception of the gospel by the pagans. Today, other young Churches excite an admiration like that of Jesus: "In all Christian lands I have not found such faith!" Truly, salvation recognizes no foreigners.

> O God, in your providence you have decreed that the Kingdom of Christ should be extended throughout the world, and that all men should share in the fruits of the redemption. Grant that your Church may be the sacrament of salvation for all men, revealing and communicating to them the mystery of your love. (*Roman Missal*. Prayer for the Church)

Tenth Sunday

"Raise Yourself from the Dead"

At the heart of the gospel and of faith is the resurrection of the dead, the pledge and assurance of which is found in the resurrection of Christ. "If for this life only we have hoped in Christ, we are the most pitiable people of all." (1 Cor 15:19, 17—Sixth Sunday).

Jesus is not a master who, on the one hand, teaches with authority and, on the other, does deeds that reveal his power, i.e., uses words, on the one hand, and demonstrations of miraculous power on the other. Words and deeds are found to be intimately linked; the former lead to the latter and vice versa. They reveal together who Jesus is, his mission, that which he brings to the world to which he has been sent: "Go and tell John what you have seen and heard: the blind regain their sight, the lame walk, lepers are cleansed, the deaf hear, the dead are raised, the poor have the good news proclaimed to them" (Luke 7:22).

Among all these signs, and in relation to them, the most decisive is that of resurrection from the dead. Not because it is a "super miracle," but because it evokes the fullness of salvation: victory over death, complete freedom from sin (1 Cor 15:54-58, 16-20—Eighth and Sixth Sundays).

Look, Your Son Is Alive

All of us know that we are moving toward death, "the way of all mankind" (1 Kgs 2:2), even if we try not to think of it. Whatever the vigor with which a person lives his or her allotted time—short or long—whatever the productivity or achievements—even the greatest—when faced with the idea of death, one can only think: "All is vanity" (Eccl 1:2). What remains of a person, of the richest life, of quickly fading memories, of material goods or work left to others over which one no longer has control, of a posterity that is subject to the same fate? Though it may be seen, even desired, as the end to the evils with which one is afflicted (Job 6:9; 7:15), can death be anything other than a defeat? The sages of the Bible constantly debated this question, thus testifying to the hesitations and contradictions involved in human thought on the subject.[14]

The absurdity of death can only lead to resignation or revolt. We must not resort to such nonsense. This refusal is expressed in one form or another, particularly by funeral rites. It is not possible that everything should come to such an end, that good and evil should end up sharing the same nothingness, that one must feverishly revel in life, according to the maxim enunciated by Paul (not without a certain oratorical exaggeration):[15] "Let us eat and drink, for tomorrow we die" (1 Cor 15:32).

However, the believers do not remain at this level of reflection; for them, death is a religious as well as metaphysical question. They believe in the living God who did not make death (Wis 1:13). They believe in a saving God whose plan of salvation cannot be obstructed, ruined, by death. It would be, in a way, deicide as well as homicide if there were an end to all knowledge and praise of God, wiped out every time a believer disappeared.[16] They believe in a just God who would not be himself if he abandoned the soul of the just person to Sheol, if he did not rescue one from its claws (Ps 16:10; 49:16). In short, it is salvation without limit, even of the dead, which is at issue here.

The episode from the First Book of Kings we read this Sunday is a concrete illustration of this (1 Kgs 17:17-24). The prophet Elijah found heroic hospitality from a poor widow of Zarephath in the territory of Sidon. His arrival was at first a blessing for this widow and her son. Elijah met her while she was collecting some sticks of wood to prepare a last morsel for herself and her son from a handful of flour and a little oil that remained to her, after which she would wait for death. Nevertheless, she readily cooked a bit of bread for the prophet who, on behalf of the Lord, promised her: "The jar of flour shall not go empty, nor the jug of oil run dry, until the day when the LORD sends rain upon the earth" (1 Kgs 17:14).

And now, behold: After a year, the son of this remarkable woman, who had exhibited such faith in God and his prophet, died! She began to waver: "Why have you done this to me, O man of God? Have you come to me to call attention to my guilt and to kill my son?" The prophet's spirit also was troubled: "O LORD, my God, will you afflict even the widow with whom I am staying by killing her son?" However, Elijah did not stop there: " 'O LORD, my God, let the life breath return to the body of this child.' The LORD heard the prayer of Elijah; the life breath returned to the child's body and he revived."

Efficacy of the prophet's prayer? Yes, to be sure. But even more crucially, a manifestation of the power of the living God, which death cannot limit, a God who wishes illness or death on no one.

To this God who raises up, who recalls from the abyss and revivifies, who changes tears into dancing, funereal garments for festive clothes, to whom the faithful give thanks by repeating his thrice-holy name:

> *I will praise you* LORD *for you have rescued me.*

> I will extol you, O LORD, for you drew me clear
>> and did not let my enemies rejoice over me. . . .
> O LORD, you brought me up from the nether world;
>> you preserved me from among those going down into the pit.
> Sing praise to the LORD, you faithful ones,
>> and give thanks to his holy name.
> For his anger lasts but a moment;
>> a lifetime, his good will.
> At nightfall, weeping enters in,
>> but with the dawn, rejoicing. . . .
> Hear, O LORD, and have pity on me;
>> O LORD, be my helper.
> You changed my mourning into dancing . . .
>> O LORD, my God, forever will I give you thanks.
> (Ps 30:3-4, 5-6, 11-12a, 13)

Paul Set Apart for the Gospel

The second reading (Gal 1:11-19) comprises the end of the first chapter of the Letter of Paul to the Galatians, begun last Sunday.[17] Paul presents himself, from his first words, as ''an apostle not from human beings nor through a human being but through Jesus Christ and God the Father who raised him from the dead'' (Gal 1:1). This is why, he says rather forcefully, there is no other gospel than the one he has announced (Gal 1:7-8). He returns to this point: ''the gospel preached by me is not of human origin. For I did not receive it from a human being nor was I taught it, but it came through a revelation of Jesus Christ.'' He recalls his former way of life in Judaism; his persecution of the Church of God; his defense, in excessive zeal, of the tradition of his fathers; his calling on the day when God chose to reveal his Son through him, for him to announce among the pagan nations; his immediate departure for Arabia; his return to Damascus and, after three years, his encounter with Peter, with whom he stayed only fifteen days.

All this could appear as a merely anecdotal recollection of a personal itinerary; interesting, but no more. A more attentive reading reveals a certain number of particularly significant features.

This is not the only time Paul recalls his past as a persecutor.[18] It is striking that he never seems to have had a bad conscience. As opposed to other Pharisees—such as his master Gamaliel, who took a "wait-and-see" attitude (Acts 5:34-39)—he took a more forceful position, impelled by his "zeal" (Phil 3:6), that is to say, his "burning jealousy" for God, which led him to combat without hesitation anything that might impinge on the divine honor. Nothing would be held back; he had personally involved himself completely. This is what made Saul seek to destroy the Church of God, going farther than most of the people of his age.

Then, suddenly, came this revelation of the Son, of which God took the initiative when "the time came." An initiative, a "grace" that had its origin in his gratuitous being "set apart" "before [he] was born." The apostle speaks of this revelation-calling in the same terms as Isaiah (49:1) and Jeremiah (1:5). They also speak of having been called, consecrated, established in their mission "from their mother's womb," "before being born," although this was only revealed to them much later.

"Set apart" has a ritual ring.[19] Not surprising when one remembers what Paul wrote elsewhere: "God is my witness, whom I serve with my spirit in proclaiming the gospel of his Son . . ." (Rom 1:9); "I have written to you rather boldly . . . because of the grace given me by God to be a minister of Christ Jesus to the Gentiles in performing the priestly service of the gospel of God, so that the offering up of the Gentiles may be acceptable, sanctified by the holy Spirit" (Rom 15:15-16).

The gospel, which it is the apostle's mission to announce, is not an abstract message or a teaching about the meaning of human destiny, but it involves a person, the Son whose "revelation" has been given him. And there is a connection between the fact that it is the "Son" and the proclamation to the nations.

Finally, because the gospel was neither given nor taught to him by a human being, Paul "immediately" started on the mission he had received: "[he] did not immediately consult with flesh and blood, nor did [he] go up to Jerusalem to those who were apostles before [him]." He did go there, but after a long time ("three years") and for only "fifteen" days.[20] This implies no contempt for Peter; on the contrary, he recognized him as the first witness of the resurrection (1 Cor 15:5—Fifth Sunday). He also met "James, the brother of the Lord," of whom the Judaizers were making use. It would not be quite accurate to see Paul as sniping at the apostolate. Rather, he affirms what was necessary in writing to the Galatians, who had been carried away by the first to come to them, namely, that he is "an apostle sent not by a human being . . . but through Jesus Christ and God the Father who raised him from the dead" (Gal 1:1). This "autonomy'' does not contradict (far from it!) the collegial and ecclesial authority of the apostles.

In the end, what counts is keeping one's eyes fixed on the Son whose Person, source of every man's unique call, is the good news of universal salvation.

Young Man, Arise

Luke reports two particularly significant manifestations of the divine power of salvation with which Jesus is invested: the resurrection of the son of the widow of Nain (Luke 7:1-17) and the pardon granted to a sinful woman (Luke 7:36–8:3—next Sunday).

In Luke, the resurrection of the dead has a notable position. One must invite to one's table the poor, the crippled, the blind, who have no way of returning the invitation, knowing that ''you will be repaid in the resurrection of the just'' (Luke 14:13-14—Twenty-second Sunday). The certitude of this resurrection cannot be subject to doubt, for the Lord, ''the God of Abraham, the God of Isaac, and the God of Jacob . . . is not the God of the dead, but of the living . . .'' (Luke 20:37-38—Thirty-second Sunday). Peter recalled to life Tabitha, a woman of Joppa, ''a disciple'' (Acts 9:36-43), and Paul did likewise to a young man of Troas called Eutychus who, sitting on a window sill while listening to Paul speak, had fallen asleep and fell to his death (Acts 20:7-12).

Luke is the only one of the evangelists to recount the resurrection of the son of the widow of Nain.[21] The story is remarkably calm and natural, without being unwieldy or artificial, without anything that rings false, without even a highlighted role for Jesus.

Two processions meet at the gate of a town: Jesus with his disciples and a large crowd, a funeral train going to bury the widow's only son.

The description reveals nothing about the dead man or his mother; nothing is said about where these people or Jesus and his disciples went on to. The focus is on a widow, a defenseless woman according to the Bible, her indigence increased by the loss of this son who was her only support. Her anonymity accentuates the fact of her being a representative of the weak, the afflicted, the defenseless, the very people for whom the Son of God has come.

There is no motive given for Jesus' intervention except his ''compassion,'' a sentiment that wells up from one's very heart. This is the only time Luke attributes it directly to Jesus. But he mentions it in two parables, those of the Samaritan (Luke 10:33) and the father who had two sons (Luke 15:20). Compassion evokes the mercy, the pity of God that Jesus revealed in his teaching and through his behavior toward the sick, the poor, the weak. This is in line with the Old Testament, which speaks, sometimes in striking terms, of the divine tenderness. Thus, for example, when one speaks to God:

> My heart stirs for him,
>   I must show him mercy, says the LORD.
> (Jer 31:20)

or when it puts this acclamation on the lips of a believer:

> Merciful and gracious is the LORD . . .
>   As a father has compassion on his children. (Ps 103:8, 13)

Though no one requested anything of him, Jesus simply says to the mother: "Do not cry." And to the dead man: "Young man, I bid you get up." What calm authority in these words! But the verb "get up [or rise up]" cannot help but hold one's attention.

In the Christian vocabulary—as Luke knows—"rise up" is used first of all for the resurrection of Christ[22] and of the elect at the end of time (Luke 20:37, for example). Its use here means that this resurrection of a young man has particular importance. It evokes the resurrection, indeed the pledge of the resurrection of the dead on the last day.

Moreover, "to rise up" applies also to the passage from death to life—the Easter resurrection[23]—which is made at baptism, as witnessed by this fragment of a baptismal hymn that we still sing today:

> Awake, O sleeper,
> arise from the dead,
> and Christ will give you light.
> (Eph 5:14—Fourth Sunday of Lent, Year A)

Clearly, there is more involved here than an extraordinary miracle; it is a sign. At least, this is what Luke wants us to learn. Moreover, the story has no follow-up. The dead man sits up and begins to speak. He is alive. Jesus returns him to his mother. Then they both disappear. Clearly, they are not the ones to whom the evangelist wishes to call our attention. He even seems to think that there would be no interest in asking questions about them. There is not the least concession to curiosity or the anecdotal. The mother and her son remain anonymous.

Instead, the evangelist reveals the importance of the miracle: that is where the key to reading this Gospel is found. "Fear seized them all and they glorified God. 'A great prophet has arisen in our midst,' and 'God has visited his people,''' they said. ''This report about him spread through the whole of Judea and in all the surrounding region.''

The ''fear'' that seized everyone is evidently not terror, but that undefinable sentiment that the manifestation of the divine excites. It leads them all to glorify God. Luke carefully underlines the fact that to glorify God is, with fear or stupor, the normal reaction to a miracle. For example, God is glorified after the healing of the paralytic (Luke 5:25-26), of the crippled woman (Luke 13:13), of the ten lepers of whom one returned ''glorifying God in a loud voice'' (Luke 17:15), of the blind man at Jericho (Luke 18:43). The centurion at the foot of the cross, ''who witnessed what had happened glorified God . . . '' (Luke 23:47).

The witnesses to the resurrection of the son of the widow of Nain recognize, in what Jesus did, a ''visit of God.'' In the Old Testament, this refers to an intervention of God to judge, punish, or grant a benefit.[24]

The expression is rarely found in the New Testament.[25] But it is in the Canticle of Zechariah after the birth of John the Baptist. That this beautiful text passed into Christian liturgy says much about the importance of the ''visit of the Lord,'' ''the daybreak from on high,'' manifestation of the kindness and love of our God who gives salvation to his people, which shines on ''those who sit in darkness and death's shadow, to guide our feet into the path of peace'' (Luke 1:68-79).

The story ends with a note typical of Luke, the evangelist of the universal mission. From Galilee, where the miracle took place in ''a town called Nain,'' the good news is spread ''through the whole of Judea and in all the surrounding region.''

Jesus is the Savior who with one phrase—''rise up''—allows believers to become ''the children of God because they are the ones who will rise'' (Luke 20:36), because he himself is the resurrection and the life.

Salvation is now universal and no longer has any limit (Ninth Sunday). It does not apply only to this life; it contains the power of resurrection that death cannot hold in check.

If God reminds us of our faults, it is not because he wishes us to die, but so that we might abandon the way that leads to death.

On our part, to recognize our sin is to turn ourselves toward God by saying to him: ''Lord, I beg of you, give me life'' with the certitude that he can and will hear us (First Reading).

His Son has come to reveal the pity and compassion of God, sentiments that arise from the heart faced with misery and affliction: ''Do not cry!''

In Jesus, we recognize the Prophet, the Lord who gives life. In and through him, "God has visited his people."

This "visit" is not a past event. It is renewed especially in all sacramental encounters, beginning with that of baptism, where, for the first time, the Lord says to us: "I bid you get up" (Gospel).

> The resurrection of this young man filled his mother, a widow, with joy. The spiritual resurrection of men each day rejoices the Church our Mother. Death had struck him in his body, then in their souls. For the former, visible death sadness was displayed on the visible face: one was not disquieted, one did not even perceive the invisible death of the latter.
>
> Only he was disturbed who knew the dead, and the only one who knew the dead was he who could make them living. For if the Lord had not come to resurrect the dead, the apostle would not have said: "Awake, O sleeper, arise from the dead, and Christ will give you light" (Eph 5:14) . . .
>
> For Christ, the one who was sleeping, to whom he said "Rise up," immediately rose. No one wakens so easily in a bed, as Christ in the tomb.[26]

We did not know the Lord during his earthly mission, or Peter or Paul, or any of the apostles. But we know nonetheless that the gospel is no mere human invention. Through the ministry of chosen people, it is from God that we hold the revelation of Jesus Christ. He has "set us apart before we were born" and "by his favor chose us." Each, according to his position and particular calling, has the mission to spread the good news of salvation, to be witnesses to it in the world (Second Reading).

> Blessed be the Lord, the God of Israel,
> for he has visited and brought redemption to his people.
> He has raised up a horn for our salvation . . .
>   salvation from our enemies . . .
>   to show mercy to our fathers
>   and to be mindful of his holy covenant . . .
> rescued from the hand of enemies,
>   without fear we might worship him
> in holiness and righteousness
>   before him all our days. . . .
>
> Prophet of the Most High,
> for you will go before the Lord to prepare his ways,
> to give his people knowledge of salvation
>   through the forgiveness of their sins,
>   because of the tender mercy of our God
>   by which the daybreak from on high will visit us
> to shine on those who sit in darkness and death's shadow,
> to guide our feet into the path of peace.
> (Canticle of Zechariah, Luke 1:68-79)

Eleventh Sunday

Salvation, Forgiveness of Sins

The healing of a man at the point of death (Ninth Sunday) and even more the recalling of a dead man to life (Tenth Sunday) inevitably lead to the question of the identity of this miracle-worker. Faith sees in him the Lord through whom "God has visited his people." Coming after the "Sermon on the Plain," this teaching in action unveils the extension of salvation: it excludes no one; it can bring the dead to life.

This healing and this resurrection arise from the fact that God uproots the source of evil through the forgiveness of sins. If such were not the case, salvation would be illusory, and we would still be awaiting the promised, announced, prefigured Savior.

The Bible often speaks of sin: original, communal, and individual. It stigmatizes the personal, communal, and cosmic consequences. To denounce sin and what follows from it, to make heard the call of God to conversion and penitence, to indicate and prepare the road of return to the one from who we have strayed, is the primary mission of the prophets.

The prayers, oracles, and poems of the Psalter are quite devoted to the discussion of sin, committed or forgiven, to the confession of the mercy and love of God that is constantly entreated, to pardon received or asked, to conversion, etc. For all people are sinners, and none can extol their own justice faced with the justice and sanctity of God. The Bible does not keep silent about the sins of its most renowned heroes. Such is the case with David, who as both man and king, is still a preeminent biblical figure. He is the chosen one of God, the hero of the people, the type of the Messiah born of his line. And yet he sinned.

The Sin and Repentance of King David
Seduced by a woman's beauty, David took her into his house. This was Bathsheba, whose husband, Uriah the Hittite, was at war. One day she told the king that she was pregnant. David recalled Uriah in order to attribute paternity to him. But the brave officer refused to go into his house while his fellow soldiers were camped out in the field. Vexed, David sent him back to the battle, dispatching an order that would render Uriah helpless in the midst of his enemies and killed. Having gotten rid of the hus-

band, the king made Bathsheba his wife, and she "bore him a son" (2 Sam 11). So it was that the chosen one of God committed adultery and premeditated murder. With a calm conscience, without realizing that "the Lord was displeased" (2 Sam 11:27)!

The intervention of the prophet Nathan was required to make David conscious of his crime. The prophet proposed a case for the king's judgment: " 'In a certain town there were two men, one rich, the other poor. The rich man had flocks and herds in great numbers. But the poor man had nothing at all except one little ewe lamb that he had bought. . . . Now, the rich man received a visitor, but he would not take from his own flocks and herds to prepare a meal for the wayfarer who had come to him. Instead he took the poor man's ewe lamb and made a meal of it for his visitor.' David grew very angry with that man and said to Nathan: 'As the Lord lives, the man who has done this merits death!'. . . . Then Nathan said to David: 'You are the man!' " (2 Sam 12:1-7).

The first reading for this Sunday begins after this declaration by the prophet (2 Sam 12:7-10, 13). By recalling all that the Lord had done for him, Nathan shows David that he truly is this rich man who not only stole from a poor man but had him killed in order to get his only possession. How can David not understand that his double crime cannot help but displease the Lord? How could he have been so blind about himself at the same time as he could, without the slightest hesitation, so well judge the action of a rich man taking the one and only lamb of a poor man?[27]

Be that as it may, the king responds to Nathan by using the classical formula of one confessing and recognizing a sin: "I have sinned against the Lord."[28] In response to this confession comes forgiveness granted by God.[29]

Since the Exodus, God defined himself as the one who forgives sinners who acknowledge their faults and accept the commensurate punishment by throwing themselves on the divine mercy (Exod 34:6-7).

Later, Ezekiel will say that God does not desire the death of sinners, but that they must renounce their conduct and live (Ezek 18:23). Likewise, if the preaching of the prophets leads to conversion and confession of guilt, acceptance of expiation also points to the forgiveness granted by God. And the beautiful Psalm 51—"Have mercy on me, O God, in your goodness"—has been put on the lips "of David when Nathan the prophet came to him after his sin with Bathsheba" as the old story recalls the sin of the king.[30]

Christians assembled today read this story in light of later revelation.
They know whence comes the love and mercy of God. So the confession
of their sin is one with the confession of the mercy of God and thanksgiving for his forgiveness: "I will give thanks to the Lord by confessing
my sins":

> LORD, *forgive the wrong I have done.*
>
> Happy is he whose fault is taken away,
>   whose sin is covered.
> Happy the man to whom the LORD imputes not guilt,
>   in whose spirit there is no guile. . . .
>
> Then I acknowledged my sin to you,
>   my guilt I covered not.
> I said, "I confess my faults to the LORD,"
>   and you took away the guilt of my sin. . . .
>
> You are my shelter; from distress you will preserve me;
>   with glad cries of freedom you will ring me round. . . .
>
> Be glad in the LORD and rejoice, you just;
>   exult, all you upright of heart.
>   (Ps 32:1-2, 5, 7, 11)

All Justified by Grace

The second reading is again an excerpt from the Letter of Paul to the Galatians (Gal 2:16, 19-21). These several verses taken from chapter 2 constitute a link between the first part, where Paul justifies his status and calling,
and the second, where he exposes his understanding of salvation by faith
and the relationship between the Law and the Cross.

One is first struck by the style and tone of this short but extremely dense
passage. Paul is not relating a thesis of dogmatic theology; he expresses
with a certain vehemence his deep involvement as an apostle of Christ.
Many of his formulas are unforgettable. But he says so many things in
such a short space that his meaning is not easy to grasp. One must refer
to the Letter to the Romans, where he deals with the subject rather more
coolly. This is not the place to make such reference. We must keep to
the Lectionary text selected for this Sunday.

Note that the use of the verb "to justify" is always in the passive tense.
It occurs three times in verse 16 and once again in verse 21. It is important to understand what is meant by the word here because the "justice" of which he speaks—as in the Old Testament in general—is not,
as it is in our modern vocabularies, one cardinal virtue among the others:
prudence, temperance, etc. It is the perfection that can come to the one

whom God declares "just," that is to say, faithful to the covenant, to the ideal that God intends.

"Justice"—this is the point on which Paul insists in various ways, always fearing he hadn't said enough—is not first and foremost the effort of a human being, but his or her observance of the Law; it comes from faith, it is received in Christ.

Faith acknowledges that we are concerned with what has come in Christ; that his death on the cross is good news, gospel, because having erased the past, it allows new life, a life completely in God through Christ. Which leads Paul to say: "I have been crucified with Christ"; "Christ is living in me"; "I still live my human life, but it is a life of faith in the Son of God, who loved me and gave himself for me."

To know oneself to be loved by Christ, loved gratuitously, with no merit! This is without doubt what contributes most to Paul's dynamism, to his passionate attachment to the Lord, to the enthusiasm of his zeal for preaching the gratuity of salvation. But is it not, for each of us, the major discovery that can raise us up and restore our dignity?

> So many people in our age are loved by no one and feel that no one cares for who they are! Many men and women feel that, if they are sought out, it is only because of the use other people can make of them: economic efficiency, commercial clientele, passing pleasure or sexual dalliance, never because of what they are themselves. They know that as soon as they stop being useful they will cease to be of interest . . . .
>
> Now, how can one find happiness if one is not recognized, esteemed, and finally loved? How can one hope for a better future for humanity if one feels that the heart of reality is personal indifference, harshness and finally "chance and necessity"? . . .
>
> Who will tell us that a man, with his hope for love, is not a bizarre being, abnormal, living by chance in a world to which he is a stranger; but that he is a subject known and loved from all eternity by the one who created him: God, whose image he bears? Who will tell us this, if not Jesus Christ?[31]

Thus, on the one hand, "I will not treat God's gracious gift as pointless." And on the other, "If justice is available through the law, then Christ died to no purpose."

We are not "justified" as by a verdict of acquittal, still less through any consideration of personal merit, but by the gift of grace acquired by the death of Christ and by the faith that makes us enter with him into the new world.

We can read here in fine print the whole mystery of the merciful love of God and charity.

The Pardon of a Sinful Woman

The Gospel that follows this text is a wonderful passage, perhaps the most beautiful written by Luke (7:36–8:3).

"A great prophet has risen among us" said the crowd after the resurrection of the widow's son of Nain (Luke 7:16—Tenth Sunday). Does not Jesus manifest himself in the most convincing manner? He speaks with authority, he heals those who appeal to him, he gives an order, and the one who was about to be buried is restored to life. It is difficult to imagine what more there could be to come.

This is a mistake, says Luke: "Jesus is prophet in a completely unknown sense: he has power over sin; he can forgive it."

A Pharisee has invited Jesus to dinner. Luke is the only one of the evangelists to recount that some Pharisees received Jesus into their homes, at their tables.[32] This is one way, for the evangelist, of reporting that Jesus considered no one, to whatever social class they belonged, as a stranger to salvation. "Friend of tax collectors and sinners"—as some said—he also accepted a seat at the table of important people and of the Pharisees, the "pure."

But see where comes, unexpectedly, "a woman in the city." Her intrusion into this house can only be a shock, throwing a chill on the gathering, appearing, if not scandalous, at least completely incongruous and annoying. And what to make of what she does? Kneeling before Jesus, who was reclining at table according to the custom for solemn meals, she wet his feet with her tears, dried them with her hair, kissed them, and poured over his feet precious perfume that she had brought with her. Unexpected behavior, even ambiguous.

The diners, especially the master of the house, can only ask: "What can we think? How can he accept these attentions from her? For we all know, she is a sinner. Jesus must know it too. It is therefore impossible that he doesn't put a stop to this. If he doesn't, he is not the prophet that we thought."

The Pharisee has enough good taste and manners to keep his reflections to himself. But there must be an intention underlying his words? What would we say—if only to ourselves—if a notorious prostitute came into one of our assemblies, went to the altar as naturally as could be, prostrated herself, weeping, bathing the cross and the altar with her tears and drying them with her hair, setting in front of the tabernacle and the altar a sumptuous bouquet of flowers, or producing a precious censer full of incense? Perhaps Luke wants to make believers ask themselves about their behavior as "pure" people, which can lead them to forget the gratuity of the call and the mercy of God by which they have benefited.

In any case, the evangelist recounts that Jesus addressed the unexpressed thoughts of Simon by proposing a parable to him: "Two people were in debt to a certain creditor . . ." Their debts are not the same, but both are unpayable and benefit by the generosity of their common creditor. "Which of them will love him more? . . . The one, I suppose, whose larger debt was forgiven. . . ." Simon's response is prudent: does he ask himself what Jesus' meaning is?

Then he turns to "the woman"; he compares the manner—polite, certainly, but no more—in which Simon received him and the "foolish" prodigality of honors rendered by "this woman" to his host's face, in his own house![33]

On the one hand, the one to whom he forgives little, showing him little love. On the other, this woman who shows great love. Why? Because "her many sins are forgiven."[34]

And this is what Jesus says to the woman: "Your sins are forgiven." Absolution or a declaration of the forgiveness granted by God? A question of little importance, for no person can either forgive sins on his or her own authority or have direct knowledge of the judgment of God.[35] Everyone rightly recognizes that Jesus, by speaking thus, places himself outside the common human condition. The guests are scandalized. The woman receives his word of pardon because she has seen in Jesus something more than an ordinary man.

> You who are seated at table like a man in good health, you ignore the physician, perhaps because a more violent fever has attacked your spirit? . . . The one who believed that Christ forgave his sins believed that Christ was not only man but God as well . . . .
> To those who say: "Who is he?" the Lord did not respond: "The Son of God, the Word of God." He did not say it, but having allowed them the thought, he resolved the difficulty that troubled them. For he who saw the diners heard their thoughts. So turning toward the woman, he said: "Your faith has saved you." How can they take me for a man, those who say: "Who is this man who forgives sins?" For you, your faith has saved you.[36]

"Your faith has been your salvation." This faith is a recognition of the gratuity of salvation, assurance that for God nothing is impossible. It was the faith of the sinless Virgin Mary that allowed the Lord to do wonders for her, and the faith of the sinful woman that gained his pardon. Both are models of believers, the latter being more like each of us, more accessible than the other.

"Go now in peace." The forgiveness of sins raises her up and sets her on her way, toward the cross and glory, toward the paschal mystery. For, Luke insists: the disciple's itinerary cannot be other than that of Jesus who "journeys" toward Jerusalem, taking us with him.[37]

The text ends with a kind of résumé or tableau of the whole activity of Jesus. Luke loves to fill his Gospel with this kind of "summary." What we have here presents particular interest. In fact, it shows Jesus traveling through towns and villages, proclaiming the good news, surrounded by the Twelve, to be sure, but also by a group of women. It is already—and Luke clearly intends this—a small Church. The evangelist insists on the presence of the women. He names three of them, but in doing so remarks that there were "many others." "Holy" women? Yes, but because "cured of evil spirits and maladies."

One of them was the wife of "Herod's steward." This first community gathered around Jesus, including several woman of diverse milieus, is made up of pardoned sinners. Isn't this the Church, and not just a community of the pure?

The women "provided for them." The verb "to provide" is used elsewhere to designate the activity of the apostles or the Seven (Acts 1:17, 25; 6:1). This is not surprising, since Jesus said during the Last Supper: "I am among you as the one who serves" (Luke 22:27).

In the ecclesial community, appeal is made to the "resources," the "goods"—not only material—of whoever assumes the role of "service," of common "ministry": men and women, sinners and sick yesterday, healed by the Lord, belonging to various social milieus, famous people, and others.

There is no salvation if one is not open to the pardon of God, before which one sees oneself as a sinner, because justice only comes by faith in Christ, who, by his paschal mystery, makes us new creatures. The three biblical readings of this Sunday throw their light, their individual but converging illumination, on these fundamental truths.

Listening attentively to the story of the pardoned sinner, one is struck by the way Jesus behaves with respect to a flagrantly sinful woman, i.e., his extraordinary gentleness.

He turns attention from her by asking everyone to think of his own debt of sin. For God does not uselessly humiliate sinners; he wants to raise them, inviting them to "journey" with him toward Jerusalem. One must think of this when one speaks of the confession of sins in the sacrament of penance and reconciliation. This admission—what other word could be used?—is not a humiliation intended to make the guilty persons prostrate in the face of their guilt.

We first of all and always confess the mercy of God, as well as our sin. "The Lord be in your heart and on your lips that you may worthily proclaim his gospel";[38] "May the Lord inspire true speech and sentiments that you may confess your sins with contrition."[39] The two benediction formulas are really parallel: the one on the deacon about to proclaim the gospel, the other on the penitent. This is perfectly intelligible, since, in both cases, it is a question of the same good news that raises up those who welcome it and that excites a worshiping love of God in them.

The Ninth, Tenth, and Eleventh Sundays of this year of Ordinary Time probe more deeply into the mystery of salvation revealed by Christ and celebrated in the liturgy.

There are no foreigners for salvation; it is resurrection and forgiveness of sins, the many sins of each.

This is why we say:

> God of love and mercy . . .
> In wonder and gratitude,
> we join our voices with the choirs of heaven
> to proclaim the power of your love
> and to sing of our salvation in Christ
> (Eucharistic Prayer for Reconciliation I).

From the Twelfth to the Fourteenth Sunday in Ordinary Time

Chapter 9 and the first half of chapter 10 mark a turning point in the Gospel According to Luke. The three passages that the Lectionary has selected for the Twelfth, Thirteenth, and Fourteenth Sundays of Ordinary Time, Year C, form a unity, and therefore must be seen in the same perspective. Luke reports first how Jesus, having asked his disciples "Who do the crowds say that I am?" then to state for themselves—"But you, who do you say that I am?"—spoke to them for the first time about his passion, and told "all" who followed him what he had to undergo on the road to the cross (Luke 9:18-24—Twelfth Sunday). From this point on, Luke's Gospel is nothing other than Jesus' long journey to Jerusalem; ten chapters of the twenty-four deal with this! A journey wherein those following him must walk "resolutely" into destitution, without casting a backward glance (Luke 9:51-62—Thirteenth Sunday). Instead, they must travel ahead of him, from town to town, preparing for the coming of the Lord. Time presses. Nothing must slow down the journey: neither discouragement because of the mission's lack of success, nor complacency because of the wonders accomplished in the name of the Lord (Luke 10:1-12, 17-20—Fourteenth Sunday).

The sequence ends with the sending not of several messengers, but of a group of disciples—the seventy-two—into not only one village but "every town and place" where Jesus intended to go. The directives for this mission share in the mission of Jesus himself. Like him, the envoys must announce "The reign of God is at hand," without being hindered by the ill will they may face, knowing that they are sent "as lambs in the midst of wolves." In this also they conform to the Lord, walking in his footsteps (Fourteenth Sunday).

Thus, this series of three passages from Luke's Gospel is arranged around what has been called "the following of Jesus" (sequela Christi) recognized as "the Messiah of God," rejected, killed, and resurrected on the third day.

In addition, we end the "semicontinuous reading" of the Letter of Paul to the Galatians (3:26-29; 5:1, 13-18; 6:14-18). The three tracts present a compressed digest of the gospel preached by the apostle. Through faith and baptism, Christians are intimately bound to Christ, they belong to him and, through him, receive the promised inheritance (Gal 3:26-29—Twelfth Sunday). Radically freed from slavery to the Law and the flesh, they can, thanks to the gift of the liberating Spirit, successfully resist the tendencies of the flesh and proceed in the ways of true freedom, not by constraint but through love (Gal 5:1, 13-18—Thirteenth Sunday). The letter ends (Gal 6:14-18—Fourteenth Sunday) with a vigorous proclamation of "the truth of the gospel," sealed by "the cross of our Lord Jesus Christ," the boast of believers, foundation of their assurance, source of peace, of mercy, of all grace.

Twelfth Sunday

Christ's Passion
and His Followers

Eyes Lifted to the Crucified One

The New Testament, tradition, and the liturgy today understand Zechariah's enigmatic prophecy as referring to the mystery of Christ, who is at once the key to and the fulfillment of it (Zech 12:10-11).

This reading is much more than simply a text where we find, three or four centuries beforehand, a description of the crucifixion on Calvary. The very force of certain expressions—"him whom they have thrust through" (v. 10)—suggest their application to Christ. Thus John: "They will look upon him whom they have pierced" (John 19:37—feast of the Sacred Heart, Year A). Likewise, the Book of Revelation completes and extends the prophecy in a joyous way by applying it to the resurrected Christ: "Behold, he is coming amid the clouds, and every eye will see him, even those who pierced him. All the peoples of the earth will lament him. Yes. Amen" (Rev 1:7).

This is one instance, among many, that shows how Christ, in surpassing the prophecies, fulfills them. For neither a prophet nor any other commentator could have imagined such a fulfillment. Moreover, chapters 9–14 of the Book of Zechariah echo numerous earlier prophecies, particularly those of Jeremiah, Isaiah, Micah, Ezekiel, and especially the four great poems of the "Suffering Servant" (Isa 42:1-9; 49:1-7; 50:4-11; 52:13–53:12).

Finally, this text—it is important to note—concerns sin and its purification. In order to overcome this evil that, directly or not, has led to the death of "him whom they have thrust through," there must be an intervention of God that grants a new spirit, a spirit of repentance with respect to the one who has suffered for all: "They shall look on him whom they have thrust through, and they shall mourn for him as one mourns for an only son, and they shall grieve over him as one grieves over a firstborn." No one can become a disciple of Jesus without having passed through the door of repentance and having shed "tears of blood."

Without true love for Christ, we will not be true disciples; and we will not know how to love if our heart is not moved with gratitude for him; and we will not properly feel this gratitude if we do not feel vividly what he has suffered for us. In fact, it seems impossible to us that anyone could attain love of Christ if he does not feel distress or heartfelt anguish at the thought of the bitter sorrows that he has suffered, and feels no remorse at having contributed to them by his sins.[1]

Zechariah is thus situated (see also 11:4-7; 13:1, 2-6) in line with the well-known text of Ezekiel: "I will sprinkle clean water upon you to cleanse you from all your impurities, and from all your idols I will cleanse you. I will give you a new heart and place a new spirit within you, taking from your bodies your stony hearts and giving you natural hearts. I will put my spirit within you" (Ezek 36:25-27—Easter Vigil).

This prophetic tradition is fulfilled in the doctrine of salvation through faith authoritatively and vigorously propounded by Paul. Sin having crucified the promised Messiah, one must simply repent and turn toward "him whom they have thrust through." Thus the salvation so long hoped for realizes the promises, gratuitously, through the grace and mercy of God, for those who rely on the Savior.

The Sunday celebration is the place par excellence for this act of faith and hope, both personal and communal:

> My soul is thirsting for you, O LORD my God.
>
> O God, you are my God whom I seek;
>   for you my flesh pines and my soul thirsts
>   like the earth, parched, lifeless and without water.
> Thus have I gazed toward you in the sanctuary
>   to see your power and your glory,
> For your kindness is a greater good than life;
>   my lips shall glorify you.
>
> Thus will I bless you while I live;
>   lifting up my hands, I will call upon your name.
> As with the riches of a banquet shall my soul be satisfied,
>   and with exultant lips my mouth shall praise you.
>
> You are my help,
>   and in the shadow of your wings I shout for joy.
> My soul clings fast to you;
>   your right hand upholds me.
>   (Ps 63:2, 3-4, 5-6, 8-9)

All Are Children of God Through Faith

In five striking sentences, the epistle for this Sunday (Gal 3:26-29) expresses quite remarkably what is at the heart of the gospel preached by

Paul. As we know, he is writing to a group of Christians who—he cannot understand how—if not abandoned, at least allowed this "truth of the gospel" to become adulterated. Who could have thus "bewitched" them (Gal 3:1)? After having given their faith to Christ and put their trust in him, the Galatians began to search elsewhere—in the Law—for the assurance of their salvation! Impossible!

To live under the order of faith is to walk with only the guarantee of God's promise, with complete confidence in him. This can be fearful. From the temptation to turn to another system of security based on fidelity to a precise set of prescriptions, to observance of minutiae, comes a kind of enslavement. This debate over justification by faith or by the Law is not a thing of the past, as one might think. It is not a question of an abstract or juridical order. It is a question of knowing whether or not we can, like Jesus Christ and in him, give to God the name of "Father": "Each one of you is a son of God." This is what is at issue.

Baptism confirms our status as sons and daughters. To enter into the water, we throw off all false apparel: religious, social, or sexual prerogatives, dignity or self-justification. On leaving the baptismal bath we put on a new garment: Christ, the raison d'être and justice of believers before God. Consequently, no other differentiation has any determinative power. Jew, Greek, slave, free man, free woman, all become one in Christ. The result is not an undifferentiated mass, but communion in a body whose reality surpasses what previously separated them. Henceforth, diversity of conditions will not change the unity of the body, but bring it out more clearly. The diversity of charisms is an instance of this. Each person will finally become him- or herself.

Also, each person is made a member of the whole of the one people of God, inheritor according to "his promise to our fathers, to Abraham and to his descendants forever" (Magnificat).

To Carry One's Cross

"One day . . . Jesus was praying in seclusion." The first sentence of the Gospel of this Sunday must hold our attention, for it is not a banal, conventional, stereotypical formula for introducing any story whatever (Luke 9:18-24).

Luke, as we know, often mentions the prayer of Jesus, the place of his encounter with the Father.[2] Each time, this prayer is situated in a moment of crucial, indeed decisive, importance for Jesus, for the present or future of his mission. It marks a climax or a turning point in the fulfillment of his mystery.[3] Knowing this, we must listen attentively to what the evangelist reports. It must be a major revelation.

"One day." This indeterminateness and the absence of locale[4] may be surprising from an author who from the very beginning (Luke 1:1-4) said he wished to do the work of a historian.[5] But this way of introducing a story is too common in Luke not to correspond to a specific intention or to have a definite meaning.[6]

Luke composed one work in two parts: Gospel and Acts. This must not be ignored, even though in our Bibles today the two books are separated. Certainly the other evangelists also intended to write, according to their own perspectives and interests, from earlier oral traditions, the good news of Jesus Christ as it was preached. They all composed their own books in light of their Easter faith and experience, the life of the Church, in a specific community, in consideration of their contemporaries and those who would read their works later. Thus, far from being dissociated, Gospels and Church are found to be intimately bound together. This is clearly the case in Matthew, Mark, and John. But in Luke, the intention of marking out the continuity between the events of Jesus' life and the missionary activity of the Church is apparent everywhere; there is not even the least hiatus between the Gospel and the Acts of the Apostles in the Christian community.

"One day" was therefore a particular date in a particular place, but also the "day" (today) when and where we are. In other words, we must do as the evangelist suggests and see the Church already present in Jesus' prayer, in the questions of "the crowd" about him, and in what he "explains" to his disciples.

Even today, what a multitude of opinions abound about Jesus! Acceptance from some, hostility, rejection, and indifference from others.

There is no cause to be surprised by this. From the beginning of his Gospel, Luke has evoked the prediction that Simeon made to Mary: "Behold, this child is destined for the fall and rise of many in Israel, and to be a sign that will be contradicted" (Luke 2:34—feast of the Holy Family, Year B). The author of the Third Gospel and the Acts of the Apostles verified the truth of this prophecy, which is still felt today. But its meaning and significance are only fully perceived in the prayer "in seclusion." One thus moves from a simple verification to the penetration of the mystery "in reference to Christ and the church," as Paul says (Eph 5:32), the Church that, not being separate from its Master, collides with incomprehension and seeming contradictions.

However, we cannot remain at this level. What is said today about Christ—and what is not said?—comes in large part from what believers themselves say of him, not so much in their words, but above all in their bearing and behavior in all areas: personal, political, and social.

Moreover, what impressions do the Church and the Christian communities give of themselves? Through their life, their way of dwelling in the world, faced with its problems, its injustices, its struggles? "Maintain good conduct among the Gentiles, so that if they speak of you as evildoers, they may observe your good works and glorify God on the day of visitation," we read in the First Letter of Peter (2:12—Thursday II of the Eighth Week).

Mustn't we admit that, frequently, what the crowds reject is the caricature we give them of Christ and of the Church?

What must we make of the impression given by the community assembled for the liturgy and the way in which it celebrates?

In any case, "But you—who do you say that I am?" calls not only for a verbal profession of faith, but an authentic witness to the faith that we profess.

Truly, this faith—professed and lived—turns out to be a quest to be followed constantly; as assured as it may be, it remains fragile in the face of trial, beginning with that of Christ himself. Jesus always knew this. That is why "one day" he explained to his disciples, that they might remember: "The Son of Man must suffer greatly and be rejected by the elders, the chief priests, and the scribes, and be killed and on the third day be raised."

The necessity of the passion of the "Messiah of God" is still an enigma and a stumbling block. The persecution of the just man, put to death because his preaching and behavior were disturbing and insupportable, one can "understand"; experience shows—alas!—that such is often the case. But the "Messiah of God!" Could he not authenticate his witness—asserting it in some way—other than by submitting to the common fate of all other prophets? Does God think, like people everywhere, that the only credible witness is the one who lets himself be killed? Was it not rather the case that from the moment that the Son was sent to confront sin in decisive combat and definitively to vanquish it, "it was necessary" that the Son of Man take on even death, the condition of the persecuted just man? And that in him is realized, by the resurrection on the third day, the promise of the victory of good over evil, grace over sin, life over death? "On that day there shall be open to the house of David and to the inhabitants of Jerusalem, a fountain to purify from sin and uncleanness'' (Zech 13:1).

The "why" of this necessity remains a mystery of the plan of God. The question of the incomprehension, systematic opposition—even hate—that is excited by the proclamation of the Kingdom, the revelation of pardon, the invitation to mercy, the necessity of the passion of Christ, had to torment Jesus' spirit; his prayer at Gethsemane is the tortured manifestation of this. How could this not haunt the heart of the believer and scandalize the nonbeliever?

In any case, faith has quite a distance to go insofar as it does not adhere to the mystery of the death and resurrection of the Son of Man. One cannot "tell to anyone" that Jesus is "the Messiah of God" if one does not announce his death and resurrection. All apologetic would be illusory, and all Christian preaching radically reduced if, for fear of scandal, it did not dare to say: "We proclaim Christ crucified" (1 Cor 1:23).

But there is more. Jesus clearly told "the crowd" that in order to "be his follower" one must "deny his very self"; that "to follow" him is to take up one's cross "each day"; that to "save his life" is to "lose it." The force of these words puts a stop to all evasion.

Here again, there is no place for an apologetic that would flatter human wisdom, for a preaching which would water down—or worse, would pass over in silence—these radical exigencies.

One cannot say: "These are exhortations for times of persecution, a program for the heros of faith." No! Jesus says this to everyone: "to the crowd." He speaks of "whoever" wishes "to be his follower," "to follow in his steps," "to save his life." And he says: take up your cross "each day."

After all, everywhere, yesterday and today—more than yesterday?—it is in fact "each day" that all disciples find themselves confronted with crucifying choices, with self-renunciation, with "losing" their lives, if they truly desire "to follow Christ." One cannot adjust to the "world," sharing in it, accommodating oneself, even if only to a certain point, to dominant values, playing the dangerous game of current morality, losing sight of Christ and letting oneself be drawn along paths that lead away from him. Whether in personal, family, social, economic, or political life, to follow the Lord is to be exposed "each day" not only to renunciations but often to the loss of "one's life" or something that, in the eye of the "world," is necessary to life and success.

"To take up one's cross" following Christ is a message that cannot be effaced from the Gospels; it occurs too often (Luke 9:23; 14:27; Matt 10:38; Mark 8:34).

This "cross" of the disciples—for they are the ones particularly in question here—evokes the sacrifices that one "must" agree to in order to follow Jesus, without excluding the possibility of a total sacrifice.

The evangelists knew—as we do—that Jesus bore a cross that was not metaphorical, but made of two pieces of wood, on which he died in order to rise again and give us life.

Since then, the cross has become the sign of those who belong to Christ: from baptism to viaticum, Christians are marked with it through every sacramental stage of their life. The cross dominates the altars of our churches, their entrances and steeples. We hang it in important places in our homes. We often wear it around our neck, as jewelry sometimes, but without forgetting what it signifies, and that it is the emblem of our faith.

The recollection of Simon of Cyrene, "pressed into service" on the road to Calvary to bear the cross of Jesus (Luke 23:26; Matt 27:32; Mark 15:21) must give a very concrete sense to this "cross" that the disciples must accept.[7]

"To follow" Christ, "to follow in his steps," is not to seek the cross or stoically resign oneself to it, still less to delight in it. These renunciations and eventual death are not desired for their own sakes, but as the necessary passage to resurrection and life in Christ, in the very footsteps of Christ.

To proclaim Jesus "Messiah of God" without "following" him, without "following in his steps," is meaningless. In this case, it would be better to say nothing of him, above all not merely to pass him off with the title "Messenger of God."

Besides, the verb "to follow" must not be understood in a figurative sense, as when one speaks of walking in the steps of another by conforming to his or her teachings, to some doctrine that influences a certain manner of thought and conduct, but in a real sense—traveling a daily road while bearing one's cross, while "denying oneself," while "losing one's life"; a road that leads to life through resurrection "on the third day."

It is not a matter of merely conforming oneself intellectually or morally to an abstract model. "In Jesus Christ," Paul reminds us, we are "each a son of God." Baptism has "united us to Christ," we have "clothed ourselves with him," we have changed our condition, no longer being other than "one in him" who has become the center of our lives and being, our justice before God.

> Consider with a frame of mind that is full of religion and faith this short definition of the Christian life: Jesus Christ is my life. If I live, it is for Jesus Christ that I live. I live only to please and obey him. I live only to continue his work. I live only to prolong his life, to extend his cares, his charity, his sufferings for his Church; to accomplish what he did not have to do himself and what he wished that his disciples, according to their ministry, their talents, their vocation, add to his preaching, his work, his ignominies, his contradictions, his trials for the establishment of his reign. This is what Paul says himself in plain terms: "Now," he says to the Colossians, "I rejoice in my sufferings for your sake, and in my flesh I am filling up what is lacking in the afflictions of Christ on behalf of his body, which is the church" (Col 1:24).
>
> The apostle does not at all mean that he adds something to the personal sufferings of Jesus Christ, to the integrity and perfection of his sacrifice, to the whole superabundant reconciliation that he merited for us by dying for us on the cross. He does not think that he can add something to his sufferings that would increase their merit. He knows that he is only an external minister, like the one who plants and waters, who is capable of success only through the grace of Jesus Christ. . . .
>
> He is thus in the form of all Christians who are worthy of the name. When they suffer, they fulfill what is lacking in the afflictions of Jesus Christ. When they work, they continue and perfect his work. When they speak, teach, give service to their brothers, they achieve as members of Jesus Christ what had been begun by their master. Or rather, he himself, as lord, fulfills in them what is lacking in the perfection of the body that grows every day through the influence of the head.[8]

From the beginning, Christians have sometimes been called members of "the Way" (Acts 9:2). This "way" is Christ the Path, the Truth and the Life. The Christ who has said: "The Son of Man must suffer greatly . . . be rejected . . . and be killed and on the third day be raised. . . . If anyone wishes to come after me, he must deny himself and take up his cross daily and follow me. For whoever wishes to save his life will lose it, but whoever loses his life for my sake will save it."

Such is our faith, such is the law written in our hearts and in our being, such is the mystery that we celebrate.

Thirteenth Sunday

Nomads Following Christ

The Gospel According to Luke contains several episodes and words of Jesus after he announced to his disciples what was to be the passion of the "Messiah of God," and had told "the crowd" that no one can follow him without bearing his cross "each day" (Luke 9:18-24—Twelfth Sunday).

First of all, "about eight days after" comes the Transfiguration (Luke 9:28-36—Second Sunday of Lent). Then the healing of a possessed child (Luke 9:37-43a), the second announcement of the passion (Luke 9:43b-45), the words about the greatest among the disciples (Luke 9:46-48), and about using the name of Jesus to work miracles (Luke 9:49-50). Many of these texts are part of the Weekday Lectionary.[9]

Thus ends, in the Third Gospel, the Galilean ministry of Jesus, framed by two solemn manifestations of God (theophanies): that which took place after the baptism in the Jordan, when a voice from heaven proclaimed that Jesus is the Son born of the Father (Luke 3:22—Baptism of the Lord), and that of the Transfiguration, where a voice is again heard to say: "This is my chosen Son; listen to him" (Luke 9:35—Second Sunday of Lent).

The other ten chapters of Luke—composed for the most part of fragments that are peculiar to the Third Gospel—make up what is known as "the journey to Jerusalem," i.e., toward the city of Jesus' passion.

Sharing in the Lord

As always during Ordinary Time, the first reading for this Sunday was chosen because of its relationship to the Gospel, and it must be read within that perspective. It recounts how Elijah, having on God's order called Elisha, son of Shaphat, to succeed him as prophet, whereupon Elisha left all to "follow Elijah as his attendant" (1 Kgs 19:16b, 19-21).

In the Bible—and such is the case elsewhere in ancient Eastern literature—personal events are recounted for reasons beyond mere anecdotal interest. The author of the story we read today wanted to show that Elisha was truly the spiritual heir of Elijah, installed as his servant-disciple after a divine intervention.[10]

What is remarkable here is the simplicity of the call made by another prophet without any direct manifestation of God.[11] Elijah merely told Elisha to "follow" him, and Elisha thereafter walked at his side. These terms hold our attention first because they were the key words of last Sunday's Gospel. Thus there is reason to believe that they are also the keys to the interpretation of this text as read in the framework of this day's liturgy.

Note also that Elisha received this call while he was busying himself with his daily tasks. This feature occurs often in the Bible: Moses, David, and Amos are guarding their sheep when God calls them (Exod 3:1; 1 Sam 16:11; Amos 7:14)); Gideon was threshing wheat (Judg 6:11); Samuel was sleeping (1 Sam 3:1); Saul was coming in from the field with his oxen (1 Sam 11:5); Simon and Andrew were washing their nets after a night of fruitless fishing (Luke 5:1-11—Fifth Sunday of Ordinary Time); Levi (Matthew) was seated at his stall collecting taxes (Luke 5:27-32—Saturday after Ash Wednesday). This happens too often not to give pause. Really, what happens to the great prophets and apostles happens also to us. Frequently, the call of God, a decisive grace, will seize us in the midst of the most banal of our daily duties.[12]

Without saying anything, Elijah merely throws his cloak—his cape— over Elisha's shoulders. Was this garment the distinctive garb of the "brotherhood of prophets" as is sometimes wondered,[13] or of Elijah himself, like the garment of camel's hair that John the Baptist wore (Mark 1:6)? It doesn't matter. The gesture alone was enough to make Elisha understand that the prophet took him under his protection, investing him to his service.[14]

"To follow," "to serve," are two verbs that have, so to speak, a technical meaning in the Bible. They imply a personal allegiance that can even involve the community in a communion of life. Such is the case even among human beings, but even more so when one speaks of "following" (or of "serving") God or other gods.[15] To speak of only one use of the word in the New Testament, "You cannot serve God and mammon" (Luke 16:13—Twenty-fifth Sunday in Ordinary Time). The reading of this text from the First Book of Kings is the occasion to become aware of all the connotations of the words "serve" and "servant" when they denote the relation of a person to God or to Christ. It is not at all a matter of slavery, or even alienation, but is instead a promotion, a grace.[16]

The delay that Elisha asks of Elijah betrays no hesitation, since he left his cattle and ran quickly after Elijah. He wanted a little time to take leave of his father and mother. What more significant gesture could point to a total renunciation of his former life than Elisha sacrificing his oxen, cooking their meat over a fire made from the wood of his plow? Like Levi (Luke 5:29), he offered a banquet to those of his household, then rose, followed Elijah, and acted as his "attendant." What an extraordinary text, full of dynamism and generosity!

Following this line, the Lectionary has chosen several verses of Psalm 16, traditionally used in the rite of ordination.

You are my inheritance, O LORD.

Keep me, O God, for in you I take refuge;
I say to the LORD, "My Lord are you. . . ."
O LORD, my allotted portion and my cup,
you it is who hold fast my lot. . . .

I bless the LORD who counsels me;
even in the night my heart exhorts me.
I set the LORD ever before me;
with him at my right hand I shall not be disturbed.
Therefore my heart is glad and my soul rejoices,
my body, too, abides in confidence;
Because you will not abandon my soul to the nether world,
nor will you suffer your faithful one to undergo corruption.
You will show me the path to life,
fullness of joys in your presence,
the delights at your right hand forever.
(Ps 16:1, 2a, 5, 7-8, 9-10, 11)

Psalm 100 also comes to mind, singing of the joy of God's servant and the thanksgiving of those who are near him:

Serve the LORD with gladness.

Sing joyfully to the LORD, all you lands;
serve the LORD with gladness;
come before him with joyful song.
Know that the LORD is God;
he made us, his we are;
his people, the flock he tends.
Enter his gates with thanksgiving,
his courts with praise;
Give thanks to him; bless his name,
for he is good:
the LORD, whose kindness endures forever,
and his faithfulness, to all generations.

To Be Truly Free

The first reading showed Elisha leaving everything to follow Elijah "as his attendant." Now see how it is first of all freedom, of liberation from a "yoke of slavery" that the epistle speaks about (Gal 5:1, 13-18).

The whole development hinges on an understanding of the double meaning—a device often found in the Bible—of the words "service" and "to serve," according to which it is a matter, on the one hand, of the submission of a human being to God or to his law or, on the other hand, of enslavement of one person by another or by that person's passions. In the first case, "service" is freedom, in the second, slavery. It is of this that Paul speaks.[17]

Between people and God, there is no mediation of a Law that would be the ultimate reference point, by which constraints would be imposed even to the point of slavery. The gospel is the announcement of salvation by Christ, gratuitously given, in the Spirit. Faith makes all believers sons of God (epistle for last Sunday). To understand the gospel as a law is to return to the slavery from which Christ has freed us.

But the proper exercise of this freedom does not consist in abandonment to egoistic impulses. On the contrary, it consists in giving "out of love, placing yourselves at one another's service"; the love with which God loves us and which we give to him is expressed by the love of one's neighbor as oneself. Outside of this is the law of the jungle; all love between people is destroyed, each seeking to be the strongest, to enslave so as not to be enslaved. A tangled web of competition, violence, and fear that we find—alas!—to be the sad and awful spectacle of our world.

Love of neighbor, rather, grows with respect to the gift not only of the one who gives, but equally of the one to whom it is given.

> The one who loves unselfishly, wholly for the other, grows in proportion to his gift; the more he forgets himself, the more he gains. God always expands his love, God obliges him to grow in order to become more effective in the service of humanity. There is no respite for the one who gives himself without holding back. Tasks are piled onto tasks. He can go on no longer, but in his infirmity, God is his strength.[18]

This freedom from egoism is in the context of a more general freedom, a freedom from what Paul calls the "flesh." He does not mean only sexual impulses, but the condition of sinful people, slaves to sin, radically stripped in order to extricate themselves from the strands of the spider's web which is woven by sin and which leads to sin.

The agent of this liberation—for it is a constant battle, involving a never-ending series of options—is the Spirit given to those who have believed in Christ, whose presence in them attests that they are children of God (Gal 4:6).

Such is the condition of believers: free men and women called to live freely, and who are made capable of doing so by the Spirit, even though in their deepest hearts they are still confronted with the "cravings of the flesh."

Without Looking Backward

"When the days for his being taken up were fulfilled, [Jesus] resolutely determined to journey to Jerusalem." Thus begins—today (Luke 9:51-62)—the second part of the Gospel According to Luke.

The road that Luke shows Jesus traveling, through these ten chapters, cannot be found on a map. It is a literary construction, to be sure, but it is more. By it, the evangelist gives us a key to reading the mystery of Jesus and vigorously turns us toward what is at its heart: the Passover of the Lord at Jerusalem, where he would die in order to rise again. How could one not be struck by the solemnity of this opening of the second part of the Third Gospel? To be sure, one enters here into a decisive phase of Jesus' itinerary. And how could one not see the clear link between the departure for Jerusalem and what Jesus said (Luke 9:22—last Sunday's Gospel) most insistently—"Pay attention to what I am telling you" (Luke 9:44)—as well as the conversation with Moses and Elijah on the mountain of the transfiguration: they "spoke of his exodus that he was going to accomplish in Jerusalem" (Luke 9:31—Second Sunday of Lent).

Jesus takes to the road to Jerusalem "resolutely," with grave determination, fully conscious of what awaits him in the city. He "set his face" (literal translation), as it is said of the mysterious person evoked in the third Song of the Servant in the Book of Isaiah: "I have not rebelled, have not turned back. . . . I have set my face like flint" (Isa 50:5-7—Passion [Palm] Sunday). Not in a kind of rigid stoicism, but because "knowing that I shall not be put to shame" (Isa 50:7). Already we see the outline of the agony of Gethsemane where Jesus, after having prayed, saying "Father . . . not my will but yours be done," rose, rejoined his sleeping disciples and said to them: "Get up" (Luke 22:42, 46—Passion [Palm] Sunday). He has said to all his disciples: "If anyone wishes to come after me . . . take up his cross daily and follow me." (Luke 9:23—Gospel for last Sunday). He spoke of a very concrete road: the road "toward Jerusalem" which he "resolutely" travels first. Luke gives this testimony that we might never forget it.

Henceforth, we are continually on the road to Jerusalem with Jesus and following him on the way to his Passover and ours.[19]

A long and tortuous road that must be taken "resolutely" at Jesus' side. A road defined by encounters, events, and stops along the way for teaching and prayer, rather than by an actual step-by-step account.[20]

The road that Jesus traveled toward Jerusalem and his Passover was located in a specific country. But each believer must do the same on other roads: wherever he may be, the believer knows that he is marching toward Jerusalem, and he takes to the road "resolutely."

If he had desired to tell us only about Jesus' itinerary on his journey to the city, the historian (Luke 1:3) Luke would have had to give us more definite road signs. It is not right for us to question his understanding of geography and chronology.[21] Indeed, his manner of speaking fits well with his intention of showing that the journey to Jerusalem accomplished previously by Jesus and the first group of disciples is still the road that disciples of all times must follow. In no way is Luke interested in a simple historical recollection; on the contrary, he discourages all attempts to fix it in time while orienting us toward the "today" of the Easter itinerary of Christ and of the believers.[22]

The evangelist first deals with the refusal of the Samaritans to receive Jesus and his companions into their village.

John recalls that Jews had nothing to do with Samaritans (4:9). This deep-seated enmity went back quite far and was the more lively as it had to do with historical circumstances, differences in worship (the sanctuary of Mount Gerezim versus the Temple of Jerusalem), ethnic mixing, etc.[23] A hereditary enmity, the most enduring and basic of all.[24]

But we remember also the enthusiastic reception of Jesus' preaching by the Samaritans of the town of Sychar (John 4:1-42—Third Sunday of Lent), the parable wherein a Samaritan is offered as a model to imitate (Luke 10:29-37—Fifteenth Sunday in Ordinary Time). Another time, Jesus showed his admiration for a Samaritan, the only one among the ten lepers whom Jesus healed to return and give thanks (Luke 17:16—Twenty-eighth Sunday).

In the Book of Acts, Luke speaks at length about Philip's mission in Samaria, where the apostles sent Peter and John to lay their hands on the new converts to receive the Holy Spirit (Acts 8:5-17—Sixth Sunday of Easter). Elsewhere, he speaks of the Church spread "throughout all

Judea, Galilee, and Samaria'' (Acts 9:31—Fifth Sunday of Easter, Year B). Finally, he says that Paul, Barnabas, and others, while going from Antioch to Jerusalem to argue with the apostles on the conditions for admitting pagans to the faith, ''passed through Phoenicia and Samaria telling of the conversion of the Gentiles, and brought great joy to all the brothers'' (Acts 15:3).

Therefore we should not see in the episode reported here any trace of animosity or distrust by the Samaritans with respect to Jesus and the gospel. After all, they are not opposing Jesus himself; they refuse to receive into their village a group of Jews en route to Jerusalem. A bit lacking in tolerance, certainly, but with respect to people who—and this is the least one could say—had not had their interests at heart. Should we, then, throw stones at them?

James and John wanted to go further: to order fire to fall from heaven to destroy them. Nothing less would do!

They are sharply rebuked by Jesus. ''Then they set off for another town,'' more hospitable. Jesus will soon tell his messengers that this is the way they must always act: leave judgment to God (Luke 10:10-12—Gospel for next Sunday).

Luke is also thinking here of the experience of the Church and its missionaries. At the time he wrote his Gospel, the question of receiving pagans into the Christian community was still being debated, despite the decisions of the Council of Jerusalem (Acts 15:5-35). Theoretically, it had been resolved a long time before. But that is not the same as being resolved in mind-sets and actions. Even today racism, anti-Semitism, xenophobia, aggressive intolerance with respect to Christians of other confessions, etc., continue to make themselves felt. We are surprised sometimes at our unconscious reflexes and unacknowledged complacency.[25] It is therefore not inopportune to hear Jesus' quick response to James and John, and to remember what he has said of the gift, without hope of return, of love of one's enemies (Luke 6:27-35—Seventh Sunday).

Without being deterred by this refusal at a Samaritan village, Jesus continued on his road. The evangelist reports three particularly significant encounters, each of which gives us food for thought.

Thus we see two men who come to find Jesus and say that they are eager ''to follow'' him, and a third to whom Jesus takes the initiative to say: ''Follow me.''

These are not three individual cases or particular callings. On the one hand, the call to ''follow Jesus'' is addressed to all (and we are among his "disciples"), those who have decided to walk in his Way (Acts 9:2). On the other hand, what is said here (vv. 58, 60, and 62) has a general significance: it is addressed to all those who wish to "follow Jesus."

These cases are memorable, or rather they express a directness that characterizes Luke. They cannot be adulterated or emended by so many "yes . . . buts," lending themselves to numerous interpretations.

Certainly the one who follows Jesus will know the joy and relief of occasional, temporary stops along the way. Jesus himself knew this and arranged for his disciples to have such pauses. Also, Luke knew well that Paul, the perfect imitator of Christ (1 Cor 4:16; 11:1; Phil 3:7), carefully prepared his missionary journeys, always offering his thanks for the help and hospitality that had been given him; that he saw to it that his collaborators lacked nothing,[26] and that he was concerned for their health (1 Tim 5:23).

Yet the Gospels—and not only Luke's—speak of the Christian as one without hearth or home, with no fixed dwelling here below, because he or she is marching toward "the one that is to come" (Heb 13:14).

"Aliens and sojourners" on this earth (1 Pet 2:11; Heb 11:13). This way of expressing the condition of the Christian here below—which is a good translation of what Jesus said—came to be familiar to the first disciples and part of the primitive catechism: "Our citizenship is in heaven" (Phil 3:20); "I urge you as aliens and sojourners to keep away from worldly desires" (1 Pet 2:11); "Think of what is above, not of what is on earth" (Col 3:2).

This way of envisaging life and leading it is not only radically opposed to that of the world, but folly in the eyes of human wisdom. This clearly arises from—and this proves to be very significant—the messages we receive from advertising: "Consider your own comfort!"; "Make sure of your security!"; "Make your life easy!"; etc. What shrugs and sneers there would be, in the midst of all this, if one would hear the message: "The foxes have lairs, the birds of the sky have nests, but the Son of Man has nowhere to lay his head." And yet, this is what Christians cannot forget without denying their faith.

What is said to the second man encountered along the way is even stronger, more shocking. First because it is Jesus himself who takes the initiative of inviting him to follow without allowing him the slightest delay to go and give his last duty to his father. One is tempted to decry this as cruelty, in flat contradiction to the piety and love for parents that is explicitly commanded by God, as well as the whole biblical and Christian tradition that regards providing for the burial of the dead as a sacred duty, a work of piety.[27]

But this is not what is at issue here. In order to understand what Jesus says, it must not be seen in the perspective of casuistry, of a conflict of duties.[28] Jesus is announcing a principle of much more general importance that is to be applied always and everywhere. It may be understood by recalling another message: "If anyone comes to me without hating his father and mother, wife and children, brothers and sisters, and even his own life, he cannot be my disciple" (Luke 14:26—Twenty-third Sunday). "Prefer nothing to the love of Christ."[29] Nothing can keep one from announcing the reign of God.

The third man that Jesus encounters along the way asks "first" to take leave of the people of his household, as Elisha did (first reading). Could we say that there is one here greater than Elijah? Certainly. But it is the word "first" we should focus on, because it leads to a response by Jesus in the form of a proverb.

Again we have the absolute priority of Christ whom one cannot claim to "follow" and to "serve" without renouncing everything, including one's past. This is what Paul understood perfectly when he said to the Philippians: "I even consider everything as a loss because of the supreme good of knowing Christ Jesus my Lord. For his sake I have accepted the loss of all things and I consider them so much rubbish, that I may gain Christ and be found in him . . . forgetting what lies behind but straining forward to what lies ahead. I continue my pursuit toward the goal, the prize of God's upward calling, in Christ Jesus" (Phil 3:8, 13-14—Fifth Sunday of Lent).

Anthony, addressing the monks gathered around him, said the same.

> This is why, my sons, we should remain firm in asceticism, fleeing spiritual sloth. The Lord works with us, as it is written: "We know that all things work for good for those who love God" (cf. Rom 8:28) . . .
>
> Having thus begun and followed the road of virtue, let us walk correctly from the beginning, straining forward with our whole being (cf. Phil 3:14). Let no one look back, like Lot's wife, for the Lord has said: "No one who sets a hand to the plow and looks to what was left behind is fit for the kingdom of God" (Luke 9:62). Looking back consists in having regrets and retaining a taste for the things of the world.[30]

To be sure, morality is not the issue in this Gospel, but rather keeping "our eyes fixed on Jesus, the leader and perfecter of faith" (Heb 12:2—Twentieth Sunday), on Christ "followed" completely.

The biblical texts of this Thirteenth Sunday of Year C, always celebrated after Pentecost, throw a particular light on the time called "Ordinary," the time of the Church and of believers who "travel with Christ." This long, winding "road" is like that of the Lord, constantly "journeying toward Jerusalem" where he was "taken from this world," throughout which he repeated to those he met and those around him: "Follow me."

To welcome this call, to respond to it, involves complete abandonment, without delay, without looking back, without being put off by the strangeness, the hardships, the difficulties of the road where we will not always find friends to receive us and lend us help. Might we not merely say that the adventure is not without risk, and that it is a frightening thing to fall into the hands of God?

> God is dangerous. God is a devouring fire. God has cast his eyes on you. Heed the warning he himself has given you: "No one who sets a hand to the plow and looks to what was left behind is fit for the kingdom of God." Whoever does not love me more than father and mother, more than beloved and homeland, more than himself, is not worthy of me. Take care, he is crafty, he begins with a little love, a small flame, and before you can realize it for what it is, he catches hold of you and you are taken. If you give over only your little finger, you are lost; there are no limits toward heaven. He is God and he is used to infinity. He whisks you toward the heights like a cyclone, he whirls you around like a typhoon. Take care: man is created for measure and limit, and finds rest and happiness only in the finite; but God knows no measure. He is a seducer.[31]

But it is worth the pain to join this adventure and follow Jesus, like nomads free from all attachments, with no other law than that of love, at the service of all, letting ourselves be led by the Spirit.

> Lord Jesus,
> You withdrew from the joy belonging to you,
> and you endured the shame of the cross.
> Do not forget that it costs men
> to follow you on this road.
> Do not forget your terror at Gethsemane.
> Forgive our fears,
> and give us the courage to follow you.[32]

Fourteenth Sunday

Messengers of the Gospel

Already, but Not Quite

The Liturgy of the Word begins with the announcement to Jerusalem of good news, of a gospel (Isa 66:10-14c).

It does not point to a distant future; it is not addressed to people faced with affliction, for they are no longer in mourning (v. 10b). In fact, the Exile has come to an end. The return to the Holy Land has begun, and through the walls of Zion the caravans continue to arrive, the people singing:

> I rejoiced because they said to me,
>   "We will go up to the house of the LORD."
>
> And now we have set foot
>   within your gates, O Jerusalem—
> Jerusalem, built as a city
>   with compact unity.
>
> To it the tribes go up,
>   the tribes of the LORD,
> According to the decree for Israel,
>   to give thanks to the name of the LORD.
> In it are set up judgment seats,
>   seats for the house of David.
> (Ps 122:1-5)
>
> When the LORD brought back the captives of Zion,
>   we were like men dreaming.
>
> Then our mouth was filled with laughter,
>   and our tongue with rejoicing.
> Then they said among the nations,
>   "The LORD has done great things for them."
> The LORD has done great things for us;
>   we are glad indeed.
> (Ps 126:1-3)

Yet, one must not forget those who have not yet begun the road back:

Restore our fortunes, O Lord,
  like the torrents in the southern desert.
(Ps 126:4)

nor be unconscious of the responsibilities that fall to exiles returning to
their home:

Pray for the peace of Jerusalem!
  May those who love you prosper!
May peace be within your walls,
  prosperity in your buildings.

Because of my relatives and friends
  I will say, "Peace be within you!"
Because of the house of the Lord, our God,
  I will pray for your good.
(Ps 122:6-9)

And yet, the flow of returnees is so great, the rebirth of the people so
marvelous and so sudden that the prophet does not hesitate to see in
Zion the Mother-City that "before she comes to labor, she gives birth;
before the pains come upon her, she safely delivers a male child":

Who ever heard of such a thing,
  or saw the like?
Can a country be brought forth in one day,
  or a nation be born in a single moment?
Yet Zion is scarcely in labor
  when she gives birth to her children.
(Isa 66:7-8)

What does it mean that they must again be urged to rejoice, as if their
joy had an aftertaste of grief or deception? Without a doubt they did not
grasp that between the "already" and the "not yet," they have a road
to follow, strengthened not only with the power of God, but with his
motherly kindness. And this is always our situation. All has "already"
been given to us, all is "yet" to come, but we can and must work in joy
that this might happen. In joy and assurance because of the kindness,
patience, forgiveness, and energy always offered from the one who is
our Father but cannot be evoked without attributing to him the qualities
and tenderness of the most motherly of mothers.

The prophet says this in an absolutely remarkable manner that, though
not the only instance of it in the Bible,[33] always excites a new admiration, indeed astonishment, that one might wish to share with the whole
universe.

Let all the earth cry out to God with joy.

Shout joyfully to God, all you on earth,
  sing praise to the glory of his name;
  proclaim his glorious praise.
Say to God, "How tremendous are your deeds!"

"Let all on earth worship and sing praise to you,
  sing praise to your name!"

Come and see the works of God,
  his tremendous deeds among men.
He has changed the sea into dry land;
  through the river they passed on foot;
  therefore let us rejoice in him.
He rules by his might forever.

Hear now, all you who fear God,
  while I declare what he has done for me.

Blessed be God who refused me not
  my prayer or his kindness!
(Ps 66:1-3a, 4-5, 6-7a, 16, 20).

The Cross of Christ, Our Boast

The epistle (Gal 6:14-18) is the conclusion of the Letter to the Galatians from which we have already read five excerpts. This letter, we remember, was written to Christian communities that were in danger of abandoning the gospel in order to seek salvation by the Law (Ninth Sunday).

Paul, who led a persecution of "the Church of God" is the witness to the gratuity of salvation and of divine election (Tenth Sunday) that the cross of Christ gains for us (Eleventh Sunday).

Consequently, to live under the rule of faith is to advance under the sole guarantee of the promise of God, with confidence in him. All believers, no matter from where they come, are children of God (Twelfth Sunday).

Under the guidance of the Spirit of God, one lives free from all constraint, under only the law of love (Thirteenth Sunday).

At the conclusion of this letter, the apostle summarizes, in several formulas of rare density and vigor, "the truth of the gospel."

"The cross of our Lord Jesus Christ," and it alone, is the guarantee of the good news of salvation given freely by the Father to all. What was a sign of disgrace has become and remains the only "boast" of the believer, the only thing by which he or she can be glorified. In fact, it frees us all from the control of the "world," from the carnal in each of us, from every exterior law.

Christ has truly been crucified; we need not blush over it. He has been crucified, we need not deny it. Rather, I must proclaim it with spirit. If I deny
it, Golgotha itself refutes me. The wood of the cross, its pieces strewn all
over the earth, also refutes me. I recognize the cross because I recognize
the resurrection. If the crucified one had remained in the realm of the dead,
I would doubtlessly not have recognized the cross and would have hidden
with my Master. But the resurrection followed the cross, and I am not
ashamed to speak of it.[34]

"All who follow this rule of life" are assured of the supreme gifts of
peace and mercy; they are "the Israel of God."[35]

Paul does not hesitate to write that he bears in his flesh the mark of
Christ's sufferings, of the cross that is his only boast. Thus has he borne
witness to Christ and defended "the gospel truth" of the death-
resurrection of the Lord. Like him he has suffered and like him he has
loved.

The letter ends with his wish for his correspondents, "the grace of our
Lord Jesus Christ." In the word "grace," we can easily see the key word
of the letter.

"Brothers" was the way Christians typically referred to each other. Paul
habitually uses this title at the beginning of his letters or of a paragraph.
The translation in the Lectionary places it at the beginning of the last sentence of the Letter. Actually, Paul put it at the end, so that it reads: "The
grace of our Lord Jesus Christ be with your spirit, brothers." This
"anomaly"—the only case of it in all Paul's letters—has intrigued exegetes.
They wonder whether such a construction reveals a specific intention of
the author. Thus we would understand: "may the grace of our Lord Jesus
Christ be with your spirit" in order that you may be truly "brothers."

The Seventy-two Messengers

On the road that goes up to Jerusalem, Jesus teaches his disciples what
"to follow" him means and implies. What he has said, what he has done,
those who have come to him, his resolution, reveal the surprising plan
of God into which disciples of all times must enter willingly, resolutely.
Clearly this is the reason that Luke recounts these words, these incidents
and encounters. He does so, as we have already noted, in the light of
the experience of Christian communities of his time, around A.D. 70–80.
In other words, what he has "handed down" (Luke 1:2), what he reports
faithfully and presents "in an orderly sequence" (Luke 1:3) is situated
and understood in the "present day" of the life of the Church. This is

what we must do in our turn when we read and listen to this Gospel (Luke 10:1-12, 17-20).

Having recalled what Jesus said about the requisite conditions for "following" him (last Sunday's Gospel), Luke comes to the instructions given by the Master to his messengers; this is the Gospel of this Sunday (Luke 10:1-12, 17-20).

In Matthew and Mark, this discourse—for it really is a discourse—is addressed to the Twelve, and it is they who are sent out (Matt 10:7-16; Mark 6:8-13).

But Luke understood that not only the small, initial group is concerned. This is not merely a personal interpretation, isolated or occurring only well after the event. Very soon, even before Pentecost, Peter suggested that among the disciples who were not of the Twelve, a replacement should be chosen for Judas. The lot fell on Matthias, who then joined the eleven apostles (Acts 1:15-26). Also rather quickly, other "messengers" were mandated to bear the good news to all the nations. Such was the "particular case" of Paul, but how many instances of this are testified to in Acts and in Paul's letters?

Luke tells us that these initiatives are in line with what Jesus himself did in appointing "seventy-two . . . whom he sent ahead of him in pairs to every town and place he intended to visit." It is a matter of more than simply designating messengers to find a sleeping-place in a village in Samaria (Luke 9:51—Thirteenth Sunday). One is in the presence here of a true mission, a mission to all places. The number "seventy-two" is itself symbolic. In fact, in the Book of Genesis, according to the Greek version (Septuagint), it is the number of people in the whole world (Gen 10).

The workers will always be too few in the huge field of the apostolate, which is as wide as the world. For the ripe harvest is already large, as the messengers testify on their return (v. 17) and as Luke reports in Acts. Hence the invitation to pray that the "Master of the harvest" will send his workers. This is in imitation of the Father, who sent his Son and gave him "all power in heaven and on earth" (Matt 28:18), especially to invest his disciples with the mission to be his "witnesses in Jerusalem, throughout Judea and Samaria, and to the ends of the earth" (Acts 1:8—Ascension of the Lord). In order that this work may be accomplished, the disciples must join their prayer to that which the Son constantly addresses to the Father.

Their mission is no less perilous than Jesus': they are sent "as lambs in the midst of wolves," with no other defense and consolation than that of the Spirit, with no other assurance than the promise that they will not be confounded. Whatever their success or the power they exert over the forces of evil, their cause of joy must be that their "names are inscribed in heaven." Luke also had experience of this, thanks to the example of Paul, whom he accompanied on several of his apostolic journeys.

The "discourse" is thus lent to the concrete instructions addressed to the missionaries of the gospel. From the beginning, they are admonished to "carry no money bag, no sack, no sandals; and greet no one along the way." In other words: "Do not bear anything that will encumber your journey. Think not of your needs; you will receive them from those who welcome you into their homes. Do not waste time in vague pleasantries. Time is short."

Their only valuable is peace, which they are to offer generously. This "peace" is a messianic gift, work of the Spirit, sign of the coming of the Kingdom: "on earth peace to those on whom his favor rests" (Luke 2:14—Nativity of the Lord, Mass during the night). Jesus granted this peace himself,[36] and it is one of the most beautiful fruits of his Easter victory.[37] Whether one rejects or accepts it—it does not depend on the messenger—it is a sign of the proximity of the kingdom, like the healing of the sick.[38]

The message the messengers must announce is this: "The reign of God is at hand." A very short message, offered to all, while allowing each to welcome it or not. Nevertheless, even for those who refuse to open their doors, the kingdom of God is at hand. This is why, shaking the dust from their feet, the missionaries repeat that "the kingdom of God is at hand." One day, perhaps, others will harvest this ground, which was at first barren. In any case, one only gathers fruit that was sown at another time. The duty of the messengers is to sow seed wherever they go. The final result? It is not theirs to see immediately; it will appear at the day of judgment. May they remember the parable of the seed and the sower! (Luke 8:4-14). It must have been inspired by Jesus' personal experience. Did not he do the same at the towns where he taught and multiplied miracles, at Capernaum (Luke 9:13-15)? But his lack of success, which he felt so keenly, never prevented him from rejoicing in the Holy Spirit and saying, " 'I give you praise, Father, Lord of heaven and earth, for although you have hidden these things from the wise and the learned you have revealed them to the childlike. Yes, Father, such has been your gracious will' " (Luke 10:21). This was, Luke tells us, at the very moment when the Seventy-two were marveling over the success of their mission. Jesus shared their enthusiasm.

But he sees further than they do, even to the final fall of Satan at the end of the battle between Good and Evil, between Light and Darkness. This will be "on the day of Judgment."

In the meantime, it falls to everyone to fulfill the mission given, knowing that, however modestly, they are working toward this victory that is "already" begun, while rejoicing to have their name written in the heavens.

Christians are those who, having recognized in Jesus the "Messiah of God" dead and risen on the third day, follow him by taking up their cross daily, knowing that "to lose one's life" for him is to save it. They are actually "clothed with Christ" at baptism. Thus conformed to him, one with him, become children of God by the Spirit that has been given to them, the heritage promised to Abraham becomes theirs (Twelfth Sunday).

Their life, whatever its duration, vicissitudes, windings, is one constant "journey to Jerusalem," begun and followed "resolutely."

With him, they know the defeats on the road. But always going forward, with never a backward glance, pilgrims without hearth or home, they travel free, under the guidance of the Spirit, with no other law than that of love for one another (Thirteenth Sunday).

But the road is long. Whatever the strength of their faith and resolution, those who "follow" Christ need to hearken to the announcement of the good news that reawakens the joy of pilgrims. May they not be discouraged! May they rely on God their father overflowing with motherly tenderness! And above all—as Paul repeats in his Letter to the Galatians—may they not yield to the temptation to seek a security other than that of "the truth of the gospel"! May they put their hope and pride in nothing other than the cross of Christ!

There is still much to do for the harvest to be gathered. Every one must pray with Christ, and through him, that the Father send workers for the harvest. But at the same time be ready oneself to labor, if one is sent.

The time is pressing. "The kingdom of God is at hand." Nothing can prevent one from proclaiming it: neither the refusal of some to listen, nor the fear of being devoured as lambs by wolves, without letting oneself become intoxicated or complacent by the success of this mission.

What counts is to have one's name written in heaven, to welcome peace oneself and to bring it into every house one enters.

Peace, the supreme benefit that comes from God, the sign of the coming of the kingdom.

"The grace of our Lord Jesus Christ be with your spirit, brothers!" (Fourteenth Sunday).

> Workers for peace,
> the harvest awaits you;
> to reconcile the world
> carry only love.
> To those who welcome you,
> and those who drive you out,
> proclaim the news:
> "The kingdom of heaven is at hand."
>
> The deaf hear,
> the dead awaken,
> the good news is announced to the poor.
>
> *The kingdom of heaven is at hand.*
>
> The blind see,
> the lame walk,
> the lepers are healed.
>
> *The kingdom of heaven is at hand.*
>
> Prisoners are freed,
> a year of favor is proclaimed.
>
> *The kingdom of heaven is at hand.*[39]

From the Fifteenth to the Seventeenth Sunday in Ordinary Time

In the Fifteenth Sunday of Ordinary Time, Year C, we begin reading four successive excerpts from the Letter of Paul to the Colossians.

This letter is relatively short: ninety-five verses in four chapters. The five passages included in the Lectionary represent a little more than a third of the total (thirty-seven percent).

The Asian proconsulary was one of the richest colonial domains of the Roman Empire. Its capital, which had been Pergamum, was at this time Ephesus, a city with a population of two hundred thousand, quite large for the time.

It was during his third missionary journey that Paul made Ephesus, where he stayed two years and three months, the seat of his apostolate in the region. From there, Christianity spread out. The Book of Revelation gives an idea of the situation, some twenty years after the evangelization done by Paul, with the letters to the Churches of Ephesus, Smyrna, Pergamum, Thyatira, Sardis, Philadelphia and Laodicea, all of which are cities in Asia (Rev 2:1–3:22).

Paul had not visited the Christian communities of Colossae. The author of the letter received his information from Epaphras, a native of the city and founder of its Church, who seems voluntarily to have shared the apostle's captivity (Col 1:7; Phlm 23; Col 4:12).

These sketchy details suffice for the moment. As we read the five passages in the Lectionary, we will have occasion to enter a bit more into the life and problems of this community, and the teaching of the apostle.[1]

In addition, during these three Sundays, we read the end of chapter 10 of Luke's Gospel (Fifteenth and Sixteenth Sundays) and the first thirteen verses of the next chapter (Seventeenth Sunday).

These are teachings of Jesus given to the many disciples who follow him on the road to Jerusalem.

The evangelist did not arrange them in any logical order, as if he were writing a treatise. He chose, rather, a different kind of presentation, one more striking: this whole section of Jesus' ministry is set in the framework of a "journey to Jerusalem," whose theological and practical import for Christian life we have already seen.

What makes the Fifteenth, Sixteenth, and Seventeenth Sundays such a distinct sequence is the concrete nature of Jesus' interventions.

Actually, several chance meetings on the road give Jesus the occasion to teach: the encounter with a doctor of the Law with a specific question (Fifteenth Sunday); an amicable dispute between the two sisters who welcome Jesus into their home, over the apparent indolence of the one who does not do her share in preparing the supper (Sixteenth Sunday); finally, seeing Jesus ''one day,'' ''in a certain place,'' in prayer, the disciples ask how they should pray (Seventeenth Sunday).

On the other hand, we notice that, on each of these occasions, the question put to Jesus and his response have to do with very concrete behavior. ''What must I *do* to inherit everlasting life?'' asks the doctor of the Law (Fifteenth Sunday). ''My sister has left me to *do* the household tasks all alone,'' says Martha; ''Tell her to help me'' (Sixteenth Sunday). And the disciples ask Jesus about praying, and even ask him to *give* them a prayer that they can recite (Seventeenth Sunday).

The recurrence of the verb ''to do'' suggests the grouping of these three passages into a coherent sequence.

We should add that the Christian must behave like Jesus, who, directly or indirectly, appears here as the model for us to imitate. It is most clear when the teaching about prayer is initiated by a question of the disciples who saw Jesus praying. But how can we avoid looking to him on reading the parable of the Good Samaritan? For Jesus is neighbor not only to someone or other but to everyone; and in what an extraordinary way! Finally, at the house of Mary and Martha, the question arises from the manner of welcoming Jesus; it is with respect to him that one can know what is necessary, indeed the only thing that is necessary.

What Must One Do to Share in Eternal Life?

Listen to the Voice of the Lord

To this fundamental question, every religion responds: "One must conform to the law—or the laws, or the commandments—that God has made known by his messenger, the one to whom he has revealed his will, who speaks in his name and with his authority."

The prophet always says, in one way or another, "Listen to the voice of the Lord, your God." So did Moses, who incessantly proclaimed: "Keep [God's] commandments and statutes that are written in this book of the Law," given by God himself at Sinai.[2] And those who follow him— the prophets in every age—say nothing else, never wearying of hearkening back to the revelation received by Moses. But like him, they always add: "Return to the Lord, your God, with all your heart and all your soul" (Deut 30:10-14).

This perpetual association of the recollection of the Law and the necessity of converting "all your heart and all your soul" is significant. This Law is not some kind of religious code, as one might speak of the "civil code" which has a value in and of itself, implying no personal allegiance to the author, much less any sort of covenant relationship with him.[3]

Only the Law of God requires true interiorization for its valid and authentic observance. A code, by contrast, demands nothing more than strict conformity to its statutes, even though it be accompanied by only minimal interior assent. It imposes sanctions against unlawful exterior acts only.

The Law of God is therefore no mere code. This is proclaimed by that text which is part of the prayer of faith—the "Shema"—that all pious Jews recite morning and evening:[4] "Hear, O Israel! The Lord is our God, the Lord alone! Therefore, you shall love the Lord, your God, with all your heart, and with all your soul and with all your strength. Take to heart these words which I enjoin on you today" (Deut 6:4-6).

Yet, a return to legalism, the temptation to reduce the Law of God— and the gospel—to a mere code, always menaces believers. They look for loopholes: "This law is quite beyond us. It is an ideal beyond our reach, up in the sky, under the sea. We are only human. We have to face reality."

Admittedly, the whole Bible teaches that the Wisdom of God remains, in itself, inaccessible. We need God himself to reveal something of it, to grant access to it gratuitously. This is the role of the Law.

And yet it is not the book of the Law, but the *Word* that Moses declares to be "very near to you." He adds that it is "in your mouths and in your hearts," which, in biblical anthropology, represent the seat of human thought and action. The Law is no dead letter, but the living Word of the living God become an interior principle written in the depths of our being, from whence come, with full knowledge and responsibility, the decisions that appear in practice.

But for all this, it is necessary that the Lord himself intervene, through grace, in order to place the Word in our hearts. This is the fruit of conversion of "all one's heart and all one's soul."

After all, only the faithful God can cause his people to be faithful. Such is the power of the word of the Lord: truth, deliverance, wisdom and joy, more desirable than anything else.

> *Turn to the LORD in your need, and you will live.*
>
> I pray to you, O LORD,
>   for the time of your favor, O God!
> In your great kindness answer me
>   with your constant help. . . .
> Answer me, O LORD, for bounteous is your kindness.
>   In your great mercy turn toward me. . . .
> I am afflicted and in pain;
>   let your saving help, O God, protect me.
> I will praise the name of God in song,
>   and I will glorify him with thanksgiving. . . .
> "See, you lowly ones, and be glad;
>   you who seek God, may your hearts be merry!
> For the LORD hears the poor,
>   and his own who are in bonds he spurns not. . . ."
> For God will save Zion
>   and rebuild the cities of Judah. . . .
>   and the descendants of his servants shall inherit it,
>   and those who love his name shall inhabit it.
> (Ps 69:14, 17, 30-31, 33-34, 36-37)

Christ at the Beginning and the End

After the salutation, thanksgiving and initial exhortation in the form of a prayer, the Letter to the Colossians contains a hymn to Christ, which is the second reading this Sunday (Col 1:15-20).

This hymn celebrates Christ's primacy in the work of creation-redemption. The form under which it appears in the Lectionary distinguishes two stanzas in this text: the primacy of Christ in creation (vv. 15-17) and in redemption (vv. 18-20), which correspond to the two themes of the text.[5] It is this double function of the Lord that we are concerned with here. For it is the creator Christ who brings about redemption, and the same redeemer Christ who is at the center of the work of creation: "He is before all else that is. In him everything continues in being"; "It is he who is the head of the body, the Church." It would be difficult to be any clearer.

To speak of "Christ" is to designate the Word of God, who, by his incarnation, has made the "invisible God" visible to our eyes. To affirm that everything has been created "through him," "in him," and "for him," is to place all creation, from the very beginning, under the sign of incarnation, since everything has been created by the Word as he was destined to become the Christ. The significance of this point of view is clear: the incarnation from all eternity in the sight of God![6]

Because everything has been created in him, through him, and for him, Christ also has primacy in the work of redemption, "to reconcile everything in his person." "Firstborn of the dead" as "firstborn of all creatures," it is "through him and for him" that God has been pleased "to reconcile everything in his person, both on earth and in the heavens." Therefore it is not in a moral or metaphorical sense that we speak of him as Lord of the universe and Head of the Church. Through him and in him, humanity and the whole cosmos find themselves henceforth radically oriented toward salvation, toward peace—the supreme gift that contains all other blessings—"through the blood of his cross" and his resurrection.

Those who proclaim this hymn can have no room for any sort of syncretism or amalgamation. Christ is the only one who can save us and, indeed, the whole universe.[7]

Who Is My Neighbor?

We all know quite well the parable of the Good Samaritan, which is the Gospel this Sunday (Luke 10:25-37). But isn't the picture we have of it often skewed, with a focus on such and such an element above the others? It is worthwhile to listen to the story once again, without prejudice, allowing oneself to be guided by the evangelist himself. We are already within the context of a "journey to Jerusalem." All the events and speeches that occur on this road are put there by the evangelist for us to read and understand as so many teachings and examples for the Easter community, marching toward the City.

The question is posed, "What must I do to inherit everlasting life?" But Jesus asks in return: "What is written in the law? How do you read it?" We know the response: "You shall love the Lord your God with all your heart, with all your soul, with all your strength, and with all your mind; and your neighbor as yourself."

In this response, uttered by a doctor of the Law, we can recognize the authentic expression of the Tradition. In fact, it combines into one sentence the commandments concerning love of God (Deut 6:5) and love of neighbor (Lev 19:18), without distinguishing a "first" and a "second" between them in hierarchical terms, that could pose a theoretical or practical problem.[8]

"You have answered correctly," says Jesus. It is an excellent response if it is taken as a rule of life and not as a basis for making subtle distinctions that would blunt the force of this "commandment" and reduce its scope of application.[9] "Do this and you shall live."

True love of God and efficacious love of neighbor form an indissoluble pair. We do not see God. He is not evident to our senses. Neighbor is clearly present, and can be acted toward efficaciously and concretely through love. Love of God is not a mere moral referent, but the source of the love one has for one's neighbor: "Be compassionate, as your Father is compassionate." One does not respect one's neighbor merely by living in proximity—especially when it is a question of those who do not love us, who do not wish us well, who show themselves to be our enemies. One must love one's neighbor because God "is good to the ungrateful and the wicked," in order that one might behave as a "son of the Most High" (Luke 6:27-38—Seventh Sunday of Ordinary Time).

"And who is my neighbor?" With this second question from the doctor of the Law, the dialogue continues. He asks it in order "to justify himself." What does this mean? Was it some sort of excuse for having asked a question to which he knew the answer? Or, rather—more likely—did he want to be just before the Law? It makes very little difference. Clearly, Luke wants to move on to Jesus' response, which will present us with something new.

He does not offer anything that looks like a definition of "neighbor," which could possibly lead to discussions, commentaries, etc. Jesus tells a story, an exemplary story, because it shows, in a concrete manner, what we must do.[10] It is a story that resembles a true anecdote; at least, it seems entirely plausible.

Behold a man—any man, an unknown—is left half-dead on the road, having been stripped and beaten by robbers.

A priest and a Levite traveling along the road[11] come to the place, in turn, and see the man lying there. They pass by on the other side.

The evangelist does not explain this indifference, which might be described as "nonassistance to a person in danger."[12] That is not important. These two personages come into the story only to point up, by contrast, the worthy example of the Samaritan, the one we must imitate. It is not worth spending much time speculating on the reasons for their behavior. On the other hand, it is not useless to ask if in some way we do not recognize ourselves in them, and if we are not sometimes tempted to think that, after all. . . . In other words, to ask if the question "Who is my neighbor?" is still relevant for us, and if we see the practical response more clearly than the priest and the Levite in the parable.[13]

"But a Samaritan . . ." One of those schismatics whom priests, Levites and other representatives of the "system" did not associate with, to say the least. He sees a man lying on the road and is "moved to pity." This verb, whose Greek etymology evokes an emotion that comes from one's inmost heart, is used in the New Testament only in the Synoptic Gospels, and always to express the compassion of Jesus or that of the Father (Luke 7:13—Jesus, for the widow of Nain, whose son was to be buried; Luke 15:20 in the parable of the father who had two sons).

Therefore, the Samaritan does not ask whether the man on the road is a countryman or stranger, a friend or a foe. It is a man who needs help, and that is enough. The traveler sees to the man's needs without a moment's hesitation.

One could even say that he automatically thinks that everyone else is prepared to act like him. He gives two pieces of silver to the innkeeper to take care of the wounded man, and promises to settle any additional expenses on his return.[14] He trusts the innkeeper as if it had not occurred to him that he might try to make a profit from the situation or neglect the wounded man.[15]

At the end of this reading, one must ask about the lesson of this parable.

"Who is my neighbor?" asks the doctor of the Law. "Anyone you encounter on your road who is in need of your help, your pity. Don't worry about whether he belongs to a list of those who have a right to your charity, whether he is of your race or a foreigner, a friend or not, worthy of interest or not. Do as the Samaritan, who asked none of these questions.''

Such is the first-level teaching of the parable, all the more striking because it was a Samaritan ''traveling'' in the land—in Judea—while the injured man must have been a Jew.

Very well. But how can such a parable be convincing for someone who has firm, entrenched ideas about those who can and should be considered a true ''neighbor?'' This story—even if personally experienced—could it convince one who believes in racial segregation that a black is just as much a neighbor as a white? Will it be enough to make others abandon their opinions and behavior with respect to Jews, Arabs, immigrants, prisoners, vagabonds, etc.? Will they not say: ''This is merely a story, though perhaps a true one. But for me to change my position, I need stronger reasons, a serious demonstration.''[16]

On the other hand, doesn't the parable say more about one's duty to respect his or her neighbor than about the definition of one? Yet this was the question posed to Jesus.

Christians, who are quite familiar with this parable, have a tendency to see it as a reminder—always timely, to be sure—of what they admit they already know: everyone is their neighbor. Thus, they constantly insist on the necessity of acting out this conviction. And they might think that the example of the Good Samaritan teaches them nothing new. This is, perhaps, why they do not pay sufficient attention to the last two verses of this Gospel passage.

The doctor of the Law asks: ''Who is my neighbor?'' Having finished the story, Jesus says to his questioner: ''Which of these three, in your opinion, was neighbor to the robbers' victim?'' The doctor of the Law does not seem to be surprised at this unexpected and curious way of reversing the question. He responds without hesitation: ''The one who treated him with mercy.''

However! The doctor of the Law, like each one of us would, spontaneously formulated the question from his own point of view: ''Whom must I, myself, consider as my neighbor?'' The answer ''everyone'' or ''whoever has need of you,'' as all-encompassing as it may be, can, because of this very same generality, give rise to casuistic argumentation, as we know only too well: ''Of course, everyone is my neighbor, and I must help whomever I find on my way. But, in this particular instance, does the duty of intervening fall upon me, personally? and must I do everything? have I no other obligations?''[17]

Jesus, after the story, invites us to pose the question another way, and it is here that we find the originality of his teaching. "To discover who is your neighbor, don't appeal to a codified list or an address book. Don't leave it as a mere generality when you say that you recognize or are ready to acknowledge everyone as your neighbor. When you encounter someone—a stranger—who has need of you, put yourself in that person's place. From your manner or behavior and action, it is they who will recognize whether you are their neighbor, whether you see them as a neighbor."

One might add that this corresponds to our own experience. We recognize our friends by their behavior toward us when we are in difficulties. And we say, "I thought they would think of me as a friend, but no! While someone on whom I had not counted, an unknown person who happened by, truly treated me as a friend, a neighbor."

What must one do to gain eternal life and accomplish what is written in the Law? To act in such a way that all people see us as their neighbor! Remember the Samaritan. "Go, and do likewise."[18]

But one could add: "Remember Jesus Christ!" Surely, the parable is not speaking of him, and there is no reason to give it an allegorical interpretation. And yet, Jesus has come into the world like an incomparable Good Samaritan. He has assisted not only one person, met by chance on the road, but all of humanity; he is the Good Shepherd who goes out to seek the lost sheep, bringing it back to the fold on his shoulders, dressing its wounds.

> The traveling Samaritan who was Christ—for he was a true traveler—saw the one lying there. He did not pass by, for the very reason he made his journey was to "visit us," us for whom he descended to earth and dwelt therein.[19]

He it is who is seen as neighbor by everyone in distress.

We know this. On Judgment Day, Christ himself will solemnly recognize as a friend whoever acted as a neighbor to those who were hungry and thirsty, who were strangers, naked, sick, or in prison (Matt 25:31-46—solemnity of Christ the King, Year A).

"What must I do to inherit everlasting life?" This question is at the heart of the liturgy of the Fifteenth Sunday of Ordinary Time; each of the readings furnishes the elements of a gradually refined response.

"The commandments and statutes" of God are "written in this book of the Law" so that we may put them into practice, knowing that nothing is prescribed that would be "too mysterious and remote."

The Law of God does not merely impose an outward submission to its obligations and interdictions. It is a principle of life that involves an inward response, to the very depths of one's being, "in our mouth and heart," as the Bible says. It is the voice of the Lord that comes to us, that we listen to, "contemplating" without end. It puts us on the right path when we would go astray: "Return to the Lord, your God, with all your heart and all your soul." This living Word that touches us and animates our daily activity allows us to march joyfully and confidently toward salvation in the ways of the Lord.[20]

The "commandment" of love of God and neighbor is, more than all the rest, the life principle that we must always have in our heart in order to put it into practice. It is also the kind of "commandment" that, unlike many others, cannot be viewed in a legalistic spirit.

There is, in fact, no theoretical definition of neighbor, no list of those who merit being called "neighbor," whether certainly a neighbor, or neighbor perhaps in certain cases, or up to a certain point, etc. My neighbor is the one to whom I draw near—though a stranger, an unknown—because I bring aid and comfort, because of the "mercy" that has "moved me to pity." Such is the teaching of the parable of the Good Samaritan.

But insofar as we listen to and meditate on the story, the features of the Lord appear more and more clearly to our eyes.

He is the Good Samaritan par excellence, beyond all comparison.

No one has been or will ever be so completely the neighbor of each and every person. He did not encounter them by chance on the road. He voluntarily came to seek them, he, the Word of God who has taken flesh. He not only did everything for them, but he handed himself over for them; he died and rose that they might have everlasting life.

In this way, he completely fulfilled the will of God and all that one reads "beginning with Moses and all the prophets" in "every passage of Scripture" (Luke 24:27).

It is toward him that, the Book of the Gospels closed, the liturgy turns our attention.[21]

He is "the image of the invisible God" by whom and in whom everything has been created and redeemed, "firstborn of all creatures," and "firstborn of the dead" in whom "absolute fullness resides"; through whom and in whom God wished "to reconcile everything," "both on earth and in the heavens."

How, then, can we not heed him when he says to us: "Go, and do likewise"?

Sixteenth Sunday

Welcoming the Lord

Immediately after Jesus, our Good Samaritan, tells this parable "on the road to Jerusalem," we see him stopping at a house. Two sisters welcome the Master. The contrast between their respective attitudes gives him the occasion to speak of what is involved first and foremost for the disciple who will welcome him when he comes. Thus, it is still a question of a disciple's proper "activity."

The Guest Sent by God

For the first reading this Sixteenth Sunday, the Lectionary contains a very beautiful story about Abraham (Gen 18:1-10a). In itself, the narrative is quite simple. Three men suddenly appear before the patriarch who was resting "in the entrance of his tent," pitched by "the terebinth of Mamre," "while the day was growing hot." Rousing himself immediately, Abraham offers them his hospitality. He readily offers them refreshment and a seat in the shade of a tree. After directing Sarah his wife to bake some fresh bread, he runs to look for a "tender, choice steer," ordering his servant to "quickly prepare it," and then, "waiting on them," serves the unknown travelers supper, which he asks them to be good enough to accept. A fine example of proverbial Eastern hospitality.[22]

But, unlike most stories of the genre, this account does not end with the travelers' departing after thanking Abraham for his generous hospitality. Instead of words of gratitude, they unexpectedly announce to Abraham that he will finally have the son he has awaited for so long, on whose birth rests the promise: "I will make of you a great nation" (Gen 12:2).

This ending may surprise modern readers, or at least lead them to regard the story as merely a beautiful fairy tale or pious legend. To say that the virtue of hospitality, so common in the Eastern world, was associated with religious virtue and that ancient cultures willingly saw the guest as a messenger of the divine, indeed God himself, situates this episode in a cultural milieu quite different from our own. Gods who visit men in this way belong to mythology! Might not this attitude be due to our own too earth-bound mentality?

Not so long ago, in our Christian countries, the traveler, the wanderer, the pilgrim who would arrive unexpectedly would be welcomed as "a messenger of God." Weren't the formulas used when they knocked, when one opened the door to them, when they left, rather ritualistic, a kind of benediction?

St. Benedict is the preeminent witness to this tradition, writing in his Rule for the monks:[23]

> Guests who arrive at the monastery are to be welcomed as Christ, for he will say to us one day: "I was a stranger and you welcomed me" (Matt 25:35). This mark of respect will be given to all, beginning with our brothers in faith and pilgrims.
>
> When a guest is announced, the superior and the brothers will go to welcome him in charity. They will first pray with him, and then exchange the kiss of peace. . . .
>
> From the moment of arrival to that of departure they will address the guest in all humility, bowing their heads or even prostrating themselves to honor Christ whom they receive in his person. Then they will lead him to prayer. The superior, or the brother who is appointed, will sit near him and read him a Scripture passage for his instruction. Then he will show him every possible form of kindness.
>
> The superior will break the fast in order to eat with him. . . . He will pour water over the hands of his guests, and assisted by the brothers, will wash all their feet. They will then recite this verse: "O God, we ponder your kindness within your temple" (Ps 48:10).
>
> A particular welcome will be reserved for the poor and pilgrims, for it is especially in them that one receives Christ. For the rich, it is pointless to insist on this: the fear they inspire will command sufficient respect.

The outward forms of welcoming have changed—even in the monasteries—but what is said here concerning the spirit in which one receives guests is very appropriate. Who, at one time or another, has not received an important or even critical message from a person met by chance? The message can come from someone who does not perceive its significance for us, but is it not God himself who appears and speaks to us on that occasion?

In the New Testament, the author of the Letter to the Hebrews, even if he is merely talking about receiving angels, suggests the theme of the mystery of hospitality: "Do not neglect hospitality, for through it some have unknowingly entertained angels" (Heb 13:2).

> This is an allusion to Abraham. The stranger, the guest, may always be an angel and is certainly always mysterious. One never knows who it is. Or rather, for us Christians, we know who it is, because Jesus Christ has told us. The guest is Jesus Christ. Jesus Christ expressly identified himself with the guest.[24]

Not that everyone must be the bearer of a major revelation. But our own personal experiences can help us to take seriously a story we have tended to relegate too quickly to the ranks of legend. In light of what has happened to us, we cannot consider the episode at Mamre a commonplace occurrence.

Yet, this story from the Book of Genesis does not intend to primarily extol the virtue of hospitality; whatever its interest morally, its central significance lies elsewhere. It is part of the long and dramatic course of the promise made by God to Abraham. It is concerned with the history and coming of salvation, a salvation whose mysterious announcement is the prelude to its marvelous fulfillment. So it is not surprising that this remarkable, luminous passage from Genesis has been endlessly meditated and commented on by the Christian tradition that has used the story as a point of departure to enlarge its contemplation, despite some of its difficulties.

Abraham sees and receives three people (v. 2); but he addresses only one (v. 3) and it is only one who, at the end, states the promise (v. 10). Where the pedantic reader might see incoherence and ask countless unanswerable questions, the believer keeps in mind the affirmation that appeared first: "The Lord appeared to Abraham by the terebinth of Mamre." Three people, only one Lord; the Christian tradition has not been shy of reading this text in light of its faith in the Trinity. One of the most beautiful representations of this unfathomable mystery, clearly inspired by the scene at Mamre, is the famous icon painted c. 1430 by Andrei Roublev.[25]

"God among men, God on our paths."[26] God who himself invites and welcomes us to the Eucharistic table, the sacrament of the feast in the kingdom:

> *He who does justice will live in the presence of the LORD.*
>
> He who walks blamelessly and does justice;
>   who thinks the truth in his heart
>   and slanders not with his tongue.
> Who harms not his fellow man,
>   nor takes up a reproach against his neighbor;
> By whom the reprobate is despised,
>   while he honors those who fear the LORD. . . .
>   who lends not his money at usury
>   and accepts no bribe against the innocent.
> He who does these things
>   shall never be disturbed.
> (Ps 15:2-4, 5)

Christ Is Here, in Our Midst

"Reading a letter of Paul's is often like hearing half of a telephone conversation; one hears the responses without quite knowing the questions that have prompted them." This remark by an exegete[27] is particularly appropriate for the Letter to the Colossians, a letter written in captivity.

This circumstance leads the author to speak of his apostolic ministry. He addresses correspondents whom he does not know personally, having neither founded nor visited their community. If he speaks of himself, it is not in order to give them his news.[28] The text read today is, from an apostle in prison, a meditation on the way in which, as a minister of God, he himself contributes to the unfolding of the divine plan for the reconciliation of the world (Col 1:24-28).

This activity is not without much suffering, in which he "finds joy." Make no mistake: there is no overtone here of spiritual masochism or stoicism. These tribulations are not accidents that could have been avoided, but the unavoidable rule of all participation in the work of redemption wrought by Christ, who continues to suffer in the apostle and the Church as he previously suffered in his physical body. Certainly, the passion of Christ needs no complement. But the Church that is united to him and constitutes his "body" experiences, like him, the mystery of death and resurrection.

Indeed, the proclamation of the gospel brings the mystery of Christ to its fulfillment, i.e., its revelation to all generations.

"Christ among us, our hope of glory." What a magnificent résumé of the gospel! We can see the preacher's ardor in proclaiming it, not letting himself be disheartened by suffering. But how is it possible that not all Christians share in this enthusiasm, and thus live the Christian life as vibrantly? Perhaps because they forget that the gospel is not a philosophy, not a collection of doctrines, not an ethics, but a person—Christ.

Thus preaching—the apostolic ministry—and witness—the responsibility of each Christian—are not supposed to convince the intellect, but to lead everyone to a personal encounter with the Lord, and to draw believers toward the full, Christian maturity of faith.

The Only Thing Required

Today's Gospel is one of the most well known, even if it is sometimes read in a superficial manner. We look to Martha and Mary's contrasting attitudes to make a case for that which we call "activity," on the one hand, and "contemplation" on the other. The pronouncement that "there is need of only one thing [and] Mary has chosen the better part and it will not be taken from her" is frequently cited, more or less appropriately, seriously or in jest. It is worth reading this Gospel again, as if it were for the first time (Luke 10:38-42).

"As they continued their journey [Jesus] entered a village where a woman whose name was Martha welcomed him. She had a sister named Mary . . . " Especially read aloud, this introduction sounds like the beginning of a ballad that will tell a story that is supposed to be an example for everyone.

By introducing two women with well-defined characters, with no details given as to time and place, the story preserves a certain freshness.[29] Martha and Mary? Not distant personages, but so near to us that we all can recognize ourselves in them.[30]

Here, then, are two sisters who welcome Jesus the "Lord," but each in her own characteristic way. Martha busies herself to receive Jesus properly. Mary, who "sat beside the Lord at his feet," stays there to hear his words, indifferent to the busy activity of her sister, who finally becomes exasperated. Her reaction is eminently understandable; who would not agree with it? Mary is taking it easy. What indolence, letting her sister do all the work! Martha, instead of confronting Mary directly, asks Jesus to intervene.

But see how the story transpires, as parables so often do. At first, we spontaneously side with Martha, agreeing with her point of view and reaction, just as we spontaneously agree with the viewpoint and reaction of the elder son (Luke 15:11-32) or those who worked all day in the vineyard (Matt 20:1-16). We say: "They are right. This is an injustice."

"No!" responds the Master. "Martha, Martha, you are anxious and worried about many things. There is need of only one thing. Mary has chosen the better part and it will not be taken from her."

What does this mean? This question has had many answers. The one that has been most influential goes back to Origen (185-254).

> One may confidently affirm that Martha symbolizes action, Mary contemplation. The mystery of charity is removed from the active life if the goal of teaching and moral exhortation is not contemplation, for action and contemplation do not exist the one without the other. One should further say that Martha has received the Logos (the Word) in a more corporeal fashion into her house, into her soul, while Mary has listened to it in a spiritual way by sitting "at his feet."[31]

According to this oft-repeated interpretation, the two sisters represent two complementary attitudes and/or stratified religious classifications: action and contemplation. Complementary, because every disciple must be at once "active" and "contemplative"; stratified, because "action" must lead to "contemplation."[32]

In the preaching we hear today, this reading is often presented in a more or less simplistic and unconvincing manner. One even sees this plea used to argue for the primacy of the "contemplative life" as opposed to the value and necessity of the kind of zeal that Martha displays. "And then, perhaps it would be better if she, too, sat for a moment at Jesus' feet to hear his word."[33]

At the beginning of the journey to Jerusalem, Luke has collected certain teachings of Jesus on the mission of the disciples (Luke 9:51-10:20—Thirteenth and Fourteenth Sundays). After the parable of the Good Samaritan (Luke 10:25-37—Fifteenth Sunday), the lesson of Martha and Mary must be of capital importance. And this is found, quite clearly, in the conclusion of the story.

Jesus—do we really need to say this?—does not condemn the zeal and generosity of Martha. He gratefully accepts her eager hospitality as he accepts that of the Pharisees (Luke 7:36; 11:37; 14:1) and solicits that of Zacchaeus (Luke 19:5). He has spoken of the hospitality given to missionaries, which they must accept in complete simplicity (Luke 10:5-9—Fourteenth Sunday). And again in Acts and the Letters of Paul, mention is made of acknowledging the welcome that has been reserved for them, the attentions of which they have been the object.

Jesus reproaches Martha for being "anxious" and "upset" "about many things." This is not the only time Jesus warns his followers against being overwhelmed with cares. One must understand what is said here in light of what was said on those other occasions.

> When they take you before synagogues and before rulers and authorities, do not worry about how or what your defense will be or about what you are to say. For the holy Spirit will teach you at that moment what you should say (Luke 12:11-12).

> . . . *do not worry* about your life and what you will eat, or about your body and what you will wear. For life is more than food and the body more than clothing. (Luke 12:22-23).

> As for the seed that fell among thorns, they are the ones who have heard, but as they go along, they are choked by the anxieties and riches and pleasures *of life*, and they fail to produce mature fruit (Luke 8:14).

> Beware that your hearts do not become drowsy from carousing and drunkenness and the *anxieties of daily life*, and that day catch you by surprise like a trap (Luke 21:34-35).

In each instance, cares are denounced because they detract from what is essential: the confession of the Son of Man before judges, the primary search for the kingdom, receiving the Word, waiting for the coming of the Son of Man (Luke 12:7-9; 12:31; 8:11-15; 21:34-36).

So it is here. The "details of hospitality" with which Martha busies herself distract her from listening to the Word that Mary understands to be essential, the "only thing required." This choice will not be denied.

There is more at issue here than a conflict of duties: it is a rule of life that makes listening to the Word in faith its first priority. That this involves certain choices is obvious.[34] But it goes beyond a division of the time allotted—or found—for "contemplation" (and prayer) and "action" (and "material" duties). There are ways of laying claim to "the better part" that betray, consciously or not, a scorn for tasks that are willingly left to others.[35] On the other hand, to be busy with all the details of hospitality can betray, if not a scorn for prayer and hearing the Word, at least a stubborn reluctance to devote oneself to the effort that contemplation requires.[36]

Clearly, this is not just an anecdote that Luke recounts, telling how one day two sisters welcomed Jesus.

The entire Bible—Old and New Testaments—extols in countless ways the virtue of hospitality. In the guest that we welcome, it is always, in some way, God who visits us and who, through the guest, may bring us a message.

The Gospels attest that at various times Jesus explicitly and solemnly declared that it is he himself that one receives in the weak, the poor, the afflicted, and also in his messengers. We will be judged according to what we have done or have failed to do with respect to those who need our welcome and assistance. We can exclude no one, since the neighbor is the one to whom we make ourselves present.

This ready and active reception of a neighbor cannot, however, dispense with the need to receive the Word and open ourselves to the mystery of the coming of the Lord. It would become a deception if it distracted from what is essential, from the "only thing required": the reception of God's gift to us of himself, of his Word, which allows us to recognize him in our neighbor.

> Happy the one who in all his works and all his travels seeks the heavenly rest. He constantly hurries, following the apostle's counsel, to enter into this rest (Heb 4:11). Because of the desire that he conceives for it, he mortifies his body, already preparing and disposing his spirit for this rest, dwelling

in peace with all men, insofar as it depends on him. He spontaneously prefers the rest and leisure of Mary, accepting out of necessity the work and duties of Martha; but he accomplishes them, as far as he can, in peace and restful spirit, and always returns to the one thing required after these multiple distractions. Such a man, even when he works, is at rest, while the impious man, even when he is at rest, works.[37]

For "Christ is in us, the hope of glory." This is "the mystery hidden from ages and generations past but now revealed to [God's] holy ones." It is Christ that the apostle and the Church announce by admonishing and instructing all people with wisdom, "hoping to make everyone complete in Christ."

He is at once the Word and the Work of God, the Lord whom we must receive by listening to his voice and putting his commandments into practice.

> I stand at the door and knock, says the Lord. If anyone hears my voice and opens the door, I will come in and sit down to supper with him, and he with me (Communion Antiphon).

Seventeenth Sunday

Prayer, the Will of God, and the Gift of the Spirit

With the parable of the Good Samaritan, Jesus teaches us that in order to fulfill the Law and have a share in eternal life, we must *make* ourselves neighbors to whomever we meet that is in need (Fifteenth Sunday).

The example of Mary, who one day with her sister Martha received the Lord into her home, reminds us that nothing, no care, no deed of service, should detract from listening to the Word. Such listening is our foremost duty, for it is what *makes* the disciple (Sixteenth Sunday).

The sequence ends, this Seventeenth Sunday, with a teaching on prayer, yet another activity of the disciple that, because of its limitless efficacy, the fruit of the gift of the Spirit, belongs to the order of *action*.

The Efficacy of the Prayer of the Just
Taken from the Book of Genesis, the first reading relates a well-known episode concerning Abraham: his intercession with God to spare Sodom (18:20-32).

The mysterious travelers to whom Abraham readily offered his hospitality told him that his hope for a line of descendants would be fulfilled (Gen 18:10—Sixteenth Sunday). Continuing on their way, they head for Sodom. The patriarch remains before the Lord, who reveals to him the purpose of his visit to this infamous city: "The inhabitants of Sodom were very wicked in the sins they committed against the Lord" (Gen 13:13). However, the Lord does not merely reveal his hidden plans to his beloved. By speaking as if he had not yet made his decision, he is really giving "a thoughtful, paternal provocation to audacious prayer."[38] Consequently, Abraham advances with humble assurance (vv. 23, 27) and begins to argue with the Lord, appealing to his justice and forgiveness. Through this "bargaining of mercy,"[39] Abraham inaugurates the ministry of intercession, which will be taken up by the prophets[40] and by Christ, who "is always able to save those who approach God through him, since he lives forever to make intercession for them" (Heb 7:25—Thirty-first Sunday of Ordinary Time, Year B).

To be more precise, this is not really a "bargaining," nor is the concern even with the fate of the just, who are in danger of being confused with the sinners if all are indiscriminately to be submitted to the same punishment. "Far be it from you to do such a thing" (Gen 18:25), which is clearly unworthy of God.

The question is what weight the just can have in the balance of judgment. Can their justice compensate for the sin of a whole society or move God to pardon? Abraham thinks yes, and it is this conviction that incites him to "bargain." Will it not suffice to avert God's punishment if there are fifty, forty-five, forty, thirty, twenty, or even only ten just people in the city? He dares not go lower. Later, Jeremiah will show God ready to pardon Jerusalem if he finds only *one* in it "who lives uprightly and seeks to be faithful" (Jer 5:1).

In the vibrant Judaism of the Diaspora, there was always a strong belief in the power of the intercession of the just, however humble they may be.

> "Do you know who revoked the heavenly decree that would have let loose a catastrophe on our people?" asked the Baal-Shem of Rabbi Nahman of Horodenko. "I will tell you. Our litanies, our fasts had no effect. It was a woman, a common woman, who saved us. See how it happened. She went to the synagogue and began weeping and praying: 'Master of the universe, are you not our father? Why do you not hear your children when they cry to you? Look at me; I am a mother, I have five children. And when they shed one tear, my heart is broken. But you, Father, have so many more. All men are your children. And they all cry and cry. Even if your heart is of stone, how can you be insensible to it?' And God," concluded the Besht, "decided in her favor."[41]

The "Songs of the Suffering Servant," in the second part of the Book of Isaiah, go even further. They proclaim the coming of a Just Man—and the words must be capitalized—who will take on himself the sins of the many, and will save them by his passion (Isa 53).

Such development of revelation and its fulfillment in Jesus Christ, the Just Savior of the world, cannot be ignored by the Christian even in hearing a much older passage from the Old Testament.

Abraham's intercession for Sodom and Gomorrah claims our attention. He was certainly not pleading for these cities insofar as they were pagan. Rather, he saw in them the type of a human community so perverted by sin that it could not escape God's supreme punishment. The remembrance of this—which is very strong throughout the Bible—must be that of an example that should always provoke our reflection.

Abraham's intercession reveals a certain universalism, such as can be seen, albeit in a different context, in his prayer for Abimelech, a pagan king.[42] But above all, one must realize that the story of the intercession for Sodom occurs under the sign of the blessing of all nations on the earth. "The Lord reflected: 'Shall I hide from Abraham what I am about to do [to Sodom], now that he is to become a great and populous nation, and all the nations of the earth are to find blessing in him?' " (Gen 18:17-18). God chose him to be the instrument of the realization of his plan and his promise of universal salvation (Gen 12:3). It is quite right to say of Abraham's intercession, "He prays with all the strength of the universal Benediction that will be received."[43]

The Christian assembly gathered around Christ the Savior and King of the universe, sings its thanksgiving for the benediction in which it shares. In the Spirit that it has been given, it proclaims its assurance of being heard by the Father when it prays that the work of salvation may be extended to the ends of the earth.

LORD, on the day I called for help, you answered me.

I will give thanks to you, O LORD, with all my heart,
  [for you have heard the words of my mouth;]
  in the presence of the angels I will sing your praise;
I will worship at your holy temple
  and give thanks to your name.
Because of your kindness and your truth;
  for you have made great above all things your name and your promise.
When I called you answered me;
  you built up strength within me. . . .

The LORD is exalted, yet the lowly he sees,
  and the proud he knows from afar.

Though I walk amid distress, you preserve me;
  against the anger of my enemies you raise your hand;
  your right hand saves me.
The LORD will complete what he has done for me;
  your kindness, O LORD, endures forever;
  forsake not the work of your hands.
(Ps 138:1-3, 6-8)

The Debt for Sin Wiped Out by God

The second reading comes again from the Letter to the Colossians (Col 2:12-14).

This passage is a new celebration of Christ's victory, a victory in which all Christians share.[44] They find themselves, here, at the center of four affirmations that bear on "sin and death," "dead and resurrected with Christ," "faith and baptism," "bond of debt and cross."

The whole biblical tradition has associated, since the very beginning, the sin and death to which we are subject as a punishment for Adam's fault (Gen 2:15; 3:19; Rom 5:12). Besides the scandal—felt by all—of this obstacle to life, death is perceived by the believer as an intolerable curse, if it brings to an end the possibility of rejoicing in God and praising him (Pss 6:6; 115:17; etc.). But no! It is not possible that the living God would permit this (Pss 16:10; 49:16; 68:21; 86:13; etc.).

Consequently, awesome though it is, it is not bodily death that we bemoan.

It is the other, which flows from sin, from which one is ransomed by the forgiveness of sin, that gives life.

This is what happens when one partakes in the mystery of the death and resurrection of Christ. Plunged into the water of baptism, one is entombed with him in order to rise with him. This new life is a gift of God— we are saved by grace (Eph 2:8)—but comes "by means of faith," by which one is turned toward the Father who has raised Jesus from the dead.

At the same time "the bond that stood against us with all its claims" is found "canceled," since God "has snatched it up and nailed it to the cross."

What should we understand by this "bond"? Recalling other passages from Paul, one will think of Mosaic law:

> Christ ransomed us from the curse of the law by becoming a curse for us . . . (Gal 3:13).

> The sting of death is sin, and the power of sin is the law (1 Cor 15:56—Eighth Sunday).

> What then can we say? That the law is sin? Of course not! Yet I did not know sin except through the Law . . . (Rom 7:7).

But it could also be the "register," where God has the account of humanity and that evokes Psalm 139:16:

> Your eyes have seen my actions; in your book they are all written; my days were limited before one of them existed.

as well as a Jewish prayer:

> Through your great mercy
> erase the writing that accuses us!

The image evokes a severe debt, not only because it cannot be honored but because the debtor is insolvent. If God does not remit it, condemnation is inevitable.

This debt is not only incommensurate with every debt that we have among ourselves, from which we might hope to be freed on payment; it is a completely different thing.[45]

Now God does not content himself simply with remitting or canceling our debt, nailing it to the cross of Christ, in whom we become just before God. He makes us his sons and daughters, his heirs, "heirs with Christ" (Rom 8:17).

The Example for Praying

This filial relationship is particularly expressed in prayer, whose efficacy is based on it, as Jesus has taught (Luke 11:1-13).

Luke, as we know, says more than any other evangelist about the prayer of Jesus. He sometimes gives us the very words. But he also mentions that Jesus was accustomed to spend the night in solitude, in prayer.[46] How could the disciples not have been impressed by their master's private moments with the Father? Certainly, they must have discussed the matter among themselves. Why would it be surprising, then, that they would have said to Jesus: "Lord, teach us to pray"?

The reference to what John the Baptist did is unexpected. Wasn't he already long gone from the scene? (Luke 3:20; 9:9). But we know that "John's disciples fast frequently and offer prayers"; and "the disciples of the Pharisees do the same" (Luke 5:33), in conformity with the customary practice to which the Bible and, especially for us, the Psalms, gives testimony.[47] In fact, in every religion there is a definite relationship between faith and prayer, between prayer and spirituality.[48]

But there is more here. Jesus is not merely one spiritual master among many, even if acknowledged the greatest. He is "the Lord," united to God by a unique relation, into the dynamic of which he brings his disciples. To learn to pray, one must listen to and contemplate his prayer, receiving from him the very words, learning the language from him.

> The more a man learns to pray as he ought, the more deeply he discovers that his stammering toward God is only a response to the word that God has addressed to him, so that we may truthfully say: the only audible thing between God and man is the language of God. God speaks first, and it is only because he "exteriorizes" himself that man can "interiorize" himself toward God.
>
> Let us simply reflect: is not the Our Father, by which we address him every day, his own word? Was it not the Son of God, who is God and the Word of God, who gave it to us? Man would never have been able to invent such a thing himself! Did not the Hail Mary come from the mouth of an angel, and is therefore also in the heavenly tongue, while Elizabeth's

addition, as she was filled with the Holy Spirit, is it not the response to the first encounter with God made man? How would we know what to say to God, if he had not first communicated himself to us in his Word, in such a way that we might have access to and dealings with him? . . .

We can be certain of it: prayer is a conversation in which the Word of God takes the initiative and we can at first be only listeners. And this is the most important thing: that we perceive the Word of God, and that from his Word we might find a way to respond to him.[49]

This is why the disciples, in their filial status through the Son, can address God as "Abba," i.e., "Father," a name that is both familiar and quite respectful.

And what should they say to this Father if not first of all that he might fulfill his plan for which he sent his Son, to which the disciples find themselves associated? "Hallowed be your name, your kingdom come." Did Jesus ever say anything other than this to his Father when he came to him in prayer? Was he ever sustained throughout his life and ministry, even in agony and on the cross, by anything other than the will to obey the Father, to glorify his name, to bring about his kingdom?

This is also what Christians must seek throughout their whole life and ask for first in prayer (or vice versa, since they go together).

This faithfulness of Christian prayer to the prayer of Jesus himself is expressed—though we don't always realize it—in the formula for the conclusion of liturgical prayers: "Through Jesus Christ, your Son, our Lord." This is more than merely an appeal to the one who "lives forever to make intercession" for us (Heb 7:25). It is an invocation (epiclesis) of the name of Jesus that makes our prayer his prayer.[50]

The request "give us each day our daily bread" is a prayer of the poor, which fits Luke's Gospel very well. A prayer not of idle vagabonds, but of the poor, who while performing the task allotted to them by the Father, know that their whole life depends on his generosity.

It is also a prayer of the community in a Church where the ideal is to hold everything in common (Acts 2:45; 4:32) in such a way that none need be poor (Acts 4:34). A prayer that implicitly refers to the sharing that God has allowed us in the bread of the Word and the Eucharist.

The obstacle both to our hope for the kingdom and our sharing of the bread is sin. May God forgive it in us, since his Son gave his life for the remission of sins, since we have received the proclamation of "repent . . . for the forgiveness of your sins" (Acts 2:38).

"For we too . . . " How could we dare to ask the Father for that which we will not grant to each other, since all are his sons? Jesus has told us:

"Be merciful, just as [also] your Father is merciful. Stop judging and you will not be judged. Stop condemning and you will not be condemned. Forgive and you will be forgiven. Give and gifts will be given to you; a good measure, packed together, shaken down, and overflowing, will be poured into your lap. For the measure with which you measure will in turn be measured out to you" (Luke 6:36-38—Seventh Sunday).

We are speaking of unbounded forgiveness, with no exclusions, since, in line with the parable of the Good Samaritan, we must be a neighbor to whomever would do us wrong. Once again we see Luke's radicalism.

In the last petition, we beg the Father that he will not submit us to temptation, if despite his grace we are not able to come through with our faithfulness unscathed. This temptation is that kind of trial which could lead us to betrayal, as it is spoken of in the parable of the sower (Luke 8:13).

Such is Luke's version of the "Our Father," noticeably shorter than the one we find in Matthew (Matt 6:13-19). The latter is more familiar to us because of its traditional use in the liturgy; we all know it by heart, in Latin or in the official modern vernacular translation.

This diversity between the traditions should not be surprising. Jesus did not teach his disciples a formula to pray word for word, as if it were a catechism, even if the words were very quickly engraved in Christian memory.

In order that the "Our Father" may be said in community, it is important to focus on only one formulation. It is fortunate that now—since January 1966—all English language Christians use the same translation, prepared by an interconfessional commission.

But nothing should hinder us from using different versions for personal prayer (such a practice could prove very profitable).[51]

In any case, prayer should not be reduced to "saying one's prayers," endlessly repeating certain formulas, however beautiful and profound they may be. The richness of the petitions of the "Our Father" opens an infinite field for prayer. Like the faith and hope from which it springs, the object of prayer is always, in one way or another, the sanctification of the Name, the coming of the kingdom, the gift of daily bread, the forgiveness of sins, and the avoidance of temptation that may overcome us. But what is its use in the concrete and unexpected situations of life?

Jesus anticipates this question with the help of two particularly transparent parables whose meaning rests on an *a fortiori* audacity. The friend who is awakened in the middle of the night, and who at first ignores the appeal for help, ends by getting up and giving what was asked for, albeit with ill grace. No father gives his son a serpent if he asks for a fish, or a scorpion if he asks for an egg. Then how could God not come to the aid of those who invoke him confidently and with perseverance? Not by freeing himself from importunate beggars who "weary" him (Luke 18:1-5—parable of the corrupt judge and the persistent widow) but because he is the Father of boundless generosity, and close to us.

But the ending is a surprise. One is waiting for Jesus to conclude: "How much more will your heavenly Father give good things to those who ask him!" This in fact is how the parable ends in Matthew (Matt 7:7-11). Luke, on the other hand, writes that God will not be remiss in giving the *Holy Spirit* to those who pray without ceasing. Let us not be mistaken, deceived by the appearance of this gift of the "spiritual" order (?), seemingly disconnected from the realities of life, into imagining that the benefit assured in prayer is, so to speak, disincarnate. Nor is it enough to say that the gift of the Spirit is the supreme grace that surpasses or contains all possible and desirable "good things."

One must rather look to the Book of Acts, the second half of Luke's work. The Spirit is the active principle of all personal and community life. It inspires decisions and the courage to take them on to the very end, even when faced with new, unexpected situations. It grants that an extraordinary human, fraternal, and ecclesial activity may be exercised in all areas. From it come many fruits. Luke saw it in the Church of his time. Acts witnesses to it. The gift of the Spirit is always the source of boundless energy and activity.

To pray is thus to act, to search, and not be inactive. It opens doors, helping to bring about whatever one hopes to see happen. It is not the efficacy of prayer that can be taken to task by the disciples, but, sometimes—often?—their passivity that, if they were to be honest about it, would reveal their unconscious fear of seeing themselves actually heard, of being taken seriously.

"Buried with Christ in baptism" and "raised to life with him," "those who have believed in the power of God" are not only freed from the debt of sin that weighs on them. Having become children of God, they are established in an intimate relationship with him, who allows them to know his plans and to be his partners in their accomplishment. Prayer is at the heart of this dialogue.

The example of Abraham and the teaching of Jesus show that in dialogue with God, any one of us can turn toward the Lord as toward a friend of whom we can ask anything, toward a father whose inexhaustible and complete generosity is well known. With the guise of simplicity and familiarity, prayer will not hesitate to be insistent and constant, to take charge in all situations, even the most difficult.

Deeply rooted in reality, our own and that of the world, prayer is the place where we discern good and evil, where we become aware of what God asks of us and what we await from God. It is a prophetic act that knows the real value of human realities as well as their ultimate scope, a true gift of the Spirit: only he on whom the Spirit rests in full can grant it, the Just Man who constantly appears before God to intercede on our behalf.

The prayer of the Christian is like that of Jesus. Far from being a flight from this world and its trials, it sets one on the road following Christ, for the glory of the Father and the coming of the kingdom. By it we obtain from his paternal generosity all that "we need each day," but it also forces us to discover what we should be looking for, opening the closed doors. For through prayer, we gain the supreme gift of the Spirit that produces abundant fruit.

The sequence of the Fifteenth, Sixteenth, and Seventeenth Sundays could be called: "What must one do?"

"You shall love the Lord your God with all your heart, with all your soul, with all your strength, and with all your mind; and your neighbor as yourself," knowing that the neighbor is the one to whom one makes oneself near (Fifteenth Sunday).

Giving absolute priority to listening to the Word is not a waste of time or idleness but a requirement, if one wishes to devote oneself to one's tasks without losing "the only thing required" (Sixteenth Sunday).

Finally, one must pray and one must strive to know God and God's will better and be open to the inspirations of the Spirit, which always urges us on (Seventeenth Sunday).

These are not just three ways of acting that one chooses from according to circumstances or one's own vocation, perhaps finding a place for each in one's life, but three ways of acting as a disciple who follows Christ on the road to Jerusalem.

> I pray like a thief begging at the door of a farmhouse that he intends to set afire. I pray like a wounded man asking for a drink from his absent mother.
>
> The Words learned from God are so holy that it is a terrible thing to use them in vain. But what of it? We have been warned for five thousand years that the name of God must not be taken in vain and that those who do so will not be regarded as innocent.[52]

From the Eighteenth to the Twenty-first Sunday in Ordinary Time

Into the framework of the "journey to Jerusalem" (9:51–19:27), Luke has incorporated certain teachings of Jesus that function as steps in Christian catechesis. It would be pointless to try to divide this melange into strict chapters that would, in an orderly fashion, deal with well-defined subjects; not according to such criteria did Luke "write [the received teachings] down in an orderly sequence" (Luke 1:3). The modern mind tends to be put off by this. But one must recognize that the evangelist's style has a certain advantage, in that his "sequence" becomes as a result more lifelike and natural. Given on the occasion of random encounters and situations, these teachings bear a striking resemblance to our own meandering "journeys." Our companions say different, even unconnected, things to us from day to day. There is nothing systematic or artificial in their words. On the contrary, things that are said by chance, often seemingly disconnected, can have a profound impact on us, indelibly written in our memories and hearts.

These remarks and teachings may appear to be disjointed and illogical, but they are not. Thus the four gospel passages read from the Eighteenth to the Twenty-first Sunday of Year C can be grouped under the heading: "In all things, consider the End (capital E)."

In the Lectionary's four excerpts from chapters 12 and 13 of Luke's Gospel, Jesus' teachings are seen from the perspective of the End of all things—eternity, the Master's return, judgment, entry into the kingdom.

The happy End of human life does not depend on wealth, and it is foolish to hoard it when what is needed is to grow rich "in what matters to God" (Luke 12:13-21—Eighteenth Sunday). One must therefore dedicate oneself to gathering a never-failing treasure, behaving as a "faithful and prudent steward" (Luke 12:32-48—Nineteenth Sunday). Such conduct and behavior contrast sharply with the world's ways of acting, often leading us to conflict with those who do not appreciate all things in the light of this "End" (Luke 12:49-53—Twentieth Sunday). Yet entry into the kingdom requires these choices (Luke 13:22-30—Twenty-first Sunday).

Eighteenth Sunday

To Grow Rich in What Matters to God

All Is Vanity

The first reading of this Sunday (Eccl 1:2; 2:21-23) is in danger of being poorly understood.

"All is vanity," all is hot air! This ancient exclamation that opens the Book of Ecclesiastes—called in Hebrew and by exegetes *Qoheleth* [1]—is very well known; it is still quoted today. And yet one might be surprised, troubled, and not a little upset to hear it proclaimed in the midst of the Sunday assembly. "What? This is Scripture?" some who have forgotten it will think. "It isn't very appropriate. We live in a sorrowful world; we try to respond helpfully to so many people who can find no meaning in life, who are broken and in despair. We come to church to find certitudes, reasons to live, to fight, to hope. And we are told: All is vanity!"

"What profit has man from all the labor which he toils at under the sun?" All his days sorrow and grief are his occupation; even at night his mind is not at rest. This also is vanity.

The incongruity is heightened when one evokes this vanity to speak of the great ones of the world.

> There are many reasons to compare ourselves to running water, as Scripture says (2 Sam 14:14). For whatever differences in size may appear among the various rivers that water the face of the earth, they all have this in common, that they come from a small source; that along their way, their waves roll on by constantly falling; and that they lose their identities as well as their water in the great bosom of the ocean, where the Rhine, the Danube, and other famous rivers are no longer distinguished from other, unknown streams: so all men begin with the same infirmities; as they age, the years jostle them together like waves: their life rolls and descends constantly to death, by its natural weight; finally, after having made, like waves, some a little more noise than others, they end up falling into the infinite gulf of nothingness, where no longer are distinguished kings, princes, captains, or any of the august titles that separate us; nothing but corruption and worms, ashes and rot, which even us out. Such is the law of nature . . .

> Everything that can make miserable people desire human greatness can do so only when they do not think of death.[2]

But when pessimism is so extreme and so general as that of Qoheleth, it can only shock us. Besides, when work is the particular focus—as here— is not such pessimism opposed to the theology and spirituality of earthly realities in general, and work in particular?

Nevertheless, it is neither to shock nor even less to discourage us that this text is read today. And it is certainly not the intention of this preacher, this Qoheleth, to speak in a despondent way of the vanity of all things.[3]

He belongs to that type of sage who does not allow himself to speak in ready-made ideas, uttering complacent or forced optimistic tirades, which claim that everything is for the best in this best of all worlds if one takes the trouble to show off one's skill, and which extols success and triumph as the supreme objective and most enviable reward. To all this he exclaims: "All things are vanity!"

He is also haunted by death. Such is the fate of all living beings, men as well as animals (Eccl 3:19-20). "As he came forth from his mother's womb, so again shall he depart, naked as he came," with nothing left in his hand (Eccl 5:14), even should he have lived "twice a thousand years" (Eccl 6:6). He is not the master of his fate (Eccl 8:8-9). Youthfulness is vanity, for at any rate, "the dust returns to the earth as it once was, and the life breath returns to God who gave it" (Eccl 11:10–12:7).

Now Ecclesiastes is not a kill-joy, who, in order to provoke, cultivates pessimism for pleasure or as a kind of aestheticism: "Songs of despair are often the most beautiful." He measures all things and their vanity in the face of the death that robs them.

Like many others—Pascal, for example—he cannot be content with what is temporary. He looks for what lasts: the Absolute. His anguish, which we sometimes share, is a heartrending appeal not to be taken in by mirages, by those things that, in the end, are only vanity, only wind.

But this anguish also—paradoxically—turns out to be an expression of a burning desire for the Absolute, and the deeply-rooted certitude that it exists, that it will reveal itself. It is like a gulf, an abyss that God alone can fill, he who is not "vanity." This is felt at least when the deception engendered by all things haunts the heart of a believer; and Ecclesiastes is definitely one of these believers, sharing much in common with other figures of the Bible.

His cry will never cease to resound and find an echo in whoever is able to see through the fundamentally empty vanity of human efforts to create something more than wind. He is irresistibly turned toward God, who not only stills his anguish, but redeems it, as George Bernanos has well said: "In a sense, you see, Fear is the daughter of God, redeemed on the night of Good Friday. It is not pretty to see—of course not!—sometimes mocked, sometimes cursed, renounced by everyone . . . And yet, do not deceive yourself: it is at the bedside of each agony, it intercedes for man."[4]

If today you hear his voice, harden not your hearts.

Come, let us sing joyfully to the LORD;
   let us acclaim the Rock of our salvation.
Let us greet him with thanksgiving;
   let us joyfully sing psalms to him. . . .
Come, let us bow down in worship;
   let us kneel before the LORD who made us.
For he is our God,
   and we are the people he shepherds, the flock he guides.
If today you hear his voice:
   "Harden not your hearts as at Meribah,
   as in the day of Massah in the desert,
Where your fathers tempted me;
   they tested me though they had seen my works."
(Ps 95:1-2, 6-9)

Given New Life, Seek the Things of Heaven

The second reading this Sunday (Col 3:1-5, 9-11) has not been selected in light of the other readings, since it is the fourth—and last—of the excerpts from the Letter to the Colossians retained in the Sunday Missal for Ordinary Time.[5] But what the apostle says here enters perfectly into the perspectives of the other two readings.

At the heart of Paul's thought and teaching we find the decisive opposition between the "old world" and the "new world," marked by the coming of Jesus Christ and especially his passion and resurrection. The real meaning of this opposition is completely different from, indeed wholly incommensurate with, what we find between two eras that are politically, socially, and culturally contrasted because of events like, for example, revolutions, world wars, etc. The death and resurrection of the Lord makes it possible for all people to die to an old world in order to be born to a new one, through their participation in the paschal mystery of Christ.

This participation occurs through faith and baptism. The condition of the believer, dead and risen with Christ, is radically transformed. It is hidden from the eyes of others, and even the one who benefits by it does not perceive it directly[6]; participation in the divine life is no more visible than God and Christ resurrected and raised to the right hand of the Father. But faith assures us of the reality of this transformation as it does of the existence of God. Besides, the rite of baptism is clearly visible, which, sacramentally, enables us to pass with Christ from death to life, from the present world to the heavenly one.

Yet, however radical the "death to sin" at baptism may be, the Christian never ceases dying to "things of earth,"[7] i.e., sin and that which leads to it.[8] He must constantly disentangle himself from "his old self with its practices," and "put on the new self, which is being renewed, for knowledge, in the image of its creator," which allows him "to live in a manner worthy of the Lord" (Col 1:10).

The image of a garment may seem weak to us, insofar as it evokes an exterior appearance that does not necessarily correspond to reality. Hence the saying: "Clothes do not make the man."

For Paul, and indeed for the whole of ancient culture, the symbolic force of the garment is such that it expresses the most unique individuality of the wearer.[9] Moreover, one should read what the author writes here, while remembering the theme of the old self and the new self, the first and the new Adam, the one shorn of the garment of the glory of God, the other clothed with the original glory through the grace of salvation.

This change of status entails a conduct that conforms to the new condition of one "raised up in company with Christ" who will restore the unity of all who are lost through sin. For from now on, all barriers—religious, cultural, social—will be transcended through Christ who "is everything in all of you."

The anguished longing of Qoheleth is here found fulfilled beyond all hope. To those who are jaded by their daily experiences of division, sin, worldly vanity, one can now say forcefully: "Set your heart on what pertains to higher realms where Christ is seated at God's right hand. Be intent on things above rather than on things of earth."

The Folly of Wealth

This is what Jesus says in a very concrete manner in response to a question of inheritance, with the help of a parable (Luke 12:13-21).

Preaching absolute detachment from the riches of the world, never missing a chance to insist on the privilege and beatitude of the poor, Luke is just as ready to recount the teachings of Jesus on the proper use of possessions.[10]

"In the crowd," someone asks Jesus to intervene so that his elder brother will give him his rightful share of the inheritance. This man realizes that Jesus' moral authority will make his brother listen to reason; he is only asking for what he is justly entitled to by law. Jesus' response must surprise him.

It is not a question of deciding a complicated dispute the younger brother's right is clear. Jesus could not have misunderstood or been uninterested or, even worse, made himself, by his silence, an accomplice to a flagrant injustice. Besides which, he explains: "Who appointed me as your judge and arbitrator?"

The response seems rather abrupt. But it is not really addressed to the one who has asked for Jesus' intervention. It is not therefore a cold refusal of his request, but a teaching of general significance given by the Master in light of what had been said to him. The situation has parallels in the Gospels. Thus, for example, when a woman in the crowd cried: "Blessed is the womb that carried you and the breasts at which you nursed!", Jesus replied, "Rather, blessed are those who hear the word of God and observe it" (Luke 11:27-28—Feast of the Assumption).

On another occasion, he declared: "My mother and my brothers are those who hear the word of God and act on it" (Luke 8:21).

Clearly, by speaking in this way, Jesus does not contest the "beatitude" of his mother, and does not set her in opposition to those who listen to the word of God, keep it, and put it into practice.

It is to the crowd that he speaks, a simple remark having occasioned a chance to present a teaching of general importance that is worthwhile for all. Here it has to do with earthly goods: "Take care to guard against all greed, for though one may be rich, one's life does not consist of possessions." The parable that follows illustrates Jesus' point very well.

To give the parables more impact, some features are forced, and others are used for dramatic effect. Thus the rich man in this scene is presented as a man of exceptional material success: his new harvest is so large that it is imperative that he build more and bigger storehouses to hoard all the grain he owns.

This man who believes that he "has it all" and says to himself, "You have so many good things stored up for so many years, rest, eat, drink, be merry," dies suddenly the very night after he had made these great plans.

What mockery! What a striking illustration of the teaching: "Though one may be rich, one's life does not consist of possessions." He has grown rich for himself; he must suddenly abandon it all. What he has put aside will go to others. To whom is not important, for his heirs will find themselves in the same situation unless they recall the parable in time and devote themselves to growing rich in "what matters to God."

To whatever problem we find ourselves confronted with, Jesus, who has not been appointed as our judge in these matters, will make the same response he did to the man who accosted him on the road to Jerusalem.

But what does it mean to grow rich "in what matters to God"? The Gospel does not here enter into a detailed examination of specific cases, which, after all, could not form an exhaustive list. But it enunciates a principle: Consider always and in everything what will remain of it after our death. We will be stripped of all material goods, though they be acquired completely legitimately. This is a universal fact. Consequently, each of us must act with respect to what will remain after our death, which can only be the quality of our work and the use we will have made of our goods, whether we owned much or little, whether we dwelt in opulence or squalor. All other behavior is "foolish," even if our death will not come upon us "this very night." It is obvious that "a man's life"—the life which is followed by death—is not guaranteed by his possessions.

This recollection is completed by the warning: "Take care to guard against all greed," that is to say, all avidity, cupidity, and lawless seeking after material gain.

Here also, taking into consideration what happens at and after death proves to be the decisive criterion. The believer cannot live like those who, denying the resurrection, act as if there is nothing after death, to whom Paul attributes this slogan: "Let us eat and drink, for tomorrow we die" (1 Cor 15:32).

Without going quite so far, surely we must recognize that in our immensely wealthy consumer society we must fight uphill in order not to succumb to that lust for gain that appears under so many false names. More or less consciously, we swallow the surrounding materialism just as we breathe the polluted air of our cities. We submit to the advertising barrage that continually solicits us to acquire more goods, laying before us reasons that are not only the most innocent, but even the most "noble and disinterested": advertising seems to tell us that our place in society depends on the acquisition of new things, the accumulation of wealth, the "quality" of life, progress; etc.[11]

> The means by which we live have superseded the ends for which we live. Our scientific power has outdistanced our spiritual strength. We have guided

missiles and misguided men. Like the rich man before us, we have fool-
ishly minimized what is interior in our lives and maximized what is exterior.
We have reduced life to life-style. Our generation will not find peace so
long as we do not relearn that "one may be rich, [but] one's life does not
consist of possessions" (Luke 12:15), as opposed to the wealth of spiritual
treasure "that no thief can reach nor moth destroy" (Luke 12:33).[12]

When we hear the Gospel proclaim "Take care to guard against all greed,"
it is easy to say that it applies to others "out there," that they are stricken
with an evil that will leave us unscathed. None of us is wholly free from
"the old self." On this earth we will never entirely put on "the new self"
or make ourselves "sowers of justice."

> Take care, brother, that the fate of the "wicked rich man" may not be yours.
> His story has been given to us so that we may avoid imitating him. Man,
> imitate the earth: like it, bear fruit; do not be inferior to that which has no
> soul. It is not for its own enjoyment that the earth nurtures its fruits; it is
> for your service.
>   But you have this advantage: the benefits of your benevolence will finally
> come back to you; for it is on the benefactor that the reward for doing good
> always returns. You have given to the poor; it is returned to you with in-
> terest. Grain, when it falls on the earth, produces for the sower. The bread
> that you give to the poor is a source of future blessings. May the end of
> your labors be the beginning of the celestial sowing: "Sow for yourselves
> justice" (Hos 10:12).
>   Why then torment yourself and make such efforts to store your riches
> in mortar and bricks? "A good name is more desirable than great riches"
> (Prov 22:1).[13]

What good is it to toil, "to labor under the sun," to live, since sooner
or later death will come? It seems impossible to avoid such a question.
This is in fact to ask about the meaning of life, the way one should live,
objectives to be pursued and their priorities, the value of earthly realities.
    Even when one really tries to discern all this, or tries to persuade one-
self about the truth of the matter, how can we be sure?[14] Is death an absolute end, with nothing after it? Or is it otherwise? Whatever may be
the conclusions and rules for living that one draws for oneself, the thought
of having only a certain amount of time left—and never being able to be
sure of its length—has given rise to philosophies of life that range, with
infinite nuances, from the most sublime human wisdom to the most rank
and hedonistic epicurism.
    The believer, of whatever sort, is always presented with the same prob-
lem. The biblical author who calls himself Qoheleth (Ecclesiastes the

Preacher) is such a one, a wise man who places himself under the patronage of Solomon.

His book begins and ends with these well-known words: "Vanity of vanities! All things are vanity" (Eccl 1:2; 12:8). Is it merely an utterance of someone despondent after having known the ridiculously insignificant weight of all things, who concludes that everything is made of wind? Is it an expression of profound sadness from a man who clothes himself in the mantle of wisdom? Without a doubt. But it is also, finally, a desperate appeal from a believer who against all hope, despite the evidence of experience, not only remains open to something but wants to believe that his desires, which he doesn't dare express, will be fulfilled. But don't we find such heartrending cries in many of the psalms as well?

In any case, one cannot forget what is written in the epilogue to the Book of Ecclesiastes: "The sayings of the wise are like goads": they stimulate curiosity and incite to action (Eccl 12:11). And these last two verses: "Fear God and keep his commandments, for this is man's all; because God will bring to judgment every work, with all its hidden qualities, whether good or bad" (Eccl 12:13-14).

In a paradoxical way, Qoheleth is a strong witness that the world is not worthy of humanity. Becoming aware of this is but one step before being turned toward God, who, in his mystery, is the absolute opposite of vanity, not wind at all, but as the psalms so often call him, an unbreakable Rock.[15] But their faith does not make believers insensitive to the questions that torment the human soul.

> Why the wind,
> If it does not sow by chance?
> Why the sea,
> If not for the sand?
> Why the fire,
> If it is not taken to the brushwood?
> And why man . . .
>
> Why the frost,
> If it does not crack in April?
> Why the night,
> If day does not rise from it?
> Why death,
> If life does not sweep it away?
> And why man . . .
>
> Why time,
> If it only passes by?

> Why love,
> If it is only to be lost?
> Why the bird,
> If it does not enchant the trees?
> And why man . . .
>
> Why the bread,
> If it is never broken?
> Why the blood,
> If it fills no cup?
> Why the body,
> If it speaks no word?
> And why man . . .[16]

Jesus could not ignore those psalms where the themes of human fragility are intermingled—"nothing more than a breath"—and the hope in God toward whom the prayer rises.[17] There are some features of it in the prayer spoken from the cross (Psalm 22 according to Matthew 27:46 and Mark 15:34; Psalm 31:6 according to Luke 23:46). He who was "greater than Solomon" (Luke 11:31) needs neither experience nor wisdom from another to recognize, in its truth and fullness, the vanity of all things. But at the same time he withheld the secret of his true end. It is thus with the authority that belongs only to him that he says: "Grow rich in what matters to God."

The apostle understood this teaching well. "Set your heart on what pertains to higher realms." Throw off the decrepitude of the "old self." "Put on the new self" that you have become in baptism. "Christ is everything in all of you."

See how from a wise man's reflection we arrive at the mystery revealed, celebrated, in which we have a share: the mystery of Christ who "became poor although he was rich, so that by his poverty you might become rich" (2 Cor 8:9), and who leads us on the way of our own Passover, through detachment from what passes away, to the attainment of the only wealth that is worth the trouble, because it not vanity, not made of wind.

> What love you show us
> as you recall mankind to its first innocence,
> and invite us to taste on earth
> the gifts of the world to come!
> (Preface of Virgins and Religious)

Nineteenth Sunday

He Will Come Like a Thief

The first reading for this Sunday comes from the Book of Wisdom, of which the Lectionary makes very little use (Wis 18:6-9).[18]

The Night of Deliverance

The passage selected for today is the beginning of a brief retelling (Wis 18:5-19) of the events experienced by the Hebrews and Egyptians during the Exodus from Egypt, as set out in chapter 12 of the Book of Exodus: the Passover meal (Wis 18:6-9), the lamentation over the loss of the first-born (Wis 18:10-13), the event itself (Wis 18:14-19). Here we have the first Passover meal, which immediately preceded the departure for the journey in the desert (Exod 12:1-28).

But the liturgy wants us to read this passage for itself, outside of its literary context.[19]

We notice first of all that "the Passover deliverance" is not regarded as a simple historical fact, whatever consequences it may still have: "For when you punished our adversaries, in this you glorified us whom you had summoned" (v. 8). It is a salvation event that happened only once, but in which we still share today, the promise of the fullness to come. This is precisely how the mystery of salvation in every liturgical and sacramental celebration is actualized in its threefold dimension of memorial, gift presentation, and anticipation of what is still to come.[20]

It is God who calls us to this Passover meal—"whom you had summoned" (v. 8)—for a covenant sacrifice that forms the people into a community of solidarity, for better or worse (v. 9).

The "Passover deliverance" realizes the promises made to "our fathers." Though a past event, it is continuously made present in the liturgical celebration.

> Understand this, beloved! Thus is the mystery of the Pasch new and old, eternal and temporal, corruptible and incorruptible, mortal and immortal; old according to the Law, but new according to the Logos; temporal by figure, eternal by grace; corruptible through the immolation of a sheep, incorruptible through the life of the Lord; mortal by burial, immortal by the resurrection from the dead. Old the Law, but new the Logos; temporal the

figure, eternal the grace; corruptible the sheep, incorruptible the Lord; immolated as lamb, resurrected as God. For "like a lamb led to the slaughter" (Isa 53:7; Acts 8:32), and yet he was not a lamb; and as a mute lamb, yet he was not a lamb. The figure has passed away and the truth has come to light. For in the place of the lamb it is God who has come, and in the place of the sheep a man, and in man, Christ who holds all. Therefore the immolation of the sheep and the rite of the Pasch and the letter of the Law have been achieved in Christ Jesus for whom everything happened in the Old Law and more still in the new order.[21]

This deliverance took place at night. It is also at night that the Son of Man will return (Gospel). That is why the Eucharistic celebration has always had the character of a vigil, waiting in expectant hope for the return of the Lord, who will not only deliver his people, but will share his blessings with his faithful servants.

"The praises of the fathers" will never cease to resound in our assemblies.

Happy the people the LORD *has chosen to be his own.*

Exult, you just, in the LORD;
    praise from the upright is fitting. . . .
Happy the nation whose God is the LORD,
    the people he has chosen for his own inheritance. . . .
But see, the eyes of the LORD are upon those who fear him,
    upon those who hope for his kindness,
To deliver them from death
    and preserve them in spite of famine.
Our soul waits for the LORD,
    who is our help and our shield.
May your kindness, O LORD, be upon us
    who have put our hope in you.
(Ps 33:1, 12, 18-19, 20, 22)

A Hymn to Faith

This year, from the Nineteenth to the Twenty-second Sunday of Ordinary Time, we read four passages from the Letter to the Hebrews.[22]

The first of these fragments (Heb 11:1-2, 8-19) lies at the beginning of chapter 11, which could be entitled, "The Gallery of our Ancestors in Faith."

First comes a definition of faith. "Faith is confident assurance concerning what we hope for and conviction about things we do not see." Faith cannot be reduced, for the author, to an interior conviction, as it has so often been called. It allows one *already* to enter into possession of what is *not yet* possessed. It brings one into communion with invisible realities. In fact in the Bible, the verb "to know" does not refer to intellectual cognition, but union, "communion" in the strongest sense of the word. John writes: "Eternal life is this: to *know* you, the only true God, and him whom you have sent, Jesus Christ" (John 17:3).

This relation between the believer and future or invisible realities is clearly not subjectively based; it is not a hope that one clings to, which, whatever its basis may be, contains no real guarantee. It rests on the Word of God that does and will do what it says; it rests on the Promise.

Hence, "Scripture testifies" to the faith-hope of our ancestors: God recognizes them as his own, as justified in his sight.

Chapter 11 of the Letter to the Hebrews recalls in particular the examples of Abel (11:4), Enoch (11:5-6), Noah (11:7), Isaac (11:20-22), Moses (11:23-29), and Rahab the harlot (11:31). But the author says that he could go on and on about Gideon, Barak, Samson, Jephthah, David, Samuel, the prophets, the multitude of women, martyrs, and others who all were "approved because of their faith" (11:32-40).

The Lectionary quite properly contains the passage concerning Abraham: on the one hand his is a well-known story; on the other hand, he is rightly considered as the father of believers not only by Christians but by Jews and Moslems as well. Scripture says: " 'Through you shall all the nations be blessed.' Consequently, those who have faith are blessed along with Abraham who had faith" (Gal 3:8-9—Second Friday of the Twenty-seventh Week).

Three events of Abraham's life are recalled: his departure "to a place that he was to receive as an inheritance," the birth of his son Isaac, and the "sacrifice" of Isaac.

These three episodes are a fine illustration of the definition of faith given at the beginning. Abraham went, "not knowing where he was going," assured only by the word of God, fully confident, both for himself and his heirs, of the promised city "whose designer and maker is God."

Despite her age, it is "by faith" that Sarah, Abraham's wife, was made capable of bearing a child. It would be difficult to find a better example of the power of faith.

Finally, though having received the message that "through Isaac descendants shall bear [his] name," Abraham shows himself ready to sacrifice his only son. His faith assures him that Isaac's death will not negate God's promise.

The author generalizes and pushes his initial affirmation even further. "Yet all these, though approved because of their faith, did not receive what had been promised." But they "saw and saluted it from afar." Their eyes did not linger on this land, this country that they had left and toward which they would have had the opportunity of returning. Faith allowed them to see invisible things. Faith enabled them to hold fast to the realities yet to come, toward which they traveled confidently; nothing, not even death, could make them doubt the reliability of these things.

The Proper Use of One's Goods

To Abraham God said: "Go forth from the land of your kinsfolk and from your father's house to a land that I will show you. I will make of you a great nation." And Abraham who was firmly rooted in Ur in Chaldea, who was very rich "in livestock, silver and gold . . . went as the Lord directed him" (Gen 12:1, 4; 13:2).

Jesus does not tell his disciples to leave their land, their families, and the houses of their fathers, but to sell what they own—those things that Abraham took with him (Gen 12:5)—and to give them to the poor.

God promised Abraham a posterity, numerous as the stars (Gen 15:5; Deut 1:10), and a country. Jesus assures his disciples: "It has pleased your Father to give you the kingdom"; to rid yourselves of earthly goods is to gain "purses . . . that do not wear out, a never-failing treasure with the Lord . . ."

In spite of the differences of circumstances and vocation—exceptional in the case of Abraham, but common to all the disciples—this is the same call to faith and confidence in the Word: Jesus assures the disciples that they have *already* received the kingdom since they can, *right now*, lay up treasure in heaven.

Abraham had no children and was, like his wife, advanced in years when God promised him a long line of descendants. The disciples are only a "little flock,"[23] but one to whom Jesus says: "Do not live in fear"; trust in my word and throw yourselves into the arena of faith!

The passage from Luke selected for the liturgy today (Luke 12:32-48) begins by once again speaking of the goods that one possesses, and of their "prudent" use. But as addressed to the community of believers— the "little flock"—it clearly concerns their preparation and vigilance for the return of their Lord.[24]

In one way or another, they are constantly admonished to "be on guard," to remain "ready," "wide-awake," busy during the master's absence, in order not to be surprised by the arrival of the Son of Man

(vv. 36, 37, 39, 40, 42, 43, 45, 46, 47: numbering at least nine verses out of the fourteen).

The meaning of each parable or comparison is clear. But it is worth the trouble to discover the way they resonate, their harmonies.

To Watch Night and Day

The first—"Awaiting their master's return from a wedding" (vv. 35-38)—has a definitely Eucharistic flavor, which appears more clearly when it is read within the Sunday liturgy. Notice the themes of the "wedding" and the "table" where the master himself serves the guests as at the Last Supper: "Happy are those who are called to his Supper." See also the exhortation to have "belts fastened," which recalls the Passover eaten by the Hebrews with loins girt and sandals on their feet (Exod 12:11). Finally, one is reminded that Jesus himself directly associated the Paschal meal with the waiting for his return (Matt 26:29; Mark 14:25; Luke 22:18; 1 Cor 11:26). In conformity with his words, we always celebrate the Eucharist in readiness "to greet him when he comes again,"[25] as proclaimed in the memorial ("anamnesis") after the words of institution.

Therefore it is within the perspective of the final manifestation (parousia) of the Lord that this first parable on vigilance is placed. "Behold, I stand at the door and knock. If anyone hears my voice and opens the door, I will enter his house and dine with him, and he with me" (Rev 3:20).

But it is not simply to any vigilance whatever that Jesus exhorts his disciples. He and he alone is the master who, upon his return, will take those faithful to his service, "seat them at table" and "proceed to wait on them."

Uncertainty of the Hour

The following parable (vv. 38-39) insists on the uncertainty as to the day and hour of this return: "Be prepared, for at an hour you do not expect, the Son of Man will come." To be sure, this can be understood as the day and hour of death, but the parable is addressed to the whole community and fundamentally alludes to the "eschatological" manifestation of the Lord.

The image of a thief may be surprising. But it occurs several times in the New Testament. It does not mean to imply that the Lord behaves like a thief, but that the day of his coming will be sudden, unforeseeable. "You know very well that the day of the Lord will come like a thief at night" (1 Thess 5:2—Thirty-third Sunday, Year A; similarly, 2 Pet 3:10—Second Sunday of Advent, Year B). "If you are not watchful, I will come like a thief" (Rev 3:3—Second Tuesday of the Thirty-third Week). "Behold, I am coming like a thief. Blessed is the one who watches and keeps his clothes ready so that he may not go naked and people see him exposed" (Rev 16:15).

The Church, far from dreading this coming, which will inaugurate the definitive Pasch, looks for it constantly, especially when it celebrates the Eucharist, exclaiming: "Come, Lord Jesus" (Rev 22:20 and memorial acclamation).

> The whole of Christian worship is merely a continuing celebration of Passover: as the sun rises it draws the Eucharist in its wake in an unbroken chain; each Mass that is celebrated is a prolongation of Passover. Each day of the liturgical year and, in each day, each moment of the life of the never-sleeping Church, continues and renews the Passover that the Lord so greatly desired to eat with his own, while awaiting that which he will share with them in his kingdom, which will last for all eternity. The yearly Passover that we commemorate and await keeps alive in us the fire of the first Christians who cried, turning toward the past: "The Lord has been raised! It is true!" (Luke 24:34) and toward the future: " 'I am coming soon!' Amen! Come, Lord Jesus!" (Rev 22:20).[26]

Faithful Servant

The third parable (vv. 42-48) is introduced by a question from Peter, who asks if what Jesus is saying is meant only for the group to which Peter belongs—"us"—that is to say the Twelve, or "for everyone" (v. 41).

Jesus then speaks of the conduct of a "steward." In the New Testament, this is one of those terms that designates those who hold authority in the communities, about whom Paul spoke most directly when he laid this charge on Titus: "For a bishop as God's steward must be blameless."[27]

This "bishop" is a "servant" of the master,[28] but one to whom the master has more particularly conferred the care of his goods and delegated a personal authority over the other servants. He must prove himself to be faithful and wise in proportion to the trust placed in him. A more rigorous account will be demanded of him, and he can look forward to a more severe punishment if he is found unworthy.[29] The other servants are "flogged," but yet receive "fewer stripes" if they conduct themselves poorly during the master's absence. He, on the other hand, will be rejected and ranked among those "undeserving of trust."

The parable speaks of what can lead a "steward" to forsake his duties: laxity, finding that his master "is taking his time about coming."

He allows himself "to abuse the housemen and servant girls, to eat and drink and get drunk." Is this an exaggeration that goes beyond the bounds of probability? Why should we think so? We sometimes see people who are delegated a certain amount of responsibility become intoxicated with their authority, become tyrannical to their subordinates, and, both out of disdain for the absent master and the very logic of their behavior, force those whom they maltreat and humiliate to witness their drunken orgies.

In any case, the parable presents the extraordinary antithesis to the service of a faithful and circumspect steward, the authentic vicar of the master who serves his servants.

> Because the Lord knew that the passage of time before his return would occasion a certain amount of hardship and anxiety, fear of discouragement, loss of vigilance, and succumbing to the fatigue of a long wait, he promises, to those who hold fast until their beatitude in heaven, to be their servant in heaven. "It will go well with those servants whom the master finds wide-awake on his return" (Luke 12:37). And that they may not be uncertain as to the character of this beatitude, he adds immediately: "I tell you, he will put on an apron, seat them at table, and proceed to wait upon them." A God will gird himself, bring his servants to table, and wait on them! Behold an unexpected inversion of things, a terrible reprimand to masters, a surprising reversal of subordination: because the servant, for a little while, remained standing, loins girt, waiting for his master and, at the cost of a little weariness, bore the weight of faith patiently, now, as a kind of recompense, divinity is shrouded in the very seat of its divinity! Ready at hand to the man seated at table, it stays standing and stands in the heavens; the servant eats and the master serves him, assisted by his domestics and servants; Christ fulfills a servile function and does so when he is already established in the glory of the Father.[30]

Each member of the community must draw the conclusion: "When much has been given a man, much will be required of him. More will be asked of a man to whom more has been entrusted." For no one is without responsibility in the community.

The life of the Church, of the Christian communities, of each believer is—must be—dynamically driven by the expectation of the full realization of the promises and the return of the Lord. This expectation is hope based on faith in the word of God, "confident assurance concerning what we hope for, and conviction about things we do not [yet] see."

This is at the heart of the celebration of the Eucharist, the Paschal supper of a people marching toward the Promised Land into which, on his return, Christ will bring them.

Such assurance banishes all fear in the "little flock" already gathered under the staff of the Shepherd who has gone before them to prepare their place in the kingdom.

For the Church, the "stewards" of the communities, for all "pilgrims to the City of God," as Augustine calls Christians, it is a time of wakefulness and vigilance, toilsome to be sure, but undertaken in joy.

Uncertainty as to the day and the hour must not lead to fretfulness or complacency, but must rather stimulate the fidelity and the hope that each Eucharist reawakens.

> Like a friend at our door,
> Jesus is about to enter.
> He is bringing his kingdom:
> May we not risk missing it.
> If a thief broke open our doors,
> We would know how to rouse ourselves.
>
> Like a friend who keeps his word,
> Jesus is returning to visit us.
> But he spoke of it in parable
> And it is reality for us:
> The one who prowls and steals from us
> Does not say when he is coming.
>
> Like a friend we have invited,
> Jesus will come when he wishes.
> The table will be quickly set
> So that he will have a place at our supper.
> The night of his sudden arrival
> Will satisfy the one who is waiting.
>
> Let us keep our lamps ever ready
> In order to receive the visitor;
> When he comes we will all celebrate.
> Like the dawn for the watchman,
> Let us watch as we await a master
> Who will serve his servants.[31]

Not Peace but Division

It is important that one be assured of being on the right path, in some measure already possessing the treasure for which one hopes, being able to see—through faith—invisible realities. Faithful vigilance in the service of the Lord who has come and will come again can nevertheless lead to distressing situations and painful, or even tragic choices.

The Crucifying Mission of the Prophet

The first reading this Sunday tells of one of those tragic episodes in which the life of Jeremiah abounded (Jer 38:4-6, 8-10).

Clearly, it has not been chosen because of its status as a mishap occurring to a famous biblical person, one that did not end up too badly. With the passage of time, this episode, sad though it is, seems to have become a mere historical anecdote of little interest. There are so many similar and worse stories that appear in the history of every nation, even today!

All this is true. But the reading is part of the montage of the Liturgy of the Word and, as we know, it has been selected with respect to the Gospel of the day, which must determine our manner of receiving, listening to, and understanding it.

Jeremiah certainly belongs to the past (six centuries before our era). But his message interests us, punctuated so often as it is by: "This word of the Lord" or "Thus says the Lord." Moreover, Jeremiah is, according to Christian tradition, one of the most striking figures of Christ.

Called to be, like Jesus, a herald of the covenant and the promise—"I will be your God, and you will be my people"—Jeremiah knows that it was never said: "I will be your God and you will be my people *exclusively*," and still less: "without taking account of your conduct." This is a constant theme of the prophets. They never cease recalling, both at convenient and inconvenient times, in no soft-spoken terms, that not only do the privileges of the covenant lead to moral obligations, but the very fulfillment of the promises always depends on the faithfulness of the people to the precepts and commandments of their God.

165

Jesus was accused of misleading the people (Luke 23:2), Jeremiah of "demoralizing the soldiers who were left in the city," of seeking "not the welfare of the people, but their ruin" (Jer 38:4). Both were arraigned before a holder of judicial power—Zedekiah, Pilate—who was unable to offer opposition to the demand for the maximum penalty, and who handed them over to their accusers (Jer 38:5; Luke 23:22, 25).

Jeremiah's innocence, like Jesus', was recognized by a pagan: the Ethiopian Ebed-melech (Jer 38:7-9), a Roman centurion (Luke 23:47).

The intervention of a palace officer saved Jeremiah from death (Jer 38:9-10). Jesus died, but was raised by God.

In reading through the text of the first reading for this Sunday, how can we not recognize Jeremiah as a figure of Christ, and indeed of all the Christian faithful, especially martyrs and persecuted missionaries?

A prophet is always, in one way or another, a "sign of contradiction" to the people. Fidelity to the Word and his mission expose him to the misunderstanding of his neighbors, often to mistreatment, sometimes even to death. The "confessions of Jeremiah"[32] testify to this: he truly experienced the fact that "God is dangerous."[33]

> Listen! he is inviting you to lose your soul in order to gain it. He always thinks in terms of love. He offers us the impossible. He does not see us as created for finite happiness: years of happy marriage, strolling through the fields, or simply a bowl of strawberries. A painting, a book, a shady bench. A comfortable chair near the fire. A hard march through the night. The joy of a fight. The majesty of a death. Always with an eternal sense, circumscribed in one perfect moment. This is enough for us; it is indescribable. In such things the world ripens and, filled with divinity, is made a perfect offering at the feet of the Eternal. Ask the poets about it.
>
> But, for ourselves, there is danger . . .
>
> If God was satisfied with the utter disproportion between his soul and ours, or was willing merely to show, before the joyful eyes of the spectators, the fire of his redeeming love, we would not object. We would be free to applaud, to shout joyfully at this unexpected gift to creation. We would be proud to witness the spectacle of the human heart, so full already of amazing things, reach its peak in the *salto mortale* of God. But that is not what he wants. He presents his victory over death as an example to be imitated, he draws us beyond our limits, into his adventure, which is inevitably fatal.[34]

The prophet willingly runs the risk of exposing himself to the "dangerous God" and his Word. This is what makes him a witness, a martyr. If thus it falls to him, he remains unshaken, secure in his faith with utmost confidence in the help of God who will never fail him, knowing that he will emerge victoriously from the trial.

> LORD, *come to my aid!*
>
> I have waited, waited for the LORD,
>> and he stooped toward me.
> The LORD heard my cry.
> He drew me out of the pit of destruction,
>> out of the mud of the swamp;
> He set my feet upon a crag;
>> he made firm my steps.
> And he put a new song into my mouth,
>> a hymn to our God.
> Many shall look on in awe
>> and trust in the LORD.
> Though I am afflicted and poor,
>> yet the LORD thinks of me.
> You are my help and my deliverer;
>> O my God, hold not back!
> (Ps 40:2-4, 18)

Eyes Fixed on Jesus

It is with a kind of meditation hymn that the author of the Letter to the Hebrews ends his recollection of the great models of faith in ancient times, this "cloud of witnesses" (Heb 12:1-4).

They are models to be imitated: "Let us rid ourselves of every burden and sin that clings to us and persevere in running the race that lies before us."

However, it is on Jesus that we must have "our eyes fixed," he whom these witnesses have prefigured or followed, because he is "the leader and perfecter of our faith."

Then in one sentence is recalled the paschal journey of Christ: "For the sake of the joy that lay before him he endured the cross, despising its shame, and has taken his seat at the right of the throne of God."

This is a traditional expression of faith, like that found in almost identical terms in Paul's famous liturgical hymn to Christ, which all Christians should know by heart (Phil 2:6-11—Passion Sunday and the feast of the Triumph of the Cross, September 14):

> Who, though he was in the form of God,
>> did not regard equality with God
>> something to be grasped.

> Rather, he emptied himself,
>   taking the form of a slave,
>   coming in human likeness;
> and found human in appearance,
> he humbled himself,
>   becoming obedient to death, even death
>   on a cross.
> Because of this,
>   God greatly exalted him
>   and bestowed on him the name that is above
>   every name,
> that at the name of Jesus
>   every knee should bend,
>   of those in heaven and on earth and under the
>   earth,
>   and every tongue confess that
> Jesus Christ is Lord, to the glory of God the Father.

These two readings prepare us to receive the proclamation of the Gospel (Luke 12:49-53), which contains three sayings of Jesus (vv. 49, 50, 51-53) which the evangelist recounts immediately after those we heard last Sunday.

A Fire

Jesus says to his disciples: "I have come to set the earth on fire, and how I wish it were already blazing!"

It is rather rare in the Synoptic Gospels (Matthew, Mark, Luke) that Jesus speaks of himself in the first person: "I have come . . . I wish . . . I must . . . ."[35] These are very involved sayings, through which Jesus not only reveals his mission but also expresses with full awareness his determination to fulfill them.

But what is this "fire" which he has come to light upon the earth, which he wishes were already kindled? Surely, not that of the divisions of which he will speak later on (vv. 52-53); Jesus clearly does not wish to willingly inspire them. And it is certainly not that of the judgment at the end of time, as it is spoken of in the prophets and the apocalyptic literature. Luke definitely wants to guard against the expectation of an imminent last day,[36] which he would not have done if he had found testimony to the contrary in Jesus.

On the other hand, in his account of Pentecost, Luke evokes the Spirit under the form of fire, and his gift as the fulfillment of the prophecy of what must come to be realized in the last days (Acts 2:3, 17, 19) as the goal of Jesus' whole mission. "God raised this Jesus; of this we are all witnesses. Exalted at the right hand of God, he received the promise of the holy Spirit from the Father and poured it forth, as you [both] see and hear" (Acts 2:32-33).

Therefore, Jesus reveals himself as filled with an ardent longing to illuminate the world by the fire of the Spirit, which is the ultimate goal of his work. Such a look into Jesus' mind is worth more than the Gospels would indicate.

A Baptism

The second saying sets against this fire a baptism that Jesus must receive, for which it is painful for him to wait. Again we must search a little to discover what is meant by this new image.[37]

This baptism has the sound of a test; it seems to be preliminary to the lighting of the fire. Mustn't we recognize in this image the passion of the Savior? Jesus spoke in a similar way with respect to his day and his glory: "For just as lightning flashes and lights up the sky from one side to the other, so will the Son of Man be [in his day]. But first he must suffer greatly and be rejected by this generation" (Luke 17:24-25); "Was it not necessary that the Messiah should suffer these things and enter into his glory?" (Luke 24:26—the road to Emmaus, Third Sunday of Easter, Year A).

When speaking of "baptism," Luke certainly cannot help thinking of the Christians of his time, just as we spontaneously think of the first of the sacraments of Christian initiation. This "baptismal bath" is in fact linked to the gift of the Spirit. Peter said, on the day of Pentecost: "Repent and be baptized, every one of you, in the name of Jesus Christ for the forgiveness of sins; and you will receive the gift of the holy Spirit" (Acts 2:38—Fourth Sunday of Easter, Year A).

Moreover, from our reading of Paul's letters, we remember what the apostle said about the Christian's baptism into the death of Christ. "Or are you unaware that we who were baptized into Christ Jesus were baptized into his death?" (Rom 6:3—Easter Vigil and Thirteenth Sunday, Year A); "You were buried with him in baptism" (Col 2:12—Seventeenth Sunday, Year C).

The baptism that Jesus must receive has an important place in his life and mission: "What anguish I feel till it is over!" Is this to say that the thought of it causes him worry or anguish? Rather, Jesus is expressing his desire to come to the end (or goal) of his mission. One must not forget that Luke recalls that Jesus frequently said: "The Son of Man must suffer."[38] Each time he does so, he testifies to a firm determination to march toward this baptism, without which his mission cannot be accomplished. So it is in strong words that he rebukes Peter when he tries to deter him from this path: "Get behind me, Satan! You are an obstacle to me. You are thinking not as God does, but as human beings do." (Matt 16:23—Twenty-second Sunday, Year A).

This then is the goal of the mission that Jesus wants to accomplish and toward which he moves by resolutely following the road to Jerusalem (Luke 9:51—Thirteenth Sunday): to engulf the earth with the fire of the Spirit after having received the baptism of his passion.

In the Church
Following him, the disciples are moved with the same desire, impatient for this fire, ready to take on the trial of a similar baptism.

The exemplary history of the early Church that Luke, as author of the Book of Acts, has left us as precious testimony, is worth meditating on.

It all begins with the descent of the Spirit on the apostles and on those who were with them on the day of Pentecost: "Then there appeared to them tongues as of fire, which parted and came to rest on each one of them. And they were all filled with the holy Spirit . . . " (Acts 2:3-4—Pentecost).

At that moment is born the missionary impulse of the Church, which announces that the last days, spoken of by the prophet Joel—"I will pour out my spirit upon all mankind" (Joel 3:1)—are accomplished. At the same time, what will be the basic message of the apostles for all time is heard: "God has made him both Lord and Messiah, this Jesus whom you crucified . . . Repent and be baptized, every one of you, in the name of Jesus Christ for the forgiveness of sins; and you will receive the gift of the holy Spirit" (Acts 2:36, 38—Fourth Sunday of Easter, Year A).

The history of the Church is that of the spreading of the Spirit, which appears in a more dazzling manner in these early times and at particularly important moments, but is no less present when its action is more subtle.

It is the Spirit who inspires saints and reformers, synods and councils, ecumenical movements. It is the Spirit who rouses missionary fervor, brings about the renewal of prayer, and is present in all that is done in good times and bad. Often blown every which way by opposing winds, the ship of the Church goes forward to the opposite shore where the Lord waits for it (Matt 14:22-33—Nineteenth Sunday, Year A). From age to age we are witnesses to it. Always, there comes a new Pentecost from somewhere; the fire is rekindled by Christ, who accomplished everything by receiving the baptism of his passion, in which we share.

Not Peace but Division

But let us continue on to the end of this Sunday's Gospel and read with equal attention Jesus' third saying: "Do you think that I have come to establish peace on the earth? No, I tell you, but rather division."

It is hard not to be astonished or taken back every time we hear this abrupt proclamation. We prefer to think, instead, of the prayer before communion: "Lord Jesus Christ, you said to your apostles: 'Peace I leave you, my peace I give to you.' Look not on our sins, but on the faith of your Church; and grant us the peace and unity of your kingdom, where you live forever and ever."

We know that Jesus said that his peace is not given "as the world gives peace" (John 14:27—Sixth Sunday of Easter, Year C), which is based on compromises, concessions, and bargaining, amounting to a balance of powers. His peace, even though it is not of this world, is still what we dream about. In any case, it is peace that is at issue, not division. How so?

This difference is crucial. To welcome the peace of the kingdom which Jesus gives and which is only attained through the cross, places believers in a situation where they are sometimes set in conflict with others. For this peace rests on faith, the choice for Christ and the kingdom, which necessarily involves detachment from, if not rejection of, all that is opposed to Christ and the Gospel or that is incompatible with the choice one makes for it.

If truth be told, this is not the only time the Gospels confront the disciple of Christ with the exigencies of this choice and the distressing consequences that can arise from it: "Let the dead bury their dead. But you, go ahead and proclaim the kingdom of God," Jesus said to the man who asked to be allowed first to bury his father (Luke 9:60—Thirteenth Sunday). To the crowds he said: "If anyone comes to me without hating his father and mother, wife and children, brothers and sisters, and even his own life, he cannot be my disciple" (Luke 14:26—Twenty-third Sunday).

Here he proclaims division even within the family: "from now on," since he is here and the choice must be made now—for or against him.

It is easy to say or think: "The way to a peaceful life is to direct oneself, today, to the gospel!" "Peaceful" perhaps, but at the price of the peace of the kingdom, the peace given by Christ. And it is because one is aware of this that one ends up desiring division instead.

Every human life is confronted, at some point or another, with choices that in some instances demand real heroism.

The situation becomes particularly distressing when one finds oneself torn between faithfulness to God, faith, and the gospel, and on the other hand, to family, friends, and country.

Often, if not always, adding to the drama of one's conscience and internal turmoil is the lack of understanding from those whom one seems not only to be abandoning, but renouncing, even betraying.

This conflict and division inevitably takes place in an atmosphere of ambiguity, of good and evil, in ourselves and in the world. By what right does anyone, the sinner and the unjust—like each of us—claim to have the final word? Such a person's pretended clarity of mind may become a source of widespread demoralization, leading to the unhappiness of family and friends?

There is a great temptation to retreat into one's own corner, refusing to choose a side or take a stand on anything. But sometimes we are remiss in not saying or doing anything about a situation to the extent that one may ultimately suffer the loss of one's soul.

Such was the drama of Jeremiah and so many others who, out of fidelity to the Word, preferred to hand themselves over rather than lose their lives. In this, they prefigure Jesus, the sign of contradiction, who had only one urgent desire: to see the fire of the Spirit come upon the earth after he had received the baptism of his passion.

We must fix our eyes on him, the beginning and the end of faith for those who have received the Spirit through baptism into his death and resurrection. He makes it possible to run "the race strongly, which leads to participation in his glory.

> In the midst of all the shouting, they asked the asiarch Philip to throw Polycarp to a lion. This he refused to do, for the wild-beast hunts had been abolished! "To the fire then!" they all cried. Thus would be fulfilled the vision of the previous days when Polycarp had, during his prayer, seen his pillow consumed by flames; so he prophesied to the faithful standing near him: "I will be burned alive!"
>
> When the fire was ready, Polycarp removed his clothes, loosened his belt, and tried to take off his shoes, which he did not ordinarily do: the faithful who followed him would always be eager to help him. This was so that they might the more quickly touch his body; he was honored for his holiness even before his martyrdom.

Immediately, then, they set around him the material to fix him to the pyre. The executioners were about to nail him to it when he said: "Do not bind me; the one who has given me the strength to face the fire will also enable me to lie still on the pyre, with no need of your nails."

They did not nail him, binding him instead. Tied to the post, hands clasped behind his back, Polycarp appeared like a choice ram, found worthy out of a great flock for sacrifice. Then raising his eyes, he said: "I bless you for having found me worthy of this day and hour, worthy of being counted among your martyrs and of sharing in the cup of Christ, for being raised to eternal life in soul and body, in the incorruptibility of the Holy Spirit.

"Grant that I may with them come today into your presence as a precious and acceptable sacrifice, as you have prepared and foretold that I shall be; you have kept your promise, God of faithfulness and truth. For this and for every blessing I praise you, I bless you, I glorify you through the eternal and heavenly high priest, Jesus Christ, your beloved son.

"Through him, who dwells with you and the Spirit, may glory be given, now and forevermore. Amen!"

When Polycarp had said this Amen concluding his prayer, the executioners lighted the fire, and the flame burnt high and bright. At this moment we witnessed a miracle; and we have been spared in order to tell it to others. The fire shaped itself like an arch, like a sail filled with wind, and it surrounded the body of the martyr. The bishop stood in the middle of it, not like burning flesh, but like baking bread or like gold or silver being tested in the fire. All this while we were aware of a delicious smell, like that of incense or precious spices.[39]

Twenty-first Sunday

The First Will Be Last and the Last Will Be First

Today's liturgy is the last in the sequence of the Eighteenth to Twenty-first Sundays. It acts as a kind of conclusion to a set of instructions given by Jesus on salvation, the type of life one should lead, and the choices required to gain salvation. In fact, it leads us here and now to the threshold of the banquet hall in the kingdom of God. The gate is narrow and will not be left open indefinitely. When it is closed, some who thought they had a right to enter will find themselves locked outside. Yet the call to the banquet has been made far and wide "from east to west, north to south."

All Are Called

Quite rightly, the first reading for the Twenty-first Sunday proclaims the universal intent of God's plan of salvation (Isa 66:18-21). The prophet reveals the will of God: "to gather nations of every language."

The true God must be God of all. This might sound like a truism; however, its proper understanding is not self-evident. History, even to the present day, provides us with examples of self-styled universalists who can only mislead or disgust us. The pretentious are almost always rooted in a desire for a personal or political gain, which has absolutely nothing in common with what God is, wants, or does. The Bible never ceases to denounce and brand such people as blasphemers and pariahs of the community.

On the other hand, for believers, those who recognize God as the only God of all, there is the temptation to focus this kind of worldly importance on themselves. Not always in such a cruel and foolish manner as Nebuchadnezzar, whose story is told in the Book of Daniel: while pretending to force all people to worship his god, it was he himself who wanted to be recognized as the only god (Dan 3). Even the naive James and John who wanted to have fire called down from heaven on those who refused to welcome Jesus (Luke 9:51-62—Thirteenth Sunday). The temptation is typically more subtle. It lies in wait for us even in our best thoughts and acts—our militant moments?—even when we are most sincere and virtuous.

The "glory" that God wants to shine on all is his power to gather together all the scattered peoples, overcoming by reconciliation the divisions between them.

For the accomplishment of this plan, God actively involves those whom he has already saved, the "fugitives." It is not enough that their community be receptive to those who come from afar. They must go "to the nations . . . the distant coastlands that have never heard of my fame, or seen my glory." The community already assembled by God must testify to the universality of salvation. Thus a "sign" will be raised in the midst of the assembly that has been set free. It will itself be this "sign," this standard, filled with the power of God, as unshakable as him because it is called together and unified by him: "As the new heavens and the new earth which I will make shall endure before me, says the LORD, so shall your race and your name endure" (Isa 66:22—the verse following today's reading).

The return to God of those dispersed throughout the nations is spoken of as an offering borne to the "house of the LORD." Such a way of speaking may be surprising and a little confusing, if one is used to thinking of missions or the apostolate in terms of "conquest" and other like words that more or less evoke a mentality somewhat tainted with colonialism, even if such is not the intent.

We forget that Paul, who is the model of missionary zeal, writes about the grace that had been conferred upon him "as the grace given to me by God to be a minister (in Greek: the *liturge*) of Christ Jesus to the Gentiles in performing the priestly service of the gospel of God, so that the offering up of the Gentiles may be acceptable, sanctified by the holy Spirit" (Rom 15:16—Friday I of the Thirty-first week). And very explicitly: "God is my witness, whom I serve with my spirit in proclaiming the gospel of his son" (Rom 1:9).

Of what must the prophet have been thinking—or dreaming—when he wrote: "Some of these I will take as priests and Levites"? How could he have foreseen such a blossoming of the sacerdotal and Levitical functions, in spite of the limited number of exiles returning to their homes? And when?[40] It doesn't matter. There are today, in the Church, bishops and priests belonging to "the distant coastlands." Not only missionaries going out from among us, but also priests who come to us with a mission that not long ago we would have taken to them. Others have responsibilities on the level of the universal Church.[41] We thank God for this, joining with all peoples in our praise, recalling the orders of the messengers:

> Go out to all the world
> and tell the Good News.

> Praise the LORD, all you nations;
>   glorify him, all you peoples!
> For steadfast is his kindness toward us,
>   and the fidelity of the LORD endures forever.
> (Ps 117:1-2)

Profit from the Lessons of the Lord

The epistle is a passage from the Letter to the Hebrews, which comes immediately after the one we read last Sunday (Heb 12:5-7, 11-13).

At the end of the preceding passage, the author invited us to turn our eyes toward Jesus who, having endured the sufferings and humiliation of the cross, entered into the glory of God (Heb 12:1-4—preceding Sunday).

The author knows that suffering can be confounding, resulting in doubt and fruitless reflection. Thus he writes to the suffering Christians: "You have . . . forgotten the exhortation addressed to you as sons."

Rather than a panacea, this is the comfort that one needs in the midst of an ordeal. Happy are those who listen to these words that, far from blocking out their troubles, help them to delve into the heart of reality, to understand what is happening to them, and thus to draw all possible good—or at least some good—from their misfortune.

This comforting message is in fact a disconcerting text from the Book of Proverbs (3:11-12):

> My sons, do not disdain the discipline of the LORD
>   nor lose heart when he reproves you;
> for whom the LORD loves, he disciplines;
>   he scourges every son he receives.[42]

What then should I be told and tell myself in my suffering? "I know God loves me, because he punishes me; my trial is his fatherly way of correcting me"!

True love is not good-natured indulgence, weakness, or compliancy that would make one say, "Yes, you have suffered greatly. I weep for you." Or worse, "You really did not deserve this." Or even, "What have you done to God that he would treat you this way?'' And if we seek the answer in ourselves, how will we receive the message "Be not discouraged. This lesson is a proof of the love of God"?

Every child must receive instruction from his or her parents. Only later—often much, much later—does the child recognize the extent to which this instruction, however harsh and painful it may have been at the time, or even because of this, has helped him or her. This is unquestionably true. But must the lesson be bitter? At what point does it become simple persecution?

One could go on and on, to the point where each response raises a new objection—on the proper means of education, the place of correction and punishment, even corporal. It must remain a theoretical discussion, for every concrete pedagogy that results from it is immediately put into question.

But this is not what is at issue, even if the author of the letter evokes the common experience of a father teaching lessons to the son whom he loves.

He is concerned with God, our relationship to the Father and the instruction that he gives us; the pains and trials of life are part of our education under him and are clearly not imposed arbitrarily, but for our own good.

What are the fruits of this lesson? Peace and justice, the messianic blessings par excellence. Gained for us by Christ in his passion, which leads to glory:

> In the days when he was in the flesh, he offered prayers and supplications with loud cries and tears to God, who was able to save him from death, and he was heard because of his reverence. Son though he was, he learned obedience from what he suffered; and when perfected, he became the source of eternal salvation for all who obey him (Heb 5:7-9—Fifth Sunday of Lent, Year B).

"All those who obey him" are those who march on the same road, who participate in his paschal mystery of death-resurrection. This is the way that leads to peace.

Hence the attitude of courage. It is not enough to hold fast in trial, to keep on the defensive, to grit one's teeth and wait for the storm to pass. One must be involved in generous action. Rise! "Strengthen your drooping hands and your weak knees." Forward! "Make straight the paths you walk on." Be confident! "That your halting limbs may not be dislocated but healed."

The Letter of James follows the same line of thought:

> Consider it all joy, my brothers, when you encounter various trials, for you
> know that the testing of your faith produces perseverance. And let per-
> severance be perfect, so that you may be perfect and complete, lacking in
> nothing (James 1:2-4—Tuesday II of the Sixth Week).

No complacent words, but a statement that demonstrates the un-
equalled depth and strength of Christian hope. Far from being foiled by
life's ordeals, it finds there the strength of confidence and new energy.
For of this we can be sure: it also is a manifestation of the love of God.

The Narrow Gate

The Gospel today is a collection of certain sayings of Jesus that acts like
a conclusion to a set of teachings. The sayings are included in the sequence
that goes from the Eighteenth to the Twenty-first Sunday of Year C (Luke
13:22-30).[43]

Luke has grouped these teachings around a question posed by someone
to Jesus while he is on his way to Jerusalem. "Lord, will only a few people
be saved?"

Such a question can come to anyone's mind who has carefully listened
to the preceding sayings and felt the weight of the demands they impose, while being conscious of one's own weakness. It is a question that
Jesus' hearers must ask themselves often, as will those who hear him
say: "It is easier for a camel to pass through the eye of a needle than
for a rich person to enter the kingdom of God" (Luke 18:25-26).

It is a question each of us asks, at some time or another, whether from
discouragement or in the hope of being reassured with little cost: "If not
many are to be saved, what chance do I have?"; "If in the end there is
room for many, indeed most, why do I need to worry about earning a
good place?"

To the question asked after his words on the obstacle that wealth places
on a person, Jesus responds only: "What is impossible for human beings is possible for God" (Luke 18:27). "Well enough, Lord. I know this.
I rely on the power of God. But allow me to ask again: Will many people
be saved?"

We should thank Luke for having gathered the sayings of Jesus dealing with this insistent question, and welcome them—studying and
meditating on them—even if they are somewhat enigmatic and contain
a serious warning.

The gate that opens on the hall of the "feast in the kingdom of God"
is narrow, says Jesus. For it is true that "many will attempt to enter but

will not be strong enough." Are the others, then, the "saved"? What does it matter? And what meaning could the answer have? What is important is that we must enter by this "narrow gate." One could add that this "hall of the feast in the kingdom" has nothing in common with a banquet room here on earth, with its limited space and place-settings, reserved tables being the "right" of those with influence; on the contrary, it is infinitely expandable, and guests are seated according to the order of their arrival. It is true that in the Book of Revelation one reads: "After this I had a vision of a great multitude, which no one could count, from every nation, race, people, and tongue. They stood before the throne and before the Lamb, wearing white robes and holding palm branches in their hands" (Rev 7:9—Fourth Sunday of Easter, Year C; Feast of All Saints). But this says nothing about the actual number of those who make up the "great multitude," and even less about how many there are of those whom Revelation castigates in virulent terms: "But as for cowards, the unfaithful, the depraved, murderers, the unchaste, sorcerers, idol-worshipers, and deceivers of every sort, their lot is in the burning pool of fire and sulphur, which is the second death." (Rev 21:8). We also read this terrible apostrophe:[44] "Outside are the dogs, the sorcerers, the unchaste, the murderers, the idol-worshipers, and all who love and practice deceit" (Rev 22:15). The power of this condemnation appears all the greater, since it is juxtaposed with this marvelous beatitude: "Blessed are they who wash their robes so as to have the right to the tree of life and enter the city through its gates!" (Rev 22:14—Seventh Sunday of Easter, Year C).

It is not a response, therefore, to the wholly theoretical question on the number of the saved or their proportion with respect to the others. But the gate is narrow; entrance is not gained easily.

What one must do in order to enter is not made clear here. But is it necessary after the instructions that precede this passage, which we have read the past three Sundays? "Do this and you will enter through the narrow gate." Accomplishing what was said there, and in the rest of the Gospel as well, does not come, as is very clear, without effort, generosity, self-denial, etc. And time is short.

The Locked Door
The day will come when the door will be locked by the master of the house. Definitively at the end of time, to be sure. But also at the end of the time of each one whom the Lord will not recognize as his own.

Then it would be completely useless to knock, to cry out "Lord, open the door for us," to say "We ate and drank in your company and you taught in our streets."

In the context of the assembly and of the Sunday Eucharist, these words provide grounds for reflection, all the more so because they are not the only instance of such in the Bible. In fact, the Bible often denounces the inanities of worship when instead of pleasing God it wrongs him, and also of listening to the Word when it is not put into practice.[45]

No evildoers can claim to enter, those who do not bear themselves like Abraham, Isaac, and Jacob, and all the prophets, figures of the faithful believers of the covenant and active servants of the Word that has inspired their life.

Instead, others will take their place at the "feast in the kingdom of heaven," coming from every corner of the world. By what right? Evidently their recognition by the master: they have done well.

This double proclamation of the exclusion of those who think they have a right to enter and the admission of others who may be surprised by the fact, recalls the passage from Matthew on the last judgment. There, too, some will be rejected for not having done what they ought, while others will receive the inheritance prepared "from the foundation of the world" for having done to the Lord what they did in serving those "least" ones who are his "brothers" (Matt 25:31-46—Christ the King, Year A).

The First and the Last

See how and why some who are last will be first and some who are first will be last.

> Listen to me, you who are few in number. I know well that many hear but few obey. I see the threshing-floor, I look for the wheat. It is hard to see the wheat when one is threshing, but it will soon be sifted out. If the saved are but few, it is only so relative to the great number of those who are lost; for their small number is, in itself, a great amount. When the winnower comes, holding his "winnowing fan in his hand. . . . he will clear his threshing floor and gather his wheat into the barn, but the chaff he will burn in unquenchable fire" (Matt 3:12).
>
> The mockery of the chaff cannot harm the wheat. This saying is true, it will lead no one into error. The amount of wheat may be great, but small in comparison to other multitudes. From this threshing floor will come enough wheat to fill the granary of heaven.
>
> Listen, my beloved, listen to what Scripture says: "I had a vision of a great multitude, which no one could count, from every nation, race, people, and tongue" (Rev 7:9). This is the wheat-pile of the saints.[46]

God wants all to be saved, every nation and tongue to gather around him to share in his glory. The prophetic oracle read at the beginning of this Sunday's liturgy insistently reaffirms that such is the plan of God.

This divine "project" has had its realization in Jesus Christ, who died at Jerusalem in order to reunite all the scattered children of God and to welcome them to the banquet table in the kingdom.

And yet, says Jesus, the gate is "narrow" and many will throw themselves uselessly at a "locked" door.

Is there a contradiction between the affirmation of a salvation open to all and the recollection of the demands that effectively limit or even close off access to it? Certainly not. On the one hand, God's call that he addresses to all with unwearying patience has always been linked to the call to faithfully observe the clauses of the covenant, the Law of the Lord. On the other hand, the Gospel is very clear: in order to have a share in the kingdom, one must accept self-denial, the need to be confronted with ordeals, even to be put to death with Christ.

But these demands do not merely place obstacles on the road to the promised glory. We must affirm the opposite, since we have been taught that everything, through the love of God who is and always shows himself to be a loving Father, can and must become a source of peace and joy. For even by means of the sufferings and deaths that are not willed by God and not imposed for our correction, a way is mysteriously opened to life.

The mystery of universal salvation: what is impossible for us is actually done by God. The mystery celebrated in the Eucharist frees us from sin and leads us toward the banquet hall in the kingdom, while we even now share in the Lord's Supper.

> Father in heaven,
> it is right that we should give you thanks and glory . . .
> Source of life and goodness, you have created all things,
> to fill your creatures with every blessing
>   and lead all men to the joyful vision of your light. . . .
>
> Even when [man] disobeyed you and lost your friendship
> you did not abandon him to the power of death,
>   but helped all men to seek and find you.
> Again and again you offered a covenant to man,
>   and through the prophets taught him to hope for salvation.
> Father, you so loved the world
>   that in the fullness of time you sent your
>   only Son to be our Savior.
> (Eucharistic Prayer IV)

The mystery that has been revealed to us, into which we enter through our celebration of it, we must proclaim so that all may hear the call.

> Come not alone to the feast of the kingdom;
> along your way, cry out the news:
> ''The promise is a bread given to be shared:
> God urges you to enter into one dwelling-place
> and gathers you in love.''
>
> *Jesus, hope of humanity,*
> *make us witnesses of your salvation.*
>
> I have come to bring fire on the earth,
> I want it to be spread and to burn.
>
> *Jesus, hope of humanity,*
> *make us witnesses of your salvation.*
>
> I have come that all might have life
> and have it to the full.
>
> *Jesus, hope of humanity,*
> *make us witnesses of your salvation.*
>
> I have come to seek for those who are lost,
> not as Judge but as Savior.
>
> *Jesus, hope of humanity,*
> *make us witnesses of your salvation.*[47]

The link—not apparent at first—between the Eighteenth, Nineteenth, Twentieth, and Twenty-first Sundays of Ordinary Time this year, has been revealed gradually. It is not a logically constructed sequence by modern literary standards. It is a progression set to the rhythm of Jesus' march to Jerusalem, an itinerary marked not by signposts on a map, but by Jesus' teachings along the way.

The teachings proclaimed in the liturgy from the Eighteenth to the Twenty-first Sunday are characterized by a deliberate gravity. They call the disciples to weigh the options and choose according to the end-goal of their life (Eighteenth Sunday), the return of their master (Nineteenth Sunday), the necessity of preferring no one to him (Twentieth Sunday); if the call to salvation is addressed to all, the gate to it is narrow and will not stay open by itself indiscriminately (Twenty-first Sunday).

In one way or another, the ''matter'' we find at the heart of each of these Sundays is about the end of all. This is what forms the internal coherence of the sequence.

The secondary personages that stand out from the crowd may change, but Jesus occupies the central place on every level. Not only because he is the one speaking, but because his words reveal himself.

No one can come close to his abandonment of riches for the sake of the whole human race, and because of his complete self-giving, he has gained the name that is above all other names and through which salvation is given for the glory of the Father (Eighteenth Sunday).

He is the master who even now invites to his table those servants who are vigilant in celebrating the liturgy, and who await his return (Nineteenth Sunday).

He has firmly adhered to the will of the Father who made him the sign of contradiction, undergoing the baptism of his passion, and who will raise him up, so that the whole world may be filled with the fire of his Spirit (Twentieth Sunday).

As the shepherd who leads his people, he is the door that opens onto the banquet hall in the kingdom; he has been sent to gather the scattered children of God. Fearless shepherd, he wants none of his lambs to be lost; he gave his life for all, even for those who refuse to hearken to his voice (Twenty-first Sunday).

These four Sundays form a sequence. But it is the totality of the mystery that we celebrate, traveling in the wake of the Lord, a stage of his journey to Jerusalem, a journey that is also ours.

From the Twenty-second to the Twenty-fourth Sunday in Ordinary Time

In the space of these three Sundays, we read a significant portion of chapter 14 and all of chapter 15 of Luke.[1] But we ought not simply to focus on the number of verses. More importantly, these two chapters contain eight of Jesus' parables, of which the Lectionary has retained six.[2]

Chapter 15—the parables on mercy—itself forms a whole: it is quite right for the Lectionary not to divide it up. It may be considered as a separate unit. But it is nonetheless true that the Gospel for the Twenty-second Sunday contains a parable that is set in the context of a meal, and that the Gospel of the Twenty-fourth Sunday—chapter 15—ends with a parable that speaks of another feast: that prepared by a father to celebrate his younger son's homecoming. This suggests that these three Sundays form their own sequence. Its framework is the great banquet at the end of time and the paradoxical conditions laid on those who wish to share in it.[3]

Twenty-second Sunday

God Raises the Humble

The first reading is taken from a book of "instruction and wisdom" whose author refers to himself as "son of (Ben) Sirach" (Sir 50:27): hence it is called the Book of Sirach.[4]

This "instruction" and "wisdom" are not merely speculative or theoretical; they are maxims that must guide the daily living-out of a well-ordered and fruitful life.

The book is a kind of "notebook" or "journal of the spiritual road" in which Ben Sirach "has gathered together the fruits of his experience and his meditation on the holy writings."[5] He has arranged his maxims by themes. Yet the progression from one to another can be rather loose, which is only typical of this "collection" genre, as one can see, for example, in Pascal's *Pensées* or, in a much different vein, La Rochefoucauld's *Maximes*.

The Lectionary has been able, without falsifying their meaning, to group six sayings on love and the search for humility (Sir 3:17-18, 20, 28-29). The first thing that strikes the reader is their forcefulness and density.

In All Things, Humility
One first notes that the author calls his interlocutor "my son."[6] Such a term is loaded with meaning. It is an invitation to adopt an attitude of attentiveness and humility—the attitude of a disciple—to the speaker. It urges an acceptance of his fatherly care. The term is used by certain spiritual masters, such as St. Benedict at the beginning of his Rule: "Listen, my son, to the teachings of the master." Whoever, at sometime or other, uses the expression "my son" or "my child" is aware of its rich connotations. Typically, whatever comes thus from an elder, one who is wise and generous, worthy of respect and attention, is not soon forgotten.

For Ben Sirach, humility is one of the fundamental attitudes of wisdom, a sure foundation for life.[7]

The humble man is better loved than a rich benefactor, who may be valued for his work but finds little affection for himself, especially if he is not "meek and humble of heart."

The humble take their proper place with respect to God. They find there true grandeur, and thus greater openness to new gifts, new graces: "My soul proclaims the greatness of the Lord . . . For he has looked upon his handmaid's lowliness . . . The Mighty One has done great things for me . . . The hungry he has filled with good things." Mary's *Magnificat* is the thanksgiving of all the humble as they give glory to God.

Contrast this with the condition of the proud: without remedy or hope of healing, they are afflicted with a deadly evil, a virus that corrupts their very being, a sin that is in itself blasphemous.[8]

The last verse of this reading might appear strange in comparison with what has been said. But on a closer look, one can see the value of this sketch (which, though roughly-drawn, still presents some very clear features) of "the wise man," the one who acts according to the truth of what he must be, endlessly meditating on and studying "the proverbs of wisdom." His ideal? To be "an ear of the heart," as St. Benedict says.[9] This is the proper attitude of the disciple that Jesus so often praised. One thinks immediately of Mary—the sister of Martha—seated at the feet of the Lord to hear his Word, whom Jesus said had chosen the better part;[10] of the beatitude: "blessed are they who hear the word of God and keep it";[11] of Jesus' mother who "treasured all these things and reflected on them in her heart."[12]

Humility—as the experience of Israel in the course of salvation history testifies—is openness to the splendor of God. The song of the humble is one of acknowledgement and thanksgiving to the God who draws them near to him.

> *God, in your goodness, you have made a home for the poor.*
>
> The just rejoice and exult before God;
> they are glad and rejoice.
> Sing to God, chant praise to his name;
>   whose name is the LORD.
>
> The father of orphans and the defender of widows
>   is God in his holy dwelling.
> God gives a home to the forsaken;
>   he leads forth prisoners to prosperity.
>
> A bountiful rain you showered down,
>   O God, upon your inheritance;
>   you restored the land when it languished;
> Your flock settled in it;
>   in your goodness, O God, you provided it for the needy.
> (Ps 68:4-5, 6-7, 10-11)

To Approach God Without Fear

This Sunday, we read the fourth and last excerpt this year from the Letter to the Hebrews (Heb 12:18-19, 22-24a).

This text is drawn from the last part of the Letter[13] that deserves, rather more than the others, the title "words of exhortation."[14] It imposes a set of demands on the Christian. These sayings are not meant to be regarded on the level of abstract morality, for they arise from the real situation of the disciples of Christ and the new spiritual relations in which they are established. This is what the passage we read today expresses.

As often occurs in the Letter to the Hebrews, the author underscores the difference between the present and an earlier situation. It is quite a contrast, since there no longer exists what characterized the first revelation and the earlier religious experience.

"Untouchable," says the Lectionary, whereas the *Jerusalem Bible* speaks of "nothing known to the senses."[15]

Then comes the evocation of something that has been consumed by fire. But the following allusions are clearer. They point to the descriptions of the revelation on Sinai.

Thus in Deuteronomy: "You came near and stood at the foot of the mountain, which blazed to the very sky with fire and was enveloped in a dense black cloud. Then the LORD spoke to you from the midst of the fire. You heard the sound of the words, but saw no form; there was only a voice" (Deut 4:11-12). In a still more detailed manner in the Book of Exodus: "On the morning of the third day there were peals of thunder and lightning, and a heavy cloud over the mountain, and a very loud trumpet blast, so that all the people in the camp trembled. Mount Sinai was all wrapped in smoke, for the LORD came down upon it in fire. The smoke rose from it as though from a furnace, and the whole mountain trembled violently. The trumpet blast grew louder and louder, while Moses was speaking and God answering him with thunder" (Exod 19:16, 18-19—Pentecost, Evening Vigil Mass). And again a little further on: "When the people witnessed the thunder and lightning, the trumpet blast and the mountain smoking, they all feared and trembled. So they took up a position much further away and said to Moses, "You speak to us, and we will listen; but let not God speak to us, or we shall die" (Exod 20:18-19).

God's approach was very restrained, as Scripture itself testifies. God said to Moses: "Set limits for the people all around the mountain . . .

Warn the people not to break through toward the LORD in order to see him; otherwise many of them will be struck down'' (Exod 19:12, 21).

With Jesus, ''the mediator of a new covenant,'' the whole situation and the resultant relationships with God are radically transformed. One comes to him without having to face manifestations that are outwardly terrifying, and to ''the city of the living God'' whose periphery is not marked with an uncrossable border.

''Come to,'' ''draw near,'' have ritual connotations: the priests ''go to'' the altar to make the sacrifices and perform the other prescribed rites (Lev 9:7-8; 21:17-23). This recalls baptism, and even more what is said of the coming to ''the assembly''—*ekklesia* (Church)—of the ''first-born,'' a title that recalls James' designation of the Christians as the ''firstfruits'' of God's creatures (Jas 1:18—Twenty-second Sunday, Year B).

In any case, the author focuses on the present condition of the Christians. It is of a spiritual order, a communion with the angels, with those ''enrolled in heaven,'' with the multitude of the ''spirits of just men made perfect.''

Fear has given way to joy that can only lead to an unrestrained yet humble generosity.

Table Talk

The first part of chapter 14 of Luke's Gospel (14:1-24) falls within the framework of a supper to which Jesus had been invited by ''one of the leading Pharisees.'' Most of the other guests are of the Pharisee and lawyer class, ''religious'' men, fervent practitioners with a sophisticated knowledge of the Law. The incident is not isolated in the Third Gospel, which, unlike the others, reports at least two other invitations of the same kind.[16] Luke has no systematic bias against the Pharisees. Was not Paul, his master, one of them and proud of the fact?[17] Perhaps the evangelist's radicalism inclines him to a certain degree of admiration for these rigorous observers of the Law: Ah! if only they could be converted like Saul of Tarsus! In any case, Luke wants to emphasize that Jesus was quite ready to bring them salvation. Indeed, he takes care not to implicate them in Jesus' death (see the Thirty-first and Thirty-second Sundays).

Luke recounts several table scenes.[18] One cannot read them without thinking of what they evoke in the Bible and for the Christian: the community at table, the sharing of food, and, finally, participation in the heavenly banquet in the kingdom, of which the Eucharist is the sacrament.[19]

It was thus at the house of "one of the leading Pharisees" that Jesus speaks what we have called "table talk," which is not limited to a collection of "catch phrases." The Gospel this Sunday recalls a portion of it (Luke 14:1a, 7-14).

This is not an ordinary meal: it takes place "on a sabbath." Did the Pharisee meet Jesus at the synagogue service and invite him to join his guests, Pharisees and lawyers, for the supper that had been prepared? It is possible, since, as we know, Jesus regularly went to the synagogue on the Sabbath.[20]

The Choice of Seats

On entering his host's house to share in the meal, Jesus sees that the guests all choose the best seats.

We do not regard this fact indignantly, even if the evangelist elsewhere speaks of the Pharisees as coveting honors.[21] After all, they were notable people: they would normally be seated in the highest places. Even if we don't dash for the chairs, none of us is surprised if we are seated in a place of honor at a supper to which we have been invited. It would be wrong to demand a place at the head of the table, or, even worse, to act out a show of humility, taking a lower place while knowing perfectly well that someone will make us move higher.[22]

> We often say that we are nothing, the worst of men, the world's refuse. But we would be sorry to have someone take us at our word or to spread our own account of ourselves. On the contrary, we make a show of retreating and hiding, so that someone may run after us and seek us out; we pretend to want to be the last, seated at the foot of the table, but only in order to move "humbly" to the head. True humility makes no pretense and speaks in no tone of humility. For it desires not merely to hide the other virtues, but first and foremost to hide itself . . . Thus my opinion, Philotheus, is, let us mouth no humble phrases, or speak them with a true interior sentiment, in conformity with what we proclaim outwardly; let us not cast down our eyes without humbling our hearts, let us only seem to wish to be last if we have the real desire for it. I hold this rule to be so general as to admit of no exception; I only add that civility requires us sometimes to give the better place to those who clearly would not take it; this has no mark of duplicity or false humility, for the offer of advantage is the beginning of honor, and since we cannot give them the whole of it, we do well by giving them the beginning. I might speak some words of honor or respect that might not seem really true, but they are nonetheless so, provided that the heart of the one who pronounces them truly intends to honor and respect the one for whom he says them. For while the words exaggerate what we

mean, it is not evil to use them when common usage requires it. True, I would wish that the words might be in accord with our affections, as closely as possible, in order to follow always and everywhere the rule of simplicity and cordial candor.[23]

It is clearly not this that is at issue here. Jesus, to whom his host undoubtedly gave not only a place of honor but the first place, offers no banal wisdom, no elementary lesson in proper behavior. Luke would certainly not have troubled to remember this episode if it had no other significance.

One notes first of all that, in the parable, it is not just any meal, but a wedding banquet. This detail is important. It is, in fact, the first and decisive key for a proper reading and understanding of the parable.

If every supper evokes for the believer the "Table of the Lord"—both of the Eucharist and the kingdom—a wedding banquet, especially when Jesus speaks of it and the evangelist records it as such, is an unambiguous reference to the "eternal wedding feast." The parable is unquestionably to be understood in this perspective.

If there is some lingering doubt, if one is tempted to regard it as a very simple, basic parable, the final proclamation will suffice: "For everyone who exalts himself shall be humbled, but the one who humbles himself shall be exalted."

The use of the passive is characteristically biblical: it allows one to refer the action to God—he who will humble and exalt—without pronouncing his ineffable name.

This dictum is found in several locations in the Gospels.[24] It must have made a deep impression on the minds of the first disciples who understood it to be a principle of life that conforms to the will of God.

"Everyone who exalts himself shall be humbled, but the one who humbles himself shall be exalted" is, in the context of this "table talk," a teaching about the kingdom of God and the revelation, by Jesus, of the path by which it must be entered.

Actually, biblical tradition already knew it. This is what one reads in Psalm 147:6: "The LORD sustains the lowly; the wicked he casts to the ground." And, in the New Testament, the *Magnificat*, gospel fulfillment, precious echo of the best biblical spiritual tradition: "He has thrown down the rulers from their thrones but lifted up the lowly" (Luke 1:52).

And yet Jesus has particularly insisted on this "law of the kingdom" that he has come to preach, to which he grants access. The Gospels speak of it forcefully: "For the one who is least among all of you is the one who is the greatest" (Luke 9:48).

Is it a "law of the kingdom," therefore, confirmed by the sovereign authority of Jesus? Yes, certainly; but even more, this saying turns our attention to the one who proclaims it, in whom it has its complete fulfillment.

"He *humbled himself*, becoming obedient to death, even death on a cross. *Because* of this, God *greatly exalted* him" (Phil 2:8-9).

St. Augustine spoke of humility as a "sign of Christ," an expression to be understood in its strongest sense: at once a "sign" that reveals Christ and allows the Christian to recognize him as by the seal of authority; which points to a greater, invisible reality—the kingdom—like a sacrament. After washing his disciples' feet at the Last Supper, Jesus told them to follow his example (John 13:15).

> Jesus Christ is a God whom one approaches without pride, before whom one may humble oneself without despair.[25]

Reading and re-reading this parable reveals another significant feature. Jesus does not address himself directly to the guests whom he saw choose the highest seats. Surely, this is not merely out of delicacy, not wishing to offend them while offering a lesson. The formulation in the second person—"When you are invited . . . do not recline at table in the place of honor . . . [instead] go and take the lowest place so that when the host comes to you he may say . . ."—gives the parable general significance, and indicates that it is not addressed only to those who heard it first. Such a formulation is familiar to us, since a number of proverbs use a similar "you."

To Choose One's Guests Well

Jesus then turns to the man who had invited him. Nevertheless, he gives—under an imperative form!—a teaching, a warning that does not merely apply to his interlocutor "that day." The "you" has the same significance it had in the parable. Jesus is speaking not only of the meal in which he is participating, but a lunch or a dinner, which means *every* lunch or *every* dinner. He is not rebuking his host, who not only invited his rich friends and relatives but also Jesus and perhaps at least some of his disciples.

The supper is taken as the most concrete expression of a broader welcoming of others. It would be absurd to interpret Jesus as saying: "Share your meal with anyone except your friends, fellows, relatives." And likewise: "Accept invitations only if they do not come from them." Not only is it absurd, it is in contradiction to what Jesus himself did. He ate in Peter's home: the Gospel recalls the day when the apostle's mother-in-law was sick with a strong fever. Jesus healed her and, "she got up immediately and waited on them" (Luke 4:38-39). He went to his friends' home in Bethany where, one day, he took part in a meal that was truly remarkable because Lazarus, whom he had raised from the dead, was one of the diners (John 12:1-11). He sat at the table of the rich: Zacchaeus (Luke 19:1-10), Levi the tax-collector (Luke 5:29-32), some Pharisees. He himself secretly prepared a last meal that he shared with his disciples (Luke 22:7-14). Nor should we forget the invitation he accepted from the two disciples at Emmaus (Luke 24:28-30) and the meal prepared on the lakeshore by the resurrected Christ for Simon Peter and his companions (John 21:9-14).

What Jesus says about one's choice of guests is valuable always and everywhere; it applies in every situation, with the invitation to dine being exemplary.[26]

Nothing about this teaching is even remotely reminiscent of a precept of human wisdom, a lesson in good manners. It is a paradox that comes from the Gospel itself, for Jesus' commandment goes counter to human wisdom, to all polite behavior.

To receive into one's communion—to invite to one's table—to love totally, not only without calculating personal gain, but in a totally disinterested manner. To turn resolutely toward "beggars and the crippled, the lame and the blind," all those who have nothing to give in return, who are deemed to be of no account, who are even excluded from participation in worship (Lev 21:18). Such is Jesus' commandment, diametrically opposed to human law and wisdom.

It would be an outrageous demand, unthinkable, impossible to take seriously, if it did not come from Jesus, if it had not been taken seriously throughout the centuries by an uninterrupted line of disciples, if it were not an imitation of God himself who grants us the grace to begin this road and to follow it to its end, the joy "at the resurrection of the dead."

Once more, it is no law that Jesus gives us in a distant way. He does not say merely: "Follow my example," but "Understand who I am, why I act thus. If you are my disciples, become what you are, Christians in the true sense of the name, this beautiful name that has been given you and which you bear. Children of God, imitate the conduct of your Father, of your family. There, and there alone, is found imperishable happiness."

Jesus, the Son of God who reveals the Father, makes himself, without reservation, without waiting for anything in return, the friend of the weak, the poor, the disinherited, the sick who need a doctor, even if they are filled with earthly goods; he does so to the point of giving his life. For, if he had one thought of avoiding death, he could act differently, in such a way that one day, in Jerusalem where he handed himself over, the crowd would prefer him to Barabbas.

One can imagine him to be speaking of himself when he says:

> If you [only] love those who love you, what credit is that to you? Even sinners love those who love them. If you do good [only] to those who do good to you, how can you claim any credit? Even sinners do the same. If you lend [only] to those from whom you expect repayment, what credit [is] that to you? Even sinners lend to sinners, and get back the same amount. Love your enemies and do good to them, and lend expecting nothing back; then your reward will be great and you will be children of the Most High, for he himself is good to the ungrateful and the wicked (Luke 6:32-35—Seventh Sunday).

In any case, these are words that the disciples must always have in their hearts and souls, in their thoughts, written over the doorways of their houses. And the Eucharistic celebration must clearly witness that such is the law of the Christian community, above all when it is gathered for the Supper par excellence.

Such, alas, is not the case! Those who watch us often say that it is nothing like that, and they are scandalized in terms that strangely recall those of the Letter of James:

> For if a man with gold rings on his fingers and in fine clothes comes into your assembly, and a poor person in shabby clothes also comes in, and you pay attention to the one wearing the fine clothes and say, "Sit here, please," while you say to the poor one, "Stand there," or "Sit at my feet," have you not made distinctions among yourselves and become judges with evil designs?" (Jas 2:2-4—Twenty-third Sunday).

St. Paul was no less severe in speaking of assemblies divided by the way they made account of individuals: "Your meetings are doing more harm than good . . . when you meet in one place, then, it is not to eat the Lord's Supper" (1 Cor 11:17, 20).

From this "table talk," which we recall today, to the last instructions given by Jesus at the Last Supper, throughout all his teaching and life, there is perfect continuity.

> When the hour came, he took his place at table with the apostles. . . . He said to them, "The kings of the Gentiles lord it over them and those in

authority over them are addressed as 'Benefactors'; but among you it shall not be so. Rather, let the greatest among you be as the youngest, and the leader as the servant. For who is greater: the one seated at table or the one who serves? Is it not the one seated at table? I am among you as the one who serves'' (Luke 22:1, 25-27—Passion [Palm] Sunday).

Charles de Foucauld said that Jesus took the last place for himself so well that no one could ever take it from him. But we know that because of this, he was exalted to the right hand of the Father in the inaccessible glory that belongs to him as Son.

And yet, he allows us to share in it by traveling, with him, a similar paschal road.

Baptized into his death and resurrection, we have ''drawn near to God,'' and ''to Jesus, the mediator of a new covenant'' who is open to the poor, the lame, the blind, and those sick with every illness that requires a doctor.

We have no right to raise or thrust ourselves into the places of honor. But God's strength is great, and it is on his grace that we rely: ''He exalts the humble,'' he seats them at his Table and, showing them the example, he, the Master, goes among them as a servant.

> Happy are those who are called to the Lord's Supper.
> Happy are those who will eat at the feast in the kingdom of God!
> Lord, I am not worthy to receive you, but only say the word, and I shall be healed.

Take Up the Cross, Renounce All Goods

Even after long and careful rereading, the demands of the gospel surprise or even shock us. They are so contrary to established human wisdom! They promote attitudes and ways of acting so opposite to our most common behavior! Shouldn't they be modified, nuanced in such a way as to be acceptable? To do so would be to appeal to basic casuistry: "Yes, but . . . rigid principles must be flexible in their concrete application."

Yet, it is in every sphere of action that these demands come into play. Besides, the gospel does not merely preach, abstractly, some general principles. It always envisages concrete situations: the choice of seats at table, for instance, or the guests that one should invite to one's supper (last Sunday's Gospel). The principles it lays out are to be applied both when convenient and inconvenient. Ultimately, the gospel poses these demands as essential conditions for having a share in the kingdom, for being truly happy.

It is impossible, consequently, to evade these obstacles, to sneak through by subterfuge and subtlety. The workings of the mind of God are beyond the capacity of our knowledge.

The Secrets of God
The first reading this Twenty-third Sunday says as much: "For what man knows God's counsel, or who can conceive what the Lord intends?" A negative response cannot be long in coming. Thus, there is no reason to be surprised if we, left to ourselves, are incapable of acknowledging as wisdom what seems to us to be absurdity (Wis 9:13-18).

The reflections—the thoughts—of mortals are weak, timid, narrow, tenuous. How could it be otherwise? We must reckon with the weight of the body, which keeps us from being lifted to the heights of God. Through "this earthen shelter," we belong to the earth. The flesh keeps us from concentrating completely on spiritual realities, solicited as we are by a multitude of earthly and contingent cares. We cannot even reach a true understanding of what falls within the senses, those things that are "within our grasp."

The author of the Book of Wisdom speaks like those philosophers who have meditated on the complete vanity of human intellectual efforts, like scientists who know that every new discovery shatters previous limits, that their explanations cannot lead one to understand, much less fully to grasp, the profound reality of people and things.

Yet the believer does not give in to extreme pessimism. The Christian is not hemmed in by a jaded view which says that the human mind, despite its intelligence and even genius, despite its ever-increasing knowledge, in the end knows only a very little of reality and is fundamentally incapable of attaining any certitude that does not rest on the "givens" of immediate experience and finds its verification there.

> For what is man in nature? Nothing with respect to infinity, everything with respect to nothing, a middle-ground between nothing and everything. Infinitely far from comprehending the extremes, the end and beginning of things must for him remain hidden in impenetrable secrecy; he is equally incapable of seeing the nothing from which he is drawn and the infinity in which he is swallowed up.
>
> What can he do, then, but perceive an appearance of the middle of things, in an eternal despair of knowing their beginning and their end? All things come from nothing and are borne to infinity. Who will trace these astonishing paths? The author of these marvels understands them. No one else can do so.[27]

The believer knows, both through faith and experience, that God has "given Wisdom and sent his holy spirit from on high." Thanks to this gift, we can attain a greater, transcendent knowledge. The revelation of this wisdom, "mysterious, hidden," enables us to understand what "eye has not seen, and ear has not heard, and what has not entered the human heart" (1 Cor 2:7-9—Sixth Sunday, Year A). This understanding comes not in a distant, speculative manner, but through the experience of faith and a holy life.

> Who will follow the Most High in his inexpressible and incomprehensible being? Who will examine the depths of God? Who will dare to draw the eternal origin of the universe? Who will pride himself on his knowledge of the infinite God who fills and surrounds, penetrates and surpasses, embraces and flies from everything, "whom no human being has ever seen or can see" (1 Tim 6:16), as he is in himself?
>
> Let no one have the presumption to plumb the impenetrable depth of God, the what, the how, the why of his being. This can be neither expressed, nor examined, nor penetrated. Believe simply, but firmly, that God is as he has been and will ever be, for he is immutable.

Therefore, search for the highest knowledge not in discussion but in leading a perfect life, not by the tongue but by the faith that springs from a simple heart and is not the product of clever constructions. If you search for the ineffable through reasoning, it will certainly be far from you; if through faith, wisdom will remain where it dwells: at your door (cf. Prov 1:21); and where it stays it can perhaps see, though only a part. In truth, it is attained the instant one believes in the invisible without yet understanding it.[28]

In its light, one discovers that "the foolishness of God is wiser than human wisdom" (1 Cor 1:25—Third Sunday of Lent, Year B).

Instead of wandering lost in an exitless labyrinth, we can forge ahead on the paths "made straight." Having learned "what was God's pleasure," we "were saved by Wisdom."

Heard in the context of the liturgy, this passage from the Book of Wisdom can reawaken an awareness of the absolute necessity of the gift of the Spirit. Believers, especially when they celebrate the Holy Mysteries, do not think of their poverty, the weakness of their intellect that must be turned toward God "their refuge through all generations." Psalm 90 is not a despairing complaint, but a hopeful prayer.

In every age, O LORD, you have been our refuge.

You turn man back to dust,
  saying, "Return, O children of men."
For a thousand years in your sight
  are as yesterday, now that it is past,
  or as a watch of the night.

You make an end of them in their sleep;
  the next morning they are like the changing grass,
Which at dawn springs up anew,
  but by evening wilts and fades.

Teach us to number our days aright,
  that we may gain wisdom of heart.
Return, O LORD! How long?
  Have pity on your servants!

Fill us at daybreak with your kindness,
  that we may shout for joy and gladness all our days.
And may the gracious care of the LORD our God be ours;
  prosper the work of our hands for us!
  [Prosper the work of our hands!]
(Ps 90: 3-4, 5-6, 12-13, 14, 17)

Christians can go still further. They have learned that "the heavenly Father give[s] the Holy Spirit to those who ask him" (Luke

11:13—Eighteenth Sunday). They remember that one day Jesus "rejoiced [in] the holy Spirit and said: 'I give you praise, Father, Lord of heaven and earth, for although you have hidden these things from the wise and the learned you have revealed them to the childlike' " (Luke 10:21). In a similar moment of exultation, the Christian, turned toward the One who has revealed to the faithful the Father and the secrets of the kingdom, prays in thanksgiving.

> Who can understand the speech of the stars,
> who can surprise the music of souls,
> who will know a heart free enough
> to know the Word of Life?

> The one in whom your Spirit dwells, Lord,
> receives the secrets of the Father.

> Happy the man whose eye
> traverses the invisible
> to seek your face.

> Happy the man whose mind
> discovers wisdom
> in the folly of the cross.

> Happy the man
> whose heart you fill
> as his first love.

> The one in whom your Spirit dwells, Lord,
> receives the secrets of the Father.[29]

Of Your Own Will, Do What Is Good

From the grand heights of such reflections, we move to a very concrete question in the text from the Letter to Philemon that forms the second reading today (Phlm 9b-10, 12-17).

This is a letter written for a specific occasion. It is the shortest of St. Paul's epistles and therefore could be understood as a personal note.[30] Though addressed to Philemon, however, it is sent to two other people as well—"Apphia our sister, to Archippus, our fellow soldier"—and to the church at the house of the beloved friend and co-worker of the apostle. Moreover, "Timothy our brother" is explicitly mentioned as co-sender (Phlm 1). Thus it is not so different from Paul's other, longer letters.

The Lectionary retains the essential, central section of the message.[31]

It is impossible not to appreciate the well-ordered composition of the text, the choice of expressions, the spirit, even the humor of the apostle, his tact and delicacy, his way of entreating Philemon that kindness might not be forced on him but might be freely bestowed. "Although I have the full right in Christ to order you to do what is proper, I rather urge you out of love" (vv. 8-9a). How could one not be touched, even today, by such a letter written by Paul, when, "an old man," he was a "prisoner for Christ Jesus"?

But the chief interest of the letter lies elsewhere. The apostle harbored an escaped slave, while he himself was in captivity! This was a crime. On his part, the slave risked punishment and prison. Paul convinced him to return to his master. But in the meantime, Onesimus was converted, and the apostle, through baptism, brought him to new life.

This baptism does not change the social condition of the slave. Paul, quite naturally, did not envisage this as a possibility. He certainly did write that in Christ "there is neither slave nor free person" (Gal 3:28—Twelfth Sunday), but such unity of the sons of God does not belong to the social order, even if the new relationships that it establishes will always tend toward equality in dignity and law.[32]

We know better than to be shocked at seeing the apostle act, in some way, in conformity with his time. We live in an age that no longer tolerates slavery, that is eager to establish human rights for everyone. How is it, then, that Christians, individually and as a community, are not always and unequivocally the defenders of those who, despite the many laws and declarations of rights, remain enslaved, or at least oppressed, treated as second-class people, with no way to exercise the rights with which they are theoretically and officially endowed? How is it possible that, after twenty centuries, societies formed in the cradle of Christianity remain so much bound by the law of class warfare? We admire Paul's letter to Philemon. How would we react to such a letter?

In the context of the liturgy this Sunday, one learns that fidelity to the gospel entails certain things that seem entirely unreasonable: compromising oneself when human wisdom suggests remaining aloof; placing renewed confidence in one who has just betrayed us; believing in the sincerity of a conversion that may well seem "convenient," or circumstantial; receiving as "a beloved brother" whom "you will know both as a man and in the Lord" someone to whom one owes nothing, who indeed has been the cause of personal injury.

Conformity to such standards does not, for the Christian, arise from a sense of morality, but an adherence to a person, communion with him. There is only one explanation, one justification: it is done "because of Christ Jesus."

Prefer Nothing to Christ

"To be my disciple" implies radical choices, says Jesus in the Gospel (Luke 14:25-33).

These demands, grouped by Luke in a new section of the "journey to Jerusalem," are consistent with the "table talk" read last Sunday.[33] There, it was a question of the only behavior proper to the feast in the kingdom. Here, the focus is the "price of grace" that the disciple pays, which is the bond with the Master. We are still clearly dealing with the concrete choices of life.

> Costly grace is the treasure hidden in the field: for its sake, the man gladly goes and sells all he has; it is the pearl of great value. For it, the merchant sells all his goods; it is the kingdom of Christ. Therefore the man plucks out his eye which is an occasion of sin; it is the call of Jesus Christ. Hearing it, the disciple leaves his nets and follows.
>
> Costly grace is the gospel that must ever be sought; it is the gift for which one must ask, it is the door at which one must knock.
>
> It is costly because it calls for obedience; it is grace because it calls for obedience to Jesus Christ; it is costly because it may cost a man his life; it is grace because only thus is man brought to new life; it is costly because it condemns sins; it is grace because it justifies the sinner. It is costly grace most of all because it has cost God dearly, because it has cost God the life of his Son—"You have been bought at a great price"—because what has been costly for God cannot be cheap for us. It is grace most of all because God did not regard his son as too precious for our life, but gave him for us. Costly grace is the incarnation of God.[34]

It is to the crowds that Jesus turns and speaks: "a great crowd was with Jesus."

Luke focuses particular attention on this multitude that followed Jesus everywhere in his endless wanderings. Such popular enthusiasm says a great deal: the insignificant people—poor, sick, downtrodden—spontaneously recognize in Jesus a Master not like others: one who is close to them, concerned with their hopes. We know that at the beginning of his ministry Jesus had solemnly proclaimed, in the synagogue at Nazareth, that "today" was accomplished the word of Scripture:

> The spirit of the Lord is upon me,
>   because he has anointed me
>   to bring glad tidings to the poor.
> He has sent me to proclaim liberty to captives
>   and recovery of sight to the blind,
>   to let the oppressed go free,
>   and to proclaim a year acceptable to the Lord"
> (Luke 4:18-19—Third Sunday).

But Jesus is no demagogue, intoxicated with popular success, who incites the crowds to follow him blindly, not knowing where he leads them, seducing them by the promise of riches near at hand. Rather, he "turns" in order to tell us, abruptly and straightforwardly, what following him entails. One cannot simply walk a stretch of the road with him, letting him go on alone or with others the rest of the way to Jerusalem. In order to be his disciple, one must follow him to the very end, not stopping along the way, as if one could pick and choose among his teachings.

Yet there is nothing of the elitist about this. He speaks to everyone, knowing from experience that the great are no more likely to receive his message: "I give you praise, Father, Lord of heaven and earth, for although you have hidden these things from the wise and the learned, you have revealed them to the childlike" (Luke 10:21).

"If anyone comes to me without hating his father and mother . . ."! Right away, this way of speaking brings to our eyes the serene majesty of Jesus' person, that no image or icon can imitate.

At the same time, we see the condition of the disciple with its unique dimension of personal attachment to the one who speaks in this way. Who else could call for this kind of allegiance? To be committed thus to another person would be immoral and unworthy of our human dignity.

"Without hating . . ."! This phrase must be understood in the strongest sense of a preference at once deliberate, absolute, complete, and deserving. It is a "devotion," that is to say an unconditional consecration in the person of Jesus.[35]

The radical nature of this exclusive attachment is more accentuated by the examples which follow: "without hating his father and mother, wife and children, brothers and sisters, and even his own life."

Neither Jesus nor Luke ignores the commandment of the Decalogue on love and duty toward one's kin. Jesus speaks of it to the man who asks him: "Good teacher, what must I do to inherit eternal life?" (Luke 18:18-20).

The demand would lose its force if the one who proclaimed it did not hold in the highest esteem love for father, mother, wife, children, brothers, and sisters.[36]

Jesus truly loved his relatives, his friends, and even his enemies. But only devotion to the Father and his will had, for him, an absolute value. Because he had to be in his Father's house, one day when he was twelve years old he abandoned his parents, who were most anxious at not finding him among their company after the pilgrimage to Jerusalem (Luke

2:41-51—Feast of St. Joseph and the Holy Family). Later, during the course of his ministry, he continued to teach those who would listen to him, while his family was outside, asking to see him (Luke 8:19-21).

Finally, he preferred obedience to the will of the Father and fidelity to his mission to his own life.

To be his disciple is to be devoted to him as he himself is devoted to the Father, toward whom he draws us. There is no other way, for Jesus himself is the Way.

To be his disciple sometimes involves painful conflicts; not only during times of persecution but also, for example, when one must respond to a vocation, a call, and prefer Christ to all those around one.

The Christian life is full of trials, events marked by constraint, uneasiness and suffering. For ages we have spoken of the "cross." In the figurative sense, "to bear one's cross" means to submit to the divine will by generously, even heroically, accepting these various trials as a sharing in the cross of Christ.

For the Christian, then as now, "to bear one's cross" has a very concrete meaning. The expression evokes the image of Christ, the man of sorrows, walking toward Calvary while staggering under the weight of the instrument of his torment. This is particularly true when, faced with the cross that dominates the altar, one celebrates the mystery of the death and resurrection of Christ.[37]

One must also renounce "all one's goods." The importance of this detachment in Luke's eyes is obvious. His ideal is, if not voluntary poverty and destitution, at least the sharing of goods so that they not become master to the person. "You cannot," he says, "serve God and mammon." (Luke 16:13—Twenty-fifth Sunday). "Sell your belongings and give alms" and provide an "inexhaustible treasure in heaven" (Luke 12:33—Nineteenth Sunday).

When in Acts he describes the model Christian community, Luke points out that the faithful had "all things in common"; they would sell their property and possessions and divide them among all according to each one's need" (Acts 2:44-45—Second Sunday of Easter, Year A). And again: "No one claimed that any of his possessions was his own, but they had everything in common. . . . There was no needy person among them, for those who owned property or houses would sell them, bring the proceeds of the sale, and put them at the feet of the apostles, and they were distributed to each according to need" (Acts 4:32, 34-35—Second Sunday of Easter, Year B).

Here again—and we must constantly emphasize the point—this demand turns our attention to Jesus, who stripped himself of everything, even his grandeur as Son of God, to share in our human condition, to give himself to us, to allow us to participate in his status as Son, in his inheritance and glory (Phil 2:6-11—Passion Sunday).

To be Jesus' disciple is to prefer him to each and every thing, and to be ready to share with others one's material, intellectual, and spiritual goods.

> Jesus breaks away from his disciples to enter into his agony; we must break with those closest to us to imitate him.
>
> Jesus being in agony and the greatest pain, let us pray at even greater length.
>
> We implore the mercy of God, not so that he will leave us peacefully in our vices, but so that he will deliver us from them.
>
> If God gave us masters from his hand, oh! how we must willingly obey them! Necessity and events come infallibly therefrom.
>
> "Be comforted; you would not seek me if you had not found me."
>
> "I thought of you in my agony, I sweated drops of blood for you."
>
> "It is tempting me more than testing yourself, if you imagine that you would act in such and such a way in the face of something that has not occurred: if it happens, I myself will act in you."
>
> "Let my rules guide you; see how I have guided the Virgin and the saints who have let me act in them."
>
> "The Father loves everything that I do."
>
> "Do you want it always to cost me the blood of my humanity, without shedding tears yourself?"[38]

Every Christian, no matter with what situation and personal vocation, must take as plain fact: "Anyone who does not take up his cross and follow me cannot be my disciple. . . . In the same way, none of you can be my disciple if he does not renounce all his possessions."

It is inescapable, for Jesus clearly announced the demands that devolve on the disciples. This is the meaning of the two parables on the man who wishes to build a tower and the king who starts a war.

Every master worthy of the name warns those who would take a vow. Thus, for example, St. Benedict, a worthy representative of the spiritual tradition. One does not receive into the novitiate someone who all of a sudden desires to join.[39] Far from opening the door to him at his first request, he is dismissed so as to learn the seriousness of his desire, admitting him only if, in spite of everything, he perseveres in his request.[40] He is informed of all the demands of the monastic life (*omnis dura et aspera per quae itur ad Deum).* So that he may realize what he is getting himself into, he reads the *Rule* first, and at the end of two months he is told: "This is the law under which you will have to live. If you can observe it, enter; if not, you are free to leave." After a second reading of the *Rule*, he is posed the same question, six months later. A third reading over the next four months. It is only at the end of a year of reflection and becoming aware of the demands of the monk's life, that the novice is allowed to commit himself.

Here, however, the situation is not quite the same, insofar as this Gospel is not read to candidates for baptism, but the assembly of the baptized.

One might expect that these two parables would end with a standard formula: "Like the man building the tower or the king starting a war, reflect carefully before committing yourself." Instead, Jesus says: "In the same way, none of you can be my disciple if he does not renounce all his possessions."

The evangelist thus reveals that these sayings are for those who, like us, have already become disciples of Christ, and not the crowds who wonder if they should commit themselves. These sayings, then, are for the baptized, not merely catechumens or those who wonder if they should take the decisive step.

All our lives we must become disciples and, consequently, we must reflect constantly on the demands of this state. Not as a kind of looking back, but so that we may always go forward.

After all, we know perfectly well that we do not have enough to pay the price, to go the distance, nor the strength needed to defeat the adversary.[41]

But we also know that the Spirit is given to us, and thus the grace that leads to doing good, to "hold fast till the end" of our vocation, to meet all requirements: to bear the cross of the disciple and renounce all our goods.

The designs and secrets of God have been revealed by the gift of Wisdom and the sending of the Holy Spirit. Knowing what is pleasing to God, we know the paths that lead to salvation.

This journey is not one of moral conduct determined by principles and rules assumed come what may. For the road that leads to salvation is a person, Jesus, the Christ. It is he whom the disciple follows, to whom he attaches himself. The disciple prefers him to each and every person, "indeed his very self." He marches behind, bearing the cross and, like Jesus, he renounces all his goods. This cannot be confused with a starry-eyed romanticism, an impulsive attachment that ends up being short-lived or conditional.

It is a radical and total choice that involves all of one's life and being. It is a calling into question of the ties that bind us to each other. For "there is neither Jew nor Greek, there is neither slave nor free person, there is not male or female"; we are one in Christ Jesus whom we follow together.

Twenty-fourth Sunday

Entering into the Joy of the Forgiving God

The Twenty-second and Twenty-third Sundays have reminded us of the demands made of the disciple. But however concrete the examples and applications offered by Jesus may be, he is never speaking solely on the level of morality.

From the very first, the central point in view is participation in the kingdom and the banquet that God prepares for his people. The "table talk" begins to trace the features of the speaker, Jesus, he who has taken the lowest place and has, because of this, been exalted in glory; he who has come to invite "beggars and the crippled, the lame and the blind" to share in the joy of the good news.

Likewise, the person of Jesus is in the forefront of what he then says to the crowds. He speaks of following him, being his disciple and, because of that, preferring him to everything else, "taking up one's cross and following him."

With chapter 15 of Luke's Gospel, proclaimed in its entirety this Sunday, the progression reaches its peak. Three parables reveal the Father who finds joy in forgiving; they invite us to share God's joy when his lost son returns.

This Sunday the Lectionary includes three excerpts from the First Letter of Paul to Timothy.[42] This letter, together with the Second Letter to Timothy and the Letter to Titus, are called the "pastoral" letters because they primarily contain instructions for the "pastors" of the Church.[43]

God's Forgiveness and the Prayer of Moses

The first reading recalls the episode of the golden calf, more specifically, the prayer of Moses that prompted God's forgiveness (Exod 32:7-11, 13-14).

The golden calf is typically referred to today as the symbol of wealth, wealth that is adored and to which one sacrifices everything. But this interpretation bespeaks a complete misreading of the story.

True, the incident has been altered through various retellings. Josephus, the famous Jewish historian (35-95), omitted it from his *Jewish Antiquities* out of a fear that anti-Jewish feeling in some pagan circles would make use of it. He merely mentioned the people's anxiety as they waited for Moses' return, and their joy when he came down from Sinai.

Stephen, in his speech recorded in Acts (7:39-43), used the story of the golden calf polemically: "He it was whom our fathers would not obey; rather, they thrust him aside and longed to return to Egypt. 'Make us gods that will be our leaders,' they said to Aaron. . . . It was then that they fashioned the calf and offered sacrifice to the idol, and had a festive celebration over the product of their own hands. But God turned away from them and abandoned them to the worship of the galaxies in the heavens" (Acts 7:39-40, 41-42).

Some years later—c. 117-130—an anonymous Christian author went even further.[44] For him, the episode of the golden calf was the end of the fidelity of the Jews; everything that came after illustrates this original apostasy. He wrote: "Did God make the covenant with the people as he promised the patriarchs? . . . Of course he did! But they were not worthy to receive it because of their sins. . . . Moses received the covenant, but they were not worthy of it."[45] This, understandably, provoked responses from rabbis, other interpretations, and new controversies.

Outrageous charges, naive reconstructions, embarrassed excuses that do no justice to the story: in short, a "good," or rather a painful example of twisting and turning the meaning of a text so that it can be used as an argument in an ill-willed quarrel. It is worth the trouble to recall the pernicious use that has been made of the text in order to guard against doing the same ourselves.[46]

In any case, it is Moses' prayer that is found at the center of the first reading today. And there, we have no need to hedge: it is a model of intercession and faith.

Moses does not argue the facts or rely on possibly extenuating circumstances; he appeals to the Lord as Lord.

God said: "Go down at once to your people, whom you brought out of the land of Egypt, for they have become depraved." Moses responds, in effect, "My people, that I, Moses, brought out of Egypt? No, Lord, you know that this is your people, that you, not I, have led them; you freed them with great power and a strong hand."

To speak thus is not the trick of an advocate or a timely declaration of humility so as to reject or share in the responsibility for what has happened. It is a proclamation of the faithfulness of the divine election that nothing can attenuate, and the indissoluble tie that it has established between God and "his people."[47] A rebellious child is still a child. Neither sin nor any possible repudiation can change this: "You are the one who has brought them forth!"

The intercession is all the more powerful since it is deeply rooted in faith, appealing more explicitly to God himself, faithful to his promise, to his "oath." God would not be God if he contradicted himself. Shall he make another covenant with Abraham's descendants, while forgetting Abraham, Isaac, and Jacob? But a new infidelity on the people's part would bring that into question too! Where will it end? Will there be an endless cycle, from promise to repudiation to a new promise? Could all these new beginnings lead anywhere? Is the ideal a pure people? Such possibilities deceive and tempt us, but not God.

It is a model of prayer and intercession, for it does not pretend to remind God of something he has forgotten; nor is it a defensive plea that looks for excuses or argues for extenuating circumstances. It is, from beginning to end, a confession of God; a filial prayer that finds in God himself its assurance, in "a merciful and gracious God, slow to anger and rich in kindness and fidelity" (Exod 34:6). And it is also a confession of the true human condition: pardoned sinfulness.

It is quite appropriate that the liturgy proposes, as an echo to this scene of the Exodus, Psalm 51: it expresses very well the priority of the divine attitude and the confidence that it can and must inspire in the sinner, whatever the fault.

It really should be sung in Hebrew; no translation can do justice to the richness expressed by this grouping of words.

Haman—to take "pity," to grant "mercy"—evokes the image of bending down, stooping, descending toward: a wholly free movement demanding no reciprocity.

Hesed—"mercy," "love"—is one of the watchwords of the covenant, practically its equivalent; not merely a sentiment of pity, but fatherly bearing, moved by active generosity.

Raham—according to your great "mercy"—designates the very seat of compassion, the voice of blood, the love that arises from the inmost heart. "O woman, motherly womb, sweet pity!" wrote Arthur Rimbaud (1854-91).

The translation of a psalm for singing imposes constraints that P. François Varillon did not experience when he translated: "Incline toward me,

O God, according to your paternal pity; according to the tenderness of your maternal breast, wipe out my offense."[48]

In any case, one must have these resonances and harmonies in mind when one sings Psalm 51:

> *I will rise and go to my Father.*
>
> Have mercy on me, O God, in your goodness;
>   in the greatness of your compassion wipe out my offense.
> Thoroughly wash me from my guilt
>   and of my sin cleanse me.
>
> A clean heart create for me, O God,
>   and a steadfast spirit renew within me.
> Cast me not out from your presence,
>   and your holy spirit take not from me.
>
> O Lord, open my lips,
>   and my mouth shall proclaim your praise.
> My sacrifice, O God, is a contrite spirit;
>   a heart contrite and humbled, O God, you will not spurn.
> (Ps 51:3-4, 12-13, 17, 19)

The Forgiven Persecutor Becomes an Apostle

From the First Letter of Paul to Timothy (six chapters, one hundred twelve verses), the Sunday Lectionary has retained three excerpts totaling twenty verses.[49] The text for the Twenty-fourth Sunday, close to the beginning of the letter, is a thanksgiving (1 Tim 1:12-17). The object of this thanksgiving situates this text in the same perspective as the readings from Exodus and the Gospel.

The trust of our Lord Jesus Christ in a man who "was once a blasphemer and a persecutor and an arrogant man," in a man who had been pardoned by the grace of the Lord who is greater than all, to whom belongs the last word.

A profession of faith in this proclamation "worthy of full acceptance: that Christ Jesus came into the world to save sinners."

The apostle was the "first" of them. Not that he was the worst; but he persecuted Jesus by deliberately and obstinately harassing his disciples, "breathing murderous threats against them."[50] This is more than enough to make of him an example of "the first" of sinners.

The sinner has been forgiven. But even more strikingly, Jesus, whom he had persecuted, has trusted him so far as to invest him with the ministry to proclaim the gospel to the Gentiles. From "first among sinners," he has thus become "first" of the pardoned, the example "to those who would later have faith in him and gain everlasting life." If such a relentless persecutor has been forgiven, what doubt can there be about the mercy of God?

For such grace—of which Paul has been "the first" beneficiary, though it fills each of us—we give thanks, endlessly repeating for ourselves the liturgical doxology with which this text concludes:

> To the king of ages, incorruptible, invisible, the only God, honor and glory forever and ever! Amen.

When God Finds What Was Lost

After these two readings comes the extraordinary chapter 15 of Luke, which has been called the heart of the Gospel (Luke 15:1-32).

There are three well-known parables. The first two are constructed in a rigorously symmetrical manner. They deal with things—a lamb, a piece of money—that are lost, sought for, and found.

Each of these two short parables deals with only one person—"one of you," "a woman"—whose story is told in a brief but captivating style: loss of a valued possession, a feverish search, and finally the experience of joy when it is recovered. Then, friends and neighbors, who were undoubtedly informed of the mishap when it happened, are "invited in." They are probably told how, after much wandering in the field, after sweeping and turning the house upside down, what was lost has, thankfully, been found. At least there is in both parables the same refrain: "Rejoice with me because I have found my lost sheep [the piece of silver]."

There is nothing extraordinary in this: such things are common occurrences. But notice that the two stories are followed by a saying of Jesus, which explains why he told the parables and in what sense they must be understood:

> I tell you, in just the same way, there will be more joy in heaven over one sinner who repents than over ninety-nine righteous people who have no need of repentance.

> I tell you, there will be rejoicing among the angels of God over one sinner who repents.

These are not simply well-told stories.

The first saying emphasizes that the shepherd "leaves" the ninety-nine other sheep "in the desert and go[es] after the lost one until he finds it." What could have been an insignificant detail becomes a significant teach-

ing, which leads to the reflection that there will be rejoicing in heaven
. . . the same kind of rejoicing among the angels of God over one repentant sinner.

This is not to say that the other sheep or the pieces of money that are
not lost are not worthy of consideration. Rather, Jesus affirms that one
sinner who is converted is of incomparable value. He appeals to common experience: one lost item claims all our attention; finding it is a cause
for great joy, as if it were unique, as if it alone mattered.

Moreover, we should remember the introduction: "The tax collectors
and sinners were all drawing near to listen to him" and he welcomed
them, going even so far as to eat with them, or in other words, to recognize them as his own, to accept them into his community. Jesus tells these
parables to respond to the recriminations of the Pharisees and scribes,
the faithful observers of the Law, as opposed to the sinners.

To be sure, nothing would scandalize them about seeing a tax collector, a prostitute, a sinner be converted. Of course it is a cause for rejoicing, especially if such a conversion had been regarded as improbable, if
not practically impossible.

What offends the Pharisees and scribes and provokes their recriminations, is that the tax collectors and sinners are not turning to the Law,
but coming to Jesus, following him, preferring him to everything. Such
a reversal of values, a justification that occurs through attachment to a
person, scandalizes those who have a different conception of justice, relation to God, religion. They cannot accept this, for they have learned
that, far from welcoming tax collectors and sinners, they are to avoid such
people.

The third parable, which is the high point of the chapter, responds still
more directly to these murmurs. The central figure is not a shepherd or
a woman, but a father with his two sons.

The story is once again very simple, at least at the beginning. We see
a son who, after having demanded his share of the inheritance, leaves
his father's house to live his own life. The plot thickens when we learn
that he "squandered his money on a life of dissipation." Thus he appears as the quintessential type of wild sinner who has abandoned all
principles of morality and honesty.

What happens to him, then, comes as no surprise. Having wasted all
his money, he must seek some means of subsistence. "Serves him right,"
one might think. But what a disgrace! Keeping pigs, an animal that an
observant Jew would never eat, no matter what the situation. Even worse,

if that were possible, he was reduced to hungering for the food that was given to the animals. But no one made a move to give him anything, not even the husks that the pigs ate.

He finally begins to reflect on his situation. He decides to return to his father's house, leaving behind this dreadful famine. He rehearses a short speech to make to his father and sets out. He acknowledges that he has "sinned against heaven and against [his father]" and no longer deserves to be called son; he will ask his father to take him on as a hired hand. But the least one could say is that he does not behave like a model of repentance and conversion. Better to be a hired hand in his father's house, assured of bread in abundance, than to die of hunger far away, in the midst of a famine, in the house of a stranger who cares nothing for him.

One would think that his father would receive him at least coolly, giving him the sharp rebuke that he deserves. If he is too kind to reject him outright—which would be perfectly understandable—he will certainly put him to the test. Wouldn't we regard this as normal behavior?

Now, as so often in the parables, having encouraged us to judge the situation in this way, Jesus ends up disconcerting us: "No! This is not what you expected to happen. The father's attitude is the complete opposite of what you yourself would have adopted."

The father sees his son while he is still far off. Did he keep lookout every day, expecting his return? Forgetting his dignity, he runs towards him to embrace him, covering him with kisses! He doesn't give him time to recite his prepared speech. Is he even listening to it? He has only one thing in mind: to celebrate a joyous reunion, to bring the most beautiful garment to clothe his pauper son, to put a ring on his finger. And so the feast begins. . . . At this point in the story comes a refrain that recalls those of the two preceding parables: "This son of mine was dead, and has come to life again. He was lost, and has been found."

The elder son enters. He is returning from the fields where, like a good son, he has been working for his father. Surprised by the noise of an unexpected celebration—"the sound of music and dancing"—he is told: "Your brother has returned and your father has slaughtered the fattened calf because he has him back safe and sound."

We are not shocked by his initial, angry response, refusing to join in the feast as if everything was normal: it is hardly surprising. Who would not have needed a moment, at least, to collect his thoughts?

The father comes out to beseech the older son. This unexpected and urgent entreaty does nothing. The son responds with a vehement outpouring of what is in the depths of his heart. It is not with the prodigal son that he is angry; he scorns this son who "swallowed up your property with prostitutes." Accusing his father and bitterly reproaching him for his injustice, the older son says, "Look, all these years I've served you and not once did I disobey your orders; yet you never gave me even a young goat to feast on with my friends," whereas the debauched one comes back and receives the fatted calf, and the whole house celebrates!

Whatever the probability of such reactions, the older son's behavior is clearly presented here as a counterpoint to that of the father, who is the central figure. We typically call this "the parable of the prodigal son." It would be more accurate to speak of it as "the parable of the father who had two sons."

Leaving aside the introduction, look at the way both sons speak certain points to the concern of the parable. Both see themselves in relation to the father as servants. "Treat me like one of your hired hands," the younger had intended to say. "For years now I have slaved for you," says the elder. The father refers to both as "my son."

Were the parable addressed to the scribes and Pharisees, one might think that it concerned only those people in Jesus' time who "remonstrated with him." But by means of these ready interlocutors, the evangelist presents a teaching of Jesus that concerns all those who, even today, and especially in the Christian community, view their relation to God in terms of service: the faithful who, living in this perspective, think of themselves as good servants of God since they have, for so many years, "never disobeyed one" of his orders. It seems incontrovertible to them that such exemplary conduct grants them rights in God's eyes. Those actions that seem to injure these rights scandalize them.

It is not the sinners who are an affront; they are merely scorned. The scandal is rather God's behavior toward the sinners. If he treats them with such mercy, what privilege can the just claim? If such is the case, does it not shake the very foundation of a religion of fidelity and obedience to God? What good is it to bother observing the commandments? What is the point?

The end of the parable, which is also the end of chapter 15—the "heart of the Gospel"—tells us. We must be attuned to the attitude of God: "We had to celebrate and rejoice! This brother of yours was dead and has returned to life. He was lost and has been found." We must share in God's concern for those whom he wishes to discover and save. We are not hired hands, but children of God.

What must we understand this father to represent? God, clearly. No one is father like him, nor as tender as him. You are his son: even if you squander what you have received from him, even if you come back naked, he will receive you, since you are returning, and he will rejoice more in your return than in all the wisdom of his other son.[51]

To each of us, God says: "My son, you are with me always, and everything I have is yours." The relation of father to son is not that of master to slave. There is to be no strict account of hours worked to ensure that the master of the vineyard gives to each a wage proportionate to his labor. Will we look askance at the master and our fellows because God himself is gracious? May everyone who responds immediately to the Lord's call share his joy at the response of those who are called at the eleventh hour, and at seeing them receive, with the others, the fullness of the "wage" that God gives to all: his love as father, participation in the joy of the kingdom.[52] God's gift is himself, and it is indivisible: "Everything I have is yours."

The parable is open-ended. It does not say whether the elder son persisted in his obstinate refusal to enter the house and join in the feast. Even after having said "no" so vehemently, he could have repented and finally done what his father begged of him.[53] In that case, we may be sure that the father, who longed for his return to better feelings, would have readily embraced him and covered him with kisses. With the same joy he expressed at the return of the prodigal, he would say "Quickly, bring the finest robe and put it on him; put a ring on his finger and sandals on his feet"; "Let us celebrate with a feast , because this son of mine was dead and has come back to life again; he was lost and has been found."

The texts we read this Sunday are wholly relevant today, for they reveal the mystery of the heart of God, his attitude toward his children, and the call to conversion of our hearts and actions that come to us from them.

In every religious community, past and present, the faithful observers of the law often tend to think of themselves as an elite to whom much is owed, and to regard others haughtily, if not scornfully.

Such an attitude is clearly opposed to the fraternal spirit that characterizes the Gospel. It leads to a pitiless intolerance for the weak, who are thought to merit no consideration.

But, more deeply, the introduction of classes into the community denotes a serious alteration of the religious attitude, based on the mercenary spirit that warps fraternal relationships at the same time as it perverts the relationship with God.

Moses already understood that in pleading to God the cause of a faithless people, pleading arguable merits or extenuating circumstances is meaningless. It is on the mercy of God, his solicitude for all, that our hope relies (First Reading).

Paul, "first" among sinners and pardoned, is a concrete example of this wonderful gratuity of the Lord, who can draw even a persecuting enemy to himself (epistle).

This liturgical sequence of Ordinary Time, Year C, contains many revelations and teachings. Its underlying theme is the banquet at the end of time in which we are called to participate. It reveals the paradoxical behavior of the Master of the feast with respect to his invited guests, so that each may prepare to share his mind, imitating his behavior.

It would be ridiculous to secretly desire to be elevated to the highest places, while pretending only to desire the lowest, leaving the host who has invited and welcomed us the responsibility of seating us. For "everyone who exalts himself shall be humbled and he who humbles himself shall be exalted." Like the Lord, always give preference to the poor and weak, to those who cannot repay us for what we offer them.

This is not sly calculation or false humility, put on for the sake of a greater honor, but a disciple's conformity to the behavior of Christ, who is preferred to everyone and everything, and whom one follows by bearing his cross.

He has not hidden his demands from us; his grace and the gift of the spirit give us what we need to march to the very end of the road on which he leads us, renouncing, like him, all our possessions.

We are all prodigal children welcomed with open arms. We cannot boast of any right, not only because we are all pardoned sinners, but first and foremost because God is not a master who keeps our accounts, but a Father full of love, tenderness and mercy. He never ceases to look for those who are lost, rejoicing when they are found, when they return to the house. Because we are his children, we must rejoice with him when one of us who was dead returns to life.

Such are God's design and will on our behalf; the Wisdom revealed to us has made them known, as has the Spirit who has been sent to us from on high.

When we intercede for ourselves and for others, we have assurance that our prayer will be heard and will move the heart of God if it appeals to his fatherly compassion, if it is addressed to him through Jesus, the mediator of the new covenant.

> I am their father, says God. *Our Father, who art in heaven,*
> My Son has clearly told them, that I am their father.
> I am their judge. My son has told them so. I am also their father.
> I am above all their father.
> In a word, I am their father. He who is father is first of all fathers.
> *Our Father, who art in heaven.* He who once has been a father can be no other than father.
> They are the brothers of my son; they are my children;
> I am their father . . .
> And now I must judge them as a father. For the one who can judge is a father. *A man had two sons.* For he is capable of judging. *A man had two sons.* One knows well how a father judges. There is a well-known example of it. One knows well how the father judged the son who was lost and who returned.
> It is still the father who wept the most.
> See what my son has told them. My son has opened to them the secret of judgment itself.[54]

The Twenty-fifth and Twenty-sixth Sundays in Ordinary Time

Chapter 16 of Luke's Gospel constitutes a clearly separate sequence in itself. It contains two parables which, with very different examples, both present a teaching on the use that one should make of money in order to store up treasure "in heaven" (16:1-13, 19-31).

Between the two are four maxims addressed by Jesus to the Pharisees. The first is of general importance (16:14-15); the other three are, respectively, the kingdom of God into which one must force an entrance (16:16), the permanency of the Law (16:17), and the indissolubility of marriage (16:18).

Their link with the parables immediately preceding and following is not immediately evident. Matthew, who also retains three of them, uses them in an entirely different context.[1] One can therefore read the two parables on money by passing directly from verse 13 to verse 19. This is what the Lectionary does, very judiciously.

This omission of the maxims that are directed to the Pharisees helps us to avoid the temptation to think that the whole chapter is addressed to the Pharisees, and that the parables on money do not directly concern us. After all, chapter 16 is introduced by these words: "Then he also said *to his disciples.*" Therefore, it is for us, today, that the evangelist recounts these two parables on the use of money. Of course, anything less would be surprising, when one remembers how insistently Luke, both in the Gospel and in Acts, speaks of the snare of riches, the necessity of sharing them, even of being stripped of them, and the beatitude of the poor, in which every disciple must share.

Twenty-fifth Sunday

Shrewd Stewards of God's Gifts

The Cry of the Voiceless Ascends to God

The Liturgy of the Word this Sunday begins with the proclamation of a short, but virulent passage from the Book of Amos (Amos 8:4-7).

These comments are just as explosive today as they were in the eighth century B.C.! What would we say of a contemporary preacher who, in front of the whole assembly, would thus challenge his hearers? Be that as it may, our task must be to place this oracle of the first prophetic "writing" in context, on the one hand to avoid abusive and arbitrary interpretations, on the other hand to better understand its real present-day import.[2] Otherwise we are in danger of regarding it as a thunderbolt directed at others, or as a rather exaggerated, strident outburst, which doesn't really concern us but should nonetheless be applauded.

The first verses of the book give us Amos' situation (1:1). He had been a shepherd not far from Bethlehem, in the southern kingdom.[3] The king there was Uzziah, while "Jeroboam, son of Joash" ruled over the northern kingdom,[4] "two years before the earthquake."[5]

In a society of great economic expansion, where not everyone's income comes from personal labor, where the small country land-owners—defenseless victims of change—quickly become a proletariat and fall so far into debt that they are at the mercy of their creditors, where commerce produces more and more loans and debts—the gulf between the rich and the poor grows ever greater. The wealth of the former increases boundlessly, while the poverty of the latter becomes harsher. Thus there is a great temptation for the rich to exploit the situation and acquire more and more, to the detriment of the poor. We know all too well what happens in consumer societies and between wealthy and poor countries. This similarity of situations then and now is why Amos interests us.[6]

How could a believer, a true champion of the weak, and moved by a prophetic spirit, do otherwise than to raise his voice to denounce injustice and oppression? Think of the Italian Dominican Savonarola (1452–1498) or the French writer Léon Bloy (1846–1917), whose virulence is reminiscent of Amos; or, among us today, though with a different tone, a Helder Camara, a Mother Theresa, and others who are less famous. It is ridiculous to claim that Amos, almost thirty centuries ago, was a kind of cryptocommunist, a generous man perhaps, but the unwitting tool of professional agitators—and that the Church is reading him today in order to destabilize society!

Amos is neither a fringe radical who preaches great societal upheaval nor a revolutionary. He certainly revolts against a lawless urban civilization and a consumerist, profit-centered society, whose logical consequences are apparent to him; but he does not, for all that, sympathize with those organizations who think they can return to the ancient morality of the nomad, dreaming naively of an idyllic egalitarian society. He is not promoting a political agenda. Nor is it by resorting to force that he wants to free the people from Money, their new, bloodthirsty god.[7]

Amos is a prophet because he speaks in the name of God. He denounces what lies in the hearts of the greedy rich, their perverse intentions that they keep well hidden while observing the rules of worship.

Yes, they celebrate the religious feasts and the sabbath like everyone else. But they resent the time taken when they could be making more money! Buy cheap and sell dear: see how these apparent law-abiders think.[8]

"Buy the lowly man for silver," sell at a good price "even the refuse of the wheat" which will find buyers among the poor; this is not ancient history but, if truth be told, the shame of the rich, of wealthy nations.

Buy the poor "for a pair of sandals," for a bagatelle, for a necessity? It may simply be a technical expression of justice.[9] In that case, Amos would also be reproaching the rich for practicing deceit in giving a legal appearance to their extortion.

This should be no cause for surprise coming from a prophet who elsewhere denounces the injustice of judges toward the poor: "[They] turn judgment to wormwood and cast justice to the ground"; "Oppressing the just, accepting bribes, repelling the needy at the gate," "Hate evil and love good, and let justice prevail at the gate"; "Can horses run across a cliff? or can one plow the sea with oxen? Yet you have turned judgment into gall, and the fruit of justice into wormwood" (Amos 5:7, 12, 15; 6:12).

We ourselves know, from our own experiences, that the poor do not always have the same chance as others of experiencing true justice, and we know that the powerful who wish to oppress them can find the means to cover their exploitation with a legal cloak, through control of the courts, certain pressures brought to bear, making judges afraid, etc.

God is the Pride, the Honor of the people, the Defender of the voiceless, the weak and the poor. He takes their part. He will not forget the evils done by the powerful and rich. He will have the last word, the supreme Judge who gives justice.

> Allow me, Lord, a special intention for my people, the world of the silenced. There are thousands upon thousands of human creatures—in poor countries and in the poor areas of rich countries—without the right to lift their voices, to shout and protest, however just the rights they seek to defend may be: those without homes, food, clothing, health, a minimum of education; those without work, future, or hope. They fall into fatalism, they are discouraged, they lose their voice, they fall silent.
>
> If we who believe in you, and in various religions, help our rich and privileged brethren—opening their eyes, rousing their consciences—injustices could not increase, the distance between poor and rich would not be so glaring, not only between individuals and groups of individuals, but between countries, and even between continents. Do, Lord, what we did not and still do not know how to do.[10]

But more than a threat, it is a call to conversion that the prophet cries out for. The worst thing that could happen would be for God to be silent, for there no longer to arise, in the people and the Church, prophets to denounce evildoing and injustice. This is the frightening situation hinted at by the psalmist: "Deeds on our behalf we do not see; there is no prophet now, and no one of us knows how long . . ." (Ps 74:9; Amos 8:11).

After this reading we are invited to raise our prayer toward God, blessing the one who lifts up the poor. It is a prayer that would condemn anyone who said it while accepting, whether by silence or inaction, what God cannot tolerate, whatever does evil and harm.

> *Praise the LORD who lifts up the poor.*
>
> Praise, you servants of the LORD,
>   praise the name of the LORD.
> Blessed be the name of the LORD
>   both now and forever.
>
> High above all nations is the LORD;
>   above the heavens is his glory.
> Who is like the LORD, our God, who is enthroned on high
>   and looks upon the heavens and the earth below?
>
> He raises up the lowly from the dust;
>   from the dunghill he lifts up the poor

To seat them with princes,
  with the princes of his own people.
(Ps 113:1-2, 4-6, 7-8)

Universal Prayer

Again today, the epistle is from the First Letter to Timothy (1 Tim 2:1-8). The choice of this passage is particularly fortunate and demands careful reading. In fact, it is characteristic of the entire letter in several ways. It offers some valuable recommendations for Christian prayer and authentic liturgy. It contains a profession of faith, a veritable Credo of the first-century Church community. Finally, it situates Christian faith and life—their certitudes and concerns—in the world and in history. All these are things that retain astonishing contemporaneity.

Very early on, certain Christian communities were menaced by a danger that can be found in nearly all ages, especially today. It is the danger of what is called "gnosticism," the search for a philosophical-religious wisdom, typically tainted with mysterious and crude orientalism, where knowledge—"gnosis"—is the way of salvation. When it arises in a Christian context, "gnosis" combines the data of faith and various "knowledges" in a syncretism that is tenuous at best; it expresses itself in a confused language that recommends it to lovers of the esoteric.

The First Letter of Timothy timely restores to us a more realistic view of salvation that is experienced concretely in human history, even day to day, particularly in family, social, and political relationships.

This realism expresses itself in liturgical prayer and indeed inspires it. It is a universal prayer of petition, intercession, and thanksgiving for all people, beginning with "kings and all in authority." "I ask" this, writes the author of the letter.

The political dimension is an integral part of human life. Christians, most of all, must be conscious of this, even in their prayer. Again, this resonates with Paul's thought: "Let every person be subordinate to the higher authorities, for there is no authority except from God, and those that exist have been established by God. Therefore, whoever resists authority opposes what God has appointed, and those who oppose it will bring judgment upon themselves" (Rom 13:1-2).

This is not to say that Christians must renounce their right, which indeed is sometimes a duty, of criticizing and challenging the public authorities, opposing their policies and decisions. That is another question.[11] Here, the focus is on prayer from which none may be excluded, that has a special place for those with responsibilities.[12] For "[God] wants all men to be saved and come to know the truth."

Pray "that we may lead a quiet and tranquil life in all devotion, piety, and dignity." In contradiction with this "tranquility" and "dignity" are the exuberance and fiery agitation of certain gnostic groups, the frivolity of their discourse and discussions, everything that can discredit religion.

Then comes a short and dense profession of faith that might well be of liturgical origin. "For there is one God": this *credo* begins like the *Shema Israel*, which pious Jews recite every day: "Hear, O Israel! The LORD our God, the LORD is one!" (cf. Deut 6:4). Such is professed by Jews, Christians, and Muslims.

"There is also one mediator between God and the human race, Christ Jesus, himself human . . ." This affirmation, which might seem banal to some Christians, must be properly appreciated. "One mediator," with whom no other person is comparable. Again, the author of the letter cuts short all fantasies and fables of the gnostic circles and—one might add—the pretensions of mediums and other gurus who set themselves up as necessary intermediaries between humanity and God or Christ.

"Christ Jesus, himself human," not a mythical person, neither angel nor spirit. "Christ Jesus . . . who gave himself as ransom for all." This proclamation of the redeeming death of Christ for all is at the heart of Christian faith and Eucharistic celebration.

The apostles are instructed to proclaim to the whole universe this death for the salvation of all. Paul is the model of this, he who was invested with the charge to announce the good news to the Gentiles, and who wished to know and preach nothing other than the cross of Christ (1 Cor 1:23; 2:2), on which has been nailed, and thus fulfilled, the debt of sin (Col 2:14—Seventeenth Sunday). Such are the faith and truth, two intertwined realities, to which we adhere by saying "Amen," a word whose root means both "Yes, it is true" and "Yes, I believe."

After the profession of faith comes a brief teaching on prayer in the liturgy.

According to ancient custom—which we are rediscovering today—the proper posture for intercession and thanksgiving is to stand with hands lifted to heaven. It is a posture at once dignified and meaningful, often seen in Christian paintings of people at prayer, particularly in the catacombs, but also later on.

The danger of this appearing as an ostentatious posture disappears when prayer is holy, that is to say, completely turned toward God, "free from anger and dissension,'' for as pardoned sinners, we cannot be resentful toward anyone; likewise, there can be no contention, because we pray together, united in the same Spirit.

Making Quick Friends with Dishonest Money

The passage that begins chapter 16 of Luke's Gospel this Sunday always catches us by surprise (Luke 16:1-13).

Every day we hear stories of managers and agents who squander the money entrusted to them and are subsequently dismissed. Accounts of falsified documents, misuse of funds, forgery and counterfeiting, etc.— Jesus had no dearth of material here. He might borrow a little here and there from some current story that his listeners might relate to, confident that they would recognize and associate it with what he would say.

What is surprising, even shocking, is what is said after the story. We expect to hear Jesus vigorously denounce this swindling—commonplace, to be sure, but no less condemnable for that—saying: ''Treat someone else's goods with scrupulous honesty.''

Such a denunciation and teaching would hardly disturb us. We know well enough the various reasons for the necessity of honesty, as well as the appropriateness of virtuous condemnations. We subscribe to such things already. And we are not slow to preach good conduct, not infrequently with such satisfaction as almost to say: ''I thank you, my God, that I am not like so many people today: thieves, crooks, cheats . . . or like this manager!''

To be sure, the Gospels condemn all forms of dishonesty. But, as we know and have already seen, they do not dwell on the commonplaces of good conduct.[13] Let us then read this passage from Luke with the assumption that Jesus is offering an unexpected lesson that might well disturb us or put us on the defensive, even those of us who behave with complete honesty with respect to money, especially if it belongs to someone else.

Was the manager in this story in fact guilty? His conduct after having received notice must make one think so. But it does not matter much. He does not waste any time trying to justify himself. He does not seem even to be under the illusion that he can find a similar position elsewhere. He immediately deals with the most pressing concern: securing his future. Ditchdigger? Never! Beggar? What a horrible disgrace that would be for a man like him!

His fertile imagination suggests an acceptable solution. He was asked to render his accounts. He does so more quickly than one would have thought. Then he approaches his master's debtors one by one. Each must think that he is the recipient of a particular favor. The manager tears up their bills and gives them new ones, in proper and due form, but for a much smaller amount.[14]

A beautiful bit of cunning! It is the master who pays the price of the transaction. The relieved debtors are at the mercy of a manager who controls a formidable means of blackmail: they will have to do what he says and hold their tongues.

We find such dealings reported in our newspapers. Typically, a long time passes before a scandal is uncovered. Those who benefit by the swindle are not all that eager—for good reason—to make their knowledge and testimony, which would unmask the culprit, a matter of public knowledge. We know perfectly well the defense that will be offered: ''All the figures are correct. Prove that there has been a falsification of the debts.'' And don't we find ourselves dumbfounded, and indeed impressed, with the cleverness of the trick, though not, of course, approving of the dishonesty and bad faith of the crook?

This is the scene Jesus sets,[15] to draw from the story an important and unexpected lesson: ''You see the resourcefulness of the children of this world? Ah! you, children of the light, would that you were as capable as they! How so? By securing your future, and without delay or dawdling. Tomorrow will be too late.''

Money—the word is capitalized, as if it were a personified idol—can only deceive: it is false, dishonest; the one who relies on it goes quickly astray. After all, it must be abandoned someday, for no one among the dead finds wealth of any more use.

What is the only way to use it profitably and be assured of a future in the eternal realm? Sharing it with those who need it to live, giving it to those who beg. We have already found the same warning in Luke's Gospel: ''Sell your belongings and give alms. Provide money bags for yourselves that do not wear out, an inexhaustible treasure in heaven that no thief can reach nor moth destroy'' (Luke 12:33—Nineteenth Sunday). This command here takes on a particular edge, after the story of the dishonest manager and his ''example.'' For it is said that the poor, who will become our friends, thanks to our almsgiving, will be there to welcome us into heaven.

Bossuet expresses this clearly and eloquently in a very few words, speaking to the rich, whom he urges to seize the chance to show their foresight:

> Come then, you rich, into his Church: its door is finally open to you; but it is open to you because of the poor, on the condition of your serving them. It is for the love of his children that Jesus Christ permits entry to strangers. Behold the miracle of poverty! Yes, the rich were strangers; but *service to the poor has naturalized them* and serves to rid them of the contagion that lies in the midst of their riches. Therefore, you rich of this age! seize as many grand titles as you please: you can wear them in the world; in the Church of Christ, you are only servants of the poor.[16]

Choose Your Master: God or Money

The first lesson of the story-parable is followed immediately by another. Jesus imparts a maxim of universal importance: "The person who is trustworthy in very small matters is also trustworthy in great ones; and the person who is dishonest in small matters is also dishonest in great ones."

Such an axiom is verified in the most diverse situations.[17] How, then, could we object to Jesus' application of it here, to the parable and the lesson he drew from it first?

If, therefore, you are not trustworthy with dishonest wealth, who will trust you with true wealth? i.e., gain for yourself friends in heaven, who will trust you with lasting wealth that will not desert you at the hour of your death? The goods of this world are only "someone else's money," given that you may manage them according to the will of God, their master. If you have not been worthy of such trust here, you deprive yourself of the heritage that you expect as your very right. Jesus repeats what he has just said. There is only one honest and prudent way to use material goods: by helping the poor with them! Thus, and only thus, will the Master say to us: "Well done, my good and faithful servant. Since you were faithful in small matters, I will give you great responsibilities. Come, share your master's joy!" (Matt 25:21, 23—Thirty-third Sunday, Year A).

As a matter of fact, this gives considerable importance to the evangelical use of money. It becomes a decisive criterion for receiving the inheritance of the kingdom! But familiarity with Luke should dispel any surprise, and we have read quite a bit of his Gospel these Sundays. No one warns about the same thing over and over like Luke. Money will burn a Christian's fingers. Far from accumulating it for oneself, though through fair and honest dealings and as the result of an enterprising spirit, one must hasten to share it with the poor, going so far as to "renounce all one's possessions" in order to become a disciple, as we heard proclaimed a short while ago (Luke 14:33—Twenty-third Sunday).

> The riches of iniquity are the riches of this world, from wherever they come. Whatever their origin, they are *mammon*, that is to say, the riches of iniquity. What does this mean, the riches of iniquity? It is money that iniquity dresses up with the name of riches. If you seek true riches, they lie elsewhere. Such are the riches that Job possessed in abundance, when, stripped of everything, his heart was full of God, and after losing everything, he offered to God, as so many priceless pearls, the tribute of his praises (Job 1:21). From what treasure-trove could he have drawn them, since he had nothing? These are the true riches. As to the others, it is iniquity that gives them this name. Your owning them, I do not call a crime; it is an inheritance that came to you; your father was rich and left you wealthy. Or you have acquired them legitimately; your house is full of the just rewards of your labor; again, I do not blame you at all. Yet be wary of calling these goods riches. For, if you give them this name, you will love them, and if you bind your heart to them, you will perish with them. Be rid of them so as not to be lost with them; give in order to receive, sow in order to reap. Never call these goods riches, for they are not true riches. They are hollow and empty and subject to a thousand mishaps. How can they be riches when you are constantly fearful that a thief or your servant will seize them when you are dead? If they were true riches, they would give you complete security.
>
> Thus, true riches are those of which we cannot be despoiled once we have them. And do not fear that thieves may take them; they will be locked away from thieves . . .
>
> O Lord, my God, Lord our God, in order draw us to yourself, make us try to find our happiness in you. We desire not to seek it in gold or silver or fine houses; we do not desire these earthly goods, goods so vain and short-lived, which belong to this fragile life. May our mouths never speak words of vanity. Make us put our happiness in you, for we cannot lose you. Once we possess you, we cannot lose you, nor ourselves.[18]

As a conclusion to this passage, Luke reports a striking saying of Jesus that one reads as well in Matthew, though in a different context (Matt 6:24): "No servant (slave) can serve two masters. He will either hate one and love the other, or be devoted to one and despise the other. You cannot serve God and mammon (money)."

One can argue over what happens when one has two masters at one time. But the slave neither chooses his master nor chooses to have more than one. He might very well detest both. To have two masters can cause tension, it is true, for it is difficult not to compare them; one may be more disagreeable than the other, or even odious. But this is not what is important. What the saying proclaims is undeniable when it is a question, as it is here, of the "service" of God and Money.

"To serve," with respect to God, has a strong significance; it implies an engagement of the whole person, an absolute preference, an undivided love with a cultural overtone. So we say in the second Eucharistic Prayer: "We thank you for choosing us to be in your presence and serve you." "Serving" amounts to adoring, worshiping.

Applied to money, the term means the same thing, for Jesus speaks of money as an idol. The Gospel here calls it "mammon," a name that personifies it as a power that rules the world.[19]

We see all too often that money can be an idol to which everything is sacrificed, a veritable Moloch. The poor and misguided destroy themselves seeking its favors; they often let themselves be bought, renouncing every human dignity for a pittance. As for the rich, the point hardly needs to be said. But it is the whole world, even today, that finds itself tempted by the cult of Mammon. Has there ever been a proselytizing movement so great as that for the worship of Money, such aggressive propaganda proclaiming its power, such publicity urging one to have as much of it as possible, always more, no matter what the cost? Those who do not slavishly follow Money or are incapable of it are viewed as more or less foolish, naive, innocent, etc. One needs a great deal of determination to resist the incessant hammering of this advertising.

Yes, this saying of Jesus is of undoubted interest for us today: "You cannot serve both God and the god Money!" Unconsciously, to be sure, we often search the Gospels for condemnation of dishonest ways of acting, along with reasons to renew our efforts not to succumb to temptation.

The Gospels certainly do rebuke dishonesty in the manipulation of money as in everything else. But it is not, for all that, a mere elementary moral code. It is not content to repeat that one must use one's money and conduct one's affairs honestly. It teaches that there is only one prudent way of making use of it: sharing it with the poor, for no one is truly the master of what he or she owns. Hoarding money is inadmissable and leads to the loss of the only true good whose possession is promised us: the eternal inheritance.

In short, one must choose: God or the god Money. It is impossible to serve both at once. No compromise may be made between them. One is faced with the unavoidable choice.

God would cease to be God if he would be friendly to the servants and idolaters of Money, with the wrongs they inflict on the poor and humble whose Defender he is. The cult of Money amounts to blasphemy. It is opposed to the very foundation of faith: "God is one."

To seek happiness in it amounts to denying that there is only "one mediator between God and the human race, Christ Jesus, human himself, who gave himself as ransom for all."

Hands that clasp money cannot be "held aloft and be free from anger and dissension."

It is impossible truly to intercede "that we lead quiet and tranquil lives in all devotion and dignity" when one is a slave to money.

One does not come to the liturgy to be comforted with platitudes, and even less to be soothed by a clean conscience. Participation in the liturgy is the demand and source of conversion to God, for he empowers us to respond "Amen" to his Word. In giving him thanks for having been chosen "to be in his presence and serve him," we can say:

> Father, we celebrate the memory of Christ, your Son.
> We, your people and your ministers,
> recall his passion,
> his resurrection from the dead,
> and his ascension into glory;
> and from the many gifts you have given us
> we offer to you, God of glory and majesty,
> this holy and perfect sacrifice:
> the bread of life
> and the cup of eternal salvation.
> (Eucharistic Prayer I)

Twenty-sixth Sunday

The Poor Man at the Banquet Doorway

One week is a short time to meditate on the word proclaimed last Sunday or to revise one's life accordingly. Hence the liturgy, without repeating itself, pursues the same thorny issue of money, and how we serve it or make use of it as skillful managers. Thus we read the last part of chapter 16 of Luke's Gospel, dwelling now on the second panel of the diptych that displays the sequence formed by the Twenty-fifth and Twenty-sixth Sundays of Ordinary Time, Year C.

The first reading is again taken from the Book of Amos.[20] Likewise, we continue our reading of the First Letter to Timothy.

The False Security of Riches
We spoke last Sunday about the social and economic situation of the country where the prophet Amos, formerly a shepherd, had been sent by the Lord (Amos 7:15).

The passage read for the Twenty-sixth Sunday is an invective—and a very strong one—against "the complacent in Zion, the overconfident on the mount of Samaria" (Amos 6:1a, 4-7). We understand these to be the leaders of the people, but also all the rich of the country who have built their fortunes through robbing the weak, through unscrupulous commerce in their dealings with the new social class of officials, functionaries, and other dignitaries. The ostentatious luxury and haughtiness of these new, complacent rich could not help but infuriate the prophet. Not only because he was the spokesman of the exploited, because of their rapid proletarianization, but also because such a way of living flatly contradicts the ideal and the prescriptions of the covenant, i.e., the will of God, who desires a people without class distinctions.

"Woe to you!" This is not a malediction, but the cry of one who sees what awaits the people he is addressing.

The description of the scandalous orgies to which these people devoted themselves surpasses any commentary. But we ought to note certain

229

specifics in the vocabulary which show us that, for Amos, these banquets are sacrilegious. "The lambs taken from the flock" and the "calves from the stall" were set aside for worship, as were the "best oils." The cultic connections implied in the improvisations to the sound of the harp and the evocation of David are obvious. These are truly scandalous parodies, caricatures of religious actions! So many things call for condemnation, even if all this extravagance did not rest on the shameless exploitation of the weak.

Nevertheless, the fundamental sin of these engorged rich, these profiteers, these "wanton revelers," consists in this: Since they think only of enjoying the present life as if their precarious security rested on themselves and their riches, they take no care for the future, their own future and that of the people.

The feast will be short and will be followed by a rude awakening: "They shall be the first to go into exile."

A virulent and straightforward denunciation of a society that produces social inequities: of the rich getting richer; of the poor getting poorer; of the impoverishment of more and more people. A foretelling of the catastrophe awaiting those who approach it carelessly, with willful blindness. Such are the features that make Amos' oracle especially interesting for us.

> We have become the wicked rich. Lazarus reclines at our table and must be satisfied with the crumbs that fall from it: a hundredth, a two-hundredth, a thousandth of our national revenue. The richest country in the world, which gives a two-hundredth, wearies us with bragging about its munificence. A few of its gifts are pure and well intentioned; the rest are cheap and self-serving. Lazarus is legion, the overwhelming majority of humanity. Lazarus used to be far away, overseas . . . Lazarus is beginning to exist for us; we are starting to discover him. To judge by our newspapers, he has become important in the life of the world. We still do not love him, but he frightens us. Lazarus has learned how to revolt. Lazarus has many children, and we have taught him, cheaply, how not to let them die. Lazarus will soon become ninety percent of the world's population. Lazarus learns to read and react. Lazarus threatens our security and peace . . . Our hearts remain closed to Lazarus, who, in the words of a delegate from a poor people, learned "of understanding and love."[21]

But one problem remains. Not everything that arises in social, economic, cultural, (i.e., historical) circles is evil. On the contrary, progress is also made. How can this be integrated with the other?

One must not ask the prophets to respond to this question, for it falls within neither their mission nor their competence. They announce and denounce. Others must figure it out. Without them, one would fall into the perpetual dissatisfaction of a protestor, who in the end has nothing to offer. But without the prophets, the technicians (political, industrial, etc.), blinded by the light of progress and, in their enthusiasm, regarding it as preeminent, might unconsciously forget those whom their marvelous inventions might well crush, and they might misunderstand the spiritual dimension of all human life that societal structures, old and new, must promote rather than abandon.[22] In other words, one must guard against too rapid an enforcement of such a message as Amos'.

In a more general way, we must not search the Bible for ready-made answers to the questions that we must deal with as responsible people.

Instead, a prophecy like Amos', and the liturgical celebration itself, situates us in the presence of the Lord who never forgets the poor and weak. He is the only solid support for anything. It is toward his reign that humanity and the world must progress.

> *Praise the LORD, my soul!*
>
> Happy he who keeps faith forever,
>   secures justice for the oppressed,
>   gives food to the hungry.
> The LORD sets captives free.
>
> The LORD gives sight to the blind.
>   The LORD raises up those that were bowed down;
> The LORD loves the just.
>   The LORD protects strangers.
>
> The fatherless and the widow he sustains,
>   but the way of the wicked he thwarts.
> The LORD shall reign forever;
>   your God, O Sion, through all generations. Alleluia.
> (Ps 146: 7, 8-9, 9-10)

The Beautiful Fight of Faith

The third and final excerpt from the First Letter to Timothy retained by the Lectionary is particularly interesting and suggestive, especially as integrated into the context of the Liturgy of the Word this Sunday.[23] In fact, it deals with the "now" of Christian life and its conscious orientation toward the manifestation of the Lord (1 Tim 6:11-16).

There are three clearly distinguished paragraphs in it, each about the same length: verses 11-12, 13-14, 15-16.

The present Christian life is a fight for faith with an eye toward the eternal life to come. This faith is associated with charity, with steadfastness (hope) and with a gentle spirit. "Man of God . . . pursue righteousness, devotion, faith, love, patience, and gentleness."

That all Christian action is rooted in faith, hope, and love, we already know. This idea is almost a commonplace of Christian discourse. The same is almost true for the pair "righteousness" and "devotion," which evoke the relation to others and to God.[24]

The mention of "gentleness" is a bit unexpected. But we remember that Jesus was "meek and humble of heart," and that it is said elsewhere that "the servant of the Lord" must know how to show "kindness" to all (2 Tim 2:24-25), including those who sin, for it is thus that one bears the burdens of others and fulfills the law of Christ (Gal 6:1-2). "Gentleness" is therefore a forceful virtue, not an anemic sweetness; it must belong to Christians as to their Lord.

"Hope" evokes that which is the source of our ability, no matter what the situation, to remain upright and face forward.

Yet for all this, such an enumeration of virtues might not seem to be striking or original, but rather like a well-worn formula with which a preacher might end his sermon.

The end of the paragraph shows that this is not the case. It situates what precedes on the level of the call of God to eternal life, for the sake of which the Christian has made, in the presence of many witnesses, "a noble confession" of faith.

"A noble confession" of faith, "beautiful fight of faith."[25] This has, in the letter's original Greek, a richness of meaning that cannot be adequately expressed in English. To the Greek mind, the beautiful always implies the good, and vice versa. "Beauty-goodness"—there is even one word in Greek that combines the two qualities—is complete perfection. Thus, the "beautiful fight" and "the noble confession" of faith are related to the absolute "beauty-goodness," the holiness, of God.

This noble profession of faith, in the presence of many witnesses, is that which is made in the presence of the ecclesial community at baptism.

We are not dealing with a mere enumeration of virtues, a list of commonplaces. What is at issue is the mystery of the Christian life as rooted in the mystery of baptism, the sacrament of faith.

Remain Faithful to the Lord

The second paragraph explains in some way what proceeds: "Before God, who gives life to all things, and before Christ Jesus, who gave testimony under Pontius Pilate for the noble confession, [I charge you] to keep the commandment without stain or reproach until the appearance of our Lord Jesus Christ."

The solemnity of this long, but well-balanced, sentence is reminiscent of a liturgical formula pronounced after the baptismal profession of faith. So it is that, at celebrations which contain a "noble confession," as for example, a taking of vows for religious life, one says, albeit more simply: "May God bring to perfection what he had begun in you."[26]

"God, who gives life to all things," for he is creator and redeemer; he gives life and revives it. This way of linking creation and redemption fits well within biblical tradition: "The LORD rebuilds Jerusalem; the dispersed of Israel he gathers. . . . He tells the number of the stars; he calls each by name" (Ps 147:2, 4); "Who made the great lights . . . split the Red Sea in twain . . . and made their land a heritage . . . the heritage of Israel his servant, for his mercy endures forever" (Ps 136:7, 13, 21, 22).

"Before Christ Jesus, who gave testimony under Pontius Pilate": the baptismal profession and the "beautiful fight" of Christian faith, the fidelity to it, recalls Jesus' testimony before Pilate and his strength to endure, secure in God, to the end of his mission.

To keep the Lord's commandment "without stain or reproach," or "living blamelessly and upright": both translations are possible. In the first case, it is a question of preserving the commandment, i.e., the doctrine and spirit of the Lord, without adding or subtracting anything from it. In the second case, it is the disciple who must stay on the right path.[27] In any case, the Lord's commandment alone is blameless and right, as faithfulness in keeping it makes one blameless and right.

The sentence ends with a fresh appeal to endurance, since one must persevere "until the appearance of our Lord Jesus Christ."

To God Be Honor and Eternal Power

The third paragraph is a magnificent profession of faith. First of all with respect to God: "The blessed and only ruler, the King of kings and Lord of lords, who alone has immortality, who dwells in unapproachable light, whom no human being has seen or can see." Then with respect to Christ and his Manifestation—his Epiphany—"at the chosen time." We must allow a text of such density and such beautiful literary craftsmanship to speak for itself. Might it have been an ancient liturgical hymn?

See that toward which Christians march, the culmination of their hope. Such is the God of their faith, the God who has called them to eternal life. "He whom no human being has seen or can see," but whom his Son has revealed by making himself one of us; he who in his turn, will bring [this appearance of Christ] to pass at his chosen time.

"To him be honor and eternal power. Amen." This solemn doxology originated in the formulas of praise in use in the synagogues of the ancient Greek world. It rises to the one who, through Christ, has restored the communion between time and eternity, between our world and the eternal kingdom.

The Thoughtless Rich Man and Lazarus

The parable of the rich man and the beggar Lazarus is very well known (Luke 16:19-31). Like the parable last Sunday, it is proper to Luke.

Jesus did not wholly invent it. One finds in rabbinic literature a similar Jewish story told in various forms, which is itself based on an older Egyptian story. But the Gospel adaptation nonetheless witnesses to a beautiful originality and is marked also by its simplicity. "There was a rich man . . . and a poor man." Nothing distinguishes them other than this difference in social status. We do not hear of a "wicked" rich man or of a "holy" poor man. The latter does, it is true, have a name. The fact is worth noting, for there is no other like case in the Gospel. Jesus calls him Lazarus, a name that suits him well. It means "God has rescued" *(El'azar)*.[28]

The rich man does nothing evil: he lives like a rich man, wears fine clothes, and throws sumptuous feasts every day.

Lazarus "lies" before the door, covered with sores. He "would gladly have eaten his fill of the scraps that fell from the rich man's table. Dogs even used to come and lick his sores."

> Ah! who would not be a beast, if he were overwhelmed with pain! The unfortunate know very well what is precious . . . The glass of water is so valuable that, even if it is given by someone who could do better, it is still of inestimable value.[29]

This can be seen every day, even in our own country. Lazarus does not beg. Doubtlessly, he does not have the strength to rummage through the trash cans for the scraps of the rich feasts. He waits for death: it comes, sure enough. And also for the rich man. He is buried "with many lamentations."[30] Perhaps even "the whole city stopped working to honor him."[31]

For Lazarus, there is nothing of the sort. He is undoubtedly thrown out of the city "rolled up in a sack, all alone, with no one following him."[32] But the parable says nothing about these funerals. It simply recounts that the angels bear the poor man to Abraham. It is solely interested in what happens later, in the afterlife. Thus come two scenes (vv. 22-26 and 27-31) punctuated by two speeches of Abraham who draws the lesson from the parable (vv. 25 and 31).

The first scene is a radical reversal of the situation. To speak in the harshness of the text, the rich man is tortured. Far off he sees Abraham and Lazarus with him. And he pleads: "Father Abraham, have pity on me. Send Lazarus to dip the tip of his finger in water and cool my tongue."

Abraham's first speech: "Remember that you received what was good during your lifetime while Lazarus likewise received what was bad; but now he is comforted here, whereas you are tormented." Abraham is saying, in effect: "Too late. Yesterday, if you had been a neighbor to Lazarus, you would have made a friend of him and he would have welcomed you to the eternal dwelling place (last Sunday's Gospel). And that is not all. Between you and us there is fixed a great abyss. You no longer have your 'elusive wealth' (Luke 16:9). Lazarus can do nothing for you. How was it that you did not see the plea in the eyes of the poor man who lay at your gate, and understood that you were fixing your own fate? Could you not read the parable at the right time?"

> Could you not give me a fifty-cent piece that would satisfy, for that moment, all my wishes? There is, on the counter, a bottle of wine from which I am separated by the vast abyss of the parable. It would cost you less than the glass of water, than the drop of water on the finger of Lazarus, who suffered all his life in order to have the right to refuse it. But you do not give the drop to me, the longing for which increases my torments, because you are satiated, because you have not known hunger and thirst, and here we are, dear sir, on the two sides of Chaos![33]

But let us not misunderstand the Gospel. Death does not invert the world so as to establish an equilibrium. He is a fool who grows rich for himself instead of growing rich in what "matters to God" (Luke 12:21—Eighteenth Sunday).

The Christian ought not to be surprised, he who has heard the proclamation:

> "Blessed are you who are poor,
>   for the kingdom of God is yours.
> Blessed are you who are now hungry,
>   for you will be satisfied. . . .
> But woe to you who are rich,
>   for you have received your consolation.
> But woe to you who are filled now,
>   for you will be hungry"
> (Luke 6:20-21, 24-25—Sixth Sunday).

And also: "If you are not trustworthy with dishonest wealth, who will trust you with true wealth? If you are not trustworthy with what belongs to another, who will give you what is yours? . . . You cannot serve God and mammon" (Luke 16:11-12, 13—Twenty-fifth Sunday).

Today's Gospel does not merely mean to remind us of this: it is above all a call to conversion that becomes more and more pressing in this life.

This is precisely what is at issue in the second scene of the parable (vv. 27-31), which is not contained in the older Egyptian and rabbinic accounts. All the more does it demand our attention.

Jesus says that the rich man, understanding the futility of any further insistence, is preoccupied with those he has left on earth: his five brothers who are in danger of blindly rushing to the same fate as belongs to him. He begs that Lazarus might be sent to warn them and, causing them to abandon their careless ways, lead them to conversion.

From someone on the other side of the great abyss, this request is more surprising even than the preceding dialogue. But their only purpose is to lead to Abraham's second speech, which summarizes the parable and its teaching: "They have Moses and the prophets . . . If they will not listen to Moses and the prophets, neither will they be persuaded if someone should rise from the dead."

The expression "Moses and the prophets" in Luke denotes the Scriptures.[34] It evokes the whole of the revealed message, the "living utterances" (Acts 7:38).

The rich man's request partakes of the same illusion suffered by many people still today: that a clear, irrefutable "sign from heaven" (Luke 11:16, 29) will make all the difference. It is an illusion, for as we well know, the miracle itself is only convincing to faith; and Scripture must authenticate it, not vice versa.

With a heart and mind impervious to faith, one cannot perceive the true significance of the most plain of signs. Some will say about Jesus himself: "It is by the power of Beelzebul, the prince of demons, that he drives out demons" (Luke 11:15).

Besides, "someone" is raised from the dead: Jesus himself. But this resurrection, the supreme sign, is also the object of faith and, as we proclaim in the creed, it is in "fulfillment of the Scriptures."

There is no way around this. We must hold with the Scriptures, the sure and only means to come to faith, and with the Word, the efficacious incitement to conversion. The miracle par excellence, the resurrection of the Lord, becomes a sign only for the one who listens to "Moses and the prophets'' and the one who has fulfilled them, Jesus, for these Scriptures culminate in his teaching.

The Gospel teaches us with extraordinary power and authority how to make the proper use of money and how to avoid being led by it into catastrophe.

Chapter 16 of Luke's Gospel forms the underlying unity of the sequence of the Twenty-fifth and Twenty-sixth Sundays.

In two parables, this chapter gives a particularly clear and strong teaching on the use of money and the privilege of the poor.

All three Synoptics report the hard saying of Jesus: "It is easier for a camel to pass through the eye of a needle than for a rich person to enter the kingdom of God" (Luke 18:25; Matt 19:24; Mark 10:25).

Both in Matthew and Luke, the beatitude of the poor comes first (Matt 5:3; Luke 6:20). For both, the announcement of the good news to the poor characterizes Jesus' mission (Matt 11:5; Luke 7:22). And both also report that one must choose between serving money and God (Matt 6:24; Luke 16:13).

Nevertheless, Luke is the herald par excellence, the one who proclaims the privilege of the poor: the *Magnificat*; the misfortune of the rich as compared to the beatitude of the poor; the repeated call to renounce riches, and to share them.

One must have these teachings in mind when one reads chapter 16, which insists on remaining mindful of death in order to teach how money is to be used in an intelligent and prudent way, so as to make friends against the time when one's wealth will have to be abandoned.

This Gospel is particularly well set forth and emphasized against the background of the Liturgy of the Word these Sundays.

The prayer of intercession is intended for the salvation of all, and it implores God particularly for those who exercise responsibility in society and the state. It is a profession of faith in Jesus Christ as the one mediator, in line with the baptismal profession of faith.

This sets the field for the ''beautiful fight'' that makes the Christian life an incessant search for justice and uprightness in relations with others and with God.

How could one then make a god of money, of mammon?

The warnings of prophets like Amos, virulent though they may be, are echoed by the Fathers of the Church and by contemporary visionaries. We must listen to them, for they perpetually rouse our consciences in a very timely manner.

Every person who has more than is indispensable for material and spiritual well-being is a millionaire, and thus a debtor of those who have nothing.[35]

Your present goods, from where have they come to you? If you say, "From chance," you are an atheist, for you do not acknowledge the Creator and you are ungrateful to the one who has provided them. If you confess that they come from God, tell us the reason you have received them. Is it so that God may be unjust, he who unequally distributes those goods necessary to life? Why are you rich, and another poor? . . . To the hungry belongs the bread that you keep; to the naked man, the cloak you keep tucked away . . . You commit as many injustices as there are people to whom you could give.[36]

The Twenty-seventh and Twenty-eighth Sundays in Ordinary Time

Chapter 17 of Luke's Gospel contains a series of Jesus' sayings and teachings on scandal (Luke 17:1-3a), forgiveness of sins (Luke 17:3b-4), the coming of the reign of God, and the Day of the Son of Man (Luke 17:20-37). Some of these texts can also be found in Matthew.[1]

But at the center of the chapter (Luke 17:5-19) are teachings on the dutiful servant and the healing of the lepers, which only Luke recounts. It is this central portion that the Lectionary contains.

The crucial emphasis is on the fact that salvation is an absolutely gratuitous gift, and that no one is *a priori* excluded from it. From this comes the unity of the sequence formed by the Twenty-seventh and Twenty-eighth Sundays.

In addition, we begin reading four excerpts from the Second Letter to Timothy (2 Tim 1:6-8, 13-14; 2:8-13; 3:14–4:2; 4:6-8, 16-18). Much shorter than the First,[2] this letter, which is addressed to the same disciple, appears to be a testament of the apostle, now old and imprisoned.

Twenty-seventh Sunday

Lord, Increase the Faith of Your Servant

Lord, Have You Forgotten Us?

The first reading comes from the Book of Habakkuk (Hab 1:2-3; 2:2-4). This is, in the Sunday Lectionary, the only text taken from this short book,[3] which is neatly divided into two parts by the titles: "The oracle which Habakkuk the prophet received in vision" (Hab 1:1) and "Prayer of Habakkuk the prophet. To a plaintive tune" (Hab 3:1). Our text this Sunday belongs to the first part.[4]

First comes a loud and audacious cry to the Lord: "How long, O LORD? I cry for help but you do not listen! . . . Why do you let me see ruin; why must I look at misery?" It is the prayer of a believer who is distressed by the triumphant appearance of evil.

But what exactly is at issue? What makes the prophet direct this "complaint" to the Lord? Is "the abomination" the shameful transgression of the Law and righteousness that can be found at large in the people? Is the "strife and clamorous discord" between neighbors who have forgotten to treat each other as such? Is the "misery," "destruction and violence" charged to a foreign aggressor? Or the injustice that reigns between people and nations? Why does God allow it? Where is his work in history?

Since these evils are spoken of in clichés, it is impossible to determine the precise nature and cause of them. But no matter, at least for us. For there was and will always be in the world—and in the Church—then as now, situations that provoke the same questions: "How long, O LORD? I cry for help but you do not listen! I cry out to you, 'Violence!' but you do not intervene. Why do you let me see ruin; why must I look at misery?"

Sometimes one will be reproached for feeling such cries of distress in the depths of one's soul, or for allowing them utterance. Such accusations indicate a lack of familiarity with the psalms, where such feelings are often echoed. Thus, for example:

240

> Why, O LORD, do you stand aloof?
>   Why hide in times of distress?
> (Ps 10:1)

> How long, O LORD? Will you utterly forget me?
>   How long will you hide your face from me?
> (Ps 13:2)

> O LORD, how long will you look on?
>   Save me from the roaring beasts; from the lions, my only life.
> (Ps 35:17)

> Awake! Why are you asleep, O LORD?
>   Arise! Cast us not off forever!
> (Ps 44:24)

> Will the LORD reject forever
>   and nevermore be favorable?
> Will his kindness utterly cease,
>   his promise fail for all generations?
> (Ps 77:8-9)

and perhaps especially Psalm 22, whose first words at least Jesus repeats on the cross:

> My God, my God, why have you forsaken me,
>   far from my prayer, from the words of my cry?
> (Ps 22:2)

These despairing calls, questions, and petitions of God do not, however, endanger the faith and trust of the believer. Let us reread Psalm 37, where the inspired psalmist, although grappling with tormenting questions, affirms his unfailing hope:

> Be not vexed over evildoers,
>   nor jealous of those who do wrong;
> For like grass they quickly wither,
>   and like green herbs they wilt.

> Trust in the LORD and do good,
>   that you may dwell in the land and enjoy security.
> Take delight in the LORD,
>   and he will grant you your heart's requests.

> Commit to the LORD your way;
>   trust in him, and he will act.
> He will make justice dawn for you like the light;
>   bright as the noonday shall be your vindication.

> Leave it to the LORD,
>   and wait for him;

> Be not vexed at the successful path
>   of the man who does malicious deeds.
>
> Give up your anger, and forsake wrath;
>   be not vexed, it will only harm you.
> For evildoers shall be cut off,
>   but those who wait for the LORD shall possess the land.
>
> Yet a little while, and the wicked man shall be no more;
>   though you mark his place he will not be there.
> But the meek shall possess the land,
>   they shall delight in abounding peace.
> (Ps 37:1-11)

Thus the prophet Habakkuk: "I will . . . keep watch to see what he will say to me," for I am sure that he will respond, and I will wait as long as necessary.[5]

The Lord responds, not by addressing the question that was put to him, but by a solemn declaration of faithfulness to the covenant, confirmed in writing. This is nothing more than a simple declaration: the Word of God accomplishes what it says, the vow written by God already begins to be fulfilled (Isa 55:10-11; Ezek 37:18-25). There is no room for impatience, and even less for doubt: "the vision still has its time," the fulfillment will surely come; to wait for it in hope is to prepare oneself to receive it; the just will live "because of faith," solidly based on God's own faithfulness.

This last declaration is the Book of Habakkuk's catchword. It has constantly been read and reread throughout Christian history, and very early on was used in catechesis.

> Even if you think you are faithful, you have not yet attained the perfection of faith. You also must say: "Lord, increase our faith." For you have hardly anything of your own, but must receive much from him . . . May you already have the faith that depends on you, so that you may be drawn by the one from whom you receive this other, who does what is beyond human power.[6]

Psalm 37, read above, expresses the hope of the believer, stronger than anything that can trouble heart or mind. It goes so far as to thank the Lord for a response that has not yet been received, but of which one is sure because, whatever happens and whatever the present situation may be—painful, distressing—he is the faithful God, on whom his people can and always will rely. "Faith is the realization of what is hoped for and evidence of things not seen" (Heb 11:1—Nineteenth Sunday). Finally, there is no proclamation of hope or profession of faith without a firm intent of conversion. Such is said in Psalm 95.

> *If today you hear his voice, harden not your hearts.*
>
> Come, let us sing joyfully to the LORD;
>   let us acclaim the Rock of our salvation.
> Let us greet him with thanksgiving;
>   let us joyfully sing psalms to him.
>
> Come, let us bow down in worship;
>   let us kneel before the LORD who made us.
> For he is our God,
>   and we are the people he shepherds, the flock he guides.
>
> Oh, that today you would hear his voice:
>   "Harden not your hearts as at Meribah,
>   as in the day of Massah in the desert,
> Where your fathers tempted me;
>   they tested me though they had seen my works."
> (Ps 95:1-2, 6-7, 8-9)

Seeing the Gift of God in Oneself

The epistle speaks once again, though in a completely different context, of faithfulness to God and trust in his Word (2 Tim 1:6-8, 13-14).

The tone is that of a "charge of ordination" and this should not be surprising. As a matter of fact, one can see, in both letters to Timothy, numerous elements that are clearly reminiscences, transpositions, even citations from liturgical texts and formulas.

The imposition of hands, a ritual gesture, goes far back in the religious tradition, not only the tradition of the Old Testament, but of all peoples. It is a gesture of investiture, a transmission of power, and bestowal of a mission. In Christian liturgy, it has always had the sense of an *epiclesis*, an invocation of God, especially of the Spirit. This gift—charism—granted and received once and for all, is not something dead, but acts rather more like a leaven, a seed that must be "reawakened" in oneself. It is a call to return to the prime of one's life with God: "Stir up the gift that you have received!"

> It is always the same journey that we must make, from year to year, not only with respect to God but with respect to our human relations. How many friendships begin in profound encounter and then become rigid or shortsighted: "I thought you were different." "Really? Then you are deceiving yourself; I was no different, but you saw me in glory, and this glory has dimmed, and you do not know how to live by faith. You wanted something clear and permanent to rely on, but sometimes there is darkness and

night.'' The same happens in our other relationships, e.g., between parents and children, husband and wife, and between the Churches.[7]

The Spirit ''that makes us strong, loving, and wise.'' The exercise of any ministry has never been an easy task, even when one does not have to deal with indifference or hostility. Paul several times asked the Christian communities to pray earnestly that he might have the courage to announce the gospel (Eph 6:19), the mystery of Christ (Col 4:3). Without the strength of the Spirit, what could human weakness accomplish?

This strength is also the spirit of love, for every charism is directed toward the exercise of charity.

''The spirit of wisdom,'' of good sense, is necessary for everyone, especially those with a ministry. Without it, how could one see well enough to be a guide to others? Hence, there is good reason not to enter a world torn asunder with thousands of doctrines, prey to the most extravagant speculations, misleading one from the demanding truth of the gospel. It was the case then, and is no less so now.

That the proclamation of the gospel could not take place without suffering, Paul knew all too well in the evening of his life, after having endured so many trials and persecutions in fidelity to his mission. And what apostle could not say the same? What thoughtful Christian can confess the faith, proclaiming Christ in words and way of life without discomfort?

Thanks to the Holy Spirit who dwells in us, everyone, no matter what the vocation, becomes a living link in the living tradition that transmits, in its purity, the teaching received form the apostles, the gospel of our Lord Jesus Christ.

This ''charge'' does not concern only those who have an ordained ministry (bishops, priests, and deacons) but the whole Christian community and each of us in it.

On the one hand, the question of ministries is not only important, then as now; it is crucial for the Church. It is not merely a theoretical debate but a concrete and vital problem. On the level of reflection and realization, it requires the active participation of all, clergy and laity.

On the other hand, what is demanded of the ordained ministries will only be possible in and through living communities animated by a ''spirit that makes us strong, loving, and wise,'' which is not ashamed to give ''testimony to our Lord,'' to participate, whatever the cost, in the proclamation of the gospel, to rule their conduct by the sure teaching received from the apostolic tradition. But though a community may be living, each member must regularly revive the initial grace of baptism.

Faith Works Wonders

Faced with such a prospect that necessitates, for everyone, a constant conversion, it is understandable that one would become rather dizzy, and turn to the Lord to plead: "Increase our faith!"

This is what the apostles did one day during the interminable "journey to Jerusalem," in the course of which Jesus taught them without ever hiding the radical involvement to which anyone who wishes "to follow him," to be his disciple, must subscribe. Thus begins this Sunday's Gospel (Luke 17:5-10).

The fact that this request is formulated by the apostles is itself very meaningful. The apostles are those who believed at Easter, and who were invested with the mission to call all people to faith, "to the ends of the world." Here they address Jesus as "Lord," a title given to him only by those who recognize in him the Christ exalted in the glory of the Father. Therefore, if these bulwarks of faith petition the Lord in this manner, how much more reason do we have to do so, who are "men of little faith."

Jesus responds by proclaiming the extraordinary power of faith. He expresses it in a way that is striking because of its paradoxical imagery: "If you had faith the size of a mustard seed" [the smallest seed of all—Matt 13:32], you could say to this sycamore, 'Be uprooted and transplanted into the sea,' and it would obey you."

Clearly he does not mean that the purpose of faith is to perform worthless and meaningless wonders. Jesus himself never did so. His miracles were not absurd demonstrations of power, but "signs" worked for salvation, for healing and life. These are the true miracles, "the trees in the sea."[8] But the miracle is also—how could Luke, the author of Acts, not think of it so?—the marvelous spreading of the good news throughout the whole world, and the multitudes of all races, peoples, and nations won over to faith and the preaching of the apostles.

In every situation, whatever the trials, difficulties, and hardships, one must remember that nothing is impossible with and for faith.

The Service of Faith

The second part of the Gospel this Sunday does not speak explicitly of faith—i.e., the word is not used—but of "service," and especially disinterested service.

"If one of you . . ." To be sure, it is difficult for us to see ourselves in the one of whom Jesus speaks. He speaks—quite naturally—within the framework of the situation of his time in speaking of the slave, who is the property of a master and has no personal rights. It has been some time in our world since any servant had the status of a slave. To say today to a servant or an employee, whatever their position, "This is what I pay you for," implies a certain hostility, or at least the deterioration of normal relations.

But the difference between the situation then and now is not the point. It cannot prevent us from understanding Jesus when he says: "When you have done all you have been commanded to do, say, 'We are useless servants. We have done no more than our duty.'"

But in what sense are we to understand this adjective that describes our quality as "servants," and what is its importance? The literal and common translation is "useless." It hardly seems to be appropriate, since these servants undoubtedly perform useful, efficient work. Other words have been tried: "poor," "ordinary" servants. Such diversity clearly indicates that the exact term has not been found. Let us instead return to what is clear: they are servants who have only "done their duty," who must be satisfied with this, who can claim no other wage, as if something were owed to them. But there is still a bit more to it than this.

Luke ignores the idea of retribution no more than the other evangelists or the writers of the Old Testament. In the fourth beatitude, that of those persecuted "because of the Son of Man," we read: "your reward will be great in heaven" (Luke 6:23); likewise in what is said about those who love their enemies, do them good and give without expecting anything in return (Luke 6:35). A little further on: "Give and gifts will be given to you; a good measure, packed together, shaken down, and overflowing, will be poured into your lap" (Luke 6:38). The servants who, having stayed awake, are ready to receive their master, will be rewarded (Luke 12:42-44), as will those who increase the talents that have been conferred on them (Luke 19:17, 19). It is also said: "Blessed indeed will you be because of their [the crippled, the lame, and the blind] inability to repay you. For you will be repaid at the resurrection of the righteous" (Luke 14:14). And Jesus one day told Peter: "There is no one who has given up house or wife or brothers or parents or children for the sake of the kingdom of God who will not receive [back] an overabundant return in this present age and eternal life in the age to come." (Luke 18:29-30). Many of these passages we have heard very recently in the liturgy.[9]

But the faithfulness of the servant, which will have its reward, is a grace given at the initiative of the one who calls, brings about a response, and enables one to endure to the very end. Consequently, one has nothing to boast of before God. One has no right to claim a wage. "We have only done our duty" through the grace of the Lord.

Every Christian knows and proclaims this in various ways in liturgical or private prayer. But it should be admitted that it is always difficult to free oneself entirely from a certain tendency to view the relationship with God more or less as a kind of give-and-take. One need not go so far as the Pharisee in the parable, who paraded his virtues before God (Luke 18:11-12—Thirtieth Sunday). But doesn't a religion experienced in terms of a right to recompense indicate a certain mercenary attitude? It doubtlessly leads to a generosity that attempts to achieve the greatest reward for the least effort. In that case, one would truly be a worthless servant, because God cannot completely rely on such a person. Jesus speaks to us of doing "everything" that God has commanded us. This proceeds not from a calculating or servile spirit but from the love whose acts are based on a total reliance on the Master one serves with a good heart.

> I am determined not to place limits to trust and to extend it to all things . . . You will be my strength, O my God, you will be my guide, my director, my counsel, my patience, my knowledge, my peace, my justice and my prudence. I will turn to you in my temptations, my dryness, my chagrin, my boredom, my fear, or rather I wish no longer to fear illusions, artifices of the devil, my own weakness, my indiscretions, nor even my suspicions; for you must be my strength in all my crosses; you promise me that you will be so in proportion to my trust, and this is wonderful, O my God, at the same time as you bring about this condition, it seems to me that you give me this confidence.[10]

"The just man, because of his faith, shall live" because of his faith in the faithful God. This is a sort of leitmotif that constantly returns throughout the Old Testament, which we must interiorize day by day.

When fortune turns against us, when trials threaten to overwhelm us, it is toward the faithfulness of God that we turn, recalling his promises and the covenant in which he takes the initiative. Our prayer can thus have despairing overtones, crying toward God our "why" and our confusion over what happens in and around us: "How long, O LORD? I cry for help but you do not listen! I cry out to you, 'Violence!' but you do not intervene."

Such a tearful prayer is really a cry of faith and trust in the God who cannot deceive, who "at the proper time" will not fail to realize what he has promised once and for all, and that is confirmed when one listens to his voice.

For it is not "a spirit of fear" that he has given us, but a spirit "that makes us strong, loving, and wise." This gift, received initially in baptism and confirmation, on which is grafted the grace of the other sacraments, makes each of us, according to our vocation, a witness of the Lord and a missionary of the gospel, a living and responsible link of the living tradition. It is awakened by the power of the Holy Spirit who dwells in us.

The extraordinary power of faith—a faith we ask God to increase—which allows us, weak and mortal though we are, to accomplish marvelous things: for God, nothing is impossible!

The joy of the believer called to the service of God performed faithfully and in a totally disinterested manner, through love.

> I know someone who so loves God, though he weeps that he does not love him as he should, that his soul constantly desires to see God glorified in him, and he himself regarded as nothing. This man hardly knows who he is, even when his praises are sung; for in his fervent desire for humility he does not think of his own worth; he celebrates the divine service as is befitting to a priest, but, in his intense love for God, he throws away the memory of his own dignity into the gulf of his charity for God, burying the glory that he might draw from it under a spirit of humility, in order to appear at all times to his own eyes and in his own estimation as only a useless servant, as excluded from his own dignity by his desire for humiliation. This is what we must do as well, in any way possible, fleeing all honor, all glory, because of the overflowing richness of love from the one who has so well loved us.[11]

The servant of God claims nothing for himself, not only because he has received all that he has but also in imitation of his Lord and Master who came not to be served but to serve (Luke 22:27). In his own frailty as "a useless servant" is displayed the power of Christ, as Paul said (2 Cor 12:9).

> He is the vanquisher of the world
> who believes;
> he subdues the universe
> for he wants nothing else,
> worthless servant,
> than to have grow in him
> the strength of Christ.

> Receive our weakness, Jesus,
> and unfold your power![12]

> Father, all-powerful and ever-living God,
> we do well always and everywhere to give you thanks.
> You are glorified in your saints,

for their glory is the crowning of your gifts.
In their lives on earth
you give us an example.
In our communion with them
you give us their friendship.
In their prayer for the Church
you give us strength and protection.
This great company of witnesses spurs us on to victory,
to share their prize of everlasting glory,
through Jesus Christ our Lord.
(Preface of Holy Men and Women I)

Twenty-eighth Sunday

Go and Give Thanks:
Your Faith Has Saved You

The Faith of a Pagan

The first reading this Sunday recalls how "Naaman, the army commander of the king of Aram . . . a leper," was healed by Elisha (2 Kgs 5:14-17).

In fact, this is only one part of the story found in the Second Book of Kings,[13] in the section sometimes called "the cycle of Elisha."[14]

What the Lectionary wants to convey today comes through this very sober story by itself. It is possible to grasp the meaning of it in the Liturgy of the Word without having to refer to what comes before or after the healing. However, one must be attentive to some of the details of the text to perceive its full meaning.

First of all—and of crucial importance—Naaman is a pagan, and even more, an Aramean general who is probably hostile to Israel itself!

He was struck with leprosy, that terrible sickness, thought to be very contagious and a divine punishment—a malediction.[15] Indeed, he is not said to be "healed" but "cleansed." His affliction was in some way, at least for the writer of the story, related to a sickness that was not more than physical.

If Naaman "went down and plunged into the Jordan seven times," it was to obey the order of the prophet who had told him, "Go and do this."

Why would Elisha command him to do this? One would have thought that he would perform the healing personally, either by laying his hands on the sick man while invoking God or by pronouncing a miraculously efficacious word such as Peter said to the invalid at the "the Beautiful Gate" of the temple. "In the name of Jesus Christ the Nazorean, [risen and] walk!" (Acts 3:6—Feast of Sts. Peter and Paul). That Naaman would have been disturbed—indeed shocked—by this is understandable.[16]

Did Elisha want to test the pagan? Did he regard this as a convenient opportunity to prove that there was a prophet in Israel (2 Kgs 5:8), rebuking a lack of faith among the people by intervening publicly on behalf of a general of the Aramean army? Like Jonah, who, after having preached at Nineveh, sat in the shade "to see what would happen to the city" (Jonah 4:5), did Elisha want to see what this man would do, whom he had sent away with such a strange order?

Whatever the case may be, Naaman finally obeyed and was "cleansed." But he had another surprise for the prophet, for "he returned with his whole retinue to the man of God."

The first thing he says could only delight the prophet. What a marvelous and sudden conversion! "Now I know that there is no God in all the earth, except in Israel."[17]

What he adds provokes a strong reaction from Elisha: "Please accept a gift from your servant." This gift was traditional. And yet the prophet emphatically refuses: "As the Lord lives whom I serve, I will not take it."

Did Elisha have some doubt about the meaning of Naaman's offer and thus the purity of his faith? Did he want him to understand that his avowal of belief must go directly to God without being mediated by a "man of God"? In any case, the prophet's disinterestedness attests to the complete gratuity of the healing: "One does not thus pay the God of Israel; one receives his gifts in thanksgiving."

Instead, the prophet accedes to Naaman's desire to cart away some of the earth of Israel to build an altar to the Lord, for he no longer wishes to "offer holocaust or sacrifice to any other god." This is a significant mark of the good intentions of this Syrian. If it seems somewhat surprising to us, it is because we have learned that God is not tied to one people, one land, one temple, nor the liturgy to one language.

How can this not be a cause for thanksgiving?

> *The LORD has revealed to the nations his saving power.*
>
> Sing to the LORD a new song,
>   for he has done wondrous deeds;
> His right hand has won victory for him,
>   his holy arm.
>
> The LORD has made his salvation known:
>   in the sight of the nations he has revealed his justice.
> He has remembered his kindness and his faithfulness
>   toward the house of Israel.
>
> All the ends of the earth have seen
>   the salvation by our God.
> Sing joyfully to the LORD, all you lands;
>   break into song; sing praise.
> (Ps 98:1, 2-3, 3-4)

Be Mindful of Jesus Christ

In this passage from the Second Letter to Timothy this Sunday, it is not difficult to recognize part of a testament of the elderly apostle in captivity (2 Tim 2:8-13).

Once again we can discern here several formulas that are at least liturgical in origin and might even be citations from hymns.

"Remember Jesus Christ, raised from the dead, a descendant of David: such is my gospel . . . " Immediately, this evokes the beginning of Psalm 132: "Remember, O LORD, for David all his anxious care." Actually, there is nothing remarkable about finding such a verse from the psalms quoted by a Christian. Isn't David a figure of Christ, the Messiah come from the line of the king par excellence? And could one speak of the "descendant of David" without affirming faith in his resurrection from the dead?

This is the gospel that Paul never ceases to preach, as do both the other apostles and the Church from age to age. It is our faith that we proclaim with the whole community, in the creed, through our life, and through liturgical celebration, particularly in the Eucharist.

> We proclaim your death, Lord Jesus,
> until you come in glory.

Nothing can restrain the gospel or the Word of God. But in order for them to be spread they must be preached: "But how can they call on him in whom they have not believed? And how can they believe in him of whom they have not heard?" (Rom 10:14).

In order to accomplish the mission of "preacher and apostle and teacher" (2 Tim 1:11) of the gospel and the Word, Paul joyfully submitted to all sorts of trials and harsh treatment, even prison and death: "Therefore, I bear with everything for the sake of those who are chosen, so that they too may obtain the salvation that is in Christ Jesus, together with eternal glory." Yet, he is well aware that he, Apollos, and the other preachers of the gospel are only "servants." They plant the seed of faith and water it, "but only God . . . causes the growth." They are nothing; everything depends on God alone (1 Cor 3:5-8).

Nothing can limit God or reduce his Word to silence. The whole history of the Church testifies to this. The grain that is sown now grows later, after it was thought to be lost.

Inspired by this certitude, every apostle, every Christian, must be able to say, like Paul, to those from whom he takes leave at the end of his life: "And now I commend you to God and to that gracious word of his that can build you up and give you the inheritance among all who are consecrated.'' (Acts 20:32).

The epistle continues with what is certainly a fragment of an Easter hymn of the primitive community.

Two things are especially noteworthy here. First, the repeated affirmation of the common destiny of the Christian and Christ. It is *with him* that we die, that we will live, that we stand the test, that we will reign.[18] Second, the expression of living hope. If we reject Christ, he will reject us as well, but he will never take the initiative.

Then comes the final sentence. Its beginning foreshadows the worst, as it sees the possibility of our infidelity. But no:

> ''But if we deny him,
>   he will deny us.
> If we are unfaithful,
>   he remains faithful,
> for he cannot deny himself.''

The Old Testament is shot through and through with this conviction that God is the ''Rock'' of his people (Deut 32:4) because he is faithful to his word, his promises, and, in the end, to himself:

> Only in God is my soul at rest;
>   from him comes my salvation.
>
> He only is my rock and my salvation,
>   my stronghold; I shall not be disturbed at all.
>
> With God is my safety and my glory,
>   he is the rock of my strength; my refuge is in God.
>   (Ps 62:2, 3, 8)

What is true of God is equally true of Christ, the ''Faithful and True'' (Rev 19:11), in whose person whatever promises God has made have been fulfilled (2 Cor 1:20—Seventh Sunday of Ordinary Time, Year B).

So we say:

> . . . but I am not ashamed, for I know him in whom I have believed and am confident that he is able to guard what has been entrusted to me until that day (2 Tim 1:12).

The Faith of a Samaritan

To remember Jesus Christ is to return constantly to the ''memoirs of the apostles,'' to what they wrote, in order that we might give a good account of the truth of the teaching we have received (Luke 1:4—Third Sunday).

Since the Thirteenth Sunday, we have followed Jesus on his "journey to Jerusalem." As we have already noted, it is more of a theological than a geographical road. In fact, we have hardly moved spatially; but what a wealth of teaching has been given us!

We are still within the confines of Galilee and Samaria in the Gospel this Sunday, the region where Jesus was born, where the Jews were so little orthodox that they were regarded as heretics, in some ways worse than the Gentiles. It is in this area of ill-repute that Luke situates one of the best-known episodes of his Gospel (Luke 17:11-19).

When Jesus is about to enter a village, ten lepers come to meet him. They keep their distance, in accordance with the laws. But what they say is extraordinary: "Jesus, Master, have pity on us!" More than a piteous petition, this is an unexpected profession of faith.

"Jesus!" It is rather uncommon in the Gospels for someone to call Jesus simply by his name.[19] Only three times does it happen, and in each case it is the beginning of an entreaty. The blind man at Jericho says: "Lord, Son of David, have pity on us" (Matt 20:31; Luke 18:38). The other two instances are found only in Luke, here and in the account of the Passion, where one of the thieves says: "Jesus, remember me when you come into your kingdom" (Luke 23:42).

The connection of this last with that of the lepers is noteworthy. They both come from sinners: a man hanging from a gibbet for his crimes, ten men struck with a sickness that was supposed to be associated with sin. Jesus' response to the thief and what he says to the Samaritan cured of his leprosy clearly indicate that prayer leads to salvation and opens the way to the kingdom: "Today you will be with me in paradise" (Luke 23:43); "Your faith has saved you." (Luke 17:19).

Thereafter, the invocation of Jesus' name becomes more common.[20] In the East the "Jesus prayer," which follows the rhythm of the breath, is a practice of the simple spiritual life: "Lord Jesus Christ, Son of God, have mercy on me, a sinner!"

"Master" also has very strong connotations. Luke is the only one to use this title as a confession of Jesus' omnipotence: Peter before the miraculous catch (Luke 5:5) and on the mountain of the transfiguration (Luke 9:33); the apostles begging for help in the midst of the storm (Luke 8:24); John expressing astonishment at having seen demons driven out at the name of Jesus by someone who does not belong to the Twelve (Luke 9:49).

What a richness of faith there is in these simple words! The lepers have nothing else to say. Jesus' response is brief: ''Go show yourselves to the priests.'' This is sufficient for the ten, who take to the road immediately to make the journey, marking a new way of expressing their faith.

Unlike Naaman, they show no disappointment at not seeing Jesus lay his hands on them to heal them directly. They rely purely and simply on his word. Why would he tell them to show themselves to the priests unless their healing would thus be verified?[21] Therefore it must already be given, even if they do not see it yet. And indeed, ''as they were going, they were cleansed.'' One thought cannot help but come to mind: it is in doing what Jesus commands that one obtains one's request. ''I say to you, rise!'' (Luke 5:24); ''Go!''; ''Blest are those who hear the word of God and observe it'' (Luke 11:28).

At this point, the plot thickens. ''One of them, realizing he had been healed, returned, glorifying God in a loud voice; and he fell at the feet of Jesus and thanked him. He was a Samaritan.''

Even if this were only a recognition of a received blessing, it would merit being singled out and set up as an example for the Christian community.[22] But there is more involved. Glorifying God, falling at Jesus' feet (prostrating oneself), speaking his praises, are all expressions that might fairly be called technical. They refer to liturgical attitudes, cultic behavior. Indeed, ''Rise,'' above all associated with ''your faith has saved you,'' is more than a mere invitation not to remain lying face down on the ground; it is reminiscent of being raised from the dead, which evokes the passage from death (sin) to the life that comes through baptism. ''Rise up'' often signifies resurrection, whether that of Christ himself or those whom God saves.

''Go your way'' also has a very strong meaning. In the context of the ''journey'' to Jerusalem, after what has been said about the necessity, for the disciple, of following Jesus wherever he goes (Luke 9:57-62—Thirteenth Sunday), and bearing one's cross (Luke 9:23—Twelfth Sunday), there is certainly more involved here than a simple leave-taking.

We note, furthermore, the abundance of verbs and terms of movement in this passage. Jesus ''journeys'' to Jerusalem, he ''enters'' a village. Ten lepers ''meet'' him. He tells them to ''go'' and show themselves to the priests. They are cured ''on their way.'' One of them ''returns,'' ''falls,'' ''stands up,'' and finally ''goes.'' This suggests that through the story, remarkably composed and structured, the evangelist wants to teach us that the encounter with Jesus overthrows not only the particular state but the ongoing life of every sinner (leper). This encounter is a ''passage,'' a Passover in faith.

In fact, it is faith that is at issue here—its gratuity, the salvation it grants that is offered to all, even to a Samaritan in the course of Jesus' ministry, to the Gentiles following Pentecost. Remember that the first "mission" took place in a town in Samaria. Philip proclaimed Christ to the people and brought them the joy of the good news. The apostles in Jerusalem learned of it. Peter and John were sent to them, "who went down and prayed for them, that they might receive the holy Spirit" through the laying on of hands (Acts 8:5-8, 14-17—Sixth Sunday of Easter, Year A).

Note also how often in his two books—Gospel and Acts—Luke insists on the universalism of salvation, and how often he points out that Jesus himself announced the good news, if not in pagan lands, at least in areas with mixed populations, like Samaria,[23] and that non-Jews also benefited by his miracles. In this, he sees the preparation for and justification of the universal mission. The Book of Acts ends with a declaration of Paul that expresses Luke's thought: "Let it be known to you that this salvation of God has been sent to the Gentiles; they will listen." (Acts 28:28).

This admonition still echoes today as a warning to the Churches.

> Just when I recognize myself in the thoughtless covetousness of these nine who pocket the healing, who lay hold of grace as something owed to them, and disappear from the Gospel, just when I see in them the faces of our forgetful and ungrateful Churches, here comes the new people of God, this Samaritan who praises God with his whole body, and thus with all his heart, this man fresh and excited in the face of the Word, this stranger to the gospel who is transformed by it and at whom Jesus is surprised: "Has none but this foreigner returned to give thanks to God?" Thus we see all our pious customs denounced as worthless, the Word dead among religious people renewed outside their small circle in a man who is a stranger to all their myths and rites; the community-prison of the gospel falls silent, and relearns it through its unexpected rising outside of all traditions and secular customs. Is it not a question of realizing that, paradoxically, I only have to do with the gospel if I deprive myself of it, if I always confess to being a stranger to it, ready to be surprised and astonished, to see it rise up, on the margin of all I have thought of as the Church, in a multitude of signs, words, and deeds that manifest the cosmic strength of the Word, free and sovereign, in the face of all division and narrowness? In him alone, this stranger, the only one to return to give thanks to God, is all the hope of Israel, the continuity of the work of reconciliation of the world, and the invitation—for whoever has eyes and ears to see and hear it—to recognize the presence and power of Christ in the world. Such is the originality of the New Testament: the Old invites the Gentiles to gaze on Israel, the New invites all pious people to see and hear in the world the truth of the journeying Christ.[24]

Whoever has faith lives by faith and obtains salvation. It is an absolutely gratuitous gift. What is done in obedience can claim a right to no other wage. The recompense itself is a gratuitous gift of the love of God that is indeed hoped for but not demanded. There is nothing servile in our service of the Lord, nor any mercenary calculation in our efforts.

> If we show ourselves to be acknowledging everything that we have received from him, we prepare a greater place in our soul for grace, and we make ourselves worthy to receive it more abundantly. In fact, the only thing that can stop our progress after our conversion is our ingratitude: the giver, regarding as lost all he has given to the ungrateful, will henceforth be more cautious, in the fear of squandering everything else that he might give to them . . . Happy the man who gives thanks from the bottom of his heart, even for the least blessings, regarding everything he receives as a purely gratuitous gift.[25]

We are the disciples of the one who has given all for us, even his own life, and received all from the Father who has resurrected and glorified him. "Remember that Jesus Christ was raised from the dead." Our hope and our joy rest on the faithfulness of God, our Rock. He cannot deceive us. His promises will be fulfilled "at the chosen time." Neither in God nor his messenger, is there the least discrimination: they distribute their gifts to all who have faith. Even a Samaritan has recognized Jesus as the Lord, has been able "to give thanks," to share in "Eucharist." The gift that we have received must constantly be awakened in ourselves, and transmitted faithfully to others.

> Ordinarily, it is through the Christian personality that the Christian truth must be recognized. One can describe the process of recognition. Dedication to it is the basis of faith, and is faith itself. It tends by its own energy to be purified and deepened. The Christian thus has the experience of the strength, life, and joy that God gives through faith. And very naturally, it shines out in his life . . .
>
> Commitment tested and contemplated tends to produce another commitment. To realize a presence and spread a call, this is the role of the witness.[26]

From the Twenty-ninth to the Thirty-first Sunday in Ordinary Time

There are only five Sundays left in the "sequence of events" of Luke's Gospel that we read throughout Ordinary Time, Year C.[1]

First—from the Twenty-ninth to Thirty-first Sundays—come three excerpts from chapters 18 and 19. The Lectionary's choice is marvelously judicious. From these two chapters it has retained the three passages that occur only in Luke: the parables of the unjust judge and the persistent widow, the Pharisee and the tax collector, and the story of Zacchaeus.[2]

The fact that after having received his information from the original "eyewitnesses," Luke alone has integrated into his "narrative" (Luke 1:1) these parables, and this episode testifies to the importance he accords them. Therefore, let us search them for valuable indications as to the evangelist's doctrine, and even the central meaning of the whole book.

We shall see as they are read that these texts form a harmonious whole. The three Sundays during which they are read therefore constitute an independent sequence in the unfolding of Ordinary Time this year.

The two parables have the obvious theme of prayer, but involve much more. The first ends with a saying of Jesus that is rather surprising: "When the Son of Man comes, will he find faith on earth?" At the end of the second, it said that the tax collector went home "justified," but the other did not, because "everyone who exalts himself will be humbled, and the one who humbles himself will be exalted."

As for Zacchaeus, "salvation has come to [his] house," and he too becomes "a descendant of Abraham." For "The Son of Man has come to seek and to save what was lost."

These, then, are three texts that, each in its own way and building to a crescendo, speak of the justification that comes from faith granted to the one who does not rely on his merits but opens himself to the gratuitous mercy of God.

At the same time, they reveal the true image of God—"the God of Jesus"[3]—who "does justice" to the defenseless (the widow of the parable), who "justifies" those who humble themselves (the tax collector), who "saves" sinners (Zacchaeus).

This revelation is found in the person and mission of the Son of Man, who is close to the weak and humble, the friend of tax collectors, of all the lost whom he has come to seek out and save.

The sequence formed by these three texts appears to be a condensation of the whole Third Gospel. In any case, everything that characterizes the message passed on by Luke is echoed here, in one way or another called forth or remembered.

Pray Always,
Without Losing Heart

God, Come to My Help! Lord, to My Rescue!

Moses, sitting on the mountain with hands uplifted while the people fight in the plain below, has become a symbol of the necessity of prayer and its efficacy (Exod 17:8-13).

It is readily made use of to illustrate that "combatants"—of the militant kind (in seeking justice), as heralds of the apostolate, etc.—need, in order to emerge victorious from the struggle here on earth, the prayer of "contemplatives" who wear themselves out by praying without rest on the mountain.

It is true that prayer (contemplation) and action are equally, reciprocally necessary.[4] It is also true that this interpretation of the scene has become the standard one, at least since Origen (185-254):[5]

> Since we must "combat principalities and powers, the rulers of this world of darkness," if you wish to vanquish and sweep them away, lift your hands, lift your actions, that your life might not be spent on the earth, but, as the apostle says "though dwelling on the earth, we live in heaven." Thus may you triumph over the people who fight against you, over Amalek, and be worthy of having it said of you: "The Lord fought in secret against Amalek." Lift your hands also toward God, put into practice the apostle's commandment: "Pray without ceasing." Thus will be fulfilled what is written: "As the calf grazes on the green grass of the fields, this people will devour the people which is on the earth." This signifies, as the ancients have told us, that the people of God fight more with tongue and voice than hands and weapons: it is in raising prayers to God that one's enemies will be routed. Also, if you wish to vanquish your enemies, lift your actions, cry to God, "persevere, be on your guard in prayer," as the apostle says. This is the battle that triumphs over the enemy.[6]

This interpretation has been taken up a great deal in iconography, in discourses, and in sermons. It is a beautiful image, and very biblical, of undeniable spiritual and pastoral interest.

And yet, our eyes are thus so fixed on Moses and his uplifted hands that we do not see that they are holding "the staff of God." This "staff" is, so to speak, the central figure. It is thanks to this that God, through his intermediary Moses, accomplishes his works: it releases the plagues of Egypt; it divides the sea to open a passage for the people; it brings forth water from the rock. And it is "the staff of God" held over the plain by Moses that gives the warriors the strength to drive off their aggressors. Moreover, at the end of the story (Exod 17:15), it is said that "Moses built an altar there, which he called *Yahweh-nissi,*" which is to say "Yahweh my banner."

It is this "banner of God" lifted by Moses over the battle that has won the victory. It is God who has fought for his people on their way to the Promised Land through the desert, as he led them through the Red Sea on dry land and gave them water from the rock, because Moses held "the staff of God" over the sea and struck the rock with it.

We should add that the theme of "Yahweh-warrior" returns at various points in the Old Testament. It is the title given him in the canticle sung by Moses and the children of Israel after their passage through the Red Sea:

The Lord is a warrior,
Lord is his name!
(Exod 15:3—Easter Vigil)

The title of "warrior" as applied to God offends our sensibilities. We no longer think that God can be invoked in this way, asking him to fight for us in our wars. Our idea of God has become more refined. But we must not ignore these texts that speak of the "Wars of the Lord."[7]

They certainly speak of the battles that the people fought with the help of God to establish themselves in the Promised Land, and throughout the centuries, to survive. These records, which are rather like epics, undoubtedly contain all sorts of exaggerations: a little skirmish with a raiding band taking on the scope of a great battle; a people small in number and fragmented into little tribes assembling such great armies; etc. This is not to say that these battles were fought without vigor, and, it must be said, without a cruel ruthlessness. But much of this comes from the literary genre of the epic.[8]

This is particularly the case regarding the Amalekites, against whom was set the strength of "the staff of God." Of these tribes, history contains almost no trace: they were quickly absorbed by their neighbors. But the Amalekites remain in the collective memory of Israel as the very type of the irreconcilable enemy, constantly rising up, whose attacks can only be met by God—by "the staff of God"—to whom his people remain faithful. They are a formidable enemy that cannot be vanquished by the sword, but only by relying on the strength of God, whom one implores hopefully in prayer. On a memorial to an unknown Jewish martyr erected in 1956 in Paris is written: "Remember Amalek!"[9]

This battle is not only a military one against an ever-aggressive outsider, but a spiritual one against the true hereditary enemy that allows no respite. There can be no victory without the help of God and his angels.

> It so happened that Father Moses had to fight strongly against fornication. Unable to remain in his cell any longer, he left and told this to Father Isidore. The old monk urged him to return to his cell. But he refused, saying: "I cannot, father." Then, taking him along, Father Isidore led him onto the roof and said: "Look toward the west." He looked and saw a vast number of demons stirring and making a loud noise, as before a battle. Father Isidore then said to him: "Look toward the east." He turned and saw a countless multitude of the holy angels shining in glory. And Father Isidore said: "Behold, these are sent to the saints by the Lord to bring them help, while those in the west are those who fight them. Those who are with us are greater in number." And Father Moses, giving thanks to God, took courage and returned to his cell.[10]

The episode of Moses on the mountain is therefore an urgent call to faithful vigilance and incessant prayer to the "the LORD, strong and mighty, the LORD, mighty in battle" (Ps 24:8).

Without God's intervention—without the "banner of God" raised above us—Amalek is stronger. But this divine protection does not free us from the need to fight: God waits for us to enter the battle ourselves before assisting us. Thus we pray and proclaim with assurance: God is our help; he who has made heaven and earth neither sleeps nor slumbers; he will protect us from all evil because he stays near us and because he desires for us to have eternal life.

> *Our help is from the LORD*
> *who made heaven and earth.*
>
> I lift up my eyes toward the mountains;
>   whence shall help come to me?
> My help is from the LORD,
>   who made heaven and earth.
>
> May he not suffer your foot to slip;
>   may he slumber not who guards you:
> Indeed he neither slumbers nor sleeps,
>   the guardian of Israel.
>
> The LORD is your guardian; the LORD is your shade;
>   he is beside you at your right hand.

The sun shall not harm you by day,
    nor the moon by night.

The LORD will guard you from all evil;
    he will guard your life.
The LORD will guard your coming and your going,
    both now and forever.
(Ps 121:1-2, 3-4, 5-6, 7-8)

The Tools for Doing Good Work

The epistle read today is from the Second Letter to Timothy, a short passage that proclaims vigorously and precisely a teaching and practice of utmost importance (2 Tim 3:14–4:2).

To proclaim the Word is certainly what is most essential in the apostolic mission. The author of the letter is not content merely to recall this; he gives Timothy certain instructions that have not and will never lose their pertinence (4:1-2).

But this announcement rests on fidelity to the Word of God transmitted by Scripture and received in the Church (3:14-17). And this is of no less permanent significance.[11] The apostle is not a schoolmaster, but a servant: he receives what he must in his turn pass on faithfully.

Before being a "static" content, the Tradition is a "living" movement, and every apostle is part of a succession of witnesses, trustees who pass on what they have received: "The things which you have heard from me through many witnesses you must hand on to trustworthy men who will be able to teach others" (2 Tim 2:2). Therefore, "You must remain faithful to what you have learned and believed." This, one might feel, has nothing to do with a strict traditionalism. The scope is historical and thus dynamic. The deposit of faith is not buried in the ground or shut up in a box; it is passed on from hand to hand.

"From your infancy you have known the sacred texts." Timothy owes this to the "faith which first belonged to his grandmother Lois and to his mother Eunice" (2 Tim 1:5). Precious testimony to the role of kinsmen—and women—in the faithful transmission of the teaching which gives life. Now, in his "infancy" Timothy was not a Christian. Thus—need we say it?—the continuity of revelation is not a privilege of the New Testament divorced from its roots in the Old. Again, there has never been a Word of God transmitted by Scripture which was not received and transmitted in the community of believers. This is the only way which "through faith in Jesus Christ leads to salvation."

Because all its passages are inspired, Scripture as received, read and understood in the living Tradition is also the primary rule for apostolic activity. The author is speaking here of what we call the Old Testament, but this must clearly be applied to the Scriptures that the Church has since recognized as equally inspired. Again, what is said here is valuable for every Christian.

Following this line of thought, it would be well to point out that Scripture is not "useful" (2 Tim 3:16), in the sense that it can be "used" at personal discretion: to justify one's own views, choices, judgments, etc. On the contrary, one must turn to it faithfully to receive—and pass on— what it teaches, its truth concerning good and evil, its admonitions, as well as to discover in its light the paths of "salvation through faith" (v. 15), and "holiness" (v. 16). One must desire faithfully to speak of the Tradition and the teaching of the Church.

Finally—an interesting point after having read the text of Exodus 17:8-13—Scripture inspired by God is the weapon which allows one to prevail in the fight of faith, the Christian life and the apostolate. Empowered by the strength of the word of God, Timothy—and every believer—not only can but must proclaim the Word.

"In the presence of God and of Christ Jesus, who is coming to judge the living and the dead, and by his appearing and his kingly power, I charge you." This charge is very solemn, particularly as it appeals to Christ, evoked as Judge in the last times, and then in his Manifestation and Reign.

Timothy must not forget that on the day of Judgment he will have to give an account of the mission which has been conferred on him. This warning is reminiscent of the parable of the faithful and farsighted steward (Luke 12:42-48—Nineteenth Sunday).

The evocation of the Manifestation and Reign emphasizes the need for missionary preaching. Remember the saying in Matthew (24:14): "This good news of the kingdom will be proclaimed throughout the world as a witness to all the nations. Only after that will the end come."[12]

The preacher of the Word must intervene "whether convenient or inconvenient," simply and audaciously. The Gospel will always be, for someone or other, "inconvenient," disturbing.

Paul remains the pre-eminent model of the preacher who proclaims the Gospel "whether convenient or inconvenient." He found all occasions to be appropriate, whatever his listeners were doing: pious Jews gathered in a synagogue, idlers strolling among the porticoes of the Agora, dock workers at Corinth, companions in his captivity, members of the Sanhedrin or the Athenean Areopagus, Roman magistrates and, clearly enough,

Christians gathered after he passed through their town. His three long missionary journeys amply demonstrate his anxiousness to bear the good news everywhere; even his journey in captivity is an occasion for preaching: "I am ruined if I do not preach the Gospel!" (1 Cor 9:16—Fifth Sunday, Year B).

There is nothing about this preaching that flatters the listener; nothing other than "Jesus Christ and him crucified," "a stumbling block to Jews, and an absurdity to Gentiles" (1 Cor 2:2; 1 Cor 1:23—Fifth Sunday, Year A; Third Sunday of Lent, Year B). Such audacity would be utterly senseless and doomed to failure if the preacher relied on his own strength, the power of his conviction alone. But just as the he uses a language that has "none of the convincing power of the Spirit," he relies on the power of God (1 Cor 2:4-5—Fifth Sunday, Year A). He is strong because he is well-armed, thanks to the "Scripture inspired of God."

Pray Without Losing Heart; God Will Respond Swiftly

"He told them a parable on the necessity of praying always and not losing heart." Thus Jesus tells the parable of the unjust judge, which is found only in Luke (Luke 18:1-8).

Luke, as we have noted at various times, lays great stress on prayer. In his second book—Acts—he emphasizes that the primitive Christian community was diligent in its practice.[13]

But discouragement can erode devotion or make it purely mechanical, thereby robbing it of its joyful spirit. To this temptation, the parable responds that prayer is never in vain.

The story is wonderfully simple. The principal figure is a judge of a small town who enjoys discretionary and absolute power. He "respects neither God nor man," being one of those whom the psalmist asks:

"How long will you judge unjustly
  and favor the cause of the wicked?
Defend the lowly and the fatherless;
  render justice to the afflicted and the destitute.
Rescue the lowly and the poor;
  from the hand of the wicked deliver them" (Ps 82:2-4).

Against this powerful man comes a widow, the type of a weak, defenseless person. What she asks is very simple: "Give me my rights against my opponent."[14] But nothing comes of it; the judge is unmoved.

Yet there comes a point when he has had enough of her, dreading the thought of her coming again. With no other consideration—neither for

God whom he does not respect, nor for other people whom he scoffs at, and certainly not for this woman—he decides to give justice, simply that she may stop boring him.

This is a clear demonstration of the fact that there is a need to "pray always and not lose heart." Not that God is comparable to such an impious judge; he himself is the just Judge. How much more, then, will he attend to those who call to him persistently! This conclusion appears with perfect clarity. But the parable's real conclusion is deeper.

We note first of all that the evangelist says, not "Jesus," but "The Lord said." The application of this name gives a solemn tone to the declaration, for it is the title the disciples attribute to the Resurrected Christ. Therefore it introduces a revelation to which one must pay close attention.

In the second place, the lesson focuses not on the need to pray without losing heart in order finally to obtain one's goal. "The Lord" declares that God does not wait for "his chosen who call out to him day and night." He does not "give justice," but "does justice," "swiftly."

"To do justice" means much more; in fact, it is something entirely different. It means "to justify," "to renew," "to make innocent," "to save."

This solemn declaration of the Lord reveals the true object of prayer made "without losing heart" and the faith which animates it. One must pray "without losing heart" in order to be "justified," or saved. And one has, through faith, the assurance that God will realize the promised salvation "swiftly." Consequently, discouragement can have only one cause: a lack, or weakness, of faith. Because one sees nothing happening, one begins to doubt God, the coming of his Reign, the promised salvation. At least, one becomes so unsure as to prefer not to think about it. But no, declares the Lord. "To those who call out to him day and night"—"without losing heart"—God "will do justice." And "swiftly."[15]

One should not be surprised, then, at the stark question that the parable leads the Lord to pose: "But when the Son of Man comes, will he find any faith on the earth?"

It is with this serious and tragic question that the Gospel today leaves us. A fearful question which none can evade, for it belongs to each one to respond to it personally.

This finale sheds light on the parable which, at first glance, may have appeared to be a simple lesson on the need to pray "without losing heart."

By her insistence, the widow of the parable shows that she remains profoundly convinced that the judge, though he respects neither God nor men, will eventually render her justice. It would be absurd to imagine that God, the just Judge, is insensible to persevering prayer. Far from it! He intervenes "swiftly" to "give us justice," to give us salvation.

Thus the issue is one of faith: faith in God who saves; faith in the Lord, the Son of Man who will come again; faith which must always be rea-wakened in us, without losing heart, because, without it, there is no salvation.

> The wait is long, in the night, Lord,
> and the bitter wind of weariness
> threatens the flame in our hearts;
> will it glow again,
> to shine on your face,
> when you knock at our door?
>
> Watch in prayer,
> I will come on you suddenly
> in the night, like a thief.
>
> When the Son of Man comes,
> will he find faith on the earth?
>
> Watch in prayer
> that you may not fall into temptation;
> who holds fast to the end will be saved.
>
> When the Son of Man comes,
> will he find faith on the earth?
>
> Watch in prayer,
> the one who is ready,
> I myself will serve in my Kingdom.
>
> When the Son of Man comes,
> will he find faith on the earth?[16]

To proclaim the Word after having studied it is the fundamental task of the Church and, in the community, of those who hold responsible positions.

This proclamation is at the heart of every liturgical celebration, that of the Sunday Eucharist in particular.

To listen to it, in the most active sense of the term, is the characteristic, the definition, one might say, of the disciple.

The proclamation and the hearing of it suppose fidelity to the Word transmitted by Scripture and received in the Church.

Thus the evangelists received and transmitted to us the sayings of Jesus, endlessly meditated on and better understood in the living Tradition of a Church community.

We must add that the Word is not a dead letter or a text on which we are merely to apply our scholarship, but living food. In the liturgy it is given us to share that we might, in a sense, eat of it; hence we speak of two Tables, of the Word and of the Eucharist.

> The Eucharistic manner of consuming the Word presupposes the epiclesis of all reading. The Word is living through the Spirit which resides in it, as it rested on the Son at Epiphany. It must be read in the measure of the Paraclete, which is that of the Body of Christ, the Church, the Tradition wherein the Word speaks. God has so ordered that Christ form the Body where his words resound as words of life; it is therefore in Christ, in the Church, that one must read and listen. Only the Church guards the Word, for it possesses the Spirit who has dictated it, as Origen teaches . . .
>
> At the Liturgy, the people are gathered first to hear, then to consume the Word. The hearing builds the people of God, forms the Eucharistic synaxis which is ready to consume the Word, to enter into substantial communion with it . . . The liturgy presents the method of ecclesial mediation where the Word is proclaimed, sung, prayed and lived. It is extended in the lives of the faithful and is found in the daily *lectio divina* which is a form of prayer and communion. Such a reading is its source and fulfillment. According to St. John Chrysostom, the reading of the Scriptures is the priesthood of the laity which leads them to holiness.[17]

Jesus tells the parable of a judge who satisfies a widow who demands justice in order to show "the necessity of praying always and not losing heart." Luke extends the teaching by adding, to a crystal-clear story, a saying of the Lord which enlarges its perspective and significance.

Prayer "without losing heart" is directed toward the salvation that God has promised to grant "swiftly" "to his chosen who call out to him day and night." It is therefore an act of faith in God and, in some way, a "school of faith," for it unfolds and expresses it, while at the same time strengthening, increasing, and expanding it.

> But, you ask, what are acts of faith? These are some of them. Going often to prayer is an act of faith . . . Trying to be attentive to your prayers is an act of faith. Behaving in the house of God otherwise than you would in an ordinary place is an act of faith . . .
>
> These are acts of faith, because they are acts that you would accomplish if you saw and understood that God is present, though your eyes and ears neither see nor hear him. But "happy are they who have not seen, and have believed!"
>
> To be sure, if we act thus, we shall, little by little, and with the grace of God, clothed with the spirit of his holy reverence. And we shall show in our way of speaking and acting, as in our religious behavior and daily conduct, that we respect and love him. Not by constraint and weary effort, but spontaneously and naturally.[18]

Without faith and prayer, who can withstand the assaults of the enemy who is always ready to assail us? "Remember Amalek!" You will only have the advantage by placing yourself under "the banner of God," the sign raised over the world.

This admonition, directed to the Church and every believer, never ceases to resound.

> God of holiness,
> you have the power to make us strong by your grace
> and vigilant by the strength of the gospel.
> Remember us in the fight of prayer
> and keep us faithful in meditating on your word.
> Thus we fervently await
> the coming of your Son, Jesus, our Lord.[19]

Thirtieth Sunday

The Prayer of the Humble Breaks Through

God Listens to the Downtrodden

The Book of Sirach is like a traditional catechism, a compendium of received truths that never attempts to expand one's reflection by opening up new perspectives.[20] The first reading today comes from this book (Sir 35:12-14, 16-18).

In the framework of the liturgical celebration, one must read these maxims in themselves, devoid of context. They present some of the thought current at the time of the Old Testament, and help us to realize what is old and what is new in other readings, being deeply rooted in ancient ground.

God "is a God of justice," the just Judge. To judge with perfect impartiality, without differentiating between individuals, truly belongs to the divine. All those who have the responsibility of exercising justice must force themselves to resemble as nearly as possible this just Judge. However, no one can match his perfection. We must reckon not only with human weakness and the pressures the rich and powerful can bring to bear on the best-intentioned judges, but also—alas!—the bad faith of those who "neither [fear] God nor [respect] any human being" (Luke 18:2, 4 —last Sunday's Gospel). For many of the poor, weak, and helpless, God, the just judge, is the only hope, for he does hear them. Even better, he has a particularly attentive ear for "the cry of the oppressed," "the wail of the orphan," "the widow when she pours out her complaint." God is the appointed defender of the powerless, at whose side he always stands. But here, the "lowly" is not only a representative of an outcast social category but one "who serves God willingly," whose poverty matches an interior disposition, an attitude of the soul.[21] Such a "poor" person can be confident of the efficacy of persevering prayer. But that very quality is also the precondition of it.

Thus we have a text that speaks with utmost simplicity of the deep and unshakable conviction of the believer of all ages. It is expressed in psalms

270

and other poems, e.g., in the *Magnificat*, which is itself bedecked with biblical reminiscences.[22] One could point to many other prayers throughout the ages, which express the true place of the human being before God; such testimony cannot fail to be moving.

> You know my misery, you know my abandonment,
> you measure my loneliness, you see my weakness
> and my infirmity, you who fashioned me, my God,
> you ignore me not, you gaze on me and know everything.
> Look at my humble heart, my contrite spirit,
> look at me approaching you in despair, my God,
> and from on high give your grace, your divine Spirit,
> give your Paraclete, O Savior, send him according to your promises,
> make him come again today over your disciple seated
>   in the upper room, O Master, truly above
> all earthly concern, beyond the whole world,
> and who searches for you, who awaits your Spirit!
>
> Do not delay, merciful Lord, do not let your eyes wander,
> compassionate, forget not the one who seeks you,
> whose soul thirsts for you,
> do not stunt the life in me, unworthy as I am of it,
> do not reject me with disgust, O God, do not abandon me!
> In your heart I take refuge, behind your pity I take shelter,
> such is your love for man
> that I call to you as intercessor.
>
> I have not toiled, I have not done the works of Justice,
> never have I kept one of your commandments,
> instead I spent my whole life in debauchery:
> yet you have not averted your glance,
> you have caught and found me in my errancy,
> you brought me back to the lost road
> and on your spotless shoulders, by the light of your grace,
> you have raised me, O Christ, you have carried me, O Merciful,
> and far from allowing me to feel the least fatigue,
> completely at my ease, as in a chariot,
> you have made me travel effortlessly the rough roads,
> until you return me to your sheepfold,
> and make me enter into communion
> and numbered among your servants.
> I proclaim your pity, I celebrate your mercy,
> I wonder and give thanks for the richness of your bounty.[23]

The Lectionary follows this text with three stanzas of Psalm 34, a psalm of no literary pretensions but typical of faith in the care of God for the "lowly" who serve him.

A psalm of praise to God who hears and saves the poor who cry to him. On the one hand, a collection of verbs that evoke an ordeal: to cry, call, deliver, be near, save, find refuge. On the other hand, those that express praise and thanksgiving: to bless, praise, glorify, feast. And all in the first stanza alone!

Then comes a profusion of terms that speak of confidence in God, in his faithfulness, his care for the "lowly."

A psalm to sing, or at least to say to oneself, to meditate on in its entirety, especially today:

> *The LORD hears the cry of the poor.*
>
> I will bless the LORD at all times;
>   his praise shall be ever in my mouth.
> Let my soul glory in the LORD;
>   the lowly will hear me and be glad.
> The LORD confronts the evildoers,
>   to destroy remembrance of them from the earth.
> When the just cry out, the LORD hears them,
>   and from all their distress he rescues them.
> The LORD is close to the brokenhearted;
>   and those who are crushed in spirit he saves.
> The LORD redeems the lives of his servants;
>   no one incurs guilt who takes refuge in him.
> (Ps 34:2-3, 17-18, 19, 23)

The Crown Belongs to God Alone

Today we read the fourth and final excerpt from the Second Letter to Timothy (2 Tim 4:6-8, 16-18).

The closing of the letter[24] is particularly moving. It must be acknowledged as an authentic echo of the apostle's testimony to his passionate love for Jesus Christ.[25]

The first part (vv. 6-8) is a short farewell discourse that successively points to the present, the past, and the future.[26]

The "time of dissolution" has come. The text uses a rare word here.[27] It evokes the image of a nomad folding up his tent, or a sailor casting off the mooring rope, the anchor already weighed.

But more remarkable is the expression he uses to speak of his approaching death: "I am already being poured out like a libation."[28] All of Christian life is spiritual worship (Rom 12:1); the apostolate even more so (Rom 1:9; 15:16): it is consummated by a libation of blood. So much for the present.

The past? One could sum it up by saying: "Mission accomplished," or like Jesus on the cross: "It is finished" (John 19:30). In fact, three verbs summarize this past. "I have fought the good fight, I have finished the race, I have kept the faith." The image refers not to war but to the contests of the stadium.[29] The apostle acted like an athlete who kept the rules (2 Tim 2:5). He was faithful to his vows.[30] Therefore, there is nothing left for him but to receive "the winner's crown" that belongs to the victor.[31]

This crown "of life" (Jas 1:12; Rev 2:10), "of glory" (1 Pet 5:4) is the eternal justice that God reserves "to all who have longed for his appearance," to those who, in fighting the good fight, will have lived in the hope of "the appearance of the glory of the great God and of our savior Jesus Christ" (Titus 2:13—Christmas, Mass at Dawn).

The second part of the text points to the apostle's concrete situation. As interesting as these details are, as well as what can be deduced from them, it is the manner in which he speaks of them that must fix our attention.[32]

Paul is alone; no one has helped to defend him since his first appearance before the tribunal. He forgives all those who have abandoned him, as did Jesus (Luke 23:34) and Stephen (Acts 7:60).

If he came out of this first ordeal, it was due to the help of the Lord.[33] Furthermore, God has "given him strength" in order to let him take this last occasion to proclaim the gospel to the pagans who are gathered together to judge him!

The coming summons will be his complete deliverance. "The Lord will rescue me from every evil threat and will bring me safe to his heavenly kingdom" (2 Tim 4:18).

What an extraordinary portrait of a condemned man waiting for death! Nothing is missing, not even the final doxology, the last echo of the great voice that, after having proclaimed the gospel "to all the nations," is already singing the canticle that resounds in heaven "to the one who sits on the throne and to the Lamb" (Rev 5:13): "To him be glory forever and ever. Amen."

God Vindicates the Humble

The parable of the Pharisee and the tax collector is found only in Luke.[34] It is well known, but for that very reason must be read carefully, avoiding the pitfall of a reading that is too shallow or clichéd (Luke 18:9-14).

First we see the figure of the Pharisee. For various reasons, the term has acquired an entirely negative connotation.[35] Thus, when the Gospel speaks of them, we immediately think of them as "hypocrites or proud men" who wish to be thought worthy by their minute observance of the rules of the Mosaic law. The synonyms of "phariseeism" are thus "duplicity, hypocrisy, double-dealing."[36]

There certainly were "bad" Pharisees; Jesus often upbraids them, in a quite lively manner, for their behavior.[37] But not every one—or even most—of them would deserve the ill-repute into which the whole sect has fallen. Besides, the Pharisees themselves castigated those who, in making use of their movement, discredited it. This can be seen in the Talmud, written at the beginning of the Christian era. With humor, and not without some very pointed remarks, they distinguish seven categories in the sect, six of which have titles that justify the accusations against them. Just as Bernanos vilified the "right-thinking," they hardly seem to have a tender spot for those possessed of a complacent bigotry:

> There are, they say in the imaginative language the Jewish mind so loves, seven sorts of Pharisees:
>
> 1. The *strong-shouldered*, who carry their deeds on their backs to receive honor from men;
>
> 2. The *stumblers*, who, in order to be noticed, drag themselves through the streets and stub their toes on rocks;
>
> 3. The *head-knockers*, who avert their eyes so that they may not see women, and knock their heads against the walls;
>
> 4. The *humiliated*, who walk doubled over;
>
> 5. The *Pharisees of calculation*, who only practice the Law so that they may reap the rewards it promises;
>
> 6. The *Pharisees of fear*, who only do good out of fear of punishment;
>
> 7. The *Pharisees of devotion*, who are the best of the lot.[38]

Among the evangelists, Luke is the one who best distinguishes between Pharisees. He tells us, for example, that one day some Pharisees came to find Jesus to tell him: "Go away, leave this area because Herod wants to kill you" (Luke 13:31). In Acts, little mention is made of the Pharisees. But one of them, called Gamaliel, "a teacher of the law, respected by all the people," played the role of a moderator when the apostles appeared before the Sanhedrin (Acts 5:34-39). Again, later on, some Pharisees were forced to acquit Paul (Acts 23:6-9). There is really only one mention of a Pharisee persecuting the first Christian community: Saul

himself, before becoming the apostle Paul! The Sadducees were the persecutors, and, with the "priestly party" bear the chief responsibility for
Jesus' death.[39]

In short, though there may have been some deviations, the Pharisees
were eminently respectable and religious people, rigorous observers of
the Law, models of piety admired and loved by the people. What the
Pharisee in the parable says is undoubtedly true: he avoids all sin, he
fasts twice a week, he gives a tenth part of all he earns.

The parable thus does not present him as a hypocrite or a pious show-
off. It is quite understandable that he would thank God for not being
"like the rest of humanity . . . or even like this tax collector" who "stood
off at a distance." Since the parable rests on a comparison, this point
must be emphasized. But it should not be accentuated to the point of
decrying the Pharisee for having a contempt for others. Who has not
thanked God for not being a worthless person, a rake, a "reputable" thief,
etc., as are so many people around us, at least according to the
newspapers? This must be admitted: such a "thanksgiving" is not necessarily perverse.

But, as we already know, this man at prayer is, in the parable, the type
of "those who were convinced of their own righteousness," to whom
Jesus addresses the story. This Pharisee seems to be entirely turned toward God. But isn't he really turned toward himself? Does he truly give
thanks to God or does he simply delight in himself? It is a question of
tone, to be sure. Psalm 131, for example, is not the self-satisfied prayer
of a Pharisee, but it could become so if one would speak it with a triumphant air and omit the last verse:

> O LORD, my heart is not proud,
>   nor are my eyes haughty;
> I busy not myself with great things,
>   nor with things too sublime for me.
>
> Nay rather, I have stilled and quieted
>   my soul like a weaned child.
> Like a weaned child on its mother's lap.
>   [so is my soul within me.]
>
> O Israel, hope in the LORD
>   both now and forever.

The comparison between the Pharisee's and tax collector's prayer illuminates the point of the parable. As the one represents "those who
believed in their own self-righteousness," the other is the very type of

the sinner: by his situation and trade dedicated to injustice and impiety (like the prostitutes—Matt 21:31-32). He sold himself to the Roman occupiers, collecting their taxes and profiting himself thereby. Tax collectors were no honest functionaries with set salaries. They had to pay their employers a fixed sum. For their own profit, they merely had to demand more than the actual rate. No control or check was put on them. The level of their cheating would vary according to their particular consciences. And as they were rather rich, like Zacchaeus . . . Indeed, this was a form of profitable prostitution. "Sinners" is quite an appropriate tag. The tax collector in the parable recognizes this. He dares not lift his eyes to heaven. Knowing his state, he turns toward God: "Be merciful to me, a sinner." That is all.

On the one hand we see a man who is thought to be, if not "just," at least in good standing with God. On the other hand, a sinner who, by confessing himself as such, simply awaits the mercy of a pitying God. The first can even enumerate his virtues. The second experiences the complete poverty of the sinner. A Pharisee who asks nothing from God, not even blessings; they come of their own accord. A tax collector who longs for everything. So this man "went home [from the temple] justified" but the other did not. His prayer, a confident appeal to the mercy of God, has pierced the clouds.

> The tax collector dared not lift his eyes toward heaven. Why did he not look at heaven? Because he was looking at himself. And by examining himself, he began to be filled with disgust, and this is what was pleasing to God. You, on the other hand, stand erect, holding your heads high. But the Lord says to the proud: "You do not wish to contemplate your wretchedness? Then I will contemplate it! Do you wish me to avert my gaze? Then do not avert your own!"
>
> Thus the tax collector does not dare to lift his eyes toward heaven: he examines and condemns himself. He makes himself his own judge, and God pleads his cause. He punishes himself, and God gives him grace. He accuses himself, and God defends him. He defends him so well that he judges him thus: "This man went home from the temple justified but the other did not. For everyone who exalts himself shall be humbled while he who humbles himself shall be exalted." He has examined his conscience, says the Lord, and I do not wish to examine him. I have heard him cry to me: "Turn your face away from my sins" (Ps 51:11). But who can pronounce such words, if not the one who says also: "My sin is before me always" (Ps 51:5)?[40]

God does not see in the tax collector virtues that he does not possess. He does not argue with the Pharisee's claims. But he is God. And "to become just" is out of human reach, it is the grace of God. It would have been sufficient for the Pharisee to see himself as "a useless servant" (Luke 17:10—Twenty-seventh Sunday) as the tax collector saw himself as a bad or misguided servant. Both would then "become just." And the Father would have invited both his sons to "celebrate and rejoice" (Luke 15:32—Twenty-fourth Sunday).

But why all these verbs in the past tense? It is to us that the parable is addressed, who are threatened by the perpetual danger of a self-satisfied phariseeism, which is all the more threatening—in an insidious way—as we demonstrate our fidelity to a rigorous practice. The temptation is perhaps not that of pride at not being like other people, or even like so many sinners around us; there is so much that is absurd in such self-satisfaction that one can manage to guard against it, at least in front of others, most often. The temptation consists rather in forgetting that even a true saint is, and remains, a sinner who must say constantly and from the depths of his heart: "O God, be merciful to me." What is finally at stake here is nothing less than the truth of God recognized by the truth of our deepest attitude before him, which is particularly expressed in our prayer. "We are only beggars," said Luther on his deathbed.

> Let the Lord cover your wounds: do not do it yourself. For if you are ashamed to show them, the doctor will not be aware of them. May he cover them with a potent salve and heal them. The wound that the doctor treats will heal. But if the sick person wishes to treat them himself, he will only succeed in hiding them. And from whom does he hide them? From the One who knows all.[41]

"For everyone who exalts himself will be humbled, and the one who humbles himself will be exalted." This is not the proclamation of a reversal of status that will occur at the end of time. It is the affirmation of what happens today, because God is God. God raises the lowly and sinners to himself by giving his grace to them, but leaves to their absurd, pretended greatness those who believe they can raise themselves. This is what the beatitudes and the *Magnificat* say.

The three readings this Sunday face us with the judgment of God, and they demonstrate the only attitude that is appropriate to us. The Lord is a judge who, far from despising the poor, heeds their prayer and gives them justice. It is from him alone that justification comes, and not from the wealth of merits on which we pride ourselves. The tax collector of the Gospel raises toward God a prayer of the poor; he returns home justified. The Pharisee, on the other hand, can receive no grace, since he seems to be ignorant of his need for it. Heeding this lesson, the Church, at the beginning of each Eucharistic celebration, has us turn toward God to beg his mercy. But all of Christian prayer must have the humility that is found in the tax collector.

> Consider also in what our prayer consists. We are certainly not worthy to receive what it belongs to friends to ask and obtain, but what is portioned out to rebellious servants and great sinners. We do not call on the Lord that he may grant us recompense or favor, but that he may be merciful to us. To ask Christ, the friend of humanity, for mercy, pardon, or remission of sins and not to go away with empty hands after this prayer, to whom does this belong if not the guilty, since "those who are well do not need a physician" (Matt 9:12). If men should raise a suppliant voice to God, this can only be the voice of those who stand in need of mercy, the sinners.[42]

The epistle, finally, shows us Paul's thoughts at the end of his life. In the prison that he would only leave to go to martyrdom, he expresses his complete confidence in "the God of justice" from whom he awaits the "winner's crown." The apostle certainly fought well for Christ, but how could this be a cause for vanity? All of us are sinners, all are deprived of the glory of God. But all may be gratuitously justified by his grace.

> For ourselves, too, we ask some share in the
> fellowship of your apostles and martyrs
> and all the saints.
> Though we are sinners,
> we trust in your mercy and love.
> Do not consider what we truly deserve,
> but grant us your forgiveness.
> Through Christ our Lord.
> (Eucharistic Prayer I)

Thirty-first Sunday

The One Who Comes for Sinners

Jesus' long journey toward Jerusalem comes to its end, and now we can mark out definite stages of it on a map. Soon, he will be near Bethphage and the town of Bethany on the mount called Olivet (Luke 19:29). Then he will enter into Jerusalem, where he will fulfill his ministry by preaching in the Temple area (Luke 19:45). Now he is at Jericho, a city of palm-trees, a pleasant oasis with three springs, a residential city and frontier town some twenty-three kilometers northeast of Jerusalem.

In terms of elevation, this is the lowest city in the world: three hundred meters below sea level. There is therefore a steep climb of some thousand meters between Jericho and the esplanade of the Temple.

We must be careful not to make too much of the symbolism of these geographical and topographical facts, or the historical associations with Jericho; this is not Luke's way. Nevertheless, there in the vale of the Jordan and in this city, Jesus encounters a leader of the tax collectors who becomes ''a son of Abraham'' because the Son of Man searches him out and saves him.

In addition, we begin this Sunday the last letter of Paul that is read during Year C.[43]

The Second Letter to the Thessalonians is short,[44] but very valuable. In fact, the two letters to the Thessalonians are the oldest writings of the New Testament era to have come down to us. The First Letter was doubtlessly sent at the beginning of A.D. 51, the second shortly afterward, therefore only twenty years after the death of Jesus.

Moreover, the Second Letter—from which we read three excerpts— forestalls all evasion of the reality of the Christians' task in the world and reminds us that Christian experience is inseparable from daily vigilance. What could be more to the point at the end of the liturgical year?

The Lord Shows Mercy to All People
The first reading comes from the Book of Wisdom (Wis 11:22–12:1).

This work is the latest of the books of the Old Testament, dating between 50 and 30 B.C. Written in Greek at Alexandria, it is one of the "deuterocanonicals."[45]

Its primary interest comes from the fact that the author, a devout Jew rooted in biblical culture, translates the message of the Bible for the people of his adopted environment, writing in Greek, the universal language, and using the rich concepts of a nonbiblical culture. A marvelous example from antiquity of what we today call acculturation!

When he retells the history of his people, it is not to discover their future or explain their destiny in it. His meditation is rather concerned with God himself and his conduct with respect to humanity. He makes an effort to better understand and to make comprehensible who God is, who always acts with wisdom and moderation even when he punishes.[46]

As always in the liturgy, the passage we read is taken out of context, and it is thus that it should be understood, having a general application and acting as good preparation for reading the Gospel. It is worthy of interest, revealing something that is important in every age.

Because he is the creator, God acts with mercy and love. The author expresses this fundamental conviction under the form of an interior prayer of adoration. If he is confident of it, it is so that the reader may also perceive the infinite love of God and may find himself drawn smoothly into a similar contemplation.

"You have mercy on all because you can do all things." The omnipotence of God, source of his mercy!

It sometimes happens today that people are embarrassed by this fundamental divine attribute. What a misunderstanding this involves! If God were not all-powerful, how could we confess our sins to him with such hope of seeing them pardoned by his mercy? How could we imagine him blessing us in such an efficacious manner?[47] "All-Powerful" in no way refers, in speaking of God, to a blind, capricious, tyrannical power. Because God can do "all," nothing is beyond his power, especially his mercy. God is merciful because he loathes nothing. "For your might is the source of justice; your mastery over all things makes you lenient to all. For you show your might when the perfection of your power is disbelieved; and in those who know you, you rebuke temerity. But though you are master of might, you judge with clemency, and with much lenience you govern us; for power, whenever you will, attends you" (Wis 12:16-18). He is "God and not man" (Hos 11:9).

We can indeed be befuddled, intoxicated, or corrupted by our power:

"All power corrupts, and absolute power corrupts absolutely." For us to close our eyes to faults can be blindness, weakness, or resignation. People can even come to hate, spurn, or destroy those that they have made, the flesh of their flesh. It can happen that, repenting of having given life in a moment of carelessness or passion, they may prevent it from being born. Not God. If he shuts his eyes, it is because he believes in the possibility of a sinner's conversion. Never does he think of anyone: "Nothing good can come from you."

"God saw how good it was . . . " (Gen 1:4, 10, 12, 18, 21, 25, 31). This refrain from the story of creation could not be forgotten by someone rooted in the Bible. The creator God is the "Lord and lover of souls," who gives life, maintains it, and returns it when it has been lost. "Do I indeed derive any pleasure from the death of the wicked? says the Lord God. Do I not rather rejoice when he turns from his evil way that he may live?" (Ezek 18:23).

To draw people to conversion ("that they may abandon their wickedness") and belief, God acts in a manner that the author summarizes in four stages, delineated by four verbs. First, he treats carefully—he "spares" says the Lectionary—"all things" because he loves them, because they "are his," because his breath moves in and through them.

If they do evil, he chastises them, he "rebukes little by little," and tells them why by "reminding them of the sins they are committing." Finally, he exhorts them.

Thus, by every possible means, God works to turn us from evil and restore us to faith, so that we discover our natural condition as creatures called to life in fidelity to the love of our creator.

This omnipotence of God is accompanied by his infinite patience.

> Truly, what great patience God has! . . . He lets the day rise and the sun shine on the good and the wicked; he waters the earth with his tears, and no one is excluded from his benefits: it rains on the just and the unjust. We see him be equally patient with the guilty and the innocent, the faithful and the impious, the grateful and the ungrateful. For all of them, the seasons obey the orders of God, the elements are put at their service, the winds blow, the springs flow, the wheat grows, the grape ripens, the trees bear fruit, the forests become green and the meadows are covered with flowers. Though God may be exacerbated by constant offenses, he tempers his indignation and waits patiently for the day set aside for retribution. And, although he may wield the sword of vengeance, he prefers to be patient for as long as possible, waiting and waiting so that, if it is possible, the evil might weaken with time and man, sunk in the miasma of his errors and crimes, finally turn himself toward God; for he tells us: "I take no pleas-

ure in the death of the wicked man, but rather in the wicked man's conversion, that he may live'' (Ezek 33:11).[48]

In the celebration of the assembly of believers, may there rise a thanksgiving to the all-powerful God, full of compassion and kindness for all! And may the whole universe join in our praise!

> *I will praise your name forever, my king and my God.*

> I will extol you, O my God and King,
>   and I will bless your name forever and ever.
> Every day will I bless you,
>   and I will praise your name forever and ever.

> The LORD is gracious and merciful,
>   slow to anger and of great kindness.
> The LORD is good to all
>   and compassionate toward all his works.

> Let all your works give you thanks, O LORD,
>   and let your faithful ones bless you.
> Let them discourse of the glory of your kingdom
>   and speak of your might.

> The LORD is faithful in all his words
>   and holy in all his works.
> The LORD lifts up all who are falling
>   and raises up all who are bowed down.
> (Ps 145:1-2, 8-9, 10-11, 13, 14)

Prayer for the Persecuted Churches

The Second Letter to the Thessalonians is addressed to a Church shaken by persecution and trial, whose faith yet ''flourishes ever more,'' while among its members ''the love of every one of [them] for one another grows ever greater.'' Here is, not only for the apostle but for all the ''Churches of God,'' a reason for pride and thanksgiving. It is also an assurance that the Thessalonians will be ''considered worthy of the kingdom of God'' for which they suffer; God will give them justice (1:3-10). Immediately thereafter comes the text that we read today (2 Thess 1:11–2:2).

It is a double encouragement addressed to Christians undergoing trials. They first of all must know that they are ''always'' being prayed for.

''I am praying for you,'' we often say to people who are sorely tried, but usually without adding anything else, because we do not know what it is appropriate to ask of God for them. We assure them, instead, of our concern and awareness, which we express especially in prayer on their behalf, an expression that is certainly not meaningless. Perhaps we run into trouble also because we do not know what we would want others to ask for us in similar circumstances. Thus our prayer comes down to this simple but very forceful formula: "God, come to their aid!"

"To this end, we always pray for you, that our God may make you worthy of his calling and powerfully bring to fulfillment every good purpose and every effort of faith . . ." In order to dare to specify thus the intention of the prayer for those who are suffering, in order to have the right to do so, one must have known at least equal suffering oneself.

But it is good for us to hear such words, even when our situation is quite different from the state of those people to whom they are addressed. They might come to mind very handily when we do have troubles, sustaining and stimulating us. Who knows? Perhaps we will then be able to say why we ask for the prayers of others.

In any case, we need to know that all Christian suffering is a participation in the mystery of Christ and, like his own passion, a promise of the glory "in accord with the gracious gift of our God and of the Lord Jesus Christ." This is the heart of our faith that we must live just as much as we proclaim it, in the expectation of the Lord's coming.

The Lord's coming does not seem to trouble the serenity of Christians today very much, and certainly does not seem to be a cause for alarm. Yet, among some people, one sees a desire for the miraculous, for pseudo-appearances, for pretended heavenly messages. It certainly is not enough to treat lightly of such anxieties, or to regard disdainfully those who preach the imminent return of the Lord and the apocalypse.

The glorious return of the Lord and "our being gathered to him" belong to faith. We proclaim this at every Eucharistic celebration. But this faith, far from legitimating any uneasiness, is the basis of our hope. It gives no grounds for restless agitation or fleeing the present; it prods us constantly to active vigilance.

He Has Come to Save the One Who Was Lost

The Lectionary has devoted a great deal of time to the section of Luke's Gospel known as "the journey to Jerusalem."[49]

The point of departure for this grand literary tract was "a Samaritan village" whose name the evangelist does not give us (Luke 9:52). Thereafter, there are no place-marks; it is said only that Jesus is "making his way to Jerusalem" (Luke 9:57; 13:22, 32; 17:11; 18:31). And here, at the end of a long journey that cannot be traced on any map,[50] Luke specifically says that Jesus approaches Jericho (Luke 18:35), enters the city and goes through it (Luke 19:1). There we find the episode of Zacchaeus' conversion that Luke alone recounts (Luke 19:1-10).

It is one of those Gospel stories that even young children know very well. This is because it does not lack picturesque elements, though they may be subject to exaggeration at times: Zacchaeus' shortness of stature, the fact that he climbed a tree to see Jesus, who lifted his eyes toward the little man, etc.

Certain Fathers of the Church seized on this chance for allegorizing; e.g., Ambrose, bishop of Milan (340-397).

> Short in height, which is to say not having the dignity of noble birth, lacking in merits like the Gentiles, when [Zacchaeus] learned of the arrival of the Savior Lord he desired to see, this One who had not been received by his own people (John 1:11). But it is not easy to see Jesus; no one can do so by being of the earth . . . And it is proper that he should climb a tree, a good tree, producing good fruit (Matt 7:17), so that, taken from the wild olive tree of his nature and grafted against his nature on the cultivated olive tree, he might bear the fruit of the Law (Rom 11:24) . . . How is it that Scripture mentions no one's height but his? Because he was short? Was he by any chance little because of wickedness, or in terms of faith? For he had been promised nothing when he climbed up; he had not yet been seen by Christ; thus he was still little . . . As for the crowd, was it not an ignorant multitude, incapable of seeing the heights of Wisdom? Thus Zacchaeus, within the crowd, did not see Christ; lifting himself above the crowd, he saw. In other words, by surpassing common ignorance, he succeeded in contemplating the One he wanted.[51]

This sort of exegesis may seem rather forced to us. We must not deny its real worth, though, and should recognize in any case that though in some ways disturbing, it is a timely reminder of a profound dimension of the mystery of grace and salvation.

Zacchaeus, by his profession and undoubtedly by his way of exercising it, found himself in the state of excommunication. How could he have become rich if he had not used his authority as a tax collector to extort the people?

But this action of his indicates a leap. He wants "to see who Jesus was." He first "ran ahead and climbed a sycamore tree." Would he have done all this if he had not foreseen—however dimly—that a chance would be offered him to leave his sinful state?

We remember that Luke, and he alone, mentions that "even tax collectors came to be baptized, and they said to [John], 'Teacher, what should we do?' He answered them, 'Stop collecting more than what is prescribed'" (Luke 3:12-13—Third Sunday of Advent, Year C).

Be that as it may, Jesus "looked up" and said: "Zacchaeus, come down quickly, for today I must stay at your house."

This is really a startling move on Jesus' part. Not only is it unexpected, but bound to shock the "right thinkers," both then and now: "He has gone to a sinner's house as a guest."[52]

Zacchaeus comes down quickly from the tree. He does not hear the recriminations, or at least does not let himself be put off by them. He does not tarry for indignant protests. He "received Jesus with joy." The joy of salvation proclaimed and received is a theme dear to Luke: the announcement of the birth of John to Zechariah (Luke 1:14), the *Magnificat* (Luke 1:47), the message of the angels to the shepherds at Bethlehem (Luke 2:10), to the apostles at the resurrection (Luke 24:41) and after the ascension (Luke 24:52-53). This joy is in itself a sign of salvation.[53] It is a joy that belongs to the angels and to the Father himself for one sinner who is converted (Luke 15:10, 32—Twenty-fourth Sunday), a joy in which each must share when they see the bounty and mercy of God, which sometimes appears in a surprising manner, as witnessed by the workers who labored all day when they received their salary (Matt 20:11). For we always find it a bit difficult to admit that God may act with the complete gratuity that one finds in the story of Zacchaeus. We remain, in spite of ourselves, governed by the notion of merit.

The unexpected conversion of Zacchaeus is wonderful and quite radical. "Half of my possessions, Lord, I shall give to the poor." See how this rich, chief tax collector immediately enters on the gospel path of the proper use of wealth. With "elusive wealth" he makes friends—the poor—who will receive him in heaven. He understands that one cannot serve both God and mammon (Luke 16:9, 13—Twenty-fifth Sunday). He firmly opts for God. And he publicly vows to make restitution to those whom he may have wronged. He will pay them back "four times over" according to the penalty that the Romans, his employers, imposed for known theft.[54]

> Whereas others accuse him of being a sinner, Zacchaeus, raising himself up, that is to say, persevering in the truth of the faith to which he has come, proves not only that he has been converted from sin, but even that he takes his place among the perfect. For since the Lord said "If you wish to be perfect, go, sell what you have and give to [the] poor" (Matt 19:21), whoever has lived honestly before his conversion can, once converted, give all to the poor. But the one who has benefited by fraud must first make restitution according to the law, then give the poor what he has left. So Zacchaeus, keeping nothing for himself, sells all his goods, gives them to the poor, and his justice remains forever (Ps 112:9).

Such is the wise folly that the tax collector had found on the sycamore, like a fruit of life: restore stolen goods, abandon one's own property, scorn visible goods in favor of the invisible, long even till death to renounce oneself and aspire to follow the footsteps of a Master who cannot yet be seen.[55]

The Gospel does not tell what were the reactions of those who "murmured" initially at seeing Jesus going to stay with a "sinner." It leaves us the responsibility of receiving for ourselves the lesson of this conversion: a man who takes it upon himself to make reparation for the wrongs he has committed by conforming to the most rigorous precepts of the law; a rich man who willingly rids himself of half his wealth.

Instead, the Gospel reports what Jesus says "to him." But it is really to everyone, and therefore to us, that he is speaking. What he says has indeed a general value for all people in all ages.

It is not belonging to a race or religion that qualifies one to be "a son of Abraham," but faith. Abraham himself was justified on account of his faith. He received circumcision "as a seal on the righteousness received through faith while he was uncircumcised." He became "the father of all the uncircumcised who believe, so that to them [also] righteousness might be credited, as well as the father of the circumcised who not only are circumcised, but also follow the path of faith that our father Abraham walked while still uncircumcised." (Rom 4:9-12).

"Realize then that it is those who have faith who are the children of Abraham"; they "are blessed along with Abraham who had faith" (Gal 3:7, 9). Jesus fully takes for his own the declaration of John the Baptist: "Produce good fruits as evidence of your repentance" (Luke 3:8). We must not forget this, for it is there that we find the foundation of the Christian condition and the sharing in the Promise. No one is excluded, though they be rich like Zacchaeus. But of everyone the same demand is made: be converted not only in words but in deeds.

Ambrose has well expressed this universalism of salvation, which excludes no one, of any social situation.

Come into favor with the rich as well; for we do not want to wound the rich, but rather, if possible, to heal the whole world. Otherwise, stigmatized by the parable of the camel, given up on more quickly than Zacchaeus was, they would have a right to be deeply offended. May they understand that the fault lies not in being rich, but in not knowing how to use riches; for the wealth that is an obstacle to a bad person is, for a good person, a means of virtue. Yes, the rich Zacchaeus has been chosen by Christ. But in giving the poor half of his goods, in restoring four times over his fraudulent gains—for one of these alone is not enough, and largesse is worthless if injustice remains, since one does not ask for spoils, but for gifts—he has received a recompense far greater than his restitution. And he is well marked as chief tax collector: who could despair of his personal situation, when this happens to such a man, who gained his wealth by fraud.[56]

The episode ends with a saying of revelation: "The Son of Man has come to seek and to save what was lost," which explains what had already appeared in the parables of the lost sheep, the coin, and the father with two sons (Luke 15:6, 9, 24, 32).

An extraordinary revelation, for Jesus applies to himself the declaration of God found in the prophet Ezekiel: "The lost I will seek out, the strayed I will bring back, the injured I will bind up, the sick I will heal [but the sleek and the strong I will destroy], shepherding them rightly" (Ezek 34:16—Solemnity of the Sacred Heart of Jesus, Year A). Thus, in Jesus' actions, one can recognize God at work; his ministry is the appearance and work of the mercy of God for sinners; he is the intermediary sworn to go to God from whom the initiative always comes.

But to the fullness of the divine gift must correspond the generosity of whoever receives it. This goes for us as for Christ: "Who, though he was in the form of God . . . he emptied himself, taking the form of a slave . . . he humbled himself, becoming obedient to death, even death on a cross" (Phil 2:6-8—Passion Sunday).

Occurring during the last stage of Jesus' life, what happened at Jericho illuminates the importance of the events that will take place at Jerusalem, and it teaches us, through a remarkable example, how we can participate in it.

One could even say that the call and the conversion of Zacchaeus constitutes a sort of summary of the whole of Luke's Gospel. In Jesus we see the true face of God the Father who forgives whomever is converted. Receiving salvation joyfully involves not only not doing evil to others but also being cheerfully rid of all that might slow one down on the road to Jerusalem, on which Jesus draws us.

Majestic temples and grandiose churches are not the only places to encounter God. Salvation also comes in our own homes.

The Church is a collection of pardoned sinners who have become children of Abraham by their faith in the one whom God has sent "to seek and to save what was lost." It must not forget this, but proclaim it to all. Not only by receiving those sinners who come of their own accord but by going out among them, lifting its eyes to see those who look on from afar, and inviting itself into their homes: "Zacchaeus, come down quickly, for today I must stay at your house."

We all find ourselves put to the test. For whatever reason, don't we sometimes treat good-willed people as the inhabitants of Jericho treated Zacchaeus? And we cannot use their excuse of ignorance, because we know and have so often proclaimed the mystery of the divine mercy revealed by Jesus.

Christians must remember, as harsh as they may be, the terrible invectives of Jesus, so that they may not earn them: "Woe to you, scribes and Pharisees, you hypocrites. You lock the kingdom of heaven before human beings. You do not enter yourselves, nor do you allow entrance to those trying to enter."

God is the all-powerful, for he has created all beings and has filled them incessantly with the imperishable breath that moves them. "Lord and lover of souls" who can do everything, he is preeminently capable of forgiving the sins of his creatures and bringing faith to birth in them. This is why we can appeal to his omnipotence when we implore his mercy. The glory of the all-powerful God is the living being!

When we, made in his image, lost his friendship by turning from him, God did not abandon us to the power of death. In his mercy he has come to the aid of all that we may search for and find him. He has made numerous covenants with them and has formed them, by the prophets, in the hope of salvation. He so loved us that he sent us his own Son, "in the fullness of time," that he might be our Savior (Eucharistic Prayer IV). He has come "to seek and to save what was lost," so that his glory may be in us. Behold what the grace of our God and the Lord Jesus Christ has reserved for us.

By continually praying "that our God may make us worthy of his call," by asking him to give us "by his power every honest intention and work of faith," we sing and bless him:

> God of power and might,
> we praise you through your Son, Jesus Christ,
> who comes in your name.
> He is the Word that brings salvation.
> He is the hand you stretch out to sinners.
> He is the way that leads to your peace.
>
> God our Father,
> we had wandered far from you,
> but through your Son you have brought us back.
> You gave him up to death
> so that we might turn again to you
> and find our way to one another.

> Therefore we celebrate the reconciliation
> Christ has gained for us.
> (Eucharistic Prayer for Masses of Reconciliation II)

God will give justice swiftly to his elect, who, with faith, cry to him day and night (Twenty-ninth Sunday).

This "justice" comes not from our own merits, but from the one who alone can raise to himself those who acknowledge their poverty and sinfulness (Thirtieth Sunday).

No one is excluded from this grace offered by the all-powerful God who has sent his Son to seek and to save what was lost (Thirty-first Sunday).

Thus the sequence constituted by the Twenty-ninth, Thirtieth, and Thirty-first Sundays centers around faith, justification, and conversion.

In giving thanks to God for what he has begun in us, in sharing the Bread of Life and the Cup of Salvation, in celebrating the mystery of Christ dead and resurrected for all, we sing with the whole Church assembly of pardoned sinners:

> The table is opened to sinners;
> Jesus calls and waits for us.
> Draw near to the Master of life;
> he alone can heal us,
> give us the joy of being saved.
>
> Near to you, Lord,
> is the abundance of forgiveness!
>
> I have come not to call the just,
> but sinners.
>
> Near to you, Lord,
> is the abundance of forgiveness!
>
> If you hear my voice,
> harden not your heart.
>
> Near to you, Lord,
> is the abundance of forgiveness!
>
> To those who thirst,
> I offer deliverance.
>
> Near to you, Lord,
> is the abundance of forgiveness!
>
> Today, the announcement of salvation
> rings in your ears.
>
> Near to you, Lord,
> is the abundance of forgiveness![57]

The Thirty-second and Thirty-third Sundays in Ordinary Time

Christian faith and life and the Church's journey point dynamically toward the resurrection of the dead and the coming of the Son of Man.

> We believe in one Lord, Jesus Christ . . .
> He will come again in glory to judge the living and the dead,
> and his kingdom will have no end . . .
> We look for the resurrection of the dead,
> and the life of the world to come.

This same tension can be found in every liturgical celebration, especially the Eucharist:

> Christ has died,
> Christ is risen,
> Christ will come again.

Each of us proclaims it in our prayer:

> Our Father who art in heaven . . .
> Thy kingdom come . . .

It may be wondered, however, whether our practical faith, our daily life, and our common perception of the Church have much to do with this. In any case, it is worth the trouble to listen carefully to the Liturgy of the Word of the Thirty-second and Thirty-third Sundays and to the respective celebrations, which are clearly marked by the idea of the end of the world. They deal explicitly with death and life after death (Thirty-second Sunday), then the events that, in the present life, are related to the final victory of the Son of Man (Thirty-third Sunday).

The idea of individual resurrection is not at the forefront of the faith of God's people. No wonder: it is such an extraordinary, unimaginable thing! We might well ask if it is not a fanciful image, a rather tenuous theory?

So was it debated when Jesus proclaimed the good news. But the debate has never ended. Even today, almost every believer expects to be questioned about it. At some time or another, we all devote ourselves to clinging strongly to a certitude that sustains our hope, but that sometimes still appears to be a wager on the future. In the present reality, the whole idea of resurrection seems so remote, even without thinking of the fact that this wager is regarded by those around us as pure foolishness, because it prevents one, so it is said, from living life to the full.

As for the end of the world, we often speak of it as a cosmic catastrophe that humanity might well set off by exhausting the forces holding the universe together. Thus we can find apocalyptic forecasts that produce in some people an anguished fear, which, paradoxically, seems also to be a source of comfort.

In Jesus' day, it was neither scientific theory nor human power over nature that caused these expectations, but messianic hopes. We no longer think much about such things, but still . . . . For it is another paradox of our age that the progress of science and technology coincides with— or inspires?—a multitude of "messianic" movements based not on revelation and faith but on the irrational, the search for security, hard and fast guarantees, all of which are detached from personal responsibility.

Such are the concerns that are opposed to the mysterious certitudes of revelation and faith, thanks to which we celebrate today, sacramentally, the realities to come.

Finally, we must point out the significance of these two powerful liturgies of the Word at the end of the liturgical year.

The Gospel According to Luke has drawn us, from Sunday to Sunday, on Jesus' journey to Jerusalem. But as we have often noted, it is no earthly road that we travel in celebrating the days of the Lord.

Jerusalem, which we enter with Jesus, is not only the end of a long journey. It is the city where the events recounted in the Gospel are unfolded, the pinnacle of the fulfillment of the mystery we never cease to celebrate.

It is fitting that there ends the earthly journey of the Son of God made flesh, he whose death is not an end but the first stage of his passage into the other Jerusalem, at the right hand of the Father. Our journey has no more ended than has his. We must travel with him the first stage of the Passover, the path of Christ and his followers. The life of each believer and of the entire Church is therefore a paschal life, which must be understood in the strongest sense, concretely as well as intellectually.

The whole liturgical year is symbolic—i.e., taking place through the work of signs and sacraments—journey through this vast trajectory that leads from the first revelation of God and his plan of salvation to the Passover of Christ—death, resurrection, ascension—drawing us along behind him.

But the fulfillment of all things is found in the return of the Son of Man, who will gather to himself the vast multitude of those who follow him.

The First Sunday of Advent sets before our eyes Jesus, who speaks to his disciples of his coming (Luke 21:25-28, 34-36). The background is thus set, from the very first, for the whole liturgical year. It returns to its beginnings in the two last Sundays before the celebration of Christ the King, like a pause before the cadence of the liturgical year.

Thirty-second Sunday

Children of the Living God, Children of the Resurrection

Die, Rather than Disobey

The Liturgy of the Word begins with a reading from the Second Book of Maccabees (2 Macc 7:1-2, 9-14).

The passage—the only verses from Maccabees in the Sunday Lectionary[1]—is particularly moving, even pathetic, which fits with the whole book, written in the first years of the first century B.C. Although the stories contained in it are based on historical fact, they are valuable as the "acts" of martyrs of all ages.[2]

It is not the admittedly edifying story of the martyrdom of seven brothers that is of interest here but their expression of faith in the resurrection. It is affirmed with shattering force, breaking through the vague and timid assertions with which the Old Testament so often treats the subject. Whoever is familiar with the psalms will be particularly conscious of this. Not so much from an awareness of the growth in consciousness of the people of God, but rather because we ourselves can take on the questions and hesitant hopes of the psalmists, as well as the assurance of the martyrs of Israel:

> For among the dead no one remembers you;
> in the nether world who gives you thanks?
> (Ps 6:6)
>
> Therefore my heart is glad and my soul rejoices,
> my body, too, abides in confidence;
> Because you will not abandon my soul to the nether world,
> nor will you suffer your faithful one to undergo corruption
> (Ps 16:9-10).
>
> Were not the LORD my help,
> I would soon dwell in the silent grave
> (Ps 94:17).
>
> It is not the dead who praise the LORD,
> nor those who go down into silence;

> But we bless the LORD,
>   both now and forever
> (Ps 115:17-18).

These prayers, taken virtually at random, express the anguish of believers haunted by the idea of emptiness after death, the miserable condition of those who, just the night before, were "living." So they ask God to prolong their life, and thank him when they escape the clutches of death. Thus King Hezekiah:

> Once I said,
>   "In the noontime of life I must depart!
>   To the gates of the nether world I shall be consigned
>   for the rest of my years."
>
> I said, "I shall see the LORD no more
>   in the land of the living.
> No longer shall I behold my fellow men
>   among those who dwell in the world."
>
> For it is not the nether world that gives you thanks,
>   nor death that praises you;
> Neither do those who go down into the pit
>   await your kindness.
> The living, the living give you thanks,
>   as I do today.
> (Isa 38:10-11, 18-19)

We still read these prayers today, because we all more or less regard death as an enigma, and we cannot help but wonder about the "silence of those who go down into the pit." But we have also received the decisive testimony of the apostles: "But now Christ has been raised from the dead, the firstfruits of those who have fallen asleep" (1 Cor 15:20—Sixth Sunday of Easter). This certitude is the foundation of our hope in the resurrection of the dead, a hope stronger than all the objections that besiege us. A hope that is not based on argumentation, that is not hesitant to acknowledge the absurdity of a life that comes to a dead end, the scandal of eternal death when one has rooted one's whole existence in God. Our assurance comes from the fact that death could not keep Jesus in the tomb.

> Previously, before the coming of the savior, death was frightening for the saints themselves, and everyone wept for the dead as if they were destined for corruption. But since the savior has risen in his body, death has no fear: all those who believe in Christ spurn it as nothing, preferring to die rather than to renounce their faith in Christ. They know very well that

in dying they will not perish, but will live, and that the resurrection will make them incorruptible . . . They scorn death so much that they rush toward it eagerly, becoming witnesses of the victory over it won by the savior in his resurrection.[3]

Nevertheless, we need the witness of the faith and the hope of our fellow human beings in faith. They are countless. Among them, those who have had to choose between clinging to life and dying in faithfulness to God are particularly significant. They have had to confront, very concretely, the critical question: Is it death or is it not the supreme misfortune that leads to nothingness? Their response is clear. They are not content to declare themselves ready to die. At the moment of expiration they confess: "It is my choice to die at the hands of men with the God-given hope of being restored to life by him."

No one can be indifferent to such testimony. It directly challenges believers, and it leads those who have looked into their hearts and know that their faith is sorely lacking into the realm of humble prayer.

> LORD, *when your glory appears,*
>   *my joy will be full.*
>
> Hear, O LORD, a just suit;
>   attend to my outcry;
>   hearken to my prayer from lips without deceit.
>
> My steps have been steadfast in your paths,
>   my feet have not faltered.
> I call upon you, for you will answer me, O God;
>   incline your ear to me; hear my word.
>
> Keep me as the apple of your eye,
>   hide me in the shadow of your wings.
> But I in justice shall behold your face;
>   on waking I shall be content in your presence.
> (Ps 17:1, 5-6, 8, 15)

May Jesus Christ and God Our Father Strengthen Our Hearts
No believer is so firm in faith as to be protected from all internal and external unrest. Nor is any Christian community. All those with authority in the Church must constantly be encouraging, responding to such questions as are asked, sometimes straightening out ideas, guarding against whatever threatens the life and peace of the community. The passage from the Second Letter to the Thessalonians read last Sunday spoke of the false rumors concerning the coming of the Lord, which were in danger of "agitating or terrifying the faithful," provoking the waywardness on which faith can become shipwrecked.

The Church cannot dispense with this vigilance: Christian communities have the right to see their leaders act zealously in these matters. But they would toil in vain if the Lord himself was not at work. This is what is spoken of in the passage from the Second Letter to the Thessalonians we read today (2 Thess 2:16–3:5).

"May our Lord Jesus Christ himself and God our Father . . . encourage your hearts." Paul wrote something like this to the Corinthians: "Be reconciled to God" (2 Cor 5:20). It is also an exhortation and a prayer, to which the Thessalonians are invited to join.

The prayer is addressed simultaneously to the Father and the only Son, source of the grace without which there is neither "encouragement" nor "hope," election nor salvation. "For those he foreknew he also predestined to be conformed to the image of his Son, so that he might be the firstborn among many brothers. And those he predestined he also called; and those he called he also justified; and those he justified he also glorified" (Rom 8:29-30—Seventeenth Sunday, Year A). Everything comes from God's love and Christ's faithfulness.

"Finally, brothers, pray for us." In many of his letters, Paul recommends himself to his correspondents' prayers,[4] as Christians often do.

This request for prayer is justified by the difficulties encountered in the exercise of the ministry: the spitefulness of those who have not faith, persecutions, ordeals of all kinds. Such adversity is hardly surprising, and Paul does not refuse it. But in order to escape it, the grace of God, beseeched in prayer, is indispensable.

It is worth noting that the first intention mentioned here has to do with the gospel itself: "that the word of the Lord may make progress." What a striking image: the Word itself must go everywhere![5]

How appropriate is this reminder of the theological—or even mystical— dimension of the Christian life and apostolate![6] The urgency that accompanies apostolic tasks, the need to act and speak well, could result in an overemphasis on worldly strategies and structures.

Note also that if the Word must "make progress," it is so that it may "be hailed by many others, even as it has been by you." This is the disinterestedness of the missionary: as tireless as he may be, he is a "useless servant" of the Word, which alone is worthy of glory![7]

Indeed, if the apostle has confidence in those to whom he spreads the good news, it is because of the Lord and his faithfulness.

Clearly such a passage has its source of inspiration in the contemplation of God and Christ the Lord, who has triumphed over evil once and for all.

I Will Not Die; I Will Live

In recounting a discussion with the Sadducees, the Gospel this Sunday reminds us of what Jesus says about the resurrection of the dead and challenges us with respect to our own position on the question (Luke 20:27-38).

The episode takes place at Jerusalem, which Jesus has finally entered and where his journey here on earth is finished. The location is significant. Jesus speaks of the resurrection in the place where he knows that, a little while later, he will die. Thus what he says takes on extraordinary power and authority.

For the first—and last—time, Luke shows Jesus speaking with the Sadducees. He says only enough about them to explain their intervention: they "deny that there is a resurrection." This must suffice for us. But our curiosity probes further: how are these newcomers different from the Pharisees whom we have often met in the course of this liturgical year? The question does not only arise from a legitimate concern to know Jesus' interlocutors. Actually, the thought of the Sadducees can be found among us.

Members of the aristocratic elite, the high priests came from their ranks. Caiaphas was one of them. According to Luke, they were the most responsible for Jesus' death. Thereafter, they persecuted the disciples. It was they who arrested Peter and John and made them appear before the Sanhedrin, then threw them in prison, from whence they were delivered at night by "an angel of the Lord" (Acts 4:1-4; 5:17-19).

Their rigorous religiosity is undoubted, but must not be confused with the Pharisees, whom they opposed and sometimes persecuted.

The root of this opposition was religious. The Sadducees were conservatives, even, so to speak, "fundamentalists."[8] At least for the "pure" among them, the whole Pentateuch and nothing but the Pentateuch was the rule. They refused to place the oral tradition on the same level as the written. Consequently, they were marked by doctrinal conservatism and liturgical narrowness.

But, paradoxically, as it often happens, they had a freer attitude, more "laicized" than can be found in the cherished observances of the Pharisees and their intransigence with respect to the foreign power. To be sure, they reproached Jesus for not respecting "the traditions of the Fathers." But not without some admiration for the demands and purity of his doctrine. Some, as we have seen, defended first him and then his apostles.[9]

The "fundamentalism" of the Sadducees made them reject what was not clearly affirmed in the Torah: the resurrection of the dead, the existence of angels, even the immortality of the soul.[10] Yet this narrow orthodoxy did not prevent them from cooperating quite closely with the Romans.

All this should awaken us to our own compromises and conflicts, which can so easily strip Scripture and tradition of the vibrancy that is so essential to them.

So the Sadducees denied the "new" doctrine of the resurrection. As may be expected, they attempt to demonstrate the absurdity of the idea by applying it to a case derived from Mosaic law. The issue concerns "levirate marriage" ("levirate"—pertaining to a "brother-in-law").[11]

The absurdity of the objection is plain to see. It cleverly points out the difficulty of imagining the life of the resurrected, and the problems that any attempt at representation must face. Who has not, at some time or other, recognized these sorts of difficulties, wondering about the quality of existence of those who have died? Where are they? What do they look like? What relationship do they bear to our memory of them? Such questions are pitfalls when we try to speak about the dead whom we believe to be living.

We must completely reject these questions. Think of a state analogous to ours in this case: the child in its mother's womb. It is totally incapable of imagining a state other than its own, how it is possible to be "outside," relating to other living beings, etc.

Jesus does not bother with analogies. He begins by pointing out that levirate marriage, and marriage in general, is a condition that belongs "to this age": perpetuating the name of the dead brother (levirate), having children so that the race will never die out (marriage). This does not apply to the "age to come," because those who are resurrected "are no longer liable to death"! Thus, the comparison fails.

"Like angels," sharing in their condition. This is not a concession to our desire to imagine the unimaginable by way of concrete comparison—not at all![12] "Like angels" as "sons of the resurrection . . . sons of God."

Jesus "was made Son of God . . . by his resurrection from the dead" (Rom 1:4). As the Word, he is eternally the Son of God. But his humanity also, by resurrection, is brought to true Life. It is in and through him that we will be "sons of the resurrection." This doctrine, which Paul states explicitly, is present implicitly here.[13] The sure guarantee of our own resurrection is, for faith, the resurrected Christ whom we celebrate in every Eucharist by being brought into communion with him, sharing sacramentally in his Passover, bringing us more and more into our own resurrection; there we see what we shall become: "a person with a wholly illuminated soul."

> Life is changed, not merely restored. It is not enough to say that what was most characteristic and essential is reestablished. You know that in the lives of those we love there are moments when they seem to be more "themselves," when what is best in them comes through; such moments we love to remember. In these moments they are closer to being children of God, realizing more nearly the idea that the heavenly Father had in calling them into existence. Thus it may be permitted to us to suppose that the future life, which our Lord describes as a clarification, will be that of a person with a wholly illuminated soul. Revelation tells us that our tears will be wiped away. But it is not only tears that will be wiped away, but everything in us that obscures—the temporal, the foreign, the profane, evil—and prevents us from experiencing only knowledge, love, good will, light, and perfume. We will be cleansed from head to toe like a little child taking a bath, carefully wiped clean.[14]

The passage is clearly more than a doctrinal reminder or a response to objections against resurrection. It sets before us Christ, with whom "we have grown into union with him through a death like his, [and] he shall also be united with him through the resurrection" (Rom 6:5).

At the same time, we return to God himself. The way this happens is worth noting. We often look for "proof texts" in the Bible, i.e., texts that support a particular argument; this is not only legitimate, but useful and necessary. Jesus, though, is not trying to prove anything. He shows or invites us to gaze on the one whom Scripture reveals, whom Moses calls "the God of Abraham, of Isaac, and of Jacob," who, after making a covenant with them, saved the patriarchs. He it is, Peter says, who "has glorified his servant Jesus," and, by his power, has "exalted him at his right hand as leader and savior" (Acts 3:13; 5:30-31—Third Sunday of Easter, Years B and C).

If he were not "the God of the living," the life of Abraham, Isaac, Jacob, Jesus, and all the disciples, all would be lost. If all were not alive "for him"—were not resurrected—he would be not only "the God of the dead," but a dead God! Then everything would be a mockery: faith, fidelity to God, worship. In that case, let us be unrestrained in our search for earthly sustenance, "Let us eat and drink, for tomorrow we die!" (1 Cor 15:32).

This sort of argumentation—if one may call it so—belongs to the liturgy and the Bible in the liturgy. In the celebration, Scripture is not "used" to present a teaching that could as well be presented in another way that might be more suitable logically or pedagogically; it is used to shed its light on the mystery we celebrate, and to draw us into the dynamic of salvation.

The liturgy can certainly act as a catechesis, even an exemplary one. But it is not purely catechesis. It is action. If it makes us think, if it nourishes our faith, it is not first of all to enrich our knowledge, to complete or supplement deficiencies in our understanding. It is revelation that calls for an active response from our faith.

Participation in the liturgy creates and presupposes moral involvement, concrete action that touches all areas of our lives. But it is first and foremost the place of personal and community encounter with the Lord, with "the God of the living." The celebration of the mystery is fundamentally mystical. Everything else—however important it may be—flows from this.[15]

We have seen many instances of this throughout the liturgical year. When he teaches, Jesus always reveals both himself and his Father. The Gospel this Sunday and the way in which Jesus responds to the question of the resurrection is at the end of the liturgical year, a particularly welcome and appropriate reminder of this.

> O love supreme, if it should happen that I die
>   without having known how I possessed you,
>   In what star your dwelling was,
> In what moment your time, in what hour I loved you,
>
> O love supreme that surpasses memory,
> Fire without home in which I have lived all my days,
>   To what destiny you draw my history,
>   In what vision your glory is seen,
>   O my abiding-place . . .
>
> When I will lose myself
>   in the infinite abyss,
>   Infinitely, when I will be broken,
> When the present with which I am clothed
>   Will have revealed,
>
>   In a universe broken into a thousand pieces,
>   With a thousand moments yet to come,
> While ashes are blown to the four winds,
>   You keep for your own time
>   Only one treasure.
>
>   You will remake my name and image
>   With a thousand pieces strewn through the day,
>   Living united without name or face,
>   Heart of the mind, O center of the shadow,
>   O love supreme![16]

There is no more common or universal experience than that of death, which no one can escape. It is present, even when we push it far from our thoughts. Yet from the beginning, history tells us that not all people have seen it as the absolute end of all life.[17] Funeral rites, spare or sumptuous tombs, ancestral sepulchers, offerings to the dead, food placed in tombs, etc., testify to the various ways in which many people express their more or less confident assurance that some form of life continues in the tomb, if not outside of it.

This is not the same as belief in an afterlife. Some people—for example, the Egyptians—came to it quite early. The people of the Bible—surprisingly enough—came to it only much later and very tentatively, only in the last few centuries before the Christian era. In Jesus' time, the problem was still being discussed. For a long time it was left up to an individual's sentiments.

But what life is there in the tomb? Certainly nothing enviable: the shadow of a full life, or a life of shadows somewhere below "the land of the living." The first problem that haunts humanity is the question of what is the relationship, possible or desired, between the living and those who have passed the gates of death. Hence those offerings that are made to them to beg their favor, appease them, or ward off their destructive power.[18]

The strict monotheism of the people of the Bible kept them from this error, although they may have remained attached to the memory of the patriarchs and their ancestral burial sites.[19] At the same time, Israel lifts its eyes to its God, in whom it trusts and hopes, God, faithful to his covenant, who will not allow his people to perish. The famous vision of the dry bones in the Book of Ezekiel is the best-known expression of this conviction (Ezek 37:1-14—Pentecost, Evening Vigil). The just God, who will not allow his servants to live lives of misery while the wicked are surfeited with good things from their birth to their death. God, whose love for humanity and those who are dedicated to him cannot be hindered by death. It is to this height that certain psalms reach, wonderful examples of a faith and hope whose simplicity and calm audacity confound us. Especially if one recites them while considering the tone and conviction that Jesus had in his prayer. "You will not abandon me to death"; "My own eyes, not another's, shall behold him"; "From my flesh I shall see God." Many people today believe in immortality, the immortality of the soul. Thus, many people and even some Christians are misled by the idea of reincarnation.[20] But resurrection? Jesus is clearly speaking of resurrection, though he is noticeably silent about the details of it. This is "the resurrection of the dead," "the resurrection of the flesh" that we proclaim in the creed.

Happy are those who through, with, and in Christ wait for the resurrection, who repeat for themselves Job's unforgettable profession of faith:

> Oh, would that my words were written down!
>   Would that they were inscribed in a record,
>
> That with an iron chisel and with lead
>   they were cut in the rock forever!
>
> But as for me, I know that my Vindicator lives,
>   and that he will at last stand forth upon the dust;
>
> Whom I myself shall see:
>   my own eyes, not another's, shall behold him,
>
> And from my flesh I shall see God;
>   my inmost being is consumed with longing
>
> (Job 19:23-27—Thursday I of the Twenty-sixth Week).

But this calls for more than a profession of faith and a line on a tombstone. One must be suspicious, especially today, of a "religion" that seems only to be an answer to the disturbing questions of life, a "faith" in life after death that "invents" a hereafter as an aid to the living of a life that is essentially absurd. "Always be ready to give an explanation to anyone who asks you for a reason for your hope" (1 Pet 3:15—Sixth Sunday of Easter, Year A).

Faith in the resurrection comes from an encounter with "God our Father, who has loved us and given us everlasting encouragement and good hope through his grace" (2 Thess 2:16). It is fundamentally rooted in the resurrection of Christ "the firstfruits of those who have fallen asleep," who by his Word inspires us to give glory to God always and everywhere (Epistle).

True witness to faith in the resurrection consists neither in an elaborate "prooftexting" of Scripture or a philosophical or theological argument with those who do not believe in it.

The only witness that is truly in accord with the good news is that of men and women who live for God here and now. Such people can say, with remarkable assurance and simplicity, like Thérèse of Lisieux at the hour of death, "I am not dying, I am beginning to live."[21]

> Father, all-powerful and ever-living God,
> we do well always and everywhere to give you thanks
> through Jesus Christ our Lord.

In him, who rose from the dead,
our hope of resurrection dawned.
The sadness of death gives way
to the bright promise of immortality.

Lord, for your faithful people life is changed, not ended.
When the body of our earthly dwelling lies in death
we gain an everlasting dwelling place in heaven.
(Preface for Christian Death I)

Awaiting the Day of the Lord

The Thirty-second and Thirty-third Sundays form a diptych. Once again this week, the Gospel is an account of a teaching given by Jesus in Jerusalem before his passion.[22] It is the last saying we hear in the Sunday assembly this year.[23] It is fitting for us to pay great attention to this "conclusion" to a book that we have heard read for so many weeks. We should come into this liturgy feeling caught up, as by a symphony, with its *fortes* and *pianos*, its alternation of quick and slow tempos.

The Day of the Lord Has Come and Is Coming

We begin with a short passage from the prophet Malachi (Mal 3:19-20a).

The Lectionary rarely uses this book, the last in the corpus of the prophetic writings.[24] In the two verses proclaimed this Sunday, "the messenger" announces the coming of the "day of the Lord."[25]

The expression is so rich with meaning that it would be impossible to give a clear, concise definition of it.[26] In the first place, it refers to a certain conception of history and God's activity in history, a conception born of the experience of his intervention in the lives of peoples and nations, especially his own people.

The history of the faithful is punctuated with "visits of God," "times," "days," "hours," singularly distinctive moments about which can be said, if not immediately, at least on reflection: "The Lord is in this spot, although I did not know it!" (Gen 28:16).

Every coming of God is a day of judgment and salvation. It points to a definitive coming when God will solemnly inaugurate his reign, the "day of the Lord" of which the prophets so often speak.[27]

They warn us against supposing that God's coming will be a show of power by which his people will be granted earthly rule. Some of the prophets, like Amos, take on quite a strong tone: "Woe to those who yearn for the day of the Lord! What will this day of the Lord mean for you? Darkness and not light!" (Amos 5:18). Likewise, Zephaniah and his fearsome *dies irae:* "A day of wrath is that day, a day of anguish and distress, a day of destruction and desolation, a day of darkness and gloom, a day of thick black clouds, a day of trumpet blasts and battle alarm against fortified cities, against battlements on high'' (Zeph 1:15-16).

Far from being a warrant for false security, knowledge of the ''day of the Lord'' is a cause, if not for alarm, at least for a sense of responsibility that devolves on each and every one of us here and now. ''That day'' will see the blazing forth of God's judgment on ''the proud and all evildoers.'' ''The day that is coming will set them on fire, leaving them neither root nor branch.'' Whereas for others, ''there will arise the sun of justice with its healing rays.''

Whatever may eventually happen, says the prophet, we must not fall prey to discouragement and doubt. Let us not say: ''How have you loved us?''; ''Where is the just God?''; ''It is vain to serve God'' (Mal 1:2; 2:17; 3:14). ''The day is coming, blazing like an oven.''

To believers who are almost ready to capitulate from weariness, to Christian communities and the Church who are occasionally tormented by fears, weakened by crises, who question the value of their fidelity to the gospel, the prophet addresses a stirring call to persevere, to prepare confidently for their encounter with the Lord. Jesus, speaking of his coming, of the disarray and confusion of the nations, of people who ''will die of fright in anticipation of what is coming upon the earth,'' will say to his disciples: ''Stand up straight and raise your heads, for your ransom is near at hand.''

May ''the inhabitants of this world'' listen to this call and enter into the song of hope and praise that the Church perpetually sings:

The LORD comes to rule the earth with justice.

Sing praise to the LORD with the harp,
  with the harp and melodious song.
With trumpets and the sound of the horn
  sing joyfully before the King, the LORD.

Let the sea and what fills it resound,
  the world and those who dwell in it;
Let the rivers clap their hands,
  the mountains shout with them for joy.

Before the LORD, for he comes,
  for he comes to rule the earth,
He will rule the world with justice
  and the peoples with equity.
(Ps 98:5-6, 7-8, 9)

Be Calm in Your Daily Tasks

It is also in the perspective of the day of the Lord that we read the exhortation at the end of the Second Letter to the Thessalonians (2 Thess 3:7-12).

We must not be "shaken" or "alarmed" when we hear from time to time that "the day of the Lord is here" (2 Thess 2:1-2—Thirty-first Sunday).

Under the pretext that the day of the Lord is near or has already happened, there are some who are not keeping busy but acting like busybodies. They readily ignore the demands and constraints of daily life, burdening others and living at their expense.

"Anyone who will not work should not eat." This is a strong and unambiguous condemnation of all forms of parasitism. Clearly, the bread that one earns by labor symbolizes everything that is necessary for life here and now, including spiritual life.

It would be a grave mistake to suppose that a "spiritual vocation" frees one from the demands of everyday life, justifying a demand of support from others. St. Benedict allows no misunderstanding: "They alone can truly be monks who live by the work of their hands like our fathers and the apostles."[28] The same is true today; indeed, there is a great need for this principle to be made explicit in the context of modern life. So it is found in contemporary monastic rules, like those of Bose (in Italy), and Taizé (in France).

> You are a man like others. You will work like them. You will seek justice and an end to exploitation and you will share in their condition. You will flee neither the world nor mankind. Living like them, you will find yourself more or less in community like them, according to circumstances. In a community, work can be quite diverse. Each will keep, if possible, the profession and work that he had when he heard the call. The community will see to it that the work of each is compatible with the common life and the individual personality. You will refrain from minimizing the value of your brother's work and making comparisons . . . When fatigue and work are not one with prayer, what should be a life of seeking God through hardships that are ultimately freeing, becomes a life of privilege.[29]

> In order that your prayer may be real, you must deal with the arduousness of work. If you live a dilettante's life, you will not be able to intercede. Your prayer becomes whole when it is of a piece with your labor.[30]

Paul is the preeminent example of this. One must not be idle; but still, the communities must provide the necessities for those who consecrate their life and service to them. More than anyone else, Paul would have had the right to receive the bread he ate. He readily devoted himself to working with his hands day and night so that he would be a burden to no one. Such was the rule he laid down.[31]

This should not be taken as a principle that would apply always and everywhere. But there are times when it would be appropriate, or even necessary, to follow Paul's example. Priests who spend their lives working so as not to be a burden to the community to which they minister, to not be dependent on anyone, to be a presence of the Church in times and places that would accept no other form of apostolate, can imitate Paul.

Never should one receive one's daily bread from others if one is not truly devoted to their service, as are the ministers of the gospel, like all those who serve their brothers and sisters, in whatever arena—political, economic, social. Otherwise, they become parasites.

In a more general way, this text, which reminds us implicitly of the "day of the Lord," presents us with the responsibilities this life entails: doing one's part "working day and night, laboring to the point of exhaustion."

In so doing, we follow the supreme example of Jesus. He never worked with his hands after beginning his public ministry. Luke speaks of "Joanna, the wife of Herod's steward Chuza, Susanna, and many others who provided for [Jesus and the Twelve] out of their resources" (Luke 8:3). But what man ever gave more to others? He, the Son of Man, who had no place to lay his head (Luke 9:58), whom the crowds come to in every house he entered "making it impossible for them even to eat," to the point that "his relatives," hearing of this, said "He is out of his mind" (Mark 3:20-21). He who gave himself for us, who gave his flesh and blood to feed us.

Persevere and You Will Gain Life

Luke's Gospel begins in the Temple of Jerusalem, with the vision of Zechariah wherein he was told that he would have a son whom he would name John, who was to be the precursor of the Lord (Luke 1:5-25, 57-80).

The infant Jesus was presented in the Temple to two prophets, Simeon and Anna, who recognized him as the anointed of the Lord (Luke 2:22-38).

Beginning at the age of twelve, he went every year to Jerusalem on the Passover pilgrimage, and Luke tells us that once he stayed three days in the Temple "sitting in the midst of the teachers, listening to them and asking them questions," and "all who heard him were astounded at his understanding and his answers" (Luke 2:41-50).

It is at the Temple that Jesus gives his disciples and the crowd his final teachings, of which today's Gospel contains the central part (Luke 21:5-19).

Some of those around Jesus were speaking about the Temple, admiring how it "was adorned with costly stones and votive offerings."[32] He certainly shared this admiration for the holy place of his people, since he, more than anyone else, understood its significance, and he could not speak of its destruction without deep emotion. Luke tells us that when Jesus came near Jerusalem, he "wept over it" at the thought that it would be destroyed and that its enemies would not "leave one stone upon another" (Luke 19:41-44—Thursday of the Thirty-third Week). Imagine what he must have felt when he spoke of the destruction of the Temple, the jewel of the city, heart of Jerusalem and unique center of worship for the people of the covenant, the sanctuary of the presence of God among his people.

The questions "Teacher, when will this happen? And what sign will there be when all these things are about to happen?" are asked lightly, as if it were any event whatever, a small catastrophe involving the destruction of an impressive building. The destruction of the Temple is tantamount to the end of the world; it is the signal of the apocalypse!

Jesus was aware of this connection, and Luke knew that there was a tendency among the Christians to expect the return of the Lord in glory very soon. So he was careful to separate the discourse on the last times from that on the Temple's ruin (Luke 17:22-37; 21:5-28). Did he suspect that such expectation would run wild in times of crisis? He would have been quite right. How many times throughout the centuries have people preached that "the end of the world is near"! Such misguided messages are prevalent even today.

Therefore, we must always remember this clear warning: "See that you not be deceived, for many will come in my name, saying, 'I am he,' and 'the time has come.' Do not follow them." Those who speak thus are impostors, who threaten the faith because they set themselves up as prophets to be followed blindly, and thus turn people from following the Lord.

Luke insists on this point. The parable of the sums of money is addressed to people who thought that the kingdom of God would appear there immediately. The rich man who gave each of his servants ten gold coins left for "a distant country" (Luke 19:11-28—Wednesday of the Thirty-third Week). In the parable of the tenants, the owner of the vineyard "went on a journey for a long time" (Luke 20:9-17). The point is clear: the return of the rich man or the vineyard owner did not occur for a long time.

Jesus explicitly states that wars and upheavals should not be interpreted as the first pangs of the end. History confirms this. The Jewish revolt in A.D. 70, the destruction of the Temple, the diaspora throughout the following centuries, did not stop the course of history. Nor did the later tumults of the "barbarian invasions" presage a destruction of the world. The same can be said about the appearance of the great heresies that shook the Church and society, as well as the dissolution of Christendom. Wars and uprisings—which still surround us today—should not even be remotely understood as signs; they have nothing to do with the end of the world. These hardships, indeed difficult to endure, should not frighten us.

Such events have nothing to do with those that will presage the end. Jesus says, "When you hear of wars and insurrections, do not be terrified; for such things must happen first, but it will not immediately be the end . . . Nation will rise against nation, and kingdom against kingdom. There will be powerful earthquakes, famines, and plagues from place to place; and awesome sights and mighty signs will come from the sky."

The Gospel here skips quickly over these upheavals to highlight their difference with the cosmic calamities to come: "There will be signs in the sun, the moon, and the stars, and on earth nations will be in dismay, perplexed by the roaring of the sea and the waves. People will die of fright in anticipation of what is coming upon the world, for the powers of the heavens will be shaken. And then they will see the Son of Man coming in a cloud with power and great glory." But even then, believers must not be afraid. "But when these signs begin to happen, stand erect and raise your heads because your redemption is at hand" (Luke 21:25-28—Thursday of the Thirty-fourth Week).

After this parenthetical remark, the Gospel returns to what will happen "before any of this," now meaning that the end is not imminent: the persecutions of the Christians do not signify that the end of the world is near. Rather, they characterize their situation in the present.

Jesus cannot be said to soften the harshness of these persecutions. "You will even be handed over by parents, brothers, relatives, and friends, and they will put some of you to death. You will be hated by all because of my name . . ." But the call to patient endurance, the assurance of gaining eternal life, is even stronger. The persecuted Christians will not even have to think about their defense! "For I myself shall give you a wisdom in speaking that all your adversaries will be powerless to resist or refute."

Surely this must make us think of Stephen; Luke tells us in Acts that his opponents "could not withstand the wisdom and the spirit with which he spoke" (Acts 6:10). Stoned to death, he died like Jesus did, crying out "in a loud voice, 'Lord, do not hold this sin against them'" (Acts 7:60).

"It will lead to your giving testimony." This translation agrees with what is said in Matthew and Mark: "And you will be led before governors and kings for my sake as a witness before them and the pagans" (Matt 10:18; Mark 13:9). Do we not call those people "martyrs" (i.e., witnesses) who confess their faith at the cost of their own life?

Luke certainly understands this mode of witnessing. He recounts many examples of it in Acts. He notes that Saul assisted in the martyrdom of Stephen, who ought to come to mind when the Lord says to him on the road to Damascus: "I am Jesus, whom you are persecuting" (Acts 9:5).

But the line could also be translated: "This opportunity will witness *for you.*"[33] Thus it refers to the benefits gained by the martyrs for themselves by their witness: the sufferings they endure speak for them before God.

Thus Christians are persecuted like Christ. Remember that it is because he was obedient unto death, death on a cross, that he has been raised to the right hand of the Father (Phil 2:8-9). His sufferings are credited to him by God; by his perseverance he has gained eternal life in the glory of the resurrection. Therefore, it is toward him that these sayings turn our attention. In the light of the paschal mystery, in which we share by being persecuted in the name of Jesus, everything else receives its full meaning, particularly the paradoxical affirmation: "They will put some of you to death . . . but not a hair on your head will be destroyed."

There is no argument or discussion in this encouragement and call to perseverance. It is enough that they implicitly evoke Christ, the faithful witness to whom God has himself given testimony, Christ whose Passover is celebrated in each Eucharist:

> When we eat this bread and drink this cup,
> We proclaim your death, Lord Jesus,
> Until you come in glory.

"Behold the coming of the day of the Lord!" This cry echoes throughout the Bible. At the beginning of his ministry, Jesus declared that he had been sent "to proclaim the good news of the kingdom of God" (Luke 4:43). Luke tells us that he has said at various times, especially on his "journey to Jerusalem," that the kingdom of heaven is at hand (Luke 10:9, 11; 21:31).

After so many "visits" in the past, "in these last days" God has visited us by sending his Son "whom he made heir of all things and through whom he created the universe," who "took his seat at the right hand of the Majesty on high" (Heb 1:1-3—Christmas, Mass During the Day).

Each time we say the creed, we proclaim that the Lord "will come in glory to judge the living and the dead; and his kingdom will have no end." We await the coming of "that day": "Come, Lord Jesus!" We wait for him in peace and confidence, while refusing to be misled by those who may come in his name, saying "I am he," those who, deducing from wars, revolutions, or persecutions of the disciples or the Church, conclude that the last day is at hand.

Our serenity is based not on our merits but on the mercy of the Lord.

> So favored is this world that our judge comes not as a stranger, but one who, being like us, can fully sympathize with our weaknesses. The one who died for love of us is given the task of giving measure and value to his work. The one who, because of his own weakness, takes the part of the weak, who wants to collect every fruit of his passion, will separate the wheat from the chaff in such a way that not one grain shall be lost. The one who has allowed us to share in his own spiritual nature, from whom we have drawn the blood vital to our souls, our brother, will judge his brothers. In the second coming, may he who is our hope and salvation in his mercy and kindness be mindful of us![34]

Knowing God and the One who intercedes for us with him, the believer can face even death calmly.

> When we decamp, without trumpet or fanfare,
> More naked than we were born, owning nothing,
> When worms and damp consume our bodies,
> We will ring, all alone, at the gate of the Garden.
> What does it matter?
> Death has been nailed to the cross
> By the hand of God who will open
> The door!
>
> Our voices will be silenced in the earth,
> Our bodies, in pieces everywhere;
> And having so long slept in the cemetery,
> Our skins will be full of a thousand holes.
> What does it matter?

Our fingers will be formed from clay
By the hand of God who will open
The door!

Will we be standing, hopping, or on crutches,
Grotesque dancing puppets?
And having lost everything all too cheaply,
Our poor hands will be as full of holes as baskets.
What does it matter?
A bleeding wound
The hand of God who will open
The door!

Sad plumes stuck in hats at the feast,
Corpse of the living unpainted and blank,
Having known no tears, we kiss the head,
Longing and yet ashamed to be seen.
What does it matter?
The tears of man will shine
In the eyes of God when he will open
The door![35]

Far from giving us a pretext to avoid the constraints and responsibilities of the present life, the view of the "day of the Lord" and his coming forces us to assume our obligations today "quietly."

Not that "that day" ought to disappear from our consciousness or cease to define the lives of believers and the Church. On the contrary, we know that God works within human history, then and now, and will never cease doing so. Nevertheless, he acts as the God who transcends history, who exists in an eternal present. That is why every day of our lives and the life of the Church is his "day."

Each liturgy—especially the Eucharist—celebrates the Lord who has come, is coming, and will come. Each liturgical and sacramental celebration is the "coming," the "visit" of God here and now.

Sunday is the "day of the Lord." The liturgical year is the unbroken procession of the "days of the Lord."

Father, all-powerful and ever-living God,
we do well always and everywhere to give you thanks
through Jesus Christ our Lord.

When he humbled himself to come among us as a man,
he fulfilled the plan you formed long ago
and opened for us the way to salvation.

Now we watch for the day,
hoping that the salvation promised us will be ours
when Christ our Lord will come again in his glory.

And so, with all the choirs of angels in heaven
we proclaim your glory
and join in their unending hymn of praise:

Holy, holy, holy Lord, God of power and might,
heaven and earth are full of your glory.
Hosanna in the highest.
Blessed is he who comes in the name of the Lord.
Hosanna in the highest.
(Preface of Advent I)

Thirty-fourth (Last) Sunday in Ordinary Time

Christ the King

Each year, the solemnity of Christ the King contains three texts chosen specifically for the day.[1] As opposed to the other Sundays of Ordinary Time, the Liturgy of the Word here takes the form of a triptych. The center, chief panel is the Gospel; the other panels, of the Old Testament and the epistle, are not quite on the same level as the first, but turned slightly toward it. Therefore, we must begin our study with the Gospel, and deal with the others later. Then we can look at the whole triptych, moving from one panel to another, in order to see the richness of the whole.

As we have already said,[2] the solemnity of Christ the King, at the end of the liturgical year, acts like the finale in a symphony. Not as a comprehensive summary of the previous thirty-three Sundays, but as a harmonizing of their main themes. Here, at this summit, we see the windings of the road we have traveled, the distinctive characteristics of our various stopping-points, the vast expanse through which we have wandered since the First Sunday of Advent. It is a summit on which to rest before finishing, at least for the time being, the Gospel According to Luke.

Our Lord and King

Though we hear in Luke's Gospel about the "reign" or the "kingdom of God," and though Jesus is often called "Lord," the title of "king" is given him only in the accounts of his triumphal entry into Jerusalem on the way to his passion.

The crowd of disciples who gathered around Jesus when he came down from Mount Olivet, riding on an ass, "began to praise God aloud with joy for all the mighty deeds they had seen. They proclaimed:

> 'Blessed is the king who comes
> in the name of the Lord.
> Peace in heaven
> and glory in the highest.'
> (Luke 19:37-38).

The evangelist says that the elders of the people, the chief priests, and the scribes, after making Jesus appear before the Sanhedrin, then "arose

314

and brought him before Pilate. They brought charges against him, saying, 'We found this man misleading our people; he opposes the payment of taxes to Caesar and maintains that he is the Messiah, a king' " (Luke 22:66; 23:1-2). Then, "Pilate asked him, 'Are you the king of the Jews?' He said to him in reply, 'You say so' " (Luke 23:3).

Then comes the Gospel reading for the solemnity of Christ the King (Luke 23:35-43).

The whole account of the Passion points toward the coming of God's kingdom. "When the hour came, he took his place at table with the apostles. He said to them, 'I have eagerly desired to eat this Passover with you before I suffer, for I tell you, I shall not eat it [again] until there is fulfillment in the kingdom of God.' Then he took a cup, gave thanks, and said, 'Take this and share it among yourselves; for I tell you that from this time on I shall not drink of the fruit of the vine until the kingdom of God comes.' Then he took the bread, said the blessing, broke it, and gave it to them, saying, 'This is my body, which will be given for you; do this in memory of me.' And likewise the cup after they had eaten, saying, 'This cup is the new covenant in my blood, which will be shed for you' " (Luke 22:14-20).

Then, as the apostles were quarreling "about which of them should be regarded as the greatest," Jesus said to them: "The kings of the Gentiles lord it over them and those who are in authority over them are addressed as 'Benefactors'; but among you it shall not be so." And he added: "I am among you as the one who serves. It is you who have stood by me in my trials; and I confer a kingdom on you, just as my Father has conferred one on me, that you may eat and drink at my table in my kingdom; and you will sit on thrones judging the twelve tribes of Israel" (Luke 22:24-30).

Questioned by the council, Jesus proclaimed: "But from this time on the Son of Man will be seated at the right hand of the power of God" (Luke 22:69).

Clearly, Jesus, according to Luke, intended to emphasize the radical difference between his kingship and that of the lords of this world who desire power, honor, or wealth. Nothing could point up the contrast more strongly than the crucifixion, the account of which we read today.

The Kingship of Christ on the Cross

Jesus hangs on the cross between two criminals who are executed along with him. He is the foremost figure in the center panel of the triptych before us. He turns first to his Father: "Father, forgive them, they know not what they do" (Luke 23:34). At this grand finale, the summit of the Gospel, we see, one last time, two groups: one sympathetic to Jesus, the other his opponents.

In the first are the people who "stood there watching," whom Luke has so often shown us at Jesus' side, though he has not always said what they thought about what was happening, their chief characteristic seeming to be a watchful expectancy. The same is the case here. These people were "watching," or better, "contemplating." In fact, Luke uses a verb—*theorein*—which in the Christian vocabulary means precisely this *(theoria*—"contemplation"). It is a subtle touch from the brush of the master painter, something requiring a bit of initiation to see. But when it is discovered, we can see ourselves in this crowd; it seems that we are invited to join it when, gathered in assembly before the triptych, we celebrate the solemnity of Christ the King.

There is also, on one of the crosses next to Jesus, a condemned man who confesses his sin, admitting the justice of his condemnation, and states that Jesus "has done nothing criminal."[3]

The other group contains first and foremost "the leaders" who have condemned Jesus. They mock him, saying: "He saved others; let him save himself if he is the chosen one, the Messiah of God." What an evil sense of irony! Into the face of Jesus on the cross they fling the wonderful names of "savior," "Messiah," "the chosen one," in order to show, ironically, that he who hangs on the cross usurped them, that God himself, who abandons him to this fate, testifies to this!

The Roman soldiers echo this. But these pagans who carry out the order of execution "know not what they do." They are merely doing their duty. They think nothing of it; a condemned man is a condemned man. They need not show him pity. Yet even with hearts dulled by familiarity, they need some inducement to jeer the one they behold, the work of their hands. They simply repeat what they hear the "leaders" of the people say.

Perhaps the same is the case with one of the criminals. He is under the same sentence. A hardened man, to be sure, with no more fear of God on the cross than he had during his life. "Are you not the Messiah? Save yourself and us." Such words are painful to hear, because they reveal the hardening of a heart, though it be of a criminal at the hour of death, and because of the anguish that must be yet to come. One might wish that he would have been silent or shed a furtive tear, like so many others who have found, at the last moment, dignity and nobility on the rack.

Remember Me, Jesus

But it is to the other side of Jesus that the evangelist has us turn our contemplative eye, along with crowd, toward the exchange between Jesus and the second criminal.

Until now, only the "leaders" have really said anything, the soldiers and the first criminal only repeating their jeers. "The people" contemplate in silence. The other criminal, clearly, cannot be castigating the authorities. Why should they listen to him? They would simply shrug and point to the justice of his condemnation, which he admits. But with his companion in misfortune, he is on an equal footing. Thus he reproaches him for his lack of "fear of God." Did the other respond? What did he say? Did he recognize the justice of the reproaches? The Gospel does not say. What it presents to us is the prayer addressed to Jesus by one who was going to die at his side: "Jesus, remember me when you come into your kingdom."

"Jesus." The familiarity of this appellation is in striking contrast to the content of the petition. Did the man know that the name means "God saves"? It doesn't matter. He is the model of all those who in anguish and distress at the moment of death utter, in an ultimate leap of faith and hope, the name that is above all other names, and from which comes salvation: "Jesus."

"Remember me." In the Old Testament especially, the subject of the verb "to remember" is more often God than a human being, while the opposite can be said of the verb "to forget." "It seems that God is always the first to remember. He remembers Noah (Gen 8:1), Abraham (Gen 19:29), Hannah (1 Sam 1:19); he remembers his covenant (Exod 2:24; 6:5), his kindness (Ps 98:3), his mercy (Luke 1:54), human beings (Ps 8:5; Heb 2:6) and the sins of his people (Hos 8:13), but also our love (Jer 2:2), our prayers (Acts 10:4), and our generosity (Acts 10:31)."[4] The psalmists say to God: "Remember."[5] It is an appeal to the living and present God, with the assurance that he desires and has the power to save. On the lips of one condemned to death by human justice, it is the striking prayer of assurance that despite one's confessed sins, God will save.

> Shall I see the broken frame of my body restored?
> The battered vessel of my soul?
> Shall I see myself united to You again, after being so far estranged?
> Shall my heart, which is now sadness and pain, be filled with joy?
> Shall I hope to see the shattered image of my nature restored?
> Unhappy as I am, shall my windblown tent be set up again?
> A prisoner in exile, shall I be free and hopeful?

> Will the light of your grace, of which I am now deprived, shine on me again?
> In your mercy, will I see your deepest majesty and splendor?
> And shall my sorrowing soul find laughter?
> Instead of the herald of bad news, shall I hear the proclamation of the good news intended for me? Vase broken in pieces, shall I see myself repaired? Will my inmost eyes see the wiping out of my debts? Will my day of anguish give way to the wondrous rising of your gracious pardon? Led by your hand, will I come to share in the festivities under the tent of light?[6]

This is the prayer of the Christian community: "Jesus, remember me when you come into your kingdom."

But it is at the same time the affirmation of the authentic sovereignty of Christ:

> Father, all powerful and ever-living God,
> we do well always and everywhere to give you thanks.
>
> You anointed Jesus Christ, your only Son, with the oil of gladness,
> as the eternal priest and universal king.
> As priest he offered his life on the altar of the cross
> and redeemed the human race
> by this one perfect sacrifice of peace.
> As king he claims dominion over all creation,
> that he may present to you, his almighty Father,
> an eternal and universal kingdom:
> a kingdom of truth and life,
> a kingdom of holiness and grace,
> a kingdom of justice, love, and peace.[7]

Today

"I assure you." Jesus' response is solemn and contains the full force of his authority. It goes even further than the petition.

"This day." The day of death is also one of salvation for whomever turns toward Jesus in hope. The time of waiting comes to an end, the time of fulfillment begins.

Luke insists on the "today" of salvation. "For today in the city of David a savior has been born for you who is Messiah and Lord" is the good news announced to the shepherds at Bethlehem (Luke 2:11).

At the beginning of his ministry, Jesus, in the synagogue of his hometown in Nazareth, having read the passage from the prophet Isaiah that announces a year of favor from the Lord, proclaimed: "Today this Scripture passage is fulfilled in your hearing" (Luke 4:21—Third Sunday).

At the house of Zacchaeus, who promised to give half his belongings to the poor and make reparation to anyone whom he had cheated, Jesus declared: "Today salvation has come to this house . . . " (Luke 19:9—Thirty-first Sunday).

This "today" must not be understood as confined to various moments in Jesus' life and ministry. "There is no salvation through anyone else, nor is there any other name under heaven given to the human race by which we are to be saved." What Peter says before the council is and will be proclaimed till the end of time. We belong, it is true, to the age of the "not yet," but equally to that of the "already," the "now," the "today" of salvation that is unfolding itself. Salvation is to be "with Jesus" through faith and the sacraments of faith, living each day at his side.

> "Amen, I say to you, today you will be with me in paradise." A marvelous indication of the need for conversion, since forgiveness is granted so quickly to the thief, even exceeding his prayer. The Lord always grants more than is asked of him. The thief asked the Lord to remember him when He entered into his kingdom; the Lord said: "Today you will be with me in paradise." Life consists of being with Christ. Where Christ is, there is the kingdom.[8]

In Paradise

"Paradise" is the heavenly dwelling that Jesus prepares for his disciples, as his Father prepared it for him (Luke 22:28-29). It is the kingdom into which Christ the King enters through his death, into which he brings "with him" those who undergo the same Passover.

"Today" is therefore the hour of decision. Gathered for the liturgy, we certainly do not belong to those who mock Jesus on the cross or speak ironically about his death. On the contrary, their blasphemous banter moves us in the depths of our hearts.

To the soldiers and the other criminal, we long to shout: "Be quiet! You don't know what you are saying. How is it possible that you have not even the slightest fear of God?"

We belong to the crowd that stands there watching in rapt contemplation, perhaps hearing nothing other than what Jesus says: "Today you will be with me in paradise," while written on our hearts so as to be constantly on our lips is this prayer: "Jesus, remember me when you come into your kingdom."

David, the Chosen One of God

Without forgetting anything of the foregoing, let us turn now to the left panel of the triptych. We read there three verses from the Second Book of Samuel (2 Sam 5:1-3).

We first experience some disorientation. The reading concerns the choice of David as king of Israel. From hearing and seeing Jesus on the cross at Golgotha, we move without transition to Hebron and the assembly of the twelve tribes of Israel.

Indeed, this side panel of the triptych is not wholly related to what appears on the center panel. It is not a prophecy of the sovereignty of Christ, who enters by death into his kingdom "today," while granting access "with him" to those whom he justifies. Instead, it reminds us, rather abruptly, of the object of today's celebration.

To be sure, however important they may be in the memory of Israel, the circumstances of David's accession to the throne are in themselves of minor importance, both for world and salvation history. One is tempted to regard them as mere facts that can be ignored without any great loss.

For Christians, David is a figure of Christ as King and Messiah. However, this does not necessarily shed any light on the feast this Sunday. But instead of passing it by, let us examine its symbolism a bit more closely. As so often in a painting, it is a detail, so easily overlooked, that reveals the meaning of what at first glance appears to be insignificant. The revealing "detail" here is in the very center of the text. It is said that "all the tribes of Israel," or more precisely "the elders," their spokesmen, chose David as king for two reasons. On the one hand, "in days past," when Saul was king, David had shown himself to be a leader of remarkable ability. But the Lord had said to him: "You shall shepherd my people Israel and shall be commander of Israel."

Thus there was, initially, a free choice by God, a choice that was, so to speak, unexpected. We know what the First Book of Samuel says. God, who had rejected Saul, told the prophet to go to the house of Jesse of Bethlehem, for he had chosen his king from among his sons. Samuel obeyed the Lord's command. Arriving in Bethlehem, he called Jesse and his sons together. On seeing Eliab, of handsome appearance, he thought that this must be the chosen one of God. "Do not judge from his appearance or from his lofty stature, because I have rejected him." Then Jesse presented six other sons to Samuel, but the Lord had chosen none of them. The prophet was perplexed. But Jesse told him that he had another son, the youngest, who was away from home tending the flocks. Samuel had him brought to him. When he appeared, the Lord said to Samuel: "There—anoint him, for this is he!" The story ends with this note: "From that day on, the spirit of the Lord rushed upon David" (1 Sam 16:1-13—Fourth Sunday of Lent, Year A). But it was necessary that the people recognize God's choice. It was necessary that "all the tribes of Israel" would want him to be king over them. What is at stake here is the union of the twelve tribes under one king, a union that would remain, after it had been lost in the schism (1 Kgs 12), the ideal that became the object of never-failing hope. Thus the prophets speak of the messianic age as the gathering of all the tribes of Israel by a descendant of David. This hope eventually developed into universal messianism, the gathering of all the nations under the aegis of the Messiah, the Son of David.

In Jesus, who was announced to Mary as the Son of the Most High (Luke 1:32), on whom descended the Holy Spirit (Luke 3:21-22), in whom the prophecy of Isaiah was realized (Isa 61:1-2; Luke 4:21), there is one greater than David. David was made king of the tribes of Israel. Jesus was made Lord and King of the universe.

Yet his election by God and universal kingship must be freely acknowledged by us. He forces himself on no one. Rather, it is through the cross that he enters into his reign and opens the doors to those who recognize him, crucified, as King of all. And if our eyes look back to the center panel of the triptych . . .

Let us eagerly join the crowd that contemplates the one who promises that we shall be with him in the heavenly Jerusalem.

While we turn to the right-hand panel, let us acclaim our King with all those who are ransomed, who enter "today" into the holy city, the dwelling-place to which he leads us.

> *I rejoiced when I heard them say:*
> *let us go to the house of the LORD.*
>
> I rejoiced because they said to me,
> "We will go up to the house of the LORD,"
> And now we have set foot
> within your gates, O Jerusalem.
>
> Jerusalem, built as a city
> with compact unity.
> To it the tribes go up,
> the tribes of the LORD.
>
> According to the decree for Israel,
> to give thanks to the name of the LORD.
> In it are set up judgment seats,
> seats for the house of David.
> (Ps 122:1-2, 3-4, 4-5)

That He May Be First in All Things

The third panel of the triptych requires a bit more attention. It is a wonderful passage, packed with meaning, a thanksgiving to the Father who "brought us into the kingdom of his beloved Son," and a hymn to Christ, who is first in all things. It is well worth the trouble of memorizing, ranking quite rightly among the great canticles of the New Testament (Col 1:12-20).

First comes the thanksgiving to the Father, which speaks of what he has already done for us through his beloved Son. Redeemed from our sins by Christ, we have been delivered "from the power of darkness" and made fit "to share in the inheritance of the holy ones in light" under the kingship of the beloved Son. Though the "not yet" must be insisted upon, we must not forget our redemption and participation in the inheritance that has occurred "already." We immediately glance back to the center panel to hear Jesus say to his companion: "Today you will be with me in paradise."

At the same time, the reality of the universal kingship of Christ is forcibly and concretely affirmed: it is neither symbolic nor "honorary,"[9] but real and effective like any other, since it is both creative and redemptive.

Such is the dual primacy in the orders of creation and redemption that the hymn to Christ sings, following naturally from the thanksgiving to the Father.[10]

The construction of this passage is inspiring. It might be a hymn that Christians of the time used in their liturgy.[11]

The work of creation and redemption are indissolubly connected. The very structure of the hymn attests to this. It is impossible to distinguish between the preexisting Word and the Word made flesh: they are both the God-man, Jesus Christ. "The first-born of all creatures" is spoken of first as the one through whom everything has been created, then he who has done the work of redemption; but the two are never separated. The Christ involved in creation is the redeemer. Inversely, the redeemer is the one through whom everything has been created. The hymn's way of expressing this is exemplary, with its literary structure of parallels and repetitions. It most admirably expresses the fullness of the mystery of Christ, while avoiding the temptation of a too-abstract formulation. Any commentary could only obscure this quality. The way to understand this text is to let it echo within oneself, reading it over and over. Each time, new features will appear; its fullness of meaning will appear ever greater. But it is not misleading to give some indications of how to read it fully.

"He is the image of the invisible God." Remember another hymn that begins with the contemplation of the Word who was "in God's presence," through whom "all things came to be," who "became flesh and made his dwelling among us" (John 1:1-18). John concludes: "No one has ever seen God. The only Son, God, who is at the Father's side, has revealed him" (John 1:18).

We know also that the personification of Wisdom is spoken of as "the refulgence of eternal light, the spotless mirror of the power of God, the image of his goodness" (Wis 7:26—Thursday I of the Thirty-second Week).

Furthermore, some of the Fathers of the Church, when they read in Genesis (1:26, 27) that "God created man in his image," connecting that text with the one we are reading here, produced the formula: We are the image of the Image (Christ) of God, the icon of his Icon.

The firstborn of all creatures, in whom everything in heaven and on earth was created, "things visible and invisible." For the whole universe, Christ is the reference and convergence point, "the Alpha and the Omega, the first and the last, the beginning and the end" (Rev 22:13). Paul goes even further. He teaches that since the beginning, all of creation is under the sign of redemption. Everything was created by the Son who would become the Christ, the "Son made man."[12]

"In him everything . . . was created . . . He is before all else that is . . . It is he who is the head of the body, the church."

"Redeemer" and "head of the church" are not titles that can be applied, as it were, in a metaphorical sense to some new David, a purely human Messiah.[13] Salvation is not a cloak thrown over our sins, a pardon that does not fundamentally transform the pardoned sinner. There is no break between the natural and supernatural, creation and redemption, that could prevent Christ's salvation from being extended to the whole universe, or the whole world from participating in the dynamism of the redemption.

We are not talking about a "fixing-up" of an accident, a sort of patching up of creation. What happens is supernatural and gratuitous, but it is rooted in the very "act" of creation, for the Christ who has redeemed us and the one through whom everything was created are the same. To call Christ "King of the universe" and "head of the Church" is not to be merely metaphorical.

The Church is not Christ, but it is the Body, of which he is the head. It becomes the Body of Christ through baptism and the Eucharist. (This is a well-known doctrine of Paul's.)[14] Christ the head of the Church is the same as Christ the King.

The Church occupies a privileged place in the world, for it is the Body of Christ. But it is called to reach to the ends of the earth, all of which lies under the rule of Christ the King. "It pleased God to make absolute fullness reside in him."

What exactly does "absolute fullness" mean? That everything is recapitulated in Christ the King, or that he is invested and filled with divinity, with the Spirit?[15] Shouldn't we rather say that Paul intends both meanings at the same time? "It pleased [God] to reconcile everything in his person . . . both on earth and in the heavens, making peace through the blood of his cross." Speaking more explicitly of the consequences of this for Christians, Paul says, in the same letter: "For in him dwells the whole fullness of the deity bodily, and you share in this fullness in him, who is the head of every principality and power" (Col 2:9-10).

This cosmic reconciliation has been brought about "through the blood of his cross." Paradoxically, it is on Calvary that Christ is enthroned—and must be recognized—as King. By this death God disarmed the principalities and powers. "He made a public spectacle of them, leading them away in triumph by it" (Col 2:15).

> O Cross, mighty love of God and light of heaven!
> Cross, eternal salvation, Cross, terror of sinners,
> support of the just, light for Christians,
> O Cross by whom on earth the God made man became our servant,
> by you, the man of heaven has become king!
> The light of truth has sprung up, the evil night has been conquered!
> You are the peaceful link that unites man to Christ, his mediator.
> You have become the ladder by which man climbs to heaven.
> May you always be for the faithful a pillar and anchor:
> Hold up our dwelling-place, guide our ship!
> In the Cross, Lord, ground our faith, as it prepares our crown![16]

The extension of redemption—its breadth and length and height and depth (Eph 3:18)—and the kingship of Christ can only be understood in so far as he is acknowledged to be creator and Lord.

Creator of humanity, he is able to turn "the power of darkness" to fit God's plan.

Creator of the universe, he brings all to salvation.

Creator of the "invisible powers," he masters them and frees us from their domination.

Now we can gaze on the triptych as a whole. Every sin is a rupture, a divergence, a split in the fabric of unity that will naturally grow ever greater. Schism in the midst of the people or the Church is the most sorrowful image of it. Every partial reunification is a rough draft and a promise of redemption. So it was when David, chosen both by God and his peers, joined together the north and south kingdoms into one Israel. It was a tenuous reunification, to be sure, which could not withstand the renewal of rivalry and hostility. Yet David is still a figure of Christ, especially in his work for unity. Like all those who do the same work, he stirs up the desire and hope for another king who will restore the lost unity of the whole universe (First Reading).

This King of the universe, through whom God "reconciles everything on earth and in the heavens" has been given to us. "Firstborn of all creatures," in whom "everything continues in being"; having "primacy in everything," through him we have received God's forgiveness and been freed not only from sin but from the "invisible powers" that tempt us to it.

Such is the fullness of the redemption brought about by the beloved Son of the Father, the image of the invisible God. The blood of his cross has reconciled earth and heaven because he was near the Father who created all things in him (Epistle).

It is on the cross that Christ has inaugurated his reign and opened the way to the kingdom. Henceforth, to everyone who turns to him and says: "Jesus, remember me," he will respond: "Today you will be with me in paradise."

He says this to us each time we encounter him in prayer and the sacraments, each time we celebrate the mystery of his death and resurrection, his passover and ours, each time we come to communion in his body and blood.

Contemplating the triptych of Christ the King, we give thanks for his reign "already here" while looking to the full realization of what is "not yet" in front of us.

> Love which waits for us
> at the end of history,
> your kingdom begins in the shadow of the cross;
> already its light
> shines in our lives.
> Jesus, Lord, make haste!
> Return and finish your work!
>
> When will we see your glory
> transform the universe?
>
> Even today, as we know,
> creation groans
> in childbirth.

When will we see your glory
transform the universe?

We await the new heavens,
the new earth,
where justice will reign.

When will we see your glory
transform the universe?

We walk in faith,
not sight,
till the hour of your return.

When will we see your glory
transform the universe?

Conclusion

Throughout the course of the liturgical year, we have been guided through the "events" of salvation as they occur in the lives of believers and the Church. Our guide has been the evangelist Luke, who has written a "narrative" so that we "may realize the certainty of the teachings [we] have received" (Luke 1:1-4—Third Sunday).

The Word of God, in both Old and New Testaments, is an important part of every Sunday assembly of the faithful who gather for the day of the Lord. We have found it to be a helpful guide in understanding our faith. However, faith is not the knowledge of a set of doctrines; it is not gnosticism.

The gospel is not a book of secrets that can be known by only the educated initiate. It is the good news, an announcement of a "year acceptable to the Lord" (Luke 4:19). This good news is addressed to the poor and to the weak, though not primarily in the sense of any social category. Luke applies the term to anyone who willingly gives up everything in order to receive lasting treasure, which belongs to God alone. The people who hear this proclamation are primarily not those who may have reason to regard themselves as just, but tax collectors, prostitutes, and sinners, who look to the Lord to "justify" them. It is also addressed to those Pharisees and rich people who are willing to do the same. Even the Gentiles who joyfully embrace the way of salvation are included.

Luke has been called "the evangelist of discipleship," urging every believer to follow the person of Jesus to Jerusalem, where, on the cross, he is revealed as king.

Of course things do not end on Calvary or with Christ's being lifted to heaven after blessing the disciples (Luke 24:50). Luke has written a second book that he begins, after the story of the ascension, by recounting how the apostles and those with them (e.g., Mary, Jesus' mother) received the gift of the Holy Spirit, which Jesus had promised, on Pentecost (Acts 1:14; 2:1-4).

Thus begins the sacred story of the Easter community who were faithful to the apostles' teaching, faithful to the community, to the breaking of the bread, and to prayer and missionary work (Acts 2:42). Of the gospel lived out and preached to every nation under the sun. Of the endless coming of the "today" of salvation. Of the baptism, Eucharist, liturgy, mission, and witness in the "ordinary time," the daily life of all people, in the cyclical rhythm of the seasons of nature, the Church, the faith, and the individual spiritual life. Of the *Days of the Lord* that have already come, are coming, and will come.

The celebration of the "standard" liturgical year is both old and new, open to all the possibilities that arise from the work of the Spirit and our response. It is a well-marked road and a path of adventure, full of the surprises that God has kept hidden for us to find. It is a journey with a set itinerary, but that always looks new, revealing something hitherto unseen, as if one were traveling a well-trodden path with a friend who points out new things, fresh perspectives, lending an aura of discovery to something we thought we knew.

As our companion on the road, Jesus explains to our dull hearts everything in Moses and the prophets that pertains to him. We recognize him in the breaking of the bread. Then he disappears before our eyes. But we know that he is at our side as we continue on. Strengthened by this encounter, we go out to spread the good news: "The Lord has truly been raised!" (Luke 24:13-35).

We celebrate in joy, wonder, and thanksgiving, if we have properly understood Luke, who returns so often, in both his books, to this theme of the past, present, and future in the lives of Christians and the Church.

We pray constantly, with an intensity appropriate to decisive moments, in order to attune us to God's will and the gift of the Spirit, following the example both of Jesus and the first Christian community.

> Blessed be the Lord, the God of Israel
> for he has visited and brought redemption to his people.
> He has raised up a horn for our salvation
> within the house of David his servant,
> even as he promised through the mouth of his holy prophets from of old:
> salvation from our enemies and from the hand
> of all who hate us,
> to show mercy to our fathers
> and to be mindful of his holy covenant
> and of the oath he swore to Abraham our father,
> and to grant us that,
> rescued from the hand of enemies,
> without fear we might worship him

in holiness and righteousness
before him all our days.
(Luke 1:68-75)

My being proclaims the greatness of the Lord;
my spirit finds joy in God my savior,
For he has looked upon his servant in her lowliness;
behold, from now on will ages call me blessed.
The Mighty One has done great things for me,
and holy is his name.
His mercy is from age to age
on those who fear him.
He has shown might with his arm,
dispersed the arrogant of mind and heart.
He has thrown down the rulers from their thrones
but lifted up the lowly.
The hungry he has filled with good things;
the rich he has sent away empty.
He has helped Israel his servant,
remembering his mercy,
according to the promise to our fathers,
to Abraham and to his descendants forever
(Luke 1:47-55)

NOTES

Ordinary Time, Year C—Page 1

1. The end of chapter 21 (vv. 1-36) is read in its entirety from Monday to Saturday of the Thirty-fourth Week.

2. We should add that an important part of Luke's Gospel is read during weekdays in Ordinary Time, from the Twenty-first to the Thirty-fourth weeks.

3. Because of the celebration of the Baptism of the Lord, there is no set of readings for the First Sunday of Ordinary Time. But the first week begins on the Monday following the Baptism of the Lord, or Epiphany if it falls on January 7 or 8 (in which case the Baptism is celebrated the next day).

4. There is an explanation of this at the beginning of Volume 4.

Practical Scheme of the Gospel According to Luke—Pages 2–10

1. The division of the books into chapters and verses that we find in our Bibles dates from the beginning of printing. We still use it because it is helpful; however, a quick glance at the text shows that our divisions are not integral to the text.

2. The second half of Luke's work is the Acts of the Apostles.

Second Sunday—Pages 11–21

1. As we have already noted (Vol. 4, *Introduction*), Ordinary Time begins the week after Epiphany, which we celebrate on the Sunday between January 2 and 8. The Sunday that introduces Ordinary Time is the feast of the Baptism of the Lord, which also closes the season of Christmas-Epiphany (Vol. 1). This celebration has its own format, and there is no other First Sunday of Ordinary Time. Hence this next Sunday is the Second.

2. The "prophetic writings" are those that have the name of the prophet applied to a particular book. Amos was without a doubt the first. Hosea dates from the third quarter of the eighth century B.C.

3. Jer 2:2-3, 23-24; 3:1; 30:14; 31:22; Isa 50:1; 54:4-7; 62:4-5; Ezek 16; 23.

4. E.g., the parable of those invited to the wedding feast of a king's son (Matt 22:1-14); John the Baptist's calling himself the groom's "best man" (John 3:29); Jesus' response to John's disciples: "Can the wedding guests fast while the bridegroom is with them?" (Mark 2:18-20); Paul's statement to the Corinthians: "I betrothed you to one husband to present you as a chaste virgin to Christ" (2 Cor 11:2); the Church as the bride of Christ (Eph 5:25); the vision of the wedding feast of the Lamb with the Church assembled in heaven (Rev 19:7-9; 21:9-10).

5. Often the subject of meditation of the Fathers, it is the thread that runs through the *Spiritual Canticle* of John of the Cross.

6. Isa 1:26; 60:14; 62:12; 62:4.

7. If one pays close attention, it becomes apparent that John's Gospel speaks of a series of events that all occur within one week. The first day, the Baptist's testimony that he is not the Messiah (John 1:19-28). "The next day," he sees Jesus coming toward him and says: "Behold, the Lamb of God . . . " (John 1:29-34). "The next day," the first two disciples follow Jesus, while Andrew leads his brother Simon to him (John 1:35-42). "The next day," Jesus leaves for Galilee, meets Philip and sends for Nathanael (John 1:43-51). Finally, "on the third day," there is the wedding at Cana (John 2:1). All in one week.

8. See L. Bouyer, *La quatrième évangile* (Paris-Tournai: Casterman, *Bible et vie chrétienne,* 1963) 82.

9. Jesus says to the Samaritan woman: "Believe me, woman . . . " (John 4:21). Likewise to the woman caught in adultery, whom he does not condemn: "Woman, where are they [her accusers] ?" (John 8:10). And to Mary Magdalene on Easter morning: "Woman, why are you weeping?" (John 20:15).

The experts say that this way of speaking conforms to Hellenic uses and thus is a part of the language in which the Fourth Gospel was written. Some modern languages use the same idiom. In Spanish, for instance, *mujer* and *hombre* are not terms of disrespect but, depending on tone of voice and circumstances, can be anything from commonplace to emphatic.

10. Ten times at least: John 2:4; 5:25, 28; 7:30; 8:20; 12:23, 27 (twice); 13:1; 17:1. One could also add: John 4:23; 16:25, 32.

11. Cyprian, bishop of Carthage who was martyred in 258, said: "No one can have God for Father if he does not have the Church for mother."

12. In the allegory of the trees who are looking for a king, the vine excused itself, saying: "Must I give up my sweetness and my good fruit, and go to wave over the trees?" (Judg 9:13—Wednesday I of the Twentieth Week).

13. Jacob blessed Isaac by saying to him: "May God give to you of the dew of the heavens and of the fertility of the earth abundance of grain and wine" (Gen 27:28—Saturday I of the Thirteenth Week).

14. Of Noah, the first to plant the vine, it is said: "Out of the very ground that the Lord has put under a curse, this one shall bring us relief from our work and the toil of our hands" (Gen 5:29).

15. "Though you have planted choice vineyards, you shall not drink their wine!" (Amos 5:11). "You shall . . . tread out . . . the grapes, yet drink no wine" (Mic 6:15). "They will . . . plant vineyards, but not drink their wine" (Zeph 1:13). "Though you plant and cultivate vineyards, you will not drink or store up the wine, for the grubs will eat the vines clean" (Deut 28:39).

16. "He tethers his donkey to the vine, his purebred ass to the choicest stem. In wine he washes his garments, his robe in the blood of grapes. His eyes are darker than wine, and his teeth are whiter than milk" (Gen 49:11-12). "Shouting, they shall mount the heights of Zion, they shall come streaming to the Lord's blessings: the grain, the wine, and the oil, the sheep and the oxen; they themselves shall be like watered gardens, never again shall they languish" (Jer 31:12). "On this mountain the Lord of hosts will provide for all peoples a feast of rich food and choice wines, juicy, rich food and pure, choice wines" (Isa 25:6—Wednesday of the First Week of Advent). "I will bring about the restoration of my people Israel; they shall . . . plant vineyards and drink the wine, set out gardens and eat the fruit" (Amos 9:14—Saturday II of the Thirteenth Week). "The Lord answered and said to his people: 'See, I will send you grain, and wine, and oil, and you shall be filled with them' " (Joel 2:19). See the article "Vin" in *Dictionnaire de théologie biblique,* col. 1357-1360.

17. Apocalypse of Baruch 29:5, P. Bogaert, *Sources chrétiennes* 144 (Paris: Cerf, 1969) 483. According to the "Tables of measures and money," *Bible de Jérusalem* (p. 2077), a "kor" equals 450 liters!

18. Ephraim, *Commentaire sur l'Evangile concordant*, XII, 2, trans. L. Leloir, *Corpus christianorum orientalium*, vol. 145, p. 115.

19. Romanus the melodist (5th c. musician, singer), *Hymnes*, XLIII, 20, *Sources chrétiennes* 110 (Paris: Cerf, 1965) 32.

20. Cana (John 2:1-11), healing of the son of a royal official (John 4:46-54), healing of the paralytic (John 5:1-9), multiplication of the loaves (John 6:1-15), healing of the man born blind (John 9:1-38), raising of Lazarus (John 11:1-44).

21. "By this is my Father glorified, that you bear much fruit and become my disciples" (John 15:8). "From his fullness we have all received, grace in place of grace . . ." (John 1:16).

From the Third to the Fifth Sunday—Pages 22-39

1. This cannot be overemphasized, for two reasons. On the one hand, there is always a tendency to interpret the Gospels in patterns to which we are accustomed, whether in terms of organization, development of themes, etc. On the other hand, such attempts will show up the apparent incomprehensibility and contradictory nature of the Gospels, thus proving themselves inadequate.

2. Note that modern historians often do the same, especially when primarily dealing with one important figure.

3. The fact that the "plans" suggested by certain exegetes do not agree with each other shows clearly that no one can claim pre-eminence. It is enough to compare the titles and subtitles of the divisions in modern Bibles to see that they are more or less fortuitously divided into "plans" of this sort.

4. As was said in the introduction to Ordinary Time (Vol. 4), none of these sequences are meant to be exclusive; all we are concerned with is that they have a sufficiently "objective" basis.

5. One ought not to suppose that Jesus "found" this text of Isaiah by chance or that he himself chose it. Originally organized in the fourth and third centuries B.C., the synagogal office has remained substantially the same till this very day. The Sabbath morning celebration—which is the principal one—is a Liturgy of the Word in two parts. The first is composed entirely of various forms of praise: morning benedictions, psalms, and canticles, concluding with the Hallel (Ps 112-117). The second contains readings: a passage from the Law (Pentateuch), then from the Prophets, followed by benedictions, which form a kind of "universal prayer." The conclusion is a set of benedictions addressed to God and a final song (Ph. Rouillard, "La lecture de l'Ecriture dans la liturgie juive," in *Paroisse et liturgie* 51 [1969] 484). In Jesus' day, this office was almost certainly not so rigorously structured, nor was there yet an "official lectionary." (A. Paul, *Intertestament*, in *Cahier évangile* 14 [Paris: Cerf, 1975] 26-33.) However, the relationship between Law and Prophets was always present. The latter, along with the later translations and commentaries (Targums), may be understood as a special instance of an actualization of the Law. Consequently, this sort of proclamation testifies to the conviction that the word of God retains a permanent value and meaning. Every person in every time and place can personally appropriate it. Take, for example, Exodus 12:25-27: by the rite of the Passover celebrated each year, God accomplishes throughout all ages what he did once in the past for his people. Our Liturgy of the Word is rooted in this biblical tradition, and preaches the same present power of the wonders of God.

6. Origen (3rd c.), *Homélies sur saint Luc*, XXXII, 6, in *Sources chrétiennes* 87 (Paris: Cerf, 1962) 391-393.

7. A monk of the Eastern Church, *Ils regarderont vers lui. Présence du Christ* (Chevetogne, 1975) 71-72. Quoted in its entirety in *Bible et vie chrétienne* 39 (1961) 62-65.

8. As pointed out in note a) of *Bible de Jérusalem*, p. 1905.

9. Thérèse of Lisieux, *Histoire d'une âme. Manuscrits autobiographiques* (Paris: Cerf-Desclée de Brouwer, 1972) 222. Letter to Sister Marie of the Sacred Heart, September 8, 1896.

10. The Marriage Lectionary suggests for the second reading, among other texts, 1 Cor 12:31–13:8 (up through "Love never fails"); many couples choose it. The text is certainly most appropriate for the liturgy of marriage, which for Christians who have been temples of the Holy Spirit since baptism (1 Cor 6:19), is "a great mystery . . . in reference to Christ and the Church" (Eph 5:32). But we should admit that in the context of a wedding, what Paul says is often understood as referring to conjugal love. To be sure, this is not excluded; however, it would be a reductive reading of Paul, insofar as the theological dimension of this love "which never fails" is, if not obscured, at least put in parentheses. At the extreme, this passage, torn from context, could be appropriated by anyone—not only a believer—for whom love is a "gift of God" or the gods.

11. Matt 13:54-58 is read Friday of the Seventeenth Week of Ordinary Time, Mark 6:1-6 Wednesday of the Fourth Week and the Fourteenth Sunday of Year B.

John, for his part, reports that "Jesus himself testified that a prophet has no honor in his native country" (John 4:44). Elsewhere, he evokes the objection "Is this not Jesus, the son of Joseph? Do we not know his father and mother?" (John 6:42). But these remarks belong to other contexts (the first is read in the Gospel of Monday of the Fourth Week of Lent, the second the Nineteenth Sunday of Ordinary Time, Year B).

The Fourth Gospel recalls the proverb about the prophet in his native country while saying that Jesus left for Galilee (from Shechem in Samaria, where he spoke to a Samaritan woman and the townspeople believed in him—John 4:1-42), where the people "welcomed him" (John 4:43, 45). The passage remains thus somewhat obscure.

As to the problem of Jesus' human origin, John presents it as an objection to the proclamation "I am the bread that came down from heaven" (John 6:41-42). It is a difficulty for faith in the Eucharist and, in a more general sense, for admitting that Jesus, true man, born of a woman, is at the same time true God, eternal Son of the Father.

12. Currently, we date the Gospel of Luke c. 80-90. But even if it is older, as some think, the same statement would hold true.

13. K. Rahner, *Une foi qui aime le monde.* Trans. R. Virion Mulhouse (Salvator, 1968) 121–123.

14. See for example in the *Vocabulaire de théologie biblique*, 2nd ed. (Paris: Cerf, 1970), the articles "Prophète" (II, 1, col. 1048) and "Vocation" (I, col. 1373–1374).

15. A figure of speech, for Isaiah knows that no one, not even Moses and Elijah, can truly see God and live (Gen 32:31; Exod 33:18-23; Judg 6:21-22). Moreover, he writes: "Woe is me, I am doomed! For I am a man of unclean lips, living among a people of unclean lips; yet my eyes have seen the King, the Lord of hosts" (v. 5).

16. See Luke 5:27, 28; 9:23, 59; 18:22, 28.

17. Ambrose, bishop of Milan (340–397), *Traité sur l'évangile de saint Luc*, IV, 76–77 in *Sources chrétiennes* 45bis (Paris: Cerf, 1971) 181.

18. Cyril, bishop of Alexandria (c. 377–444), *Commentaire sur Luc*, 1, 11, quoted in *Le livre d'heures d'En-Calcat* (Dourgne, 1952) 370.

From the Sixth to the Eighth Sunday—Pages 40–65

1. In Deuteronomy (30:15-20—Thursday after Ash Wednesday), we read a text nearly contemporary with Jeremiah and very close to his spirit. There, all Israel is placed at the crossroads, faced with the choice between life and happiness or death and unhappiness. But God wants his people to live: "Choose life, then, that you and your descendants may live, by loving the Lord, your God, heeding his voice, and holding fast to him. For that will mean life for you, a long life for you to live on the land which the Lord swore he would

give to your fathers Abraham, Isaac and Jacob'' (Deut 30:19-20). See also, for example, Isa 31:1-3; Jer 2:18-19; 9:22; Ezek 16:15; 33:13; Pss 1; 44:7; 49:7-8, 14; 52:9- 10; 118:8-9; etc.

2. See also Pss 1:3; 46:2-3; 112:7-8; etc.

3. Ambrose, bishop of Milan (340–397); *De Excessu fratris* II, 90–91, 102–103. Trans. Fiches d'Orval (F 8).

4. Luke 3:21: after the baptism when the Spirit descended on Jesus; 5:16: after healing a leper when, avoiding the crowds, Jesus went into the desert; 9:18: before announcing to the disciples that he must die; 9:28-29: at the Transfiguration; 10:21: after the seventy-two had reported on the success of their mission; 11:1: before teaching his disciples how to pray; 22:40-46: on Mount Olivet; 23:34, 46: on the cross.

5. This text—Luke 6:12-16—is read on Tuesday of the Twenty-third Week of Ordinary Time.

6. Luke adds here the list of the Twelve from "Simon, to whom he gave the name Peter" to Judas Iscariot whom he calls, like the other evangelists (Matt 10:1-4; Mark 3:16-19), "the one who betrayed him."

7. Verses 20-23 contain five sentences, but only four "beatitudes," verse 23 not really being a fifth.

8. Origen (185–254), *Commentaire de la Lettre aux Romains*, 7, 11. Quoted in G. Bardy, *La vie spirituelle d'après les Pères des trois premiers siècles* (Paris: Bloud et Gay, 1935) 247–248.

9. Cardinal E. Pironio, "Méditation pour des temps difficiles," in *L'osservatore romano*, French edition (January 11, 1977) 7.

10. Such a cutting-up of a text—verses 2, 7-9, 12-13, 22-23—may be surprising: what could be the justification for a reading with so many gaps in it? The First Book of Samuel spends all of chapter 26 (twenty-five verses) on this story. The Lectionary contains only eight of the verses. Those omitted speak of certain details that refer to the where, when, and how of what happens (vv. 1, 3-5), discourse of David and his men (vv. 6, 10-11), Saul's men (vv. 14-16) and Saul himself (vv. 17-21, 24-25). The omission of these verses does not produce a slanted or lifeless reading. The Lectionary retains everything in chapter 26 that deals with the central point: David, when he had a chance to kill Saul, who was pursuing him in the desert of Ziph, spared him because he had received the Lord's anointing. Moreover, this is what is important for our liturgy.

11. This ignores the question of the exercise of justice, which a society cannot do without. There are many complex problems—theoretical and practical—involved in the exercise of justice, beginning with the question of whether the intent of punishment should be punitive or rehabilitative.

12. *Te Deum* is the classic, Latin title of this psalm; the words in quotes come from the psalm's subtitle.

13. The first two have been read during the Fifth and Sixth Sundays.

14. Theodore of Mopsuestia (4th c.), *Commentaire sur saint Jean*, book II, C.S.C.O., 116, p. 55.

15. We remember that Matthew says (Matt 25:31-46—Thirty-fourth Sunday of Ordinary Time, Year A) that at the last judgment this reward will also be given to those who gave food and drink to the hungry and thirsty, welcomed the stranger, clothed the naked, visited the sick and imprisoned, without knowing that in doing these things they were serving Christ.

16. Rabban Youssef Bousnaya, Syrian monk of the tenth century. Quoted in P. Deseille, *L'Evangile au desert* (Paris: Cerf, 1965) 244.

17. Augustine (354–430), *Homélie 56 sur le pardon des péchés*. Quoted in *Bible et vie chrétienne* 29 (1959) 9–10.

18. Jesus, son of Eleazar, son of (Ben) Sirach, was a Palestinian Jew who wrote c. 190 B.C.

19. The first part (1:1–42:14) is a collection of maxims in the style of the Book of Proverbs. The second (42:15-51:38) is a hymn to the glory of God.

20. E.g., this apothegm: "Some brothers went from Scete to see Father Anthony. On the boat, they met an old man who was going that way too. The brothers did not know him. Seated together in the boat, they talked about the sayings of the Fathers and Scripture, as well as their work manuals. The old man kept silent. Arriving in port, they discovered that the old man was also going to Father Anthony. When they came to him, Anthony said: 'You have found in this old man a good companion for the journey.' To the old man he said: 'You have found some very good brothers, father.' The old man said: 'Yes, they are good, but their barn has no door, and anyone may go inside and untie their donkey.' He said this because the brothers spoke everything that occurred to them." N. Devilliers, *Antoine le Grand, père des moines* (Abbaye de Bellefontaine, 1971) 75. The *Rule of St. Benedict* has one chapter (VI) entitled *De taciturnitate* ("restraint of speech"). The Church has never entirely approved of monastic rules that require absolute silence.

21. Though translated "hypocrite," the term does not necessarily refer to conscious dissimulation or lying. The Greek word—*hypokrites*—occurs only twice in the Septuagint, the Greek translation of the Old Testament made between 250 and 130 B.C.—in the Book of Job (34:36; 36:13).

22. John Chrysostom, patriarch of Constantinople (c. 344–407), *Homélie sur les Actes des Apôtres*, 29:3. Quoted in *Une nuée de témoins* (Paris: Cerf-Droguet et Ardant, Langage des hommes/Parole de Dieu 1, 1974) 62–63.

23. Such is the teaching of the parable of the sower (Luke 8:4-15—Saturday of the Twenty-fourth Week; Matt 13:1-23—Fifteenth Sunday, Year A; Mark 4:1-20—Wednesday of the Third Week). Luke clearly indicates that Mary is the model of the disciple when he says that "Mary kept all these things, reflecting on them in her heart" (Luke 2:19—Christmas, Mass at Dawn); ". . . and his mother kept all these things in her heart" (Luke 2:51—Holy Family, Year C).

From the Ninth to the Eleventh Sunday—Pages 66–91

1. The first set of parables is not contained in the Sunday Lectionary: Luke 8:1-21 is read from Friday of the Twenty-fourth Week in Ordinary Time to Tuesday of the Twenty-fifth.

2. This refers to the episode when John the Baptist, in prison, sent two of his disciples to ask the Lord: "Are you the one who is to come, or should we look for another?" (Luke 7:18-20).

3. Jesus' response to John's messengers says precisely this: "Go and tell John what you have seen and heard" (Luke 7:22).

4. Jesus declares: "And blessed is the one who takes no offense at me" (Luke 7:23). And after John's messengers have left, he speaks sadly of the blindness of the "men of today": "For John the Baptist came neither eating food nor drinking wine, and you said, 'He is possessed by a demon.' The Son of Man came eating and drinking and you said, 'Look, he is a glutton and a drunkard, a friend of tax collectors and sinners!' " (Luke 7:33-34).

5. Certain portions of chapters 3 (four out of twenty-nine verses), 5 (seven out of twenty-six verses) and 6 (five out of eighteen verses) will be read on the Twelfth, Thirteenth and Fourteenth Sundays.

6. It is true that in the text from the Book of Kings, as we find it in the Bible, the prayer for strangers is followed by another intercession for Israel (vv. 44-51), an invocation that God might receive the supplication of his servant and the people (vv. 52-53), and a solemn benediction by Solomon over the people (vv. 54-61).

However, the consensus among exegetes is that this last part (vv. 44-61) was added later, after the Exile. Therefore, the prayer for strangers might well be understood as the end of Solomon's prayer, which successively deals with the king, the people, and the other nations.

7. The difference between these two categories is often emphasized in the Bible. Cf. Deut 14:21: "You must not eat any animal that had died of itself . . . But you may give it to an alien who belongs to your community *(ger)*, and he may eat it, or you may sell it to a foreigner *(nokri)."*
Some of the laws concerning liturgical (Num 15:14-16) or social order (Exod 22:20; Lev 19:33-34; Ezek 47:22) deal with strangers *(nokri).*

8. To be exact, Galatia is a hilly region in Asia Minor where the Gauls, before crossing the Bosporus, appeared at the beginning of the third century B.C. The chief city was Ancyra (today Ankara, in Turkey).
The Roman province of Galatia in the time of Paul included other territories, particularly Pisidia, where Paul spread the good news on his first missionary journey (Acts 13–14).

9. There is a notable difference between this address and those of all the other letters where Paul mentions his status as an apostle of Christ.

10. In writing this, Paul is obviously thinking of the time when, as he says to the Galatians, he persecuted the Church of God and tried to destroy it (Gal 1:13). He has not forgotten the voice that said to him on the road to Damascus, where he was going to arrest the faithful: "I am Jesus, whom you are persecuting" (Acts 9:5).

11. In specifying that the officer was a Roman centurion, the Lectionary goes beyond the text. He was probably a mercenary recruited by the governor of the region, Herod Antipas. The Romans typically left it to their subordinates to keep order in an area, preferring not to use their own troops for that purpose. His occupation indicates that he was a pagan, as does the praise that Jesus gives him: "Amen, I say to you, in no one in Israel have I found such faith" (v. 9).

12. The question of what faith—or what beginning of faith—these words reveal in the centurion is secondary. Likewise, the meaning that he would have attributed to the title "Lord." What is important is that believers acknowledged this title, confessing in faith that Jesus is the Lord.

13. K. Rahner (died 1986), *Homélies bibliques,* (Mulhouse: Salvator, 1967) 20–21.

14. For a treatment of death in the Bible, see *Vocabulaire de théologie biblique,* 2nd revised and expanded ed. (Paris: Cerf, 1970) col. 795–807.

15. Paul knows—indeed he says in some verses earlier—that one can renounce material pleasures for purely human reasons, such as a concern for good health.

16. This "argument," if one may call it such, occurs frequently in the prayer of believers of the Old Testament, the psalmists in particular: Psalms 6; 30; 88; etc.

17. Actually, this text does not extend quite to the end of the chapter, falling five verses short: "As to what I am writing to you, behold, before God, I am not lying. Then I went into the regions of Syria and Cilicia. And I was unknown personally to the churches of Judea that are in Christ; they only kept hearing that 'the one who once was persecuting us is now preaching the faith he once tried to destroy,' So they glorified God because of me."

18. See 1 Cor 15:9; Phil 3:6; 1 Tim 1:13; and also Acts 8:3; 9:1-30; 22:5- 16; 26:9-18.

19. The firstfruits and firstborn (Exod 13:12), the portions of the victim for the holocaust (Exod 29:24, 26, 27) were set apart.

20. We know that on his first trip to Jerusalem, Paul received a vision in the Temple that confirmed his ministry to the Gentiles (Acts 22:17-21).

21. The raising of Jairus' daughter (Luke 8:40-56) is recounted also by Matthew (9:18-26) and Mark (5:21-43—Thirteenth Sunday of Ordinary Time, Year B).

22. Acts 3:15; 5:30; 13:37; 1 Cor 15:4; Luke 24:6; Mark 16:6; etc.

23. See Col 2:12 and 3:1.

24. Sometimes it refers to the final judgment (Wis 3:7, 13). God "visits" those whom he tests: "Though you test my heart, searching [visiting] it in the night, though you try me with fire, you shall find no malice in me" (Ps 17:3). "To visit" is often synonymous

with "to punish," which is clear in modern translations (Exod 32:34; Isa 10:3; 23:17; Jer 6:15; 11:22-23; Ps 59:6; Zech 10:3; etc.). But "the visit of God" is also evoked when he "comes" to grant a blessing, or salvation: to a woman whom he causes to have a child (Gen 21:1; 1 Sam 2:21), to those who are faithful to him (Jer 15:15; Job 10:12; Ps 106:4: "Remember me, O Lord, as you favor your people; visit me with your saving help"), to the people he led out of Egypt (Gen 50:24; Exod 3:16; 4:31; 13:19), whom he led back from exile (Jer 29:10; Ezek 34:11-12; Ps 80:15: "Once again, O Lord of hosts, look down from heaven, and see; take care of this vine").

25. Luke speaks four times of the "visit" of God (or of Christ): 1:68, 78; 7:16; 19:44. The reference occurs only once more in the whole New Testament: "Though the pagans may slander you as troublemakers, conduct yourselves blamelessly among them. By observing your good works they may give glory to God on the day of visitation" (1 Pet 2:12).

26. Augustine (354-430), *Sermon 98 au people*, P.L. 988, 591-592. In H. Tissot, *Les Pères vous parlent de l'Evangile* I (Bruges: Apostolat liturgique, 1954) 781.

27. The parallelism with Nathan's story is not only clear but virtually *a fortiori*. The king, who in accordance with the morals of the times had a harem, took Uriah's only wife. Moreover, what is at issue here is not a little "lamb" but a human being! The crime is similar, but not proportionate.

28. The prodigal son will use the same formula: "Father, I have sinned against heaven and against you" (Luke 15:21—Twenty-fourth Sunday).

29. Verses 11-12 are rightly omitted by the Lectionary. Exegetes have concluded that they were a later addition to presage a later episode: Absalom visiting his father's concubines (2 Sam 16:22).

30. The title of Psalm 51 as it is found in ancient Hebrew and Greek Bibles.

31. A. Brien, *Jésus Christ inutile et pourtant nécessaire*. Conference de Notre-Dame de Paris, February 28, 1971 (Paris: Bayard-Press, 1971) 22-24.

32. He mentions three occasions when Jesus ate with Pharisees: here, and in chapters 11 (vv. 37-52) and 14 (vv. 1-24).

33. One cannot accuse the Pharisee of slighting Jesus in his manner of receiving him. He welcomed Jesus according to custom, though without showing him a special mark of honor.

34. There is a difficulty with verse 47. It is readily understood as: "Her sins are forgiven her *because* she has shown much love." Love is therefore the cause of forgiveness, which runs counter to the meaning of the parable. Exegetes explain that love must be understood as the consequence of the forgiveness, and that it is much greater than the "debt of sin."

35. Remember that Nathan was sent by God to David to tell him that he had sinned and that God forgave him. He did not speak on his own account, as Jesus does here.

In the case of the paralytic (Luke 5:18-26), it is clear that Jesus himself forgives the man's sins, and that he has the right to do so: " 'Which is easier, to say, "Your sins are forgiven," or to say, "Rise and walk"? But that you may know that the Son of Man has authority on earth to forgive sins'—he said to the man who was paralyzed, 'I say to you, rise, pick up your stretcher, and go home.' "

36. Augustine (354-430), *Sermon 99*. In H. Tissot, *Les Pères vous parlent de l'Evangile* II (Bruges: Apostolat liturgique, 1955) 295-296.

37. The whole latter portion of Luke's Gospel from 9:51 on deals with Jesus' "journey" toward the place of his passion and resurrection.

38. *Missel romain, Liturgie de la parole*, n. 11.

39. *Célébrer la pénitence et la réconciliation*. *Nouveau rituel* (1978), n. 61.

From the Twelfth to the Fourteenth Sunday—Pages 92–119

1. Cardinal J. Newman (1801–1890), *Douze sermons sur le Christ* (Paris: Egloff, 1943) 145–146.

2. Thus Luke 10:21; 22:42; 23:34, 46.

3. See the Sixth Sunday of Ordinary Time, p. 335, note 4. This is not to say that Luke is the only one of the evangelists to note that Jesus prays or that he ignores or minimizes the value of this prayer as the manifestation of the union of Son and Father, or that he forgets that Jesus, in praying, taught his disciples the necessity of prayer and the way in which they themselves must pray. See, for example, in *Bible de Jérusalem,* p. 1635, the note on Matthew 14:23.

4. Matthew 16:13 and Mark 8:27 situate the scene in the region of Caesarea of Philippi, while Peter's profession in John 6:67-71 takes place in Capernaum (John 6:59).

5. See above, introduction to the Third to Fifth Sundays, p. 22.

6. This is a formula characteristic of Luke (he uses it thirty-six or thirty-seven times; it occurs only three times in Mark and six in Matthew), which is formed of three parts: "It happened" (or: "it came to pass" or "one day"), a specifying of time or circumstance, and an active verb in the past tense.

7. See X. Léon-Dufour, "Perdre sa vie selon l'Evangile," in *Etudes,* October 1979, pp. 395–409.

8. J.-J. Duguet, *Jésus crucifié,* Paris, 1728, pp. 491–494. Quoted in *Et la vie jaillira,* Orval, Eveils 1, 1976, pp. 100–101.

9. Saturday of the Twenty-fifth Week of Ordinary Time, Monday of the Twenty-sixth Week.

10. Similarly, Joshua was made servant-disciple and later on leader after Moses. Elijah is often associated with Moses in the New Testament, especially in the Transfiguration (Luke 9:30—Second Sunday of Lent).

11. "Remarkable" because though it is akin in a literary sense to the stories of the calling of the great prophets (cf. Isa 6; Jer 1; Ezek 1-3), it is distinguished from them by its simplicity and absence of "theophany."

12. This should not be understood as referring only to the "call" or vocation to the religious or priestly life, but rather to times when the hand of God can be felt within the framework of everyday life. Because we do not have an adequate appreciation for this kind of call, however, we speak of these things as happening by chance or coincidence. Ask many couples about the circumstances that led to their choice to make a life together.

13. For example, 1 Sam 28:13-14; Zech 13:4.

14. The cloak symbolizes the personality and rights of its owner, as well as the owner's protection. Thus the man spread a corner of it over the woman that he chose for a wife (Ruth 3:9; Ezek 16:8). The gift of a cloak was a sign of unity, communion, and friendship: Jonathan made a gift of his cloak and weapons to David (1 Sam 18:4).

Insofar as it was a sign of a function (the royal cloak, for example: Jonah 3:6), it shared in the "charism" of the one who wore it, and the imposition of this cloak was an investiture. When Elijah was lifted to heaven, Elisha picked it up and was thus able to perform the same miracle as Elijah (2 Kgs 2:8, 13-14).

The liturgy retains this symbolism: imposition of the habit of the religious, the stole of the deacon, the chasuble of the priest.

15. The expression occurs often in the Bible: 1 Kgs 14:8; 18:21; Deut 6:14; 8:19; etc.

16. Note also that the mutual service owed between the faithful involves communal charity, which is something entirely other than the condescension of the false "charity" that humiliates those who receive it.

17. See, for example, the article "Servir" in the *Vocabulaire de Théologie biblique,* 2nd ed. (Paris: Cerf, 1970) col. 1218.

18. L.-J. Lebret, *Dimensions de la charité,* Paris, Ed. ouvrières, 1958, p. 73.

19. The word "road" is found here five times in seven verses!

20. Indications as to places are infrequent and vague. If one was pressed on the point, one would have to say that Jesus was either going in circles or that he was not sticking to the Jerusalem road. At the beginning of chapter 17 (v. 11), Jesus is continuing his journey, traveling through Samaria and Galilee, though the evangelist says at various times (e.g., Luke 10:38; 13:22) that he was traveling "to Jerusalem." One must wait for chapter 19 (v. 28) to see him finally proceeding "on his journey up to Jerusalem." In fact, he arrives quickly with his disciples at "Bethphage and Bethany at the place called the Mount of Olives" (Luke 19:29).

21. The second volume of his work—the Acts of the Apostles—does not share this feature. Most of its events, discourses, etc., are placed very precisely. Many Bibles today provide maps of Paul's missionary journeys and his voyage in captivity.

22. The reader is struck by the formulas used, which, if they are not intentional, reveal a singular carelessness of style that is totally uncharacteristic of Luke: "After this" (10:1); "On one occasion" (10:25); "One day" (11:1); "Another time," "Jesus said to them" (12:54; 13:6, 20; 15:11; 16:1; 18:9; 19:11); "At that time" (13:1); "In a synagogue" (13:10); "He went through cities and towns" (13:22); etc.

Whom does Jesus not encounter on this road? He talks to a lawyer (Luke 10:25-37), Pharisees and scribes (11:37-53; 13:31-33; 14:1-24; 15:2; 16:14-15; 17:20-21), tax collectors (15:1), and various anonymous people. Meanwhile, he is always surrounded by crowds.

23. The archaeological findings at Samaria confirm the mixed character of its population. There are, among others things, many household account books containing names compounded with Baal or El.

24. To call someone a "Samaritan" (". . . you are a Samaritan and are possessed?" John 8:48) is to imply that he is under the influence of perverse forces.

25. How often does one hear: "I am not a racist, but . . ."!

26. Cf. 1 Cor 16:3-11 where all these concerns are expressed.

27. Burial is the primary duty of the children of a dead parent (Gen 25:8-10; 35:29; 50:12-13; Tob 4:3-4; 6:15; 14:10). It is a work of piety that falls to the army in wartime (1 Kgs 11:15) and to all faithful Israelites (the Book of Tobit insists on this duty: Tob 1:17-20; 2:4-8; 12:12-14).

The *Rule of St. Benedict* testifies to this in the Christian tradition. The chapter entitled "The tools for good works" groups together the following "good works": "Relieve the poor. Clothe the naked. Visit the sick. Bury the dead. Help the troubled. Console the afflicted" (édition "du centenaire." Rochefort, 1980, ch. 4, ll. 14, 15, 16, 17, 18 and 19).

28. Casuistry here can only lead to two opposed attitudes that betray a misapprehension of Jesus' demands. On the one hand is an accumulation of circumstances that turn these words into the sort of "commandment" that is admirable (and performable by a select few) but not generally applicable.

On the other hand, they can be understood as calling for a kind of behavior that does not fit the gospel. For example, when "in the name of renunciation," men and women entering religious orders abandon their parents. Fortunately, such practices no longer exist and, indeed, are hardly imaginable.

29. *Rule of St. Benedict,* ch. 4, line 21, ed. cited, note 27.

30. Athanasius (c. 295–373), *Vie de saint Antoine,* 16–20. Modified translation of Père Placide Deseille, in *Les saints moines d'Orient* (Namur: Edition du Soleil Levant, 1958) 31–32.

31. H. Urs von Balthasar, *Le coeur du monde* (Paris: Desclée de Brouwer, 1956) 124–125.

32. N Berthet—R. Gantoy, *Intercessions,* coll. "Vivante liturgie" 95 (Paris: Centurion, 1980) 141.

33. One should mention, among others, all those texts that speak of the "tenderness of God" See *Vocabulaire de théologie biblique,* 2nd ed. (Paris: Cerf, 1970) 1284–1286.

34. Cyril, bishop of Jerusalem (c. 315–386), *13ᵉ Catéchèse baptismale*, 1–4: PG 33, 771–778.

35. This does not mean that for Paul there is an Israel of the flesh opposed to an Israel of the spirit. Besides, he never calls the Church a "new Israel." On the contrary, he emphasizes that "the gifts and the call of God are irrevocable." Hence he concludes: ". . . a hardening has come upon Israel in part, until the full number of the Gentiles comes in, and thus all Israel will be saved" (Rom 11:29, 25). This fits well with the prophetic tradition that announces the complete purification of Israel through the coming of the Messiah, and speaks of the "remnant of Israel." For Paul, this purification, which is already begun in the conversion of the Gentiles, includes the conversion of the Jewish people.

36. Thus to the woman with a hemorrhage (Luke 7:50) and the sinful woman (Luke 8:48).

37. Luke 19:38; 24:36; John 20:19; Acts 7:26; 9:31; Eph 2:14-22; John 16:33.

38. Note how Jesus healed so many people without, so to speak, forethought, calculation, or condition. For example, though he was pleased with the Samaritan who was healed from leprosy and returned to give glory to God, he shows no regret at having healed the other nine (Luke 17:11-19—Twenty-eighth Sunday). In any case, the Gospel says absolutely nothing about what happened to most of the sick people whom Luke says that Jesus healed: the paralytic (5:17-26), the man with a withered hand (6:6-11), the centurion's servant (7:1-10), the Gerasene demoniac (8:26-39), the woman with a hemorrhage (8:43-48), the possessed boy (9:37-43), the infirm woman (13:10-13), the man with dropsy (14:1-6), the blind man at Jericho (18:35-43), nor even those whom he raised from the dead: the young man at Nain (7:11-17), Jairus' daughter (8:40-42, 49-55).

39. *Tropaires pour les dimanches* (Dourgne, *Livre d'Heures d'En-Calcat*, 1980) 87 (Fiche de chant T 61).

From the Fifteenth to the Seventeenth Sunday—Pages 120–146

1. For a more detailed analysis of this letter and its theology, see, for example, *Introduction à la Bible*, under the editorship of A. Robert and A Feuillet, t. II. *Nouveau Testament* (Paris: Desclée, 1959) ch. IV: "Les épîtres de la captivité" by M. Cerfaux, pp. 487–496. More recently: A. George and P. Grelot, *Introduction à la Bible*, new edition, T. III, *Le Nouveau Testament*, vol. 3, *Les lettre apostoliques* (Paris: Desclée, 1977) ch. VII, "Paul et l'Eglise de Colosses," by M. Carrez, pp. 153–163.

2. As soon as the "prophet" draws attention to himself and his own words instead of focusing on the Other whose mouthpiece he is, things begin to go awry. Such is often the case today. Only Jesus can say: "I tell you."

3. We speak of the "Napoleonic Code" even though the political regime is long gone.

4. The "Shema" is formed by the combination of Deut 6:4-9; 11:13-21; Num 15:37-41 and several benedictions.

5. Exegetes vary in dividing this hymn into two or five strophes. See M. Carrez, in A. George and P. Grelot, *op. cit.* (note 1) p. 149.

6. The term "image" has a double meaning and usage. In Trinitarian theology, the Word is called the "image of the Father," so as to affirm their perfect union: "Eternally begotten of the Father. God from God, light from light, true God from true God, begotten, not made, one in being with the Father, through him all things were made." Here, in light of this faith, "image" suggests that "the Word made flesh," makes the invisible God visible.

Commenting on the story of creation (Gen 1:26-27), the Fathers loved to say that man is "the image of the Image (Christ) of God."

7. We might rightly wonder here—as in the case of Philippians 2:6-11—about the origin of this text, its context, its author, and particularly whether it is a hymn from the baptismal liturgy or a Eucharistic thanksgiving (see in A. George and P. Grelot, *op. cit.*, p. 157).

In any case, today it has been integrated into the Liturgy of the Hours (Wednesday evening). The passage from Philippians 2 is found on Saturday evening.

8. In Matthew (22:36) and Mark (12:28), a similar question is put to Jesus, but there it is a question of "Which commandment in the law is the greatest?" He responds by citing Deuteronomy 6:5 and Leviticus 19:18 in succession to point out that both commandments are important (Matt 22:39; Mark 12:31).

9. Note that Luke does not even use the term "commandment."

10. It is a "story" rather than a "parable," although the latter term is often applied to it. There is no need of interpretation because the lesson concerning proper behavior to others is merely reinforced by the contrast between the conduct of the Samaritan and that of the priest and the Levite. So Jesus can conclude: "Go and do the same as the Samaritan who found a man half-dead along the road."

11. It is nineteen miles from Jerusalem to Jericho, with a "descent" of thirty-six hundred feet. One crosses a desert zone that is very impressive even today, driving along the modern road. P. Ternant—who lives at St. Anne in Jerusalem—speaks of "the Turkish road" near the gorge of Ouadi el-Quelt, as particularly dangerous for meeting an ambush, especially if one is traveling on foot and alone, P. Ternant, "Le Bon Samaritain," in *Assemblées du Seigneur*, 2nd series, n. 46 (Paris: Cerf, 1974) 70.

12. It would be too harsh to accuse them of acting in this way out of carelessness or disdain. Coming from the holy city, perhaps after having completed their service in the Temple (see Luke 1:8 with notes in the *Bible de Jérusalem*) they may have been afraid of contracting legal impurity if the man lying motionless was already dead (see: Lev 21:1; Num 19:11). The hypothesis is of interest only insofar as the reader remembers that mercy is more important than sacrifice (Hos 6:6), which the priest and Levite forgot.

13. One need not levy a charge of bad will against them. Take this example: Two friends, a pharmacist and a priest, were hurrying from their car through the rain along a small, deserted street in a large city to one of their apartments. Across the sidewalk lay a man: a vagrant? dead drunk? Maybe, but why was he lying there without moving, in this rain? Should they go over to him? Should they call the police and be forced to justify their worry? Should they pass by, reasoning that if they intervened every time they saw a vagrant . . . who might after all be angry with them for calling the police? Fortunately, before they came to a decision, a police car came by, doubtlessly having been called by someone else who was careful not to remain on the spot. The pharmacist and the priest went away, relieved, turning around only to be sure that the man, laid on a stretcher, was in the hands of the competent public authority.

14. A "piece of silver" (= a denarius) was the daily wage of an agricultural worker (see the parable of the "workers in the vineyard": Matt 20:2).

15. These are marginal reflections. But what he says to the innkeeper and his paying of two silver pieces shows that the Samaritan was truly concerned for the wounded man and took him completely in charge. If necessary, he will settle accounts on his return. What more could he do? Even this was not without some risk.

We may know, personally or by report, instances of a similar "compasssion" on the part of persons—Christian or not—in our midst: the concierge who finds a baby in a garbage can and, with his wife, requests to adopt it; students who receive into their "community house" an old man who runs away from institutions, who without them would have no place to stay, etc.

16. Everyone has personally witnessed such edifying examples. Some admire them but think that they are not able to imitate them. Others take exception to them with all sorts of charges: "subversion," "lack of propriety," "undermining of the established order," etc. We know such reactions all too well. Sadly, these who give voice to them are Christians by baptism, and often are among the loudest in proclaiming their faith!

17. At one time or another, who does not reason this way? And who, in a particular case, could condemn the one who holds this? As soon as one admits casuistry, this type of debate becomes legitimate and necessary.

18. Since the patristic period, this parable has been regarded as an allegory, with each detail having symbolic meaning. The Samaritan would be Jesus; the wounded man, Adam or humanity; Jerusalem, paradise; Jericho, the world; the thieves, demons; the innkeeper, the Church; etc. Although such a reading can boast of several distinguished names such as Clement of Alexandria (c. 150–216), Origen (185–254), and Augustine (354–430), and though it has been taken up by many authors and preachers, this sort of allegory, though suggestive, does not fit with the meaning intended by Jesus or Luke. The parable has no need of such grand allegorizing to be worthwhile.

19. Severus of Antioch (6th c.) *Homélie* 89, quoted by H. de Lubac, *Catholicisme. Les aspects sociaux du dogme* (Paris: Cerf, Unam sanctam 2, 1954) 377.

20. Such is proclaimed in Psalm 118.

21. Need we point out that to see the face of Christ in the parable does not require an allegorical reading (cf. n. 18, *supra*)?

22. A tradition that has not been lost. Though one may have heard about it, experiencing it always comes as a surprise, beginning with the fact that the host does "wait" on the guests.

23. Chapter 53, trans. F. Debuyst, in *Saint Benoît. Prie et travaille au milieu de les frères* (Paris: Centurion, Fontaine vive, 1980) 65–66.

24. J. Daniélou, "Pour une théologie de l'hospitalité," in *La vie spirituelle* n. 367 (November 1951), p. 345. See Matt 10:40; 25:36-40; John 13:20.

25. One should mention that the Trinitarian interpretation of the episode at Mamre appeared early on, but not right away. It is found in the fourth century in Gregory of Nyssa, in the fifth century in Cyril of Alexandria, and in the sixth century in Procopius of Gaza. Before the end of the fourth century it came into the Latin milieu, first in Ambrose, then in Augustine. In the Syrian Church, it is found in Ephraim, perhaps dating from the fourth century. However, this exegesis has never been exclusive, and perhaps not even dominant.

26. Text by M. Scouarnec, music by J. Akepsimas, fiche de chant E 118.

27. P. Federle, in *Assemblées du Seigneur*, 2nd series, n. 47, (Paris: Cerf, 1970) 70.

28. It is worth pointing out the terms and perspectives in which the letter speaks of the prisoner's situation. "Pray for us, too, that God may open a door to us for the word, to speak of the mystery of Christ, for which I am in prison, that I may make it clear, as I must speak." (4:3-4). "Aristarchus, my fellow prisoner, sends you greetings, as does Mark the cousin of Barnabas (concerning whom you have received instructions; if he comes to you, receive him" (4:10). "The greeting is in my own hand, Paul's. Remember my chains" (4:18).

29. This is not to suggest that this is a fictional story. On the contrary, "the density of the text and the absence of all imaginative details" are "proofs of its historicity." When exegetes speak of "legend," it must be understood "in the technical sense of a story centered around a person" See A. George, "L'accueil du Seigneur." Luke 10:38-42, in *Assemblées du Seigneur*, 2nd series, n. 47 (Paris: Cerf, 1970) 82.

30. The connection between the episode recounted here by Luke and the story of the raising of Lazarus in John (11:1-45) comes easily enough. In the house at Bethany, there were also two sisters, Martha and Mary, with character traits that match those of the two women who, "in a village" one day, gave hospitality to Jesus. But we should not push the connection, since the two stories are very different. After all, John's account is not requisite to an understanding of Luke's.

31. Origen, *Homélie sur saint Luc*, frag. 72 in *Sources chrétiennes* 87 (Paris: Cerf, 1962) 521–522.

32. In the tradition, this interpretation has been very nuanced. Among others, Augustine speaks of the two successive states of the Church: militant ("active") now, glorious ("contemplative") hereafter. Some see this rather as a lesson on hospitality, particularly with

respect to missionaries who do not need "many things" when they are welcomed, for frugality suits them. Clearly, this interpretation is not complete.

33. We should point out that many women, overworked with household tasks, are justly affronted by a "simplistic" representation of the lesson of the episode, especially if they are admonished about the "better part" by people who do not have many responsibilities. Even more so if they are told: "You would find it beneficial to take a little time to read, meditate, and pray."

The validity of these objections indicates that this cannot be the lesson of the text. Note also that the Fathers did not preach such an "irresponsible" reading.

34. We can think here of the choice the apostles made between the service of the Word, which was their first responsibility, and the service at table that could not be neglected, for which they instituted the Seven (Acts 6:1-7).

35. A master of novices once said: "If contemplation consists in doing nothing, I know a number of sloths who are great contemplatives."

36. It is often the case that when people who complain that they have no time to rest, read, pray, reflect, etc., are given some leisure time, they fill it up by inventing things to do.

37. Guerricus of Igny (12th c.), Sermons II, in Sources chrétiennes 202 (Paris: Cerf, 1973) 445.

38. L. Bloy, Le salut par les Juifs (Paris, 1946) 171.

39. H. Gaubert, Abraham l'ami de Dieu (Tours, 1964) 166.

40. Thus Moses: "Why, O Lord, should your wrath blaze up against your own people?" (Exod 32:11); "I will go up to the Lord, then; perhaps I may be able to make atonement for your sin." Moses then returned to the Lord and said: "Ah, this people has indeed committed a grave sin in making a god of gold for themselves! If you would only forgive their sin! If you will not, then strike me out of the book that you have written" (Exod 32:30-32); "When the people cried out to Moses, he prayed to the Lord" (Num 11:2); "Then the people came to Moses and said, 'We have sinned in complaining against the Lord and you. Pray the Lord to take the serpents from us' " (Num 21:7).

"Moses and Aaron were among his priests, and Samuel among those who called upon his name; they called upon the Lord, and he answered them" (Ps 99:6).

"This is God's prophet Jeremiah, who loves his brethren and fervently prays for his people and their holy city" (2 Macc 15:14).

" 'I said: "Forgive, O Lord God! How can Jacob stand? He is so small!" And the Lord repented of this. "It shall not be," said the Lord God' " (Amos 7:2-3).

41. E. Wiesel, Célébration hassidique. Portraits et légendes (Paris: Seuil, 1972) 54–55.

42. Genesis 20:1-18. Coming to a place where "there would surely be no fear of God," Abraham was afraid that someone would kill him for his wife. Thus he made Sarah pose as his sister. In fact, the king did take her, but did not touch her, kept by God from sin (although "in good faith"). One might say then that Abraham's intercession for Abimelech and his harem, smitten with impotence and sterility because of Sarah, was both a recompense for his "deception" as well as a response to the king's restoration of his wife. God, in fact, said to Abimelech: "Yes, I know you did it in good faith. In fact, it was I who kept you from sinning against me; that is why I did not let you touch her. Therefore, return the man's wife—as a spokesman he will intercede for you—that your life may be saved. If you do not return her, you can be sure that you and all who are yours will certainly die" (Gen 20:6-7).

43. L. Bloy, Le salut par les Juifs, p. 172.

44. Remember that the first extract from this letter, read on the Fifteenth Sunday, was a hymn to Christ (Col 1:15-20; see above, pp. 123–24).

45. This is connected with the parable of the merciless debtor (Matt 18:23-35).

46. See the Sixth Sunday above, p. 335, note 4.

47. On "La prière dans l'histoire d'Israel," see the article "Prière" in Vocabulaire de théologie biblique (Paris: Cerf, 1970) col. 1024–1028.

48. Today, prayer is still the source and expression of every spiritual tradition, united in one faith and basic evangelical tradition, even if, these days, "liturgical spirituality" has a greater impact on all spiritual traditions.

49. H. Urs von Balthasar, *La prière contemplative* (Paris: Desclée de Brouwer, 1959) 10–11.

50. Some people, in order to "rectify" the "strange" character of this formula, change the sentence, beginning it with "We ask (or pray) you . . ." There certainly is justification for this, but nevertheless, the end result does not have the sense of invocation (epiclesis) of the formula that is found in the Missal or the Office.

51. Matthew's, to be sure, but also others, even paraphrased renditions as one finds in Dante (*La divine Comédie*, Purgatory, canto XI, 1–21, trans. Lucienne Portier [Paris: Cerf, 1987] 246): Our Father, who art in heaven, not circumscribed, but because you love more what you first did there, hallowed be your name and majesty by every creature as it is able to give thanks. May the peace of your kingdom come to us, for we ourselves cannot attain it, however skillful we are, if it does not first approach us. As your angels, of their own will, offer sacrifice to you in singing hosanna, may men do likewise. Give us this day our daily manna without which in this harsh wasteland the man who strives most to advance goes steadily backward, and as we forgive the wrongs done to us, so may you graciously forgive us, taking no account of our merits. Do not submit our faltering virtue to the test of the ancient foe, but from the tempter deliver us.

52. *Léon Bloy en verve. Mots, propos, aphorismes. Présentation et choix de textes* by H. Juin (Paris: Horay, 1972) 56–57.

From the Eighteenth to the Twenty-first Sunday— Pages 147–183

1. This is what the author calls himself. But Qoheleth is not a proper name. It refers to the function, the profession of someone who speaks in the public assembly: a preacher. In Latin, the assembly is called *ecclesia*, hence Ecclesiastes.

The author puts his sayings under the patronage of Solomon, the greatest of Israel's sages. Clearly, this is merely a literary device.

2. Bossuet (1637–1704), "Oraison funèbre de Henry de Gormay," in *Oeuvres oratoires de Bossuet*, tome 2 (Paris: Desclée de Brouwer, 1914) 526.

3. The word "vanity" occurs forty times in this book, and twenty-five times it is rendered: "It is vanity." Note that this book has only twelve chapters, two hundred twenty-two verses in all.

The Sunday Lectionary contains only the four verses we read this Sunday. The Weekday Lectionary has three excerpts (31 verses): 1:2-11; 3:1-11; 11:9–12:8, Thursday, Friday and Saturday of the Twenty-fifth Week, even years.

4. G. Bernanos, *La joie* (Paris: Plon, 1929) 237.

5. We have read 1:15-20 on the Fifteenth Sunday; 1:24-28 on the Sixteenth, and 2:12-14 on the Seventeenth.

6. Through the Spirit of truth that dwells in us, we can have only one conscience (see John 14:17), but one that is confused, imperfect, like a reflection in a mirror (see 1 Cor 13:12; 2 Cor 5:6-7).

7. In this respect, Paul often speaks of the "flesh" (1 Cor 15:50; Rom 8:8) or the "body," indeed the "sinful body" (Rom 6:6), or "carnal body" (Col 2:11). To this he opposes the "spirit" or "spiritual body" (1 Cor 15:35-49), etc. Make no mistake: in Paul's vocabulary, the terms "flesh" ("body") and "spirit" do not denote the makeup of a person in the sense of body and soul. "Flesh" (or "body") means the person enslaved by sin; "spirit" is the same person transfigured by the Holy Spirit, by grace.

8. We need not dwell on the sins and vices enumerated here and elsewhere (cf. Rom 1:29-31) by the Apostle (see the note in the *Bible de Jérusalem,* p. 1869).

9. We must not exaggerate the difference in mindset between then and now. We have not become entirely indifferent to the signification of clothing, what it reveals about a person. We move easily from "He (or she) dresses like . . ." to "He (or she) is . . . ." And who has never said: "When I saw him (or her) dressed that way, I naturally thought . . . ." All this merely shows that clothing is still regarded as having symbolic significance. See E. Haulotte, "Symbolique du vêtement," in *Assemblées du Seigneur,* 1st series, No. 43 (Bruges: Publications de Saint-André, 1964) 49-75.

10. The passage from the Gospel read this Sunday has no parallel in Matthew and Mark.

11. Advertising agencies are quite open about their objectives: encouraging people to buy. The best of them are able to do it very well, with a sense of public psychology and a mastery of the proper wording of advertisements, producing quite fine art (publicity). Properly speaking, this profession should not be overly chastised, when the buying public bears at least as much guilt. Isn't it really the public greed that sets the rules for the game?

12. Martin Luther King Jr. (died 1968), *La force d'aimer* (Tournai: Casterman, 1968) 97.

13. Basil (329-379), *Homélie sur la charité,* P.G. 31, col. 266-267. Quoted in *Lectures pour notre temps,* fiche X 1, Orval, 1969.

14. This is not to say that those who deny an afterlife are not sincere. But their denial can only be a "confession," like that of faith.

15. See note g) in the *Bible de Jérusalem,* p. 1026.

16. D. Rimaud, *Les arbres dan la mer* (Paris: Desclée, 1975) 159. (Fiche de chant D 204).

17. See, for example, Psalm 38.

18. This book has nineteen chapters with four hundred thirty-five verses.
The Sunday Lectionary makes use of it eight times (Year A: Sixteenth and Thirty-second Sundays of Ordinary Time; Year B: Thirteenth, Twenty-fifth, and Twenty-eighth Sundays; Year C: Nineteenth, Twenty-third, and Thirty-first Sundays), totaling one hundred forty-one verses.
The Weekday Lectionary uses it seven times (Friday of the Fourth Week of Lent; every day of the Thirty-second Week of Ordinary Time, odd years), totaling sixty-seven verses.
It is one of the "deuterocanonical" books, so called because they were added much later to the official list ("canon") of biblical writings. They are not part of the Hebrew Bible used today by the Jews. It was written in Greek during the first century B.C.

19. The first reading, chosen from the Old Testament in relationship to the Gospel, is always to be understood, not in its literary context, but as part of the montage of the Liturgy of the Word.

20. The Eucharist is obviously the fulfillment of this definition of the mystery-sacrament, as is said so well in the antiphon "O sacrum convivium": *Recolitur memoria passionis; mens impletur gratia; et futurae gloriae nobis pignus datur:* "The memorial of the passion is celebrated; our soul is filled with its grace; and the promise of future glory is given to us" (Antiphon of the *Magnificat* for the feast of the Body and Blood of Christ).

21. Melito of Sardis (died before 190), *Sur la Pâque,* 1-6, in *Sources chrétiennes* 123 (Paris: Cerf, 1966) 61-65.

22. Seven other extracts are read from the Twenty-seventh to the Thirty-third Sunday of Ordinary Time, Year B. In addition, there are eighteen "discontinuous" references to this letter in the Sunday Lectionary, totaling ninety verses out of the three hundred three that make up the text. This is not very much.
However, the Weekday Lectionary contains twenty-eight excerpts from the Letter to the Hebrews, totaling one hundred eighty-six verses.

23. It is "little" (i.e., small in number), to be sure. But "flock of God" is an expression that refers to the people of God whom he has chosen, assembled, protected, and loved,

according to the traditional imagery of the Old Testament, which is often used in the Gospels. Many texts testify to this. See the article "Pasteur et troupeau" in *Vocabulaire de théologie biblique*, 2nd ed. (Paris: Cerf, 1970) 917–1021.

24. In the Gospel According to Luke, the text read last Sunday—"Grow rich in what matters to God" (Luke 12:13-21)—is followed by a teaching regarding reliance on Providence. "Do not worry about your life . . . All the nations of the world seek for these things, and your Father knows that you need them. Instead, seek his kingdom, and these things will be given you besides." (Luke 12:22-31).

When one reads Luke in this way, the beginning of the Gospel this Nineteenth Sunday (Luke 12:32-48)—"Do not be afraid any longer, little flock, for your Father is pleased to give you the kingdom"—seems like a conclusion to what goes before, prolonged by the two following verses: "Sell your belongings . . . For where your treasure is, there also will your heart be" (vv. 33-34).

But since this passage (12:22-31) has been omitted, it can be taken as the beginning of today's Gospel. Nevertheless, however proper it may be, the dividing of the Gospel into chapters and paragraphs, some with their own subtitles, is always a point for discussion. Often, but not always: there can be no such doubt concerning Luke 12:35-48, a section entitled "On being ready for the Master's return" in the *Bible de Jérusalem*.

25. Eucharistic Prayer III: "Father, calling to mind the death your Son endured for our salvation, his glorious resurrection and ascension into heaven, *and ready to greet him when he comes again*, we offer you in thanksgiving this holy and living sacrifice." Likewise Eucharistic Prayer IV: "Father, we now celebrate this memorial of our redemption. We recall Christ's death . . . *and, looking forward to his coming in glory*." And the prayer after the Our Father: "In your mercy keep us free from sin and protect us from all anxiety *as we wait in joyful hope for the coming of our Savior, Jesus Christ*."

26. L. Bouyer, *Le mystère pascal* (Paris: Cerf, 1947) 9.

27. Titus 1:7. The translation in the Weekday Lectionary (Thirty-second Week, Monday II) explains most clearly: "For a bishop, as God's steward . . ." This paraphrase merely explains in several words, instead of one, in what the function consists. Of course, it is true that the term "bishop" too readily evokes the understanding of "bishop" in the Church today, which would have been anachronistic in the apostolic Church. To Titus 1:7 one could add 1 Cor 4:1-2; 9:17; 1 Pet 4:10.

28. Though they may have a distinctive ministry (or service), neither the apostles nor those who in the Church today exercise a great deal of authority can be regarded as separate from the "crowd" of disciples (see Luke 6:17; 19:37).

"For you I am bishop, with you I am a Christian," said Augustine in one of his sermons (*Sermon* 340:1, quoted in *Missel dominical de l'assemblée* [Paris: Brepols, 1981] 1479). Again, the Second Vatican council has insisted on the place of pope, bishop, and priest in the Church, the community, the assembly: at its head, to be sure, but not above or beyond it.

29. The Christian tradition is unanimous on this point. One reads, for example, in the *Rule of St. Benedict*, "The abbot must remember that at the final judgment of the Lord he will have to give an exact account of two things: his teaching and the obedience of his disciples. He must know that the shepherd will be held responsible for all that the Father finds lacking among his sheep" (ch. 2:6-7; trans. Ph. Schmitz, Brepols, 5th ed. 1987, p. 15). "The abbot must always remember who he is and the position he holds; that more is demanded of those to whom more is entrusted" (ch. 2:30; *ibid.*, p. 19). "He must think constantly of the nature of the load that he has received and the one to whom he will have to give an account of his administration" (ch. 64:7; *ibid.*, p. 147).

30. Peter Chrysologus (406–450), *Sermon* 24, *P.L.* 52, col. 266–267. Quoted in H. Tissot, *Les Pères vous parlent de l'Evangile*, II (Bruges: Apostolat liturgique, 1955) 435–436.

31. Cl. Duchesneau, in *Eglise qui chante* 167 (May–June 1978), 17–18 (Fiche de chant T 58, disques Cantoral 2, UD 30 1299 and EqC 167).

32. These are the passages where the prophet speaks movingly about the internal crises he has experienced and which he evokes in the style of "Psalms of lamentation": Jer 11:18–12:6; 15:10-21; 17:3-18; 18:18-23; 20:7-18.

33. "Dieu est dangereux" is the title of chapter 5 of H. Urs von Balthasar, *Le coeur du monde* (Paris: Desclée de Brouwer, 1956) 124–141.

34. *Ibid.*, pp. 125–126.

35. This way of speaking in the first person is quite different from "I tell you," which he says fairly frequently.

36. "While they were listening to him speak, he proceeded to tell a parable because he was near Jerusalem and they thought that the kingdom of God would appear there immediately" (Luke 19:11). "See that you not be deceived, for many will come in my name, saying, 'I am he,' and 'the time has come.' Do not follow them!" (Luke 21:8—Thirty-third Sunday, Year C). See also Luke 17:23; Acts 1:6-7.

37. In all other cases where the New Testament uses the word "baptism," it refers to a "ritual bath," whether that of John the Baptist or the Church. Clearly, Jesus is not speaking here of a baptismal rite that he himself must undergo. Exegetes have noted that the substantive *baptisma* does not occur in Greek before the New Testament, neither in the Greek version of the Old Testament (the Septuagint) nor in any other, earlier, secular writings. One might suggest that the New Testament authors found it in the language of their era; but this has not been proven.

38. Luke 9:22; 17:25; 24:7, 26, 44.

39. "Martyre de Polycarpe," 13–15. Trans. A.G. Hamman, *Les prémiers martyrs de l'Eglise* (Paris: Desclée de Brouwer, "Les Pères dans la foi," 1979) 30–31.

40. Today, there are Jewish rabbis of every nationality.

41. Only recently has there been an indigenous ordination to the priesthood and episcopate in the Church, especially in the Far East, India, Africa—indeed most of the Third World. However, we should not forget the diversity in origin of the Fathers of the Church. Many Africans gained great status: Tertullian, Cyprian, Lactanius, Augustine. In the official list of the popes, in addition to eleven Greeks and twenty-two Europeans (in the present definition of the term), not including the Italians and John Paul II, there are six Syrians (from the seventh and eighth centuries) and three Africans (from the second, third and fourth centuries).

42. The translation varies from one Bible to another. However, in nearly every case, the fact that God reprimands and chastises those he loves is made clear.

43. Note that all these sayings may be found in Matthew, but in different contexts: v. 24 = Matthew 7:13-14 (during the Sermon on the Mount); v. 25 = Matthew 25:10-12 (at the end of the parable of the ten virgins); vv. 26-27 = Matthew 7:22-23 (again, during the Sermon on the Mount); vv. 28-29 = Matthew 8:11-12 (in the story of the healing of the centurion's servant, at Capernaum). The last saying—v. 30—is a kind of proverb that is repeated many times in various circumstances: Matthew 19:30 and Mark 10:31 (in the encounter with the rich young man); Matthew 20:16 (at the end of the parable of the workers in the vineyard); this is a quite typical use of a proverb.

The fact that Luke may have created a mosaic out of the sayings of Jesus that Matthew and Mark recount at different times and places is worth noting. It is a clear indication that the evangelists had no intention of writing a *"life of Jesus,"* otherwise, there would not be such discrepancies concerning places, times, and circumstances. Either that, or one would have to say that the disagreements between the evangelists indicate that they were careless, misinformed, etc. We say such things about historians when they disagree with one another, waiting for someone to come along with better information to show that one historian was right, or that they all were wrong.

Just as the evangelists did not write a *"life of Jesus,"* so it would be misguided to try to reduce the Four Gospels into one, either by taking one as normative or trying various ways to reconstruct one. It would be as if one took four great paintings of Christ and tried to create a fifth by retaining only those elements common to all four. The result would not even be a recognizable picture.

Clearly, each of the evangelists intended, with his own goals or questions in mind, to write a "narrative" of the "events" (words and deeds) "that have been fulfilled among us, just as those who were eyewitnesses from the beginning and ministers of the word have handed them down to us . . . so that you may realize the certainty of the teachings you have received" (Luke 1:1-3—Third Sunday). Their concordance is greater than if they were simply repeating the same text. This is precisely what P. M.-J. Lagrange points out, in his famous study *L'évangile de Jesus Christ* (Paris: Gabalda, 1928), by quoting this saying of Heraclitus: "Tacit agreement is better than explicit agreement."

44. No current lectionaries have retained these verses, and quite rightly so. Not because they are untenable in themselves; no one should forget the warning given in the epilogue of Revelation: "I warn everyone who hears the prophetic words in this book: if anyone adds to them, God will add to him the plagues described in this book, and if anyone take away from the words in this prophetic book, God will take away his share in the tree of life and in the holy city described in this book" (Rev 22:18-19). But rather so that these texts not be misunderstood, one would have to explain the genre of apocalyptic writing, and indeed the whole book.

45. See the article "Culte" in *Vocabulaire de théologie biblique*, 2nd ed. (Paris: Cerf, 1970) 238-239 especially.

46. Augustine (354-430), *Sermon sur la porte étroite*. Trans. in *Bible et vie chrétienne* 51 (May-June 1963), pp. 15-16.

47. Commission Francophone Cistercienne, *Tropaires des dimanches* (Dourgne, le Livre d'Heures d'En-Calcat, 1980), "Temps ordinaire, 21e dimanche C," p. 105.

From the Twenty-second to the Twenty-fourth Sunday— Pages 184-216

1. Chapter 14 is thirty-five verses long. We read 1a, 7-14 (Tweny-second Sunday) and 25-33 (Twenty-third Sunday), totaling eighteen verses.

2. These are the parables (properly so-called) and similes of chapter 14: on the choice of seats at a banquet (14:7-11), on the replacing of the discourteous guests with the poor (14:15-24), on the building of a tower (14:28-30), on the king who wondered whether he was strong enough to give battle (14:31-33), on salt (14:34-35). We read in the assembly the first (vv. 7-14), third (vv. 28-30) and fourth (vv. 31-33). Following that, we read in chapter 15 three parables on mercy.

3. Exegetes have pointed out the tripartite structure of chapters 14 and 15 in Luke's Gospel: 14:1-24 = two parables and one saying addressed by Jesus to the Pharisee who had invited him; chapter 15 = three parables; 14:25-35 (which seems a little out of place) = two sayings (punctuated by the same warning: "Anyone who does not—take up his cross/renounce all his possessions—cannot be my disciple") and one parable. Therefore: 2 + 1; 3; 2 + 1. This is another example of the way in which Luke wrote a "narrative" of the events and sayings that he reports (Luke 1:3).

4. The *Bible latine* and the *Bible de Jérusalem* today still refer to it as "Ecclesiasticus." This title undoubtedly comes from the fact that the Church has given it official status although it does not appear in the Jewish canon: it is one of the "deuterocanonicals," so called because their place in the canon of Scripture has been a subject of debate throughout the ages. They are: Judith, Tobit, 1 and 2 Maccabees, Wisdom, Sirach, Baruch, the Letter of Jere-

miah (= Bar 6), as well as some passages in Esther and Daniel which occur only in the Greek translation.

Yet the Book of Sirach was written in Hebrew. Approximately two-thirds of the Hebrew text was found, in 1896, in a medieval manuscript that came from an old synagogue in Cairo. Also was found, in 1964, a long extract containing 39:27–44:17.

See: *Bible de Jérusalem*, pp. 1076–1078. The numbering of the verses—particularly in chapter 3—differs between the Vulgate and the Greek text followed here: 3:19-21, 30-31 (Vulgate), 3:17-18 (skipping v. 19), 20, 28-29 (Greek).

5. M.-F. Lacan, ''L'humilité et ses fruits'' (Sir 3:17-29), in *Assemblées du Seigneur*, 2nd Series, n. 53, p. 66. This experience is especially of the tradition.

6. The Greek term—*teknon*—is neuter: it can mean both son and daughter. John, in his first letter, will use it—*teknion*, diminutive of *teknon*—''little ones'' (1 John 2:1, 12, 28; 3:7, 18; 4:4; 5:21) as did Jesus in his ''farewell discourse'' (John 13:33).

In Sirach, the term is used twenty times.

7. He will return to the themes of the fate of the humble as opposed to the proud (10:14-15; 35:17), and the castigation of pride (10:7-8). But everything that is needed is said here.

8. Of course, all sin can be forgiven. But pride must be eradicated. Note also that ''pride'' here does not refer to the sinful tendency that each one of us is subject to. It refers to the ''condition'' of a person. Remember that Ben Sirach is always concerned with a concrete situation and aim.

9. First sentence in the *Rule* (Prologue): ''Listen, my son, to the teachings of the Master and hear with the ear of your heart.''

10. Luke 10:38-42—Sixteenth Sunday.

11. Luke 11:28—Vigil of the Assumption.

12. Luke 2:19—Christmas, Mass at Dawn; January 1, feast of Mary, mother of God.

13. After chapter 12 comes only one chapter (13:1-25) whose last verses (20-25) contain some news—particularly the release of Timothy (v. 23)—some prayers, and salutations.

Chapter 13 is entitled, in the *Bible de Jérusalem*, ''Appendix'' (with three paragraphs: ''Final recommendations,'' ''Faithfulness,'' ''Obedience to religious leaders'').

14. ''Brothers, I ask you to bear with this message of encouragement'' (Heb 13:22).

15. The term refers to the way blind people apprehend objects by feeling them.

16. 7:36-50: a supper during which a sinful woman came to Jesus and was told by him: ''Go, and sin no more''; 11:37-52: a supper during which he appraises the legalism of the Pharisees and lawyers.

17. ''If anyone else thinks he can be confident in flesh, all the more can I . . . in observance [I was] a Pharisee . . . in righteousness blamed on the law I was blameless'' (Phil 3:4-6); speaking to the Sanhedrin, he said: ''My brothers, I am a Pharisee, the son of Pharisees'' (Acts 23:6); speaking of his accusers before king Agrippa: ''They have known about me from the start, if they are willing to testify, that I have lived my life as a Pharisee, the strictest party of our religion'' (Acts 26:5).

18. Besides 7:36-50 and 11:37-52 (see note 17), 10:38-42: the supper at Martha and Mary's house (Sixteenth Sunday); 19:1-10: a supper at Zacchaeus' house (Thirty-first Sunday); and certainly 22:14-38: the Last Supper.

19. See the article ''Repas'' in the *Vocabulaire de théologie biblique*. It deals with the meaning of the prayer that frames the supper, especially when it is more developed, as it is today in some monasteries and communities. It is not simply a prayer addressed to God before eating, and still less a blessing of the food, but it is really a ''Eucharist''—a blessing of God, a thanksgiving—which more or less explicitly evokes the feast in the kingdom.

20. Luke 4:16—Third Sunday. Jesus' presence would not have gone unnoticed even if on ''that day'' he did not read the Word during the Office like he did at Nazareth and af-

terward (Luke 4:15). In fact, a sick man suffering from dropsy came to the house of the Pharisee who had invited Jesus (Luke 14:1-2).

Even today, an invitation to Sunday dinner made and accepted after Mass is not without particular significance.

21. The first places in synagogues (Luke 11:43; 20:46), at feasts (20:46), and greetings in public places (Luke 11:43).

22. Some people have the habit of always taking the best places. If one asks them to "give way" to "someone more important," they do so as naturally as they took the place.

23. Francis de Sales (1567-1622), *Introduction à la vie dévote,* III, chapter 5 (Tours: Mame, 1956) 145-146.

24. Matthew 23:12 (Thirty-first Sunday, Year A), in the "apostrophe to the Pharisees" Luke 18:14 (Thirtieth Sunday) at the conclusion of the parable of the Pharisee and the tax collector who went up to the Temple to pray.

25. B. Pascal (1623-1662), Pensée 678 (Brunschvicg 528), J. Chevalier, ed. (Paris: NRF, Bibliothèque de la Pléiade, 1939) 1046.0

26. It is because of this metaphor that exegetes sometimes speak of "the parable of the choice of guests."

27. B. Pascal, Pensée 84 (Brunschvicg 72), *op. cit.,* p. 842.

28. Columban (c. 540-615), *Instruction* 1:2-4, *P.L.* 80, col. 231-232.

29. Commission Francophone Cistercienne, *Tropaires des dimanches,* p. 111.

30. This Letter has only twenty-five verses.

31. Note that verse 11 has been omitted. It contains a play on words that is virtually impossible to translate into English, without which the sentence becomes meaningless. Onesimus means "useful." Paul writes: "He was once useless to you": especially in that he escaped from his master and stole from him, as verse 18 implies ("And if he has done you any injustice or owes you anything, charge it to me"). And he adds: ". . . [he] is now useful to [both] you and me."

One other time (Phil 4:3), the apostle made a similar play on words with the name Syzygos, which means "companion."

32. It was not until the nineteenth century that slavery was abolished.

33. On Luke's reordering of sayings and maxims that are found in other contexts, particularly in Matthew, see above, p. 178 ff.

34. D. Bonhoeffer, *Le prix de la grâce* (Paris: Cerf—"Labor et fides, Traditions chrétiennes" 20, 1985) 20-21.

35. Luke says: "without hating," a Hebrew idiom, for which we have no equivalent. "Preferring" makes more sense, given our understanding of the terms.

36. Matthew 10:37 mentions only "father, mother, son, daughter" ("children" in Luke's version). Luke adds "wife, brothers and sisters, his very self."

37. See what was said regarding Luke 9:23, which we read on the Twelfth Sunday: above, p. 99 ff.

38. B. Pascal, Pensée 736 (Brunschvicg 553), Pléiade, *op. cit.,* pp. 1060-1061.

39. *Rule of Saint Benedict,* ch. 58, "De la manière de recevoir les frères." In one way or another, every rule of a religious order or institution prescribes similar prudence.

40. This is in contrast to what is prescribed for the welcome of guests and the poor. When one of them knocks at the door of the monastery, the porter must hurry to open it (ch. 66: "Du portier du monastère"). The superior, indeed the whole community, must make haste to welcome the guest (ch. 53: "De la manière de recevoir les hôtes").

41. Using the example of the "king about to march on another king to do battle" might be surprising. But this would be to forget that Christian life is also a battle against the Adversary, the ever-threatening prince of darkness. Remember the warning in the First Letter of Peter (5:8-9), which was read previously at every Compline, and still is on Tuesday: "Your

opponent the devil is prowling like a roaring lion looking for someone to devour. Resist him, solid in your faith.''

42. We read eight passages from it, from Friday of the Twenty-third Week to Saturday of the Twenty-fourth Week, odd years.

43. For an introduction to the ''pastoral epistles'' in general and the Second Letter to Timothy in particular, see the brief introduction in the *Bible de Jérusalem*, pp. 1862–1863.

44. The author is known as Pseudo-Barnabas.

45. Pseudo-Barnabas, 14:1-3.

46. The meaning of the incident is not immediately clear. First, the people asked Aaron: ''Come, make us a god who will be our leader; as for the man Moses who brought us out of the land of Egypt, we do not know what has happened to him.'' Aaron assented to this and built ''a molten calf.'' But this was not apostasy, since Aaron gathered the people to celebrate ''a feast of the Lord,'' offering holocausts and peace offerings. Besides a lack of confidence in God who apparently carried Moses away on the mountain, the people were guilty, in contravention of the prescription of Exodus 20:4, of making an image of the invisible God.

47. Note that Paul will reaffirm this in his Letter to the Romans, for example, when he writes: ''In respect to the gospel, they are enemies on your account; but in respect to election, they are beloved because of the patriarchs. For the gifts and the call of God are irrevocable'' (Rom 11:28-29).

48. F. Varillon, *Eléments de doctrine chrétienne*, tome 1 (Paris: Epi, 1961) 259–260.

49. The Weekday Lectionary contains fifty-two verses, making a total of seventy-two verses that we read out of one hundred twelve, or fifty-nine percent.

50. There are three accounts given of the conversion of Paul and his activity as a persecutor: Acts 9:1-19; 22:4-21; 26:9-18. To which one could add what the apostle says about his ''former way of life'' in Galatians 1:13-14 and in passing in 1 Corinthians 15:9 and Philippians 3:6.

51. Tertullian (c. 155–220), *Traité de la pénitence*, VIII, 7–8. Trans. P. de Labriolle (Paris: Picard, Textes et documents, 1906) 39.

52. The parable of the workers in the vineyard (Matt 20:1-16—Twenty-fifth Sunday, Year A) is not really a parallel of the parable of the father who had two sons. But it deals with the same perspectives: a mercenary religion, the complaints of those who think they deserve more rights than others because they have done more, the justification of God's and Jesus' conduct, and a reminder of what we are and what we must be.

53. The parable of the two sons (Matt 21:28-32—Twenty-sixth Sunday, Year A) attests to the possibility and value of such a conversion.

54. Ch. Péguy, *Le mystère des saints innocents*, in *Oeuvres poétiques complètes* (Paris: Bibliothèque de la Pliade, 1957) 693, 694.

The Twenty-fifth and Twenty-sixth Sundays—Pages 217–238

1. Luke 16:16 = Matt 11:12-13; Luke 16:17 = Matt 5:18; Luke 16:18 = Matt 5:32; 19:9 (and Mark 10:11-12).

2. Amos is ''the first prophetic writing'' because he is the earliest of the prophets whose acts and sayings have been collected into a particular biblical book.

3. At Tekoa, five miles southeast of Bethlehem.

4. Amos calls these two kingdoms respectively Judah and Israel, or ''house of Isaac'' (7:16) and ''house of Jacob'' (3:13; 9:8) or ''house of Joseph'' (5:6), or simply ''Isaac'' (7:9) and ''Jacob'' (6:8; 7:2, 5), ''Joseph'' (5:15; 6:6). The sudden division of the twelve tribes

into two kingdoms—Judah and Samaria—in 931 destroyed the unity of the people, who awaited a restoration.

5. Archaeologists have discovered evidence that may point to an earthquake in the eighth century B.C. (c. 746). In any case, this shock was long remembered. But the mention in the Book of Amos does not refer to it as a point on a time-line. It is seen as a sign of God, a divine manifestation that confirms Amos' message and the seriousness of his threats: "Remember the earthquake!"

6. Once again the archaeological evidence testifies to the situation of the northern kingdom experienced by Amos. Not far from Naplouse (nowadays Tell el Farah), one can see a site where a section of large, well-built houses is separated from an extremely poor section. And this was in the eighth century B.C.! See: R. de Vaux, *Les institutions de l'Ancien Testament* I (Paris, 1961) 114.

The prophets also testify to this. "How rich I have become; I have made a fortune" says Hosea (12:9) of Ephraim (Israel). They denounce luxurious dwellings (Hos 8:14; Amos 3:15; 5:11), banquets (Isa 5:11-12; Amos 6:4), clothing (Isa 3:16-24).

"Woe to you who join house to house, who connect field with field, till no room remains, and you are left to dwell alone in the midst of the land" (Isa 5:8). "They covet fields, and seize them; houses, and they take them; they cheat an owner of his house, a man of his inheritance" (Mic 2:2).

7. There is nothing in common here with the bloody and savage revolution of Jehu, who, with the approbation of Elisha, purged the country of the cult of Baal. Jehu did not preach; he destroyed the temple of Baal and made it "into a latrine, as it remains today"; he was a merciless butcher. The account of this can be found in the Second Book of Kings, chapter 10.

8. The balance referred to is the one used in the market to determine the weight, and therefore the price, of something. Cheating with the balance is a guarantee of profit. Today, there are laws that require companies to list the accurate weight and price/unit of weight on products. Clearly, then, we do not have to deal with the same kind of deception that the people in Amos' day did. Nevertheless, advertising and packaging can often deceive unwary, uneducated people. Perhaps the need to inform people how not to be taken advantage of by the marketplace is a lesson we can learn from Amos.

9. In Psalm 60:10 (= 107:10) we read: "Upon Edom I will set my shoe." This certainly signifies a "taking possession of." The "taking possession of" gains a violent character, as if one were to say, "I set my boot," an option that clarifies the meaning. But the question rests on the probable juridical sense. In some ancient texts—discovered at Nuzi in Iraq—an object of little value seems to be a gesture that validates a transaction by giving it a legal appearance: "to throw one's shoe."

10. H. Camara, *La voix du monde sans voix* (Zurich: Pendo, 1971) 109–110.

11. We often today hear Church authorities reproached for accommodating themselves to every regime and maintaining "normal" relations with them, uncritically, forgetful of the way in which they came to power, their political dealings, etc. It isn't always as cut and dried as that; it is worth the trouble to look closer. Be that as it may, the principle remains: "There is no authority which does not come from God." Paul did not say this in an age which was the best of all possible worlds, particularly for the Church. Political responsibility belongs to the citizens, and the Christians among them have the right and duty to criticize the "established authorities," to fight for political change, having recourse to ways and means of which the gospel does not disapprove. If bishops, the pope, and Christian communities inspire, approve, and animate resistance movements, it is always at the risk of being wrong and "seeing themselves condemned."

There was a time when bishops and popes excommunicated emperors, kings, and princes, restoring to their subjects the oath of fidelity. We need not regret the downfall of such an age where the political maturity of the subjects was so denigrated.

The use made of the so-called "theology of the absolute power of the divine right" led to a refutation of any "theology" of another power.

12. The formulation of this sort of petition sometimes indicates a kind of pride, when it has the tone of a denunciation of others for their failing. It is unthinkable that Christians should pray as if they thought: "We are not like those for whom we intercede."

13. E.g., regarding the choice of places at table: Luke 14:1-10 (Twenty-third Sunday).

14. To get an idea of the size of these "gifts," refer to the "Tables of measures and money" in the *Bible de Jérusalem*, pp. 2077-2078. The first amounts to fifty times forty-five liters of oil; the second, twenty times four hundred fifty liters of wheat! Quite a gift: it amounts to the cost of six hundred days of work! One would be indebted to the manager for far less than this.

15. For he is the "master" who praises the cleverness of his deceitful manager. Such praise would be too unlikely in the mouth of the one who was the victim of such criminal acts. If he acknowledged the adroitness of his dishonest manager, it would be with great anger. Probably, he would conclude that such a man was more of a thief that he had at first thought.

16. Bossuet, "Sermon sur l'éminente dignité des pauvres dans l'Eglise," in *Oeuvres complètes*, tome 3 (Paris: Méquignon et Leroux-Gaume, 1845) 190-191.

17. Note that Jesus says: "If you can *trust* a man" and not "If he is capable of fulfilling a responsibility." Competence in "little things" is not enough to guarantee competence in "greater things." Although very similar, the lesson of the "sums of money" (Luke 19:17) is somewhat different. It is a question of "faithfulness" in the management of "little things" (five or ten pieces of money) and "authority" given over the towns. The perspective here is of the coming of the kingdom, which is not immediately apparent, and the judgment that will affirm one's fidelity or infidelity in increasing one's gifts.

18. Augustine (354-430), *Sermon*, 113, IV, 4; V, 5; ed. Vives (Paris, 1873, tome 17) 181-182, 184.

19. The Lectionary prefers to avoid this dated term. The *Bible de Jérusalem* mentions it only in a note. By avoiding the use of a strange name, one makes sure that it will be understood that we are speaking here of Money. Thus we capitalize this word, which is very well for reading, but perhaps not for simply hearing. The point is: "One cannot serve both God and the god Money."

20. From this short book (nine chapters, one hundred forty-six verses), only three extracts have been retained in the Sunday Lectionary: those of the Twenty-fifth and Twenty-sixth Sundays, and the one we read on the Fifteenth Sunday, Year B. There, it is a passage—Amos 7:12-15—where it is said that Amazias, priest of Bethel, on the road from Jerusalem to Sichem, but in the northern kingdom, urged Amos to leave these places: "Off with you, visionary, flee to the land of Judah (the southern kingdom, where he came from)! There earn your bread by prophesying, but never again prophesy in Bethel; for it is the king's sanctuary and a royal temple (of the northern kingdom)."

21. L.-J. Lebret, *Dimensions de la charité*, Paris, ed. ouvrières, 1957, p. 48.

22. For a careful analysis of prophetic denunciation (its movement, its necessity, its conditions of validity, its insufficiency) and political construction (its movement, its temptation, the qualities it requires) see P. Jouguelet, "Conception chrétienne de la paix," in *Semaines sociales de France, 40e Session, Pau 1953, Guerre et paix* (Lyon, 1953) 151-166: "As authentic as it may be, the prophetic attitude is insufficient so long as it is not complemented by action of a different kind. It destroys without creating anything as a replacement. The prophet must be surrounded by more prosaic men who will build less faulty structures on the ruins he leaves behind. When such men are not present, the ruins prove to be a breeding ground for new injustices and a cover for the old ones. Both in times of war and peace, any imperfect undertaking is liable to be denounced for its faults, which apparently discredit the whole enterprise. There will always be unscrupulous men ready to use the prophet for their own

ends. His greatest weakness is to seem merely mysterious; the first duty of his community is to surround him with those who can build on the wreckage left by his prophecy; if this does not happen, the crusade that begins as a recovery of Christ's tomb ends in the sacking of Byzantium: the crusaders will be amazed at the metamorphosis of their cause" (p. 161). "Political activity is marked by its relativity. It seeks *hic et nunc* the path of greatest justice; clearly, its decisions are not on the level of the absolute. Hence the natural and necessary tension between prophet and politician, the man of witness and the man of efficiency. It goes without saying that the classic temptation of the builder is idolatry. He always wants to believe that his achievements are definitive and perfect, that everything must be sacrificed to them, that heaven has come to earth" (p. 162).

23. The epistle is not chosen as a function of the other readings. But the fact that it makes a part of the liturgical montage invites us to understand it in this context. Frequently, such may be not only possible but called for; such is certainly the case today.

24. Some Bibles have: "Follow justice, piety." Our translation tries to avoid the word "piety," which, in its most typical sense, does not express clearly enough the sense of "relation to God."

25. "Beautiful fight" is a literal translation of the Greek. "Good fight" rather evokes the quality of combat.

26. *"Quod coepit in te Deus, ipse perficiat!"*

27. Most modern Bibles opt for the first construction.

28. Lazarus is a symbolic name rather than one of a particular person. This person here has nothing to do with Lazarus the brother of Martha and Mary.

29. L. Bloy (1846–1917), *Le sang du pauvre* (Paris: Stock, 1922) 76.

30. In the Egyptian story mentioned above.

31. In the story in the *Palestinian Talmud*.

32. Egyptian story.

33. L. Bloy, *op. cit.*, p. 77.

34. Thus in the well-known story of the road to Emmaus (Luke 24:27, 44), Paul's discourse before king Agrippa (Acts 26:22) and his declaration to the Jews at Rome (Acts 28:23).

35. L. Bloy, *op. cit.*, p. 77.

36. Basil (329–379), *Homélie* 6:7; PG 31, 275–278.

The Twenty-seventh and Twenty-eighth Sundays— Pages 239–257

1. The parallel texts from Matthew are read during Year A: Matthew 15:21-22, Twentieth Sunday of Ordinary Time; Matthew 24:37-39, First Sunday of Advent.

2. Four chapters, eighty-three verses. Here we read twenty-one of them. Another short passage (2 Tim 1:8b-10) is read on the Second Sunday of Lent, Year A.

3. The Book of Habakkuk is only three chapters, fifty-six verses long. The Weekday Lectionary contains only one passage from it: Habakkuk 1:12–2:4 (ten verses), Saturday II, Eighteenth Week of Ordinary Time.

4. This is an example of how the first printers made a more or less uncertain division into chapters and verses of the biblical books that had been written on scrolls or parchment leaves. Two titles within the text divided the Book of Habakkuk clearly into two parts; yet there are three chapters. This is not to say that these divisions were made haphazardly or unwisely. But at least we should understand why, today, exegetes and commentators will sometimes speak of sections of text that do not exactly correspond to chapter divisions.

5. This is a good opportunity to point out how valuable praying the psalms is, with their congruence with the human condition and the struggles of faith. It is rightly said that to pray the psalms is to travel the road from Psalm 1 ("Happy the man who follows not the

counsel of the wicked, nor walks in the way of sinners, nor sits in the company of the insolent, but delights in the law of the Lord and meditates on his law day and night") to Psalm 150 ("Alleluia! Praise the Lord in his sanctuary"), a road of which no step can be avoided or belittled, neither that of the "despairing" psalms nor that of the psalms of "imprecation."

6. Cyril of Jerusalem (c. 315–386), *Catéchèse*, 5:9-11; *P.G.* 33, 315–320.

7. Metropolitan Anthony Bloom, "L'éxpérience, le doute et la foi," in *Lumen vitae* (1971) 24–25.

8. A collection of texts of D. Rimaud is entitled precisely *Les arbres dans la mer* (Paris: Desclée, 1975). This title is drawn from the text of pages 99–100. The author well understood and expressed the significance of the saying. Trees in the sea? "Beggars as kings, powers overturned, hoarded gold shared with all! . . . Hangmen without work, rusted manacles, empty prisons! . . . buried guns, disbanded armies, dancing mountains!"

9. Sixth, Seventh, Nineteenth and Twenty-second Sundays.

10. Cl. la Colombière (1641–1682), *Ecrits spirituels* (Paris: Desclée de Brouwer, Christus, 1962) 163.

11. Diadochus of Photice, *Cent chapitres sur la perfection spirituelle*, XIII, trans. E. des Places, in *Sources chrétiennes* 5 (Paris: Cerf, 1943) 81–82.

12. Commission Francophone Cistercienne, *Tropaires des dimanches* (Dourgne, Livre d'heures d'En-Calcat, 1980) 123.

13. The healing of Naaman covers nineteen verses (2 Kgs 5:1-19). Afterward comes the incident of Gehazi, Elisha's servant, who was struck with leprosy for soliciting a gift from Naaman and lying to Elisha about it (2 Kgs 5:20-27).

The Lectionary retains only four of the nineteen (or twenty-seven) verses. Again, this shows us that we do not read the Old Testament each Sunday to satisfy an (albeit valid) historical interest, but because of its relation to the Gospel of the day.

14. The "cycle of Elisha" covers 2 Kings 2:1–13:21.

The Sunday Lectionary reads from this book only twice: 4:8-11, 14-16a (Thirteenth Sunday of Ordinary Time, Year A); 4:24-44 (Seventeenth Sunday of Ordinary Time, Year B). Since all the readings from this book come from the cycle of Elisha, it may be worthwhile to list the various episodes within this section: the solemn investiture of Elisha as a prophet (2:1-18); healing of the water at Jericho (2:19-22); the curse of the small boys (2:23-25); the miracle of the water during the campaign against Moab (3:9-20); the increase of the widow's oil (4:1-7); promise of a son to the Shunammite woman (4:8-17); the resurrection of that son (4:18-37); the poisoned stew (4:38-41); cure of Naaman the Syrian (5:1-27); recovery of the lost ax (6:1-7); capture of the Aramean soldiers (6:8-23); siege of Samaria and death of the king's adjutant (6:24– 7:20); prediction of famine to the Shunammite woman (8:1-6); prediction of the death of Ben-hadad (8:7-15); anointing of Jehu as king (9:1-10); predictions to king Joash (13:14-19); the resurrection of the dead man thrown into Elisha's tomb (13:20-21).

15. See the article in *Vocabulaire de théologie biblique*, 2nd ed. (Paris: Cerf, 1970) col. 655–656.

The term covers a number of skin diseases. How was it that Naaman, though a "leper," held the highest post in the Aramean army? At any rate, the disease was regarded as incurable.

16. "I thought that he would surely come out and stand there to invoke the Lord his God, and would move his hand over the spot, and thus cure the leprosy" (2 Kgs 5:11).

17. It is difficult to determine precisely what this sudden profession of faith means. Is it strict monotheism ("the God of Israel is the only God")? or monolatry ("there are other gods, but only the God of Israel is worthy of worship")? What Naaman says immediately thereafter—"I will no longer offer holocaust or sacrifice to any other god except to the Lord"—is not enough to settle the issue. For he adds: "But I trust the Lord will forgive your servant this: when my master enters the temple of Rimmon to worship there, then

I, too, as his adjutant, must bow down in the temple of Rimmon. May the Lord forgive your servant this" (2 Kgs 5:18). This is completely inadmissable for a true monotheist. Yet the prophet Elisha does not condemn this overtly idolatrous gesture; he simply says: "Go in peace" (2 Kgs 5:19).

Again, this does not mean that Elisha was less intransigent about monotheism than his master Elijah, who, after the sacrifice on Mount Carmel, slaughtered the prophets of Baal (1 Kgs 18:20-40). The two situations are not really the same. In the latter, it was a matter of wiping out the pagan practices in the midst of the people, forcing a choice between Yahweh and Baal: "How long will you straddle the issue? If the Lord is God, follow him; if Baal, follow him" (1 Kgs 18:21: Wednesday II of the Tenth Week).

In the former, Naaman is a foreigner. What could he have done on returning to his own country, after having acknowledged that the Lord alone is God? The fact that Elisha refused any gift for the healing could help this pagan to grow in the purity of his faith.

18. In Paul's letters we often find verbs that are compounds with the preposition "with" (in Greek, sun): "suffer with" (Rom 8:17; 1 Cor 12:26); "crucified with" (Rom 6:8; Gal 2:19); "buried with" (Rom 6:4; Col 2:12); "raised to life with" (Eph 2:6; Col 2:12; 3:1); "to be given new life with" (Eph 2:5; Col 2:13); "glorified with" (Rom 8:17); "seated with" (Eph 2:6).

19. It occurs exactly five times. Three instances are common to Mark and Luke: Mark 1:24 (= Luke 4:34) and Mark 5:7 (= Luke 8:28) from a demon; Mark 10:47 (= Luke 18:38) from the blind man at Jericho. The other two occur only in Luke: here, and at 23:42, from the repentant criminal.

20. See *Bible de Jérusalem*, note b) on Acts 3:16.

21. According to the law, he must go to the priest to verify the sickness and the healing. Jesus therefore shows his own obedience to the Law.

22. Think of the image of the two altars: the one at which we beg for graces is always crowded, while the one at which we give thanks is scarcely used.

23. Archaeological evidence in Samaria confirms the presence of a mixed population. Especially telling are the household account books with names compounded either with "El" ("Elohim") or Baal.

24. G. Casalis, *Prédication et acte politique* (Paris: Cerf, 1970) 24–25.

25. Bernard (1090–1153), *Sermon 27 de diversis*, (Dourgne: *Lectionnaire de l'Abbaye d'En-Calcat*, 1952) 475–76.

26. J. Mouroux, *Je crois en toi. La rencontre avec le Dieu vivant* (Paris: Cerf, Foi vivante 3, 1965) 98–101.

From the Twenty-ninth to the Thirty-first Sunday—Pages 258-289

1. The Gospel According to Luke is divided into twenty-four chapters. His "narrative" ends with chapter 21. The last three are devoted to the Passion of the Lord (chs. 22 and 23) and the events between the discovery of the empty tomb and the ascension (ch. 24).

2. Respectively, Luke 18:1-8 (Twenty-ninth Sunday), Luke 18:9-14 (Thirtieth Sunday) and Luke 19:1-10 (Thirty-first Sunday).

3. "Le Dieu de Jésus" is the title of an exegetical study by P. Jacques Dupont in *La nouvelle revue théologique* 109 (1987) 321–344.

4. Often—and wrongly—we speak as if the one had only to pray on the mountain and the others to fight in the plain. Always we find this dichotomy: Martha or Mary, the fighters or Moses, discussing endlessly (and fruitlessly) which is the more important. It would be valuable to remember what Paul wrote on the need for the different members of the body (1 Cor 12:12-30).

5. This interpretation was also ascribed to by Gregory the Great (c. 540–604).

6. Origen, *Homélies sur l'Exode* XI, 4, in *Sources chrétiennes* 16 (Paris: Cerf, 1947) 235–236.

7. Numbers 21:14 cites a text from the "Book of the Wars of the Lord," doubtlessly an ancient collection of epic songs of which only this fragment remains. In the First Book of Samuel (25:28), it is said that David "fought the battles of the Lord."

8. A well-known example of this is *La chanson de Roland*. From an ambush laid by some Basque mountaineers for the rearguard of Charlemagne's army on its passage through the Pyrenees, a chronicler—Eginhard—made an epic legend: Roland, the nephew of the emperor, became the hero of a great battle against the Moors, in which he died gloriously after having defeated the enemy. We ought neither to be fooled nor shocked at this.

9. This is not the place, but it would be interesting and instructive (cf. J.-L. Declais, in *Assemblées du Seigneur* n. 60, p. 58): "to follow rabbinic thought in all its nuances and to undertake with it a reflection on violence, its roots and implications, and on reconciliation, the fruit of justice, not of resignation or cowardice." Also worth citing are a few lines from the contemporary Jewish philosopher, Emmanuel Levinas: "Certainly, the whole grandeur of the so-called 'Old Testament' consists in being aware of the blood spilled, the justice of the cry of vengeance, the proper indignation at forgiveness granted by proxy when only the victim has the right to forgive" (*Quatre lectures talmudiques*, Ed. de Minuit, p. 58). "Sin committed against God can be forgiven by divine pardon. Sin against man cannot . . . No one, not even God, can take the place of the victim. The world where pardon is all-powerful is inhuman" (*Difficile liberté*, Albin Michel, p. 37).

To forgive is clearly not to forget; rather, forgiveness demands recollection.

See also *Concilium*, n. 204, 1986 ("Le pardon"), particularly the article by Raymond Studzinski, "Memory and Forgiveness. The Psychological Dimension of Forgiveness" (pp. 23–34): "To forgive is to remember the past and make it part of our history. The commemoration that is forgiveness is a creative work and not the mere mental repetition of a past event" (p. 30). See also the article by P. Ch. Duquoc ("Le pardon de Dieu," pp. 49–58): "To forgive is not to forget the past, it is to hazard another future than the one imposed by the past or memory. It is an invitation to the imagination" (p. 55); "Only the victim has the right to forgive his persecutor" (p. 56).

10. *Les apophtegmes des Pères du désert, Série alphabétique*, trans. J.-Cl. Guy, Abbaye de Bellefontaine, Textes de spiritualité orientale 1, 1966, p. 183.

11. We sometimes speak of a "double fidelity to Scripture and tradition." This is true. But despite the sense expressed both by the word "double" and the copula "and," it is all too common for Scripture and tradition to be understood as two paths that, though they certainly converge, are more or less distinct, even by those people who do not imagine that one can have one entirely without the other. The debate on this relationship is not as fierce today as it was in the sixteenth century, but remnants of that conflict linger on in the way we talk about the issue.

To speak of "fidelity only to the word of God transmitted by Scripture and received in the Church" cuts through any ambiguity.

12. Exegetes differ on the meaning of "the end": the fall of Jerusalem (*Bible de Jérusalem*, p. 1651, note u); or the end of the present order and the definitive inauguration of the reign of God. The same word has both senses: Matthew 10:22; 24:6, 13. Be that as it may, the Church orients itself toward the manifestation and return of the Lord, which always implies a certain amount of urgency.

13. See note q) in the *Bible de Jérusalem*, p. 1799. Paul also insists on this point in similar terms and formulas: to the Romans, he recommends that they "persevere in prayer" (Rom 12:12); to the Ephesians, he writes "Giving thanks always and for everything in the name of our Lord Jesus Christ to God the Father" (Eph 5:20); to the Philippians, ". . . in everything, by prayer and petition, make your requests known to God" (Phil 4:6); to the Colos-

sians, "Persevere in prayer, being watchful in it with thanksgiving" (Col 4:2); to the Thessalonians, "Pray without ceasing" (1 Thess 5:17).

14. The psalmist addresses God in similar terms: "Do me justice, O God, and fight my fight against a faithless people; from the deceitful and impious man rescue me" (Ps 43:1).

15. The use of the word "immediately" is surprising, coming from Luke. Typically, he is careful to warn against expecting an imminent return of the Son of Man (Luke 17:23; 19:11; 21:8-9). But this is not at issue here. To the objection, that God will not do justice to his chosen ones who call out to him day and night, Jesus responds: ". . . he will see to it that justice is done for them speedily," as opposed to the wicked judge who turned a deaf ear to the widow. This does not alleviate any of the uncertainty of the day and hour of Judgment.

16. Commission Francophone Cistercienne, *Tropaires des Dimanches* (Dourgne: *Le Livre d'heures d'En-Calcat*, 1980) 101 (Fiche E 239-1).

17. P. Evdokimov (died 1970), *Les âges de la vie spirituelle* (Paris: Desclée de Brouwer, 1964) 206-208.

18. J.-H. Newman, *Parochial and Plain Sermons*, V, 2 (unpublished translation).

19. Commission Francophone Cistercienne, *Prières au fil des heures*, Vivante liturgie, n. 99 (Paris: Publications de Saint-André, Centurion, 1982) 12.

20. The Sunday Lectionary contains only seven excerpts (forty-four verses from this book that has fifty-one chapters and fourteen hundred verses). The Weekday Lectionary gives it a larger place: fifteen excerpts totaling one hundred forty-five verses.

21. See the article "Pauvres" in the *Vocabulaire de théologie biblique*, col. 927-932.

22. It is sufficient to look at the numerous marginal references to Luke 1:46-55.

23. Symeon the New Theologian (11th c.), *Hymnes* XLI in *Sources chrétiennes* 196 (Paris: Cerf, 1973) 11-13.

24. The last verses of this letter (vv. 19-22) are devoted to greetings and the final wish: "The Lord be with your spirit. Grace be with you."

25. Some exegetes question whether this letter could have been entirely and directly written by Paul himself.

26. We remember the other "farewell discourse," more developed, addressed by Paul to the "presbyters" of the Church of Ephesus, to whom he wrote from Miletus (Acts 20:18-35).

27. It occurs nowhere else in the New Testament. Philologists determine its meaning partly from etymology, partly by comparing it to other terms with the same root, etc.

28. Ignatius of Antioch, on the road to Rome and martyrdom, wrote to the Christians of this city: "I ask only one thing of you: to allow me to offer God the libation of my blood" (*Aux Romans* 2:2).

29. "Do you not know that the runners in the stadium all run in the race, but only one wins the prize? Run so as to win. Every athlete exercises discipline in every way. They do it to win a perishable crown, but we an imperishable one. Thus I do not run aimlessly: I do not fight as if I were shadowboxing. No, I drive my body and train it, for fear that, after having preached to others, I myself should be disqualified." (1 Cor 9:24-27; see Phil 2:16; 3:12-14).

30. At the Olympic games, each athlete swears that he has undergone the required training and, under pain of immediate disqualification, takes an oath to abide by the rules of the games.

31. The image of the "crown" is found in the text of 1 Corinthians 9:25, quoted in note 29 above.

32. This situation is very different from that of his first imprisonment at Rome. Then, the apostle had his own house, and could come and go under guard (Acts 28:16). One might call it "military custody." Now, he is in a prison; Onesiphorus has been trying to find him (2 Tim 1:17). There is little hope of his being freed.

33. In other words, Paul has already appeared once; this was the *prima actio* of Roman law. The magistrate would have determined that in the present state of the matter he was not able to make a judgment *(non liquet)*, and authorized the procuring of more information *(amplius)*. Now he has it. In the first stage of the trial, the Apostle escaped "the lion's jaws," a favorite expression in the Psalms (Pss 7:3; 17:12; 22:22; 35:17). He is waiting for his second appearance *(secunda actio)* and the certain pronunciation of the death sentence.

34. All in all, there are fifty parables in the Synoptics; Luke recounts forty of them. These numbers are approximate, because it may be argued whether a specific text is a parable in the strict sense of the term. At any rate, fifteen of them are proper to the Third Gospel.

35. See the definitions of "Pharisee," "Phariseeism," "Pharisaic" in any dictionary.

36. It is fair to say that the connotation of "Pharisee" has changed quite a bit over the years.

37. Thus, for example, to the Pharisees who mocked him after hearing the parable of the faithless manager (Luke 16:1-13), Jesus says: "You justify yourselves in the sight of others, but God knows your hearts; for what is of human esteem is an abomination in the sight of God" (Luke 16:15).

38. R. Aron, *Les années obscures de Jésus* (Paris: Grasset, 1960) 150–151. The author adds: "Among the good Pharisees of the time (the ones of the seventh category), some went even further than this passage from the *Talmud*. Rabbi Hachman said, 'The supreme Magistrate will punish those hypocrites who wrap themselves in their *talliths* in bad imitations of true Pharisees.' Likewise, an adversary of the sect, Alexander Jannaeus, said to his wife before he died: 'Do not fear the true Pharisees, nor those who are not Pharisees; rather, fear the corrupt Pharisees, those who are not Pharisees but wish to appear as such' " *(Ibid.,* p. 152–153).

39. At least according to Luke. Neither can one forget the Pharisee Nicodemus who came to Jesus at night and brought one hundred pounds of myrrh and aloes for his burial (John 3:1-21; 19:39), nor Joseph of Arimathea, "secretly a disciple of Jesus," who asked Pilate for the body (John 19:38), nor the scribe to whom Jesus said: "You are not far from the kingdom of God" (Mark 12:34).

40. Augustine (354–430), *Commentaire sur le psaume 31*, L. 36, col. 266.

41. *Ibid.*

42. Nicholas Cabasilas (14th c.), *La vie en Jésus Christ*, livre 6, *P.G.* 150, col. 682–683.

43. On the Thirty-fourth Sunday, we read an excerpt from the Letter to the Colossians. However, that text has been chosen specifically for the celebration of Christ the King.

44. Three chapters, forty-seven verses, of which seventeen have been retained by the Lectionary for the Thirty-first, Thirty-second and Thirty-third Sundays of Year A.

45. See above, p. 346, note 18.

46. The text retained here by the Lectionary is part of a meditation on the Exodus in the last part of the book (11:2–19:22), and it attempts to show God's moderation toward Egypt.

47. "I confess to almighty God"; "May almighty God have mercy on us"; "May almighty God bless you."

48. Cyprian, bishop of Carthage (martyred in 258), *Du bienfait de la patience*, 3–5, *P.L.* 4, col. 624–625.

49. Luke 9:51–19:27; four hundred four of the one thousand one hundred fifty-one verses that make up the Third Gospel.

50. The absence of geographical markers should not be surprising. It acts as a literary device. Luke the historian could hardly want us to try to follow Jesus on roads that he had not marked out. It is a spiritual (or theological) path that he wants us to travel. What need have we then of physical maps?

51. *Traité sur l'Evangile de saint Luc*, VIII 81, 87, 90, trans. G. Tissot, in *Sources chrétiennes* 52 (Paris: Cerf) 136–138.

52. Familiarity means that some of Jesus' actions and words no longer shock us. It is rather

the response he provokes that scandalizes us: "How could one recriminate with Jesus for going to the house of a sinner?"

But what would we say, today, if a bishop or a priest, traveling through one of our Jerichos instead of staying somewhere we would have expected, said to a modern "publican" along the way: "Come quickly, for I mean to stay at your house today"? Is it not true that certain terms—"sinners," "prostitutes"—when we read them in the Gospels, do not strike us in their full sense? "The Son of Man came eating and drinking and you said, 'Look, he is a glutton and a drunkard, a friend of tax collectors and sinners.' " (Luke 7:34). "Amen, I say to you, tax collectors and prostitutes are entering the kingdom of God before you. When John came to you in the way of righteousness, you did not believe him; but tax collectors and the prostitutes did" (Matt 21:31-32—Twenty-sixth Sunday, Year A).

53. See the article "Joie" in the *Vocabulaire de théologie biblique*, col. 613–616.

54. Exodus (21:37) foresees such a sanction in only one case: "When a man steals an ox or a sheep and slaughters or sells it, he shall restore five oxen for the one ox, and four sheep for the one sheep."

55. Bede the Venerable (672/673–735), *Commentaire sur saint Luc*; in H. Tissot, *Les Pères vous parlent de l'Evangile*, II (Bruges: Apostolat liturgique, 1955) 715–716.

56. *Traité sur l'évangile de saint Luc*, VIII, 84–86, op. cit., p. 137, note 47.

57. Commission Francophone Cistercienne, *Tropaires des dimanches* (Dourgne: Le Livre d'Heures d'En-Calcat, 1980) 73.

The Thirty-second and Thirty-third Sundays—Pages 290–313

1. This book contains fifteen chapters with five hundred fifty-five verses.

The Weekday Lectionary uses only two other excerpts from it (twenty-seven verses in all), occurring on the Tuesday and Wednesday I of the Thirty-third Week. It is also used twice for saints' celebrations: St. Pancras (May 12) and St. Charles Lwanga and Companions (June 3), and there is a passage from it in the funeral Lectionary.

2. For the historical context of the Books of Maccabees, see the introduction in the *Bible de Jérusalem* (pp. 674–677). However, the following note is generally sufficient: "After a long period of at least relative security, if not tranquility, in the institutions of the Torah (accepted as the Law of the Jews first by the Persians, then the Greeks), came the sudden and violent crisis of the persecution of Antiochus IV Epiphanes (175-164). This Greek ruler thought that the Jewish population was hellenized enough to be forced to abandon the Torah and its religious traditions. He wanted to secure the unity of the Greek state through a unity of religion. He proscribed circumcision, destroyed the scrolls of the holy books, abolished the liturgical feasts, and profaned the Temple and the altar by placing on it a statue of the Olympian Jupiter, "the horrible abomination" (1 Macc 1:54; cf. Dan 9:27). Thus came massacres and martyrdoms: men who saved the holy books, women who had their children circumcised, older people who would not eat forbidden meat . . . Thus Mattathias and his sons, including Judas Maccabeus, fled to the hills and began the long series of battles that ended with the restoration of a national state under the Hasmonean dynasty of the Maccabees" (H. Cazelles, in *Assemblées du Seigneur* n. 63 [Paris: Cerf-Publication de Saint-André, 1971] 73–74).

3. Athanasius (c. 295–373), *Traité de l'incarnation du Verbe*, in *Sources chrétiennes* 18 (Paris: Cerf, 1947) 261–262.

4. 1 Thess 5:25; Rom 15:30-33; 2 Cor 1:11; Col 4:3-4; Phil 1:19; Phlm 22.

5. The race is a favorite image of Paul's: Phil 2:16; Gal 2:2; 5:7.

6. The third part of this epistle (2 Thess 2:23-3:5) "is formed of small units. There is no general teaching or argument, but rather a set of prayer recommendations, requests . . .

But, as it so often happens, the doctrinal background is very rich'' (B. Rigaud, *Les épîtres aux Thessaloniciens* [Paris: Gabalda, Etudes bibliques, 1956] 680).

7. Paul never backs down on this principle: "What is Apollos, after all, and what is Paul? Ministers through whom you became believers, just as the Lord assigned each one. I planted, Apollos watered, but God caused the growth. Therefore neither the one who plants nor the one who waters is anything, but only God, who causes the growth. The one who plants and the one who waters are equal, and each will receive wages in proportion to his labor. For we are God's co-workers; you are God's field, God's building" (1 Cor 3:5-9). "Thus should one regard us: as servants of Christ and stewards of the mysteries of God. Now it is of course required of stewards that they be found trustworthy" (1 Cor 4:1-2). He goes so far as to write: ". . . the majority of my brothers, having taken encouragement from the Lord from my imprisonment, dare more than ever to proclaim the word fearlessly. Of course, some preach Christ from envy and rivalry, others from good will. The latter act out of love, aware that I am here for the defense of the gospel; the former proclaim Christ out of selfish ambition, not from pure motives, thinking that they will cause me trouble in prison. What difference does it make, as long as in every way, whether in pretense or in truth, Christ is being proclaimed? And in that I rejoice" (Phil 1:14-18).

8. Today, this term refers to Christians who take as normative only a literal reading of Scripture. Such an attitude has always been present in the major Christian Churches, both Catholic and Protestant, as well as in Islam. People who hold this position are very often sectarian, and dialogue with them amounts to an impossibility.

9. See above, Thirtieth Sunday, p. 328.

10. See Matthew 22:23; Acts 4:2; 23:8.

The Jewish historian Flavius Josephus (37–95) speaks of the Sadducees: *Antiquités juives*, 12:173; 18:16; *Guerre juive*, 2:164-166. He claims that they deny divine providence and the freedom of the soul, and can only persuade the rich. But such charges should be treated warily, since Josephus was a sworn enemy of the Sadducees.

11. "When brothers live together and one of them dies without a son, the widow of the deceased shall not marry anyone outside the family; but her husband's brother shall go to her and perform the duty of a brother-in-law by marrying her. The firstborn son she bears shall continue the line of the deceased brother, that his name may not be blotted out from Israel" (Deut 25:5-6). It goes without saying that the brother-in-law is not married himself.

12. Paul speaks of the "spiritual body" of the resurrected (1 Cor 15:44), a paradoxical way of speaking that defies all attempts at clear representation, while affirming that the person is both a "fleshly body" and a "spiritual body."

13. Read, for example, Romans 6:3-11 on Easter Vigil.

14. P. Claudel, *Je crois en Dieu*, texts collected and presented by A. du Sarment (Paris: NRF, 1961) 390.

15. This should indicate how ill-informed are those charges against the Liturgy of the Word which complain that the readings have no logical or pedagogical order.

We have explained our way of dealing with the readings in the introduction to Ordinary Time (Volume 4). To try to see the readings each Sunday within a more logical framework is not inappropriate. One could even argue that the gospel, the summit of Scripture, is the key to the Old Testament, and the apostolic writings are the preaching of the good news, often in order to explain this. However, we have dealt with the readings as they occur in the liturgy, only dealing strictly in the conclusion with their coherence.

We should add that the liturgy, especially the Eucharistic liturgy, is not a "thematic celebration." There is a great temptation to regard it as such, but that ends up being a reductionist reading. The fullness of meaning contained in it is always greater than can be defined. It can be neither fully mastered nor limited. To attempt to do so would be to unduly restrict the spiritual freedom of the participants in the liturgy.

16. C. Pozzi, "Ave," in J. Mambrino, *La poésie mystique française* (Paris: Seghers, 1973) 190–191.

17. Of course, there have always been people who have thought otherwise. And of course our information is limited to that portion of human history after the invention of writing.

18. The Bible always castigates those who consult the dead. It tells how one day Saul, who "had driven mediums and fortune-tellers out of the land," nevertheless went to Endor to ask a witch to raise up the spirit of Samuel, who had died (1 Sam 28:1-25). But, "Saul died because of his rebellion against the Lord in disobeying his command, and also because he had sought the counsel of a necromancer, and had not rather inquired of the Lord. Therefore the Lord slew him, and transferred his kingdom to David, the son of Jesse" (1 Chr 10:13-14).

19. For example: Isaac and Rebecca buried near the tombs of Abraham and Sarah by Joseph (Gen 49:31; 50:12), whose bones Moses took out of Egypt (Exod 13:19).

20. P. Thomas, *La réincarnation oui ou non?* (Paris: Centurion, 1987) 151 pp.: "La réincarnation et ses enjeux"; "Quand on croit en la réincarnation"; "Les points d'appui de la réincarnation"; "La réincarnation et sa version occidentale"; "Les malentendus de la réincarnation"; "Est-il question de la réincarnation dans la Bible?"; "Réincarnation et résurrection: ressemblances"; "Réincarnation et résurrection: différences et incompatibilité"; "Conclusion: la réincarnation et la foi chrétienne"; "Bibliographie brève."

21. R. Troisfontaines has used this text for his two works: *"Je ne meurs pas"* (Namur: Presses universitaires de Namur, 1960); *"J'entre dans la vien"* (Paris: Editions universitaires, 115, 1963, réimpression anastatique, 1984).

22. Thus, whereas in Luke's Gospel the "journey to Jerusalem" occupies a great deal of space (Luke 9:51-19:27), the final ministry in the city is recounted in a relatively brief manner (Luke 19:45-21:37). From this last part, the Lectionary retains the teaching on resurrection (Luke 20:27-38—last Sunday's Gospel), and the most important part of the discourse on the destruction of Jerusalem (Luke 21:5-19).

In the Gospel, this last text is followed by a warning ("When you see Jerusalem surrounded by armies . . . Luke 21:20-23), a saying concerning the relationship between this catastrophe and "the times of the Gentiles" (Luke 21:24-27), the parable of the fig tree (Luke 21:29-33), and an exhortation to keep awake, so as not to be surprised (Luke 21:34-36).

The last two verses are a kind of summary of Jesus' activity in Jerusalem: "During the day, Jesus was teaching in the temple area, but at night he would leave and stay at the place called the Mount of Olives. And all the people would get up early each morning to listen to him in the temple area" (Luke 21:37-38).

23. All three readings for the Thirty-fourth and Last Sunday of Ordinary Time are selected specifically for the celebration of the solemnity of Christ the King.

Note also that the rest of chapter 21—vv. 1-4; 5-11; 12-19; 20-29; 29-33 and 34-36—are read during the Masses of the Thirty-fourth Week.

24. Of course, the Book of Malachi (5th c. B.C.) has only three chapters and fifty-five verses (three pages in the *Bible de Jérusalem*). The Sunday and feastday Lectionary contains twelve verses of it: 1:14b-2:2b, 8, 10 (Thirty-first Sunday, Year A); 3:1-4 (Presentation of the Lord); and 3:19-20a (this Sunday). The Weekday Lectionary uses it twice: December 23 (Mal 3:1-4; 4:5-6) and Thursday I of the Twenty-seventh Week (3:13-4:2a).

All in all, we read twenty verses of the fifty-five, nearly thirty-six percent of the whole.

25. "Malachi" means "my messenger." It is no doubt a symbolic name given to an anonymous prophet. He is likened to the precursor of the Messiah. In fact, Luke (7:27), Matthew (11:10), and Mark (1:2) apply Malachi 3:1 to John the Baptist: "I send my messenger before you to prepare your way."

26. It is sometimes referred to briefly as: "the Day," or "that Day."

27. See the article "Jour du Seigneur" in the *Vocabulaire de théologie biblique*, col. 618-625.

28. *Rule of St. Benedict*, ch. 48.

29. *Règle de Bose*, 24 and 25. Trans. F. Debuyst in *Saint Benoit. Prie et travaille au milieu de tes frères* (Paris: Centurion, Fontaine vive, 1980) 57.

30. *Règle de Taizé*, 31–32, cited *ibid.*, p. 62.

31. The only exception being the help he accepted from the Philippians: "You Philippians indeed know that at the beginning of the gospel, when I left Macedonia, not a single church shared with me in an account of giving and receiving, except you alone" (Phil 4:15: Saturday II of the Thirty-first Week).

32. Note that the Gospel refers to the people who were saying this merely as "some," meaning certain anonymous people around Jesus, not the disciples. Moreover, the title that they give to Jesus—*Didaskale, Magister,* translated as Master—is reserved by Luke to these others; the disciples call him *Epistata, Praeceptor.*

This is not merely a semantic detail. It shows us that the discourse on the end of time in Luke 17:22–18:8 is addressed to the disciples, while this one here is meant for all.

33. This is the translation favored by exegetes.

34. J.-H. Newman (1801–1890), *Douze sermons sur le Christ,* trans. P. de Leyris (Paris: Egloff, 1943) 39.

35. D. Rimaud, "Quand nous décamperons," in *Des grillons et des anges* (Paris: Desclée, 1979) 116–117.

The Thirty-fourth Sunday—Pages 314–326

1. See Volume 4 for the origins and evolution of this feast since its institution in 1925 by Pope Pius XI.

2. *Ibid.*

3. In the story of the Passion According to Luke, we read three times that Pilate said of Jesus: "I find this man not guilty." He even adds: ". . . nor [has] Herod" (Luke 23:15). Nonetheless, however, he does accede to the request of the chief priests and the people, decreeing that "their demand should be granted" (Luke 23:24).

This public declaration of innocence by a representative of the Roman authority is important: even when he is judged, Jesus is condemned "though he had done nothing wrong." But it is another condemned man who, dying near Jesus, proclaims that this just man hanging on the cross can save him, and begs him to do so!

Remember also that after Jesus' death, a Roman officer, the centurion who had presided over the execution silently to this point, "witnessed what had happened . . . and said, 'This man was innocent beyond doubt.' When all the people who had gathered for this spectacle saw what had happened, they returned home beating their breasts" (Luke 23:47-48).

4. J. Corbon, "Le Souvenir ou l'Esprit Saint mémoire de l'Eglise," in *Assemblées du Seigneur,* 1st series, n. 50 (Bruges: Publications de Saint-André-Biblica, 1966) 42.

5. This prayer occurs at least fifteen times in the psalms.

6. Gregory Narekatzi (10th/11th c.), in J.-P. Foucher, *Poésie liturgique* (Paris: Mame, 1963) 237.

7. Preface of Christ the King.

8. Ambrose (340–397), *Traité sur l'Evangile de saint Luc,* in *Sources chrétiennes* 52 (Paris: Cerf, 1958) 195–196.

9. An expression used by an exegete: P. Lamarche, "La primauté du Christ;" in *Assemblées du Seigneur* n. 46 (Paris: Cerf, Publications de Saint-André, 1974) 59.

10. Note that this is the typical structure of prefaces: "Father, . . . we do well always and everywhere to give you thanks through Jesus Christ your Son."

11. This fragment is disconnected from what precedes and follows it. Therefore modern Bibles set this hymn apart and in stanzas.

12. In scholasticism, theologians asked whether the Word would have become incarnate if man had not sinned. It was a question that led to lengthy and impassioned discussion. Thomas Aquinas spoke of it in his *Summa theologica* III, 9, 1, art. 3. Surely, he said, "he could have become incarnate in the absence of sin," for God's power is unlimited. But "that which depends only on the will of God and to which the creature has no right, can only be known to us insofar as it is contained in Sacred Scripture, which makes the will of God known to us." Now, "in Sacred Scripture, the reason for the incarnation is always attributed to the sin of the first man."

This is a sound lesson that is worth keeping in mind. One ought to be suspicious of hypothetical theologizing based on a great many "ifs." What often happens is that the view of the speaker is substituted for that of God.

13. And yet it is in such a sense that we often apply the title of "king" to Christ.

14. See the article "Corps du Christ" in *Vocabulaire de théologie biblique,* col. 213–216.

15. This second interpretation is favored by what is said a little further on: "For in [Christ] dwells the whole fullness of the deity bodily" (Col 2:9—Tuesday II of the Twenty-third Week). We recall the Letter to the Philippians (2:7, 9): "He emptied himself . . . Because of this, God greatly exalted him . . . " "Fullness" is thus opposed to "emptiness." Christ renounced it "taking the form of a slave," "obediently accepting even death, death on a cross." It is given to him when "God greatly exalted him." It comes from the "emptiness," the abyss bridged by the "negation" of the incarnation and the death on the cross.

16. Paulinus of Nola (353–431), Chant 19, 718–730, in *Corpus scriptorum ecclesiasticorum latinorum* 30, p. 143.

17. Commission Francophone Cistercienne, *Tropaires des dimanches* (Dourgne, 1980) 142 (Fiche E 173-1).